# The French Revolution

'This is more than a history of the French Revolution. It covers all Europe during the revolutionary period, though events in France naturally take first place. It is particularly good on the social and intellectual background. Surprisingly enough, considering that Lefebvre was primarily an economic historian, it also breaks new ground in its account of international relations, and sets the wars of intervention in their true light. The French have a taste for what they call works of synthesis, great general summaries of received knowledge. We might call them textbooks, though of the highest level. At any rate, in its class, whether synthesis or textbook, this is one of the best ever produced.'

*A. J. P. Taylor*

'Probably the greatest study ever written of the earthquake of 1789 and its aftermath.'

*John Banville, Irish Times*

Routledge Classics contains the very best of Routledge publishing over the past century or so, books that have, by popular consent, become established as classics in their field. Drawing on a fantastic heritage of innovative writing published by Routledge and its associated imprints, this series makes available in attractive, affordable form some of the most important works of modern times.

For a complete list of titles visit
www.routledgeclassics.com

Georges
# Lefebvre

## The French Revolution

From its origins to 1793

Translated by Elizabeth Moss Evanson

With a foreword by Paul H. Beik

London and New York

*La Révolution française* was first published in 1930 by Presses Universitaires de France. A new, entirely rewritten, version was published in 1951. The present work is a translation of the first three parts of the revised edition of 1957.

First published in the United Kingdom 1962
by Routledge and Kegan Paul

First published in Routledge Classics 2001
by Routledge
11 New Fetter Lane, London EC4P 4EE

Reprinted 2002, 2004

*Routledge is an imprint of the Taylor & Francis Group*

© 1962 Columbia University Press

Typeset in Joanna by RefineCatch Limited, Bungay, Suffolk
Printed and bound in Great Britain by
TJ International Ltd, Padstow, Cornwall

*British Library Cataloguing in Publication Data*
A catalogue record for this book is available from the British Library

ISBN 0–415–25547–3 (hbk)
ISBN 0–415–25393–4 (pbk)

# Contents

# FOREWORD

Georges Lefebvre, when he died in August, 1959, in his eighty-sixth year, was internationally known as the greatest authority on the French Revolution. His career had been extraordinary in its enduring creativity. Born at Lille, the son of a small commercial employee, he obtained secondary and university training with the help of scholarships, taught for more than twenty-five years in secondary schools, and entered university teaching at the age of fifty, after completing a monumental doctoral thesis, *Les paysans du Nord pendant la Révolution française*.[1]

In the French educational system a period of secondary teaching is not uncommon on the part of scholars awaiting opportunities at the university level. Lefebvre's contribution at each stage far exceeded the usual limits. After the quarter century of labour in provincial archives which paralleled his secondary teaching, he broke new ground by demonstrating in depth what the revolution had meant to the peasants. In the university career which followed, he proved himself, in the art of exposition, the equal of his famous predecessors Alphonse Aulard and Albert Mathiez, and produced syntheses which have ranked him, for

---

[1] Lille, C. Robbe, 1924. A second edition with the same text but omitting many notes and statistical tables has been issued by an Italian publisher, Laterza (Bari, 1959; Preface by Armando Saitta and Albert Soboul).

some, with the great historians. Lefebvre also played an important
institutional role as the recognized leader in his field, reviewer of its
important books and guide to innumerable research projects, a man
around whom gathered a whole generation of scholars who continued
to acknowledge his learning, lucidity, and balance.

Georges Lefebvre's first university teaching was at Clermont-Ferrand
and Strasbourg. Another decade passed before he was called to Paris in
1935. Upon the death of Albert Mathiez in 1932, Lefebvre was named
president of the Société des Études robespierristes and director of the
*Annales historiques de la Révolution française*, centres of his service to the profession during the following decades. In 1937 he succeeded to the
Chair of the History of the French Revolution at the Sorbonne, the
professorship made famous by Aulard and Mathiez. Although Lefebvre
appeared to be following in the footsteps of the dynamic Mathiez, he
was not his disciple. The two were, within a few months, the same age,
but while Mathiez in the early years of the century was becoming
famous, first as the brilliant pupil of Aulard and then as his critic,
Lefebvre was busy elsewhere. He translated Stubbs's *Constitutional History
of England* into a French edition in three volumes (1907, 1923, and
1927) and together with the medievalist Charles Petit-Dutaillis, under
whom he had studied at Lille, wrote many pages of notes and commen-
tary. As early as 1914 he published a collection of documents, titled
*Documents relatifs à l'histoire des subsistances dans le district de Bergues pendant la
Révolution (1788–An V)*.[1] As the title shows, he was already taking the
direction indicated by Jean Jaurès, the socialist historian who was to
be martyred by an assassin in 1914 and whose *Histoire socialiste de la
Révolution française* had appeared in four volumes between 1901 and
1904. Lefebvre always acknowledged that Jaurès was his model: 'I saw
and heard Jaurès only two times, lost in the crowd . . . but if anyone
cares to assign me a *maître*, I recognize only him.'[2]

[1] Lille, C. Robbe, 1914. A second volume appeared in 1921.

[2] Cited in Albert Soboul, 'Georges Lefebvre historien de la Révolution française 1874–
1959', *Annales historiques de la Révolution française*, No. 159 (Janvier–Mars, 1960), p. 3. This
entire issue is devoted to 'Hommage à Georges Lefebvre' on the part of his students and
friends. See also Beatrice F. Hyslop, 'Georges Lefebvre, Historian', *French Historical Studies*,
Vol. I, No. 3 (Spring, 1960), pp. 265–82, a perceptive appraisal by one who perhaps of all
American historians knew Georges Lefebvre best; and Robert R. Palmer, 'Georges

It may have been coincidental that Lefebvre chose 86 Boulevard Jean-Jaurès in Boulogne-sur-Seine, a plebeian suburb of Paris, as his residence; yet one suspects that his close friends were not surprised, for Lefebvre, like Jaurès, had deep emotional commitments. Both men were rationalist humanitarians in the tradition of the Enlightenment, who thought that the times called for democratic socialism. Lefebvre always remained true to this ideal. He was also a French patriot in the Jacobin tradition, who admired Robespierre for upholding civic virtue as essential to national independence. He could see Robespierre's weaknesses, as he could see weaknesses in Jaurès and Marx. Lefebvre was deeply influenced by Marx, and, like many of his generation, had passed through the experience of having to decide which parts of Marxism to accept and which to reject. He retained a strong tendency to wring the utmost in the way of historical explanations out of social and economic material. He had, however, an exquisite sense of balance and a deep appreciation for all kinds of evidence, and was above all an empiricist whose art consisted in telling the truth as his researches and fine understanding disclosed it to him. Lefebvre cared more for the exact statement of truth than for any other cause. 'His historical integrity,' as Beatrice Hyslop has written, 'was unimpeachable, and like Robespierre, incorruptible'.[1]

In his university career, Georges Lefebvre wrote works of synthesis and was drawn into a multitude of services to scholars and scholarship. He never ceased, however, to value above all the finding and publishing of new material, as is illustrated by his collection of documents *Questions agraires au temps de la Terreur* (1932), by his work for the Commission de recherche et de publication des documents relatifs à la vie économique de la Révolution, by his activities in connection with the hundred and fiftieth anniversary of the Revolution, and by the Institut d'histoire de la Révolution française, which he founded and kept going in spite of the Second World War and the post-war

Lefebvre: The Peasants and the French Revolution', *Journal of Modern History*, XXXI (March–December, 1959), pp. 329–42.

[1] Beatrice Hyslop, 'Georges Lefebvre, Historian', *French Historical Studies*, Vol. I, No. 3 (Spring, 1960), p. 278.

inflation.[1] His retirement in 1945 from his chair at the Sorbonne neither diminished his zeal nor curbed his influence. As the decade of the 1950s, and his own lifetime, drew to a close, Lefebvre was promoting a great collective effort of historical research designed literally to 'count', as he was fond of saying, the numbers, kinds, and resources of Frenchmen at the end of the Old Regime. His own unfinished *Études sur l'histoire économique et sociale d'Orléans et du département du Loiret pendant la Révolution française* was associated with this project. Meanwhile, year by year, Lefebvre took account in the columns of the *Annales historiques* of every important publication related to the French Revolution. He also furnished direct personal guidance to scholars from many lands who visited him at 86 Boulevard Jean-Jaurès.

Lefebvre's success as a writer of more general works may have occasioned some surprise, for he took this direction in his fifties, after having become known as a scholarly master of statistical tables and economic details. At that time, in the late 1920s, it could not have been foreseen that a whole career lay ahead for him. In any case, Lefebvre's works of synthesis revealed him as an unusually perceptive observer of human nature and of moods and ideas at all levels of society. His studies of peasant landholding led him to crowd psychology in *La Grande Peur de 1789* (Paris, A. Colin, 1932, 2d ed. 1956) and in his famous lecture, 'Foules révolutionnaires,' published in 1933.[2]

---

[1] A revised and enlarged edition of the *Questions agraires* was published in 1954 (Strasbourg, F. Lenig). Concerning the Commission, see the article by Marc Bouloiseau, 'De Jaurès à Lefebvre', *Annales historiques de la Révolution française*, No. 159 (Janvier–Mars, 1960), pp. 57–66, which summarizes Lefebvre's views concerning the value of systematically planned group research projects using statistics. The Institut d'histoire de la Révolution française, although reduced to a small, part-time research staff, produced in 1953 the first volume of a *Recueil de documents relatifs aux séances des États généraux, mai–juin 1789*, edited by Georges Lefebvre and Anne Terroine. Lefebvre also published, in collaboration with Marc Bouloiseau, Albert Soboul, and J. Dautry, the *Discours de Maximilien Robespierre* (4 vols., Paris, Presses Universitaires de France, 1950–59). The fourth volume reaches July, 1793.

[2] This and other important articles, for example 'La Révolution française et les paysans' and 'La Révolution française dans l'histoire du monde', together with a brief biographical note and a list of his principal publications, were published in honour of Georges Lefebvre's eightieth birthday as *Études sur la Révolution française* (Paris, Presses Universitaires de France, 1954). A recent book by an English historian, George Rudé, *The Crowd in the French Revolution* (Oxford, Oxford University Press, 1959), is dedicated to Lefebvre and acknowledges his influence.

*Quatre-Vingt-Neuf*, a little book about the year 1789, published in 1939 as part of the sesquicentennial celebration of the Revolution, is completely successful as a popular narrative and yet manages to impart the essence of scholarly findings together with a general statement about the significance of the Revolution. Lefebvre's eye for particulars combines here with his power to organize quantities of material without losing sight of the drama of long-term trends. 'This book had the misfortune to appear at the start of the Second World War and to be suppressed by the Vichy regime during the Nazi occupation. Only a few copies survived. Since 1947 an English translation by Robert R. Palmer[1] has acquainted many thousands of American students with Lefebvre and with the French Revolution.

As early as 1930 Lefebvre, in collaboration with Raymond Guyot and Philippe Sagnac, published *La Révolution française*, Volume XIII of the outstanding 'Peuples et Civilisations' series edited by Louis Halphen and Philippe Sagnac. For two decades the book was widely believed to be the best on its subject. In the next few years after its publication Lefebvre's attention turned to Napoleon Bonaparte and his relationship to the Revolution, and in 1935 he published as Volume XIV in the 'Peuples et Civilisations' series his *Napoléon*, which has had four editions, the latest in 1953. This study is still considered by many historians to be the most judicious evaluation of Napoleon's career. It also illustrates the author's ability to use social material without failing to appreciate the importance of individual will and character. After completing his *Napoléon*, Lefebvre went to work on the period from 1794 to 1799, years which had been least satisfactorily explained by historians and into which Albert Mathiez had been directing his researches at the time of his death in 1932. Mathiez's three-volume history of the Revolution having ended with the downfall of Robespierre, Lefebvre was requested by the publishers to carry the story forward, and did so in *Les Thermidoriens* (1937) and *Le Directoire* (1946). It was this work, together with the fresh researches of which he continuously took account in the *Annales*, which enabled Lefebvre to bring out in 1951 a new version, entirely rewritten by himself, of *La Révolution française*. The 1957 edition of this book, from which the present translation was made,

---

[1] *The Coming of the French Revolution* (Princeton, N.J., Princeton University Press).

incorporates some further revisions and bibliographical additions, and may be said to sum up more than half a century of research in its field. Seldom has any work been so consistently held at the crest of current scholarship.[1]

The 'Peuples et Civilisations' volumes, with their global setting and extensive diplomatic and cultural materials, offer a severe challenge to the literary craftsmanship of their authors. This series pioneered in the comparative study of institutions and cultures which has since the Second World War become more commonplace although scarcely less difficult. In the process of comparing developments in various parts of Europe and the world, Lefebvre's *La Révolution française* achieved a perspective denied to earlier historians of the Revolution. The author was, of course, best informed and most effective in the European area, which he knew best and to which most of his pages were devoted. He had an unusual knowledge of world history, however, and a talent for comparative descriptions. This aspect of his work may be said to have pointed the way to continued research in the field of comparative studies of institutions.[2]

Lefebvre's erudition and conscientious reporting led him to pack his 'Peuples et Civilisations' volumes rather tightly in places, but his sense of relevance was very keen. His direct style had a powerful, cumulative effect, and when he broke free into summary passages and interpretation he was extraordinarily eloquent.

Georges Lefebvre gave his consent to the present translation project, and discussed it with the translator, Elizabeth Moss Evanson, but he did

---

[1] Lefebvre in his turn took account of the discoveries of friends and disciples who had continued to emphasize economic and social materials, for example C. E. Labrousse, *La crise de l'économie française à la fin de l'ancien régime et au début de la Révolution* (Paris, Presses Universitaires de France, 1944), and Albert Soboul, *Les sans-culottes parisiens en l'an II. Mouvement populaire et gouvernement révolutionnaire, 2 juin, 1793–9 thermidor an II* (Paris, Librairie Clavreuil, 1958). Other long-time associates of Lefebvre have been Marc Bouloiseau, author of *Robespierre* (Paris, Presses Universitaires de France, 1957) and other studies, and Jacques Godechot, whose most recent books are *Les institutions de la France sous la Révolution et l'Empire* (Paris, Presses Universitaires de France, 1951) and *La grande nation. L'expansion révolutionnaire de la France dans le monde de 1789 à 1799*, 2 vols. (Paris, Aubier, 1956).

[2] See, for example, Robert R. Palmer's *The Age of the Democratic Revolution. A Political History of Europe and America, 1760–1800.* Vol. I: *The Challenge* (Princeton, N.J., Princeton University Press, 1959).

not live to see the finished product. Mrs. Evanson, an Editor at the Columbia University Press, was graduated from Swarthmore College and studied history there as well as in the graduate school of Columbia University and in the course of several periods of residence in France.

PAUL H. BEIK

*Swarthmore College,*
*Swarthmore, Pa.*

# Preface

This book is a translation of the first half of Georges Lefebvre's history of the French Revolution. The original was first published in 1951, and my translation is based on the 1957 reprinting, which contains additions to the Bibliography, corrections of printing errors, emendations, and one new footnote.

I have followed the French text as closely as possible within the limits inherent in rendering French syntax into English, and where word changes or shifts seemed justified, I have made them. Terms such as *bourgeoisie* have been translated literally, as I have considered it worthwhile to preserve the flavour of the original. In some cases, however, clarifying phrases have been run into the text—as, for example, when I have translated *généralités* as 'fiscal districts called *généralités*'. In rare instances I have added footnotes to explain terms which may not be familiar to the English-speaking reader.

The Bibliography has not been changed except to bring facts of publication up to date wherever such information could be obtained. Like the text, it represents French scholarship, and in both cases I have tried not to alter the French point of view.

I am especially indebted to Paul H. Beik, who was my teacher at Swarthmore College and who has encouraged this translation from the beginning. Without his help and consistent criticism the book could not have been prepared. I also wish to thank Professors Beatrice F. Hyslop, of Hunter College, John Hall Stewart, of Western Reserve University, and Shepard B. Clough, of Columbia University, who have offered helpful suggestions and useful comments.

ELIZABETH MOSS EVANSON

New York
June, 1961

# INTRODUCTION

The origins of the Revolution of 1789 lie deep in French history; the basic outcome of the Revolution hastened the nation's development without altering its historical direction. Begun by the 'patricians', as Chateaubriand remarked, the Revolution seemed to be the final episode in the aristocracy's struggle against the Capetian monarchy, and thereby it ended the long history of the kingdom. Completed by the 'plebeians', it made certain the advent of the bourgeoisie. Thus it inaugurated the history of modern France, but nonetheless capped the era preceding it, for the germination of that class within the feudal world it undermined was one major aspect of a long-term development.

Neither of these features sets France apart from Europe. All European states were formed similarly, at the expense of the lords, and all were sooner or later dominated by the rising bourgeoisie. The French Revolution was not the first which benefited a middle-class—before it, two revolutions in England and one in America were landmarks in that evolution.

Viewed in the broad development of civilization, the Revolution has greater significance. After the barbarian invasions ended, a passion for conquest drove Europeans towards domination of the globe, towards discovery and control of natural forces. At the same time a bold determination to govern the economy, society, and manners grew stronger—for the welfare of the individual and the improvement of mankind. The bourgeoisie of 1789 guaranteed freedom of research to the scholar, freedom of enterprise to the producer, and at the same time undertook to rationalize the ordering of politics and society. The French Revolution denotes one step in the destiny of the Western world.

Nevertheless, as its power grew the bourgeoisie could have stepped into government without breaking with the aristocracy. In England, after the revolutions of the seventeenth century, gentlemen and bourgeois joined to share power with the king; in the United States they dispensed with the monarch by common agreement; on the continent hereditary kings, yielding to historical change during the nineteenth century, retained control and arranged compromises. In France, on the contrary, the nobility intended both to impose itself on the king and to hold the bourgeoisie down. To oppose the aristocracy, the bourgeoisie became the apostle of the equality of rights, and when popular force stepped in the Old Regime abruptly gave way. The aristocracy lost not only its privileges but also a portion of its wealth and, consequently, of its social authority. Artisans and peasants, however, supporting the 'notables' in their struggle, turned the same principle of equal rights upon the bourgeois, who had used it to arm themselves, and the Revolution for a time led first to political democracy and then to an embryonic social democracy.

Accelerating its development with these sharp changes, the Revolution stirred fervent hopes beyond its frontiers. It also, however, aroused violent reaction from threatened kings and aristocrats. Thus, from 1789 to 1815, the history of countries of European culture was to a large extent determined by this great event.

Its influence has not yet ceased to play a role in men's lives. Nevertheless, if we today are for that reason inclined to view the French Revolution as one chapter in world history, the reader must not expect that feature to characterize the Revolution at the time it took place. Then, much of the world lay outside European dominion; the great civilizations which had developed under Islam and those in India, China, and Japan had not yet opened to the European spirit. The greater part of contemporary humanity was unaware of the flame that had been kindled in a small area of the world, or else did not feel its heat. The unity of the world is beginning to be realized in our time; only when it is achieved will a truly universal history begin.

# Part I

The World on the Eve of the
French Revolution

# 1

# EUROPEAN EXPANSION

The European spirit of conquest, so marked in all spheres from the twelfth century onward, dominant in the sixteenth, was then checked by religious and royal reaction. It was again released in the eighteenth century, termed by Michelet the 'great century' and in any terms the century of true renaissance. Let us look first at Europe's progress in exploration and in acquiring new territories overseas, as well as at the limits, still relatively narrow, which marked its extent.

## KNOWLEDGE OF THE GLOBE

Maritime exploration lagged during the seventeenth century, but was revived and systematized under the impulse of scientific knowledge and with technical improvements. One of the era's most important innovations was the ability to fix position, a development essential to navigation as well as to measurement of the globe and to cartography. New nautical instruments such as the compass, the sextant, and Borda's circle determined latitudes. Construction of the chronometer and maritime clocks and basic establishment of astronomical charts meant that longitudes could be calculated rather than simply estimated. These were revolutionary advances.

On the basis of knowledge gained during his second voyage

(1772–76), Cook dismissed the theory that a southern continent bordered on the antarctic pole. Many explored the waters of the Pacific, which covered one-third the globe's surface; Cook devoted his first and third voyages to the Pacific, and La Pérouse sailed the length of its American and Asiatic coasts. Many new islands were being discovered and had yet to be enumerated and visited. In addition, the search for polar areas and for the arctic passages of north-west and north-east remained in abeyance.

Continental expanses posed greater obstacles to penetration and were explored at a slower pace. Canadians reached Lake Winnipeg, the Great Slave Lake, and the Columbia River, then pushed over the Rockies and at Nootka Sound met Russians from Alaska and Spaniards from California. Squatters in the United States settled on the Ohio plains, but the area between the Mississippi and California was unknown, and knowledge of the Amazon basin was sketchy. Asia was known only superficially; of Africa nothing was familiar but the Mediterranean shores. The advent of the machine era had not yet shortened distances between points of the globe, and vast reaches of the earth were shrouded in mystery. The main outlines of continents and seas were nevertheless registered upon new maps; the face of the earth was emerging from shadow. In France Méchain, Delambre, and Lalande were about to undertake measuring a meridian.

## THE PARTITION OF OVERSEAS TERRITORIES

These new advances did not immediately affect the destiny of Europe, in contrast to the discoveries of the fifteenth and sixteenth centuries, which had produced an overseas empire. The congenital fragmentation of that empire reflected the disharmony of its rulers: Europe faced the new territories as a single conquering power, yet this was not the unity with which it had confronted Islam at the time of the early Crusades. Christianity still reigned, but religious differences were growing more pronounced; the East was Orthodox, the North, Protestant, the South, Catholic; the central regions were mixed; and free-thinkers were scattered through all areas. Political dissension was even older in origin. The formation of large states and their eastward expansion during the eighteenth century signified the disintegration of Europe as a political entity, for the drive towards power which spurred the dynasties responsible for state building also pitted ruler against ruler.

Discovery of new lands presented a larger stage for the play of rivalry among great powers. This had two results: continental hostilities expanded overseas in the form of increasingly complex naval and colonial warfare; and the powers bordering on, or having access to, the Atlantic profited most from the sharing of new spoils, which stimulated their economies and strengthened Western supremacy. The farther a nation lay from the Atlantic the lower was its level of prosperity, if not of civilization. Losing its monopoly over connections with Asia, the Mediterranean ceased to be the dynamic centre it once had been, a change hastened by the facts that part of its shores belonged to Islam and that it lacked anything like the natural resources of the West. Now only local traffic passed over the once great trading route running from Venice to Bruges and Antwerp by way of the Brenner Pass, Augsburg, and the Rhine valley. Italy and Germany lost their primacy in Europe's economy, and neither shared in the acquisition of colonies overseas. Italy still preserved a part of the wealth it had acquired, but Germany, ruined by the Thirty Years War, had to wait until the last decades of the eighteenth century for a revival.

Eastern Europe was even less fortunate: its only access to international trade lay through the Baltic, and the efforts of eighteenth-century enlightened despots could not alleviate its poverty. Its backwardness in comparison to the West grew more pronounced. Not until relatively late was it decided that the schismatic Muscovites could be considered Europeans. No one suspected that, in occupying Siberia, Russia was building its own kind of colonial empire, for Russian Asia then contained scarcely half a million inhabitants.

The diversity of Europe and the warring anarchy to which it was subject produced two visible results by the end of the Old Regime. Not only had the partitioning of new territories slackened since the sixteenth century; European supremacy was not yet contested, but colonial empires seemed faced with the threat of internal decomposition. And, although Europe continued to expand, dissension among its rulers curbed its overseas growth. The majority of the world's population lay outside its grasp.

## THE COLONIAL EMPIRES

Portugal and Holland were minor imperial powers left with fragments of their former possessions. Portugal now had Brazil and a few ports in Africa and Asia. Holland could boast of part of the West Indies, Dutch Guiana, settlements around the Cape of Good Hope, Ceylon, chiefly of Java and the Spice Islands. Spain, in contrast, not only retained its imperial boundaries but was expanding them by occupying California, where San Francisco had just been founded, and by acquiring Louisiana and along with it the Mississippi delta and New Orleans. It thus controlled the shores of the Gulf of Mexico and of the Caribbean Sea as well as two jewels in the Caribbean's belt of islands.

Last to become colonial powers, England and France had vied for North America, India, and the smaller West Indian islands. As the losing competitor, France possessed only Haiti, Martinique, Guadeloupe, and Île-de-France; in addition, it regained Saint Lucia, Tobago, and commercial agencies in the Senegal in 1783. Despite its losses, it therefore possessed a good part of the sugar-producing areas. The newly founded British Empire appeared shaken by the secession of its thirteen American colonies, and its conquest of India had slowed. Britain still controlled all of Bengal, received tribute from Oudh, and with Calcutta ruled Bombay and Madras. But Cornwallis, successor to Warren Hastings, had undertaken reform of the civil administration and was conciliatory in mood; he declined to support the Nizam, sovereign of Hyderabad, when that ruler was attacked by Tippoo, ruler of Mysore. Another threat was posed by the alliance of feudal Marathas led by Sindhia, whom the Great Mogul recognized as his hereditary lieutenant. Britain nevertheless held an ascendant position among European colonial powers.

The exploitation of all these empires led to similar ruthless mercantile practices. Each mother country imported the products it lacked and sent back part of its usual exports. In principle it did not allow its colonies to raise or manufacture anything that might compete with its own goods or to trade with other countries, and it permitted no ships other than its own to be used. In France this was called l'*exclusif* or exclusive colonial rights. Overseas territories thus supplied Europe with a mandatory clientele and with two of the basic resources that stimulated its economy: precious metals and tropical produce.

Three-fourths of the world's gold and more than nine-tenths of its white metals were provided by Latin America. The once rich Potosí mines of Bolivia were being exhausted, and Mexico was now the chief source of silver. As new lode veins were opened and the price of mercury dropped 50 per cent, after a group of Germans reorganized the working of Almadén, the production of silver jumped after 1760 and reached its greatest annual rate of 900 tons between 1780 and 1800. Gold had to be obtained by panning, and even though Brazil and the Guinea coast of Africa added rich sources, production declined.

The planting of food crops spread and stock farming expanded with the opening up of vast grasslands. Leather goods were exported, and the port of Buenos Aires, declared open in 1778, began to prosper. But Europeans were really interested only in tropical crops, primarily sugar cane and secondarily coffee, cacao, cotton and indigo, and tobacco. Sugar, coffee, and cotton from Brazil were added to shipments from Spanish colonies. Among native plants, vanilla and quinine, logwood and mahogany were sent to Europe. The labour force consisted mostly of Indians, who were compelled to reside in specific places and to perform forced labour. Charles III freed them in principle from the *mita* in mines and from the *encomienda*, which grouped them in villages serving plantations, but wage earners, such as the peons of Mexico, were in fact little more than slaves. In addition, the natives were required to pay a direct tax and to buy whatever European manufactured goods the managers wished to distribute. Many workers fled to the savanna, the mountains, or the impenetrable forests, so Negro slaves, who were, furthermore, stronger, were also employed. According to Humboldt, however, there were not many Negroes: he estimated that they constituted 5 per cent (as compared to an Indian population of 47 per cent) of the 16 million inhabitants he attributed to Latin America. But he added a category of 'mixed blood' forming 32 per cent.

The West Indies, Louisiana, the Atlantic coast from Florida to Maryland, and the Mascarene Islands in the Indian Ocean had no mines; there agricultural production found no rival. A large part of Europe's sugar and coffee came from the West Indies. France and England jealously regarded the islands as their most valuable colonies. The United States exported tobacco, but not yet cotton: introduction of the long-staple cotton called 'sea island' dated only from 1786. Because the Carib Indians had been exterminated in the West Indies and because colonists on the American continent were pushing the natives back from the coast, the entire economy of these areas depended upon Negro slave labour. Humboldt estimated that 40 per cent of the West Indies population was Negro, a figure which seems small in view of the fact that Necker recorded 85 per cent in the French islands. In Louisiana they were thought to constitute half of the total population; the United States had at least 500,000. In 1790 it was estimated that slave traders transported 74,000 Negroes to America each year. Africa was the 'ebony reservoir' for the New World. Europeans decimated the population with their raids on the mainland; a part of those captured died later at sea. The white men in Africa who ran commercial agencies sometimes traded with natives, but did not try to subjugate them.

A similar relationship, purely commercial, prevailed in Asia, where the main concern was not conquest but trade. Europeans paid native rulers for the right to establish trading stations, some of which remained in the eighteenth century. There had been many chartered trading companies in America, but now they were important only in Canada, where they dealt in furs. In contrast, the various East India companies retained their monopolies—the Dutch East India Company, which had gone in debt during the American war and was still having financial difficulties; the French Company, recently (1785) reorganized by Calonne; and the British Company, reformed by Pitt in 1784, which held the dominant position.

These companies sold little and bought much in the Far East. The exports of the French East India Company rose over a four-year period to 7 million livres, and the returns rose to 50 million. In the same period the British East India Company brought in a few woollen goods and hardwares, took back cotton goods, indigo, sugar, rice, and some saltpetre, and left an annual balance of about 2 million pounds sterling. The companies' monopoly did not extend to China: in 1789 twenty-five ships flying various flags, another fifty under the English flag, and yet another fifty serving inter-Indies traffic put in at Canton. The Chinese balance sheet, however, was similar to the European: they bought only a little opium and sold full cargoes of tea, china, and lacquer wares. Whereas Europe grew rich from America, the contrary was true of its relation to Asia, where it spent its money. Stockholders did not suffer from this arrangement, for sale of imported goods brought them huge profits at their compatriots' expense.

On the eve of the French Revolution the Dutch and the English were adding other strings to their bows. By subjugating native populations, as they had in America, they could exploit the inhabitants without having to import Negro slaves. The Dutch forced Malayans to work their plantations, imposed certain crops on the rural communities, and availed themselves of a portion of the harvest. The British East India Company exercised monopolies on salt, opium, and saltpetre, concluded unconscionable bargains with weavers by granting them advances, and after dispossessing native rulers collected a land tax in their stead. The exactions of the Company's agents aroused indignation within England: the trials of Clive and Warren Hastings brought to light a few of the practices—excused on grounds of services rendered—illustrating the extent to which subalterns were willing to push their authority. Asia did not know slave traders, but it experienced techniques which recalled those employed by the conquistadors.

In his *Philosophic History of the Two Indies* the abbé Raynal had recently published an indictment of overbearing masters, but only slavery itself was beginning to arouse religious or philanthropic scruples. For a long time the Quakers were the sole group to stigmatize the slave trade; the *philosophes* then joined their protests; finally a London Society of Friends of the Negroes was founded in 1787, and a sister organization was established in Paris during the following year. Wilberforce and Pitt grew interested in their programme, which aimed not at immediate suppression but at gradual disappearance by abolition of the trade.

Politicians and businessmen were too closely involved in the colonial system to consider giving it up, and, moreover, there were pleaders of its cause. Few on the continent defended the British colonists in India or those in North America who waged war against the Indians to push them westward and settle in their place. But as for Latin America, Raynal was reminded that the natives evidently benefited from prohibition of internecine wars, from undeniable advances in techniques and development of the economy, since the native population was increasing despite famine and epidemics. Reforms intended to alter colonial abuses were cited, as well as the paternalistic benevolence practised by some planters and the enthusiasm of monks who, like the earlier Jesuits in Paraguay, brought Indians into the missions to educate them. Colonial defenders pointed to the development of an embryonic middle class composed of Indians, half-breeds, and moneyed and educated mulattoes. Undeniable, nevertheless, was the fact that Europeans and planters supplied the colonies and developed production only to augment their own profits, doing nothing to improve the condition of the natives in the belief that it was sufficient to impose Catholicism upon them. While Western languages and customs spread through natural contact, personal interest, and social differentiation, the whites, imbued with racial prejudice, pushed aside the assimilated—even the half-breeds and mulattoes whom they had sired. Yet most of the subjugated peoples never entirely conformed to a European pattern. They transformed foreign languages into native dialects, secretly practised their religious rites, such as the Voodoo cult at Santo Domingo, and even preserved their legal customs.

White men did not attempt to establish residence in tropical Asia and Africa, where the climate was unfavourable and a frightening mortality rate reduced the ranks of company agents and employees. But in America and the Mascarene Islands there were, in addition to officials and military personnel, resident Europeans—planters, traders, supervisors, and 'petty whites' of various professions and circumstances. Many of them put down roots, and by the end of the eighteenth century colonial-born Europeans far outnumbered those from the mother country.

According to Humboldt, Spanish America was 19 per cent white and the proportion of European-born residents in Mexico was 7 per cent. Necker stated that 12 per cent of the French West Indies population was white; 3 per cent he classified as free 'people of colour'. Overseas, a minority of masters confronted a huge majority of subjects. In either long- or short-range terms a potential threat to the encroachers could not be denied. From time to time a leader arose to foment rebellion: the Peruvian Tupac Amaru in 1781; the Brazilian Tiradentes, executed in 1792. From their black slaves, planters feared domestic crimes and sporadic revolts. Yet in their eyes such perils inevitably accompanied the system, and by adjusting to conditions transplanted Europeans grew confident enough of the future to secede from their homeland.

## THE EMPIRES IN JEOPARDY AND THE AMERICAN REVOLUTION

Europe exported its methods of governing to the overseas territories: absolutism, bureaucratic centralism, military and police rule, religious intolerance. Only England, having evolved a constitutional system, granted its American nationals a certain degree of autonomy through charters. Aspects of the social structure of the older continent were also transplanted to Latin America: clerical privileges and certain noble pretensions, even the manorial regime in French Canada. These features were being attenuated, however, at least in the towns. In the French West Indies, for example, direct taxes were based on landholdings and admitted no exemptions; the Church did not have a great deal of property; nobles and commoners mingled in a modern, propertied bourgeoisie, characterized by wealth and forming a class distinct from the 'petty whites'.

The white men of Africa and Asia, few in number, residing temporarily, concerned only with achieving personal profit rapidly and at any risk, were not tempted to contest the discretionary authority of their companies. Whatever conflicts existed arose from competition and personal resentment, tensions characteristic of the mother country as well. Colonial-born residents, however, took a different stand. They grew impatient with a ministerial bureaucracy which undertook to decide the most important questions concerning them; they were jealous of crown representatives and aspired to self-government, if not to independence. Above all, they resented exclusive rights and wanted particularly to trade freely abroad. The West Indies especially would have profited from setting up a regular exchange of supplies from New England in return for sugar and rum. To these material issues were joined those of the enlightened philosophy that reached America. The colonists had schools and universities; even in Spanish and Portuguese territories books circulated freely despite the Inquisition. Rodríguez, master of Bolívar, was a disciple of Rousseau. Some of the colonials went to Europe to pursue their studies. The American Revolution occurred when the moment was ripe to convince others that speculation was not enough.

In contrast to the varied population of Latin America, the North Atlantic coast was peopled by white men alone—workers in search of land or employment who had nothing to do with black slaves or Indian servants and who were led by a bourgeoisie of modest pretensions, itself dominated by businessmen. This constituted a third type of European expansion. The throngs of Anglo-Saxons who left Europe formed the nucleus of a new Western world and developed an 'American personality' that was distinguished by a spirit of adventure and enterprise familiar to Europe, but also by a nonconformist individualism hostile to religious intolerance, to aristocracy, to the Old World despotism that Puritans had fled. The colonists of New England and Pennsylvania joined port traders, planters from Virginia and even from southern states, where the American personality was qualified by plantations and slavery, in the common task of expelling the Indians and pushing back French colonists, execrated as Papists, and also in opposing authoritarian mercantilism and representatives of the mother country. The Puritan spirit of independence preserved the concept of natural right, and charters granted to various colonies carried on the tradition of British common law. Refusing to be taxed by the London Parliament, where they had no representatives, the colonists severed relations with their homeland. The republic of the United States came into being.

Its example captivated European minds and made a powerful contribution to preliminary steps towards social and political reform. But it also forecast disruption of the authority commanded by all colonial powers. First and foremost, this act of secession indicated that England would have to plan an entirely new imperial structure if it were to establish white colonies in the future. A new solution was not, however, urgent, since no danger threatened from the French-speaking Canadians, obedient to their Catholic clergy and isolated by their religion, which itself guaranteed their cohesion. Nor was there any threat from the American loyalists who had emigrated to regions north of the Great Lakes. The important task was to keep these two Canadian elements from clashing, and Pitt achieved this in 1791 by dividing the area into two autonomous provinces.

On the other hand, Latin powers faced in United States independence the threat of a colonial amputation such as that suffered by Great Britain. American-born colonials stirred and instinctively turned their attention to the Anglo-Saxons, who, since the sixteenth century, had opposed Catholic states out of material interest and religious fanaticism. The English coveted the excellent markets which would be available if Spanish America were opened to trade, and they envied the sugar islands no less. It was hardly doubtful that the United States would soon favour the eviction of Europeans from the New World; in the interim it obtained access to several French West Indies ports in 1784. Miranda, a Venezuelan, would soon make overtures to Washington and Pitt; the Brazilian Maia tried to win Jefferson while at Nîmes in 1787.

Actually, the insurgents of the thirteen colonies owed their success to the desire of European powers to damage each other's interests. France, Spain, and Holland had supported the rebellious colonies against England; colonists could therefore count upon other coalitions some day to play into their hands. Europe stamped its imprint upon overseas conquests, and one could foresee that a humanity in its own image would take form throughout the world. If the hour of the people of colour was not yet at hand, Europe was beginning to realize that by transporting its sons across the seas it taught them to break off from their mother continent. At the same time its own internal dissension gave a respite to other parts of the world.

## FOREIGN CIVILIZATIONS

For centuries Moslems and Christians had been as if inseparable. The same fanaticism had engendered holy war between them. As the heir of Graeco-Roman civilization and as the mediator between Asia and Europe, Islam had been the catalyst of Europe's medieval Renaissance. Mediterranean commerce bound them together. In the eighteenth century Islam continued to recruit followers in the Sudan and the Malay Archipelago, but on the European front it had been thrown on the defensive and was falling back. Trade with Asia had turned away from the Moslem world; its economy was stagnant, its intellectual and artistic life fading.

At the dawn of the modern world the Ottoman sultan had seemed about to restore Islamic unity, but he had failed. At the end of the eighteenth century he had not regained Morocco; Shiitic Persia resisted him; the Berbers no longer obeyed him; and in central Arabia, after Abd-el-Wahab had preached return to primitive austerity, Saud was preparing to fight a holy war. The size of the Grand Turk's empire encouraged an appearance of power, but its decadence was manifest. The unique military and administrative system which recruited its personnel from Christian converts had deteriorated as Turkish warriors, grown accustomed to sedentary life in their 'timars', pushed their sons, who were trained at schools, into office. Provincial pashas were slipping towards autonomy; Ali Pasha had just made himself master of Yannina; in Egypt the Mamelukes ruled as they pleased. The Turks did not try to convert or assimilate Christians, letting them live under the administration of their own priests and notables. The Greeks and Armenians of the port towns formed a commercial and banking bourgeoisie, which dealt with European merchants protected by the Turkish capitulations granting extra-territorial rights; and Greek ships, the only merchant marine of the empire, were to be seen everywhere in the Mediterranean. Finally, Christian powers were becoming more influential: France was the protector of Catholics; the Serbs turned to Austria, the Montenegrins and Greeks to Russia. Austria was the first to profit from Osmanli weakness, by reconquering Hungary. Recently Catherine II, having pushed down to the coast of the Black Sea (as far west as the Bug River), annexed the Crimea and the Caucasus, thus ending Tartar raids and opening up the black-earth region to her peasants. The Turkish empire was no longer capable of keeping Europe out of the Moslem world.

Europeans visited only the coasts of Negro Africa, particularly Senegal and the Gulf of Guinea, in their search for slaves. With the exception of Dutch settlers on the Cape, the only outsiders to venture inland were Arab traders from the Sudan and eastern regions. Native empires of varying stability still existed: the Benin kingdom boasted of bronze art in the sixteenth and seventeenth centuries and regained some of its prosperity in the eighteenth century; east of the Niger the Hausa states had flourished since the seventeenth century; the Sokoto, Bornu, and Kanem states grew stronger early in the nineteenth century. But these played no role in general history.

Asia, to the contrary, with its fabled riches and its great civilizations which had reached their height long before that of Europe, continued to evoke curiosity. The magnificence and treasures of the shah of Persia and of the Great Mogul still kept a legendary character, but Europe had begun to discover that, having failed to advance for many centuries, this part of the world was easy prey. India was already passing into English hands. Burma and Cambodia could offer little resistance; in Annam Bishop Pigneau de Béhaine and the merchants of Pondichéry took advantage of domestic anarchy to try their luck. When Cochin China was attacked by the Taj-Suns, a rebellious mountain people who had taken Tonkin and Hué in 1787, Nguyen-Anh signed a treaty with France ceding Tourane and Poulo-Condore to the French and granting them a monopoly on trade. Louis XVI did not, however, ratify the treaty. Europeans found Indochina less tempting than Japan and China, where missionaries and merchants had penetrated in the sixteenth century but had been shut out since the seventeenth.

In China the reign of Ch'ien Lung was drawing to a close. This great sovereign and conqueror was a highly cultured ruler and a talented administrator who, after ascending the throne in 1736, successfully continued the work of K'ang-Hsi. In his lifetime the Manchu dynasty reached its height: he subdued Mongolia and Turkestan, whose nomad bands had plagued both China and Europe, and imposed his suzerainty on Tibet, Nepal, and Annam. China's influence spread through emigration as well. The Chinese were the only foreigners admitted to Japan. They settled in Cochin China, reached Bengal and the Philippines, and prospered everywhere through commerce and usury. Ch'ien Lung did not admit foreigners, and he dealt severely with those of his subjects whom the Jesuits and then the Lazarists had converted. The Son of Heaven deigned to authorize the barbarians, whose currency he pocketed, to trade with his subjects, but only at Canton. The West admired China for its highly moral philosophy, its enlightened emperor, the democratic features of a society in which nobility was purely honorific—with no privileges or duties—and state service was open to all competitors. The mandarinate was indeed unique in the world, and China had in the past possessed its share of inventors and thinkers.

It had, however, long ago hardened in its traditions. The mandarins received only a formal education. An abundant labour supply had discouraged technical advances and even the use of animal power. As was true throughout Asia, the emperor's authority stemmed from his person and was not buttressed by institutions. Absolute in theory, it depended upon the good will of provincial governors, who had charge of the militia and of proceeds from duties, only a small part of which went into the central treasury. The imperial troops encamped around Peking and a few of the larger cities were supplied with obsolete equipment. Finally, although the Manchus had treated the Chinese well and had given them administrative posts, a national movement smouldered in many secret societies. Ch'ien-Lung had to suppress several revolts at the end of his long reign. His huge empire could offer little effective resistance to Europeans.

Japan was even more hostile to Westerners. It sold only a little copper to the Dutch, confined upon an island opposite Nagasaki, and bought nothing in return. The ruling Tokugawa family had restored order by imposing its authority upon the daimyo (feudal lords) to the extent of forcing the lords to sell surplus crops from their domains only through the state, but the Tokugawas supported Japan's feudal and military aristocracy by abandoning the peasants to aristocratic discretion and by prohibiting emigration in order to assure the nobles a labour force. The Japanese artisan was highly skilled and, under noble patronage, the art of painting and printmaking reached its height with Kujonaga, Utamaro, and Hokusai. Like China, however, Japan was ignorant of technical progress and experimental science. The samurai remained a medieval warrior.

The country seemed prosperous in the seventeenth century, when its population is estimated to have been 23 millions. But terrible famines ravaged its people, crowded into the various islands, during the following century. Revenue ceased to flow to the state and to the daimyo. Duties, labour services, and land rents grew more oppressive to the peasants; currency weakened and dropped. The impoverished daimyo could no longer support the samurai, who began to break away from their class. Some entered trades, others left in search of employment, still others adopted the errant life of the ronin, warriors who lived on the fringes of society.

Under Ieharu, degenerate descendant of the great Tokugawas, the shogunate and its bureaucracy not only failed to check the country's decadence but added to it through wastefulness. At Kyoto the court helped them by selling guarantees of the emperor's submission. When Ienari, a minor, acceded in 1786, his brother Hitotsubachi became regent. He and his minister Tanuma, considered a reformer, were deposed by the Tokugawas in 1788. The new regent, Sadanobu, undertook to restore the regime—or at least its treasury—by issuing sumptuary ordinances, reducing debts, and stabilizing the currency. But, having quarrelled with the court and encountered opposition from his predecessor, he had to retire when Ienari came of age in 1793.

A bourgeoisie of merchants and financiers who had influence but were denied landed property and government office existed in the large towns, chiefly at Osaka. We do not know if they learned from Chinese émigrés of rationalist Confucianism, which evidently dared to assert that the gods made no distinction among men and which contested the solar origins of the Mikado. Neither do we know if Tanuma and Sadanobu came to terms with this class, an event that would indicate resemblance to the enlightened despots of the West. It is none the less true that a mystical and nationalistic reaction, supported with a legendary history taught by Motoori Norinaga, the disciple of Kamo Mabuchi (who died in 1769), had taken root. Mabuchi purified the language, preached a return to Shinto, and opposed Chinese influence. Motoori reminded his listeners that the empire on earth belonged to Tenno, descendant of Atamerasu. The lettered samurai gave their approval while waiting for better times. Politically, this romanticism meant that the shogun was a usurper. The European intervention which was to provoke his fall, however, did not come for another seventy-five years.

The technical inferiority of these peoples left them vulnerable to foreign conquest, but their distance from Europe protected them in an era when vessels depended upon wind and sail and the round trip to China took eighteen to twenty months. Separation by water did not shield Mediterranean Islam from Europe; furthermore, Russia, following Austria's lead, attacked the Ottoman empire overland. Yet internal rivalries slowed the conquest of new lands. Europe embraced 200 million inhabitants, America 25 million. The Africans—100 million—and most Asians—500–600 million—were not under Europe's sway.

Consequently the great majority of the earth's population lived and died without suspecting that in one corner of the world, in France, a revolution had occurred which was to leave a spiritual legacy to their descendants.

# 2

## EUROPEAN ECONOMY

The European economy developed steadily through the final centuries of the Middle Ages, then gained momentum from the mercantilist policies of great states and the exploitation of new lands overseas. In England during the eighteenth century economic progress gained revolutionary force, brought in the reign of the steam engine and of mechanized power, and on the eve of the French Revolution gave Britain a superiority which was to play an essential role during the long struggle that followed. With the advantage of historical perspective we label this economic surge the industrial revolution because we can perceive in it the germ of world transformation. Its development was slow, nevertheless, even in the country of its origin, and the fact that England owed its superiority merely to the first stages of industrialism implies that the continent was as yet scarcely affected. Europe's economy in the concluding years of the eighteenth century seemed, despite its relative prosperity, to share much in common with the past.

## THE TRADITIONAL ECONOMY AND ITS DEVELOPMENT

The old methods of production yielded a slow and meagre output. Agriculture was governed by climatic caprice; industry was restricted by the scarcity of raw materials and the inadequacy of power resources.

The peasant laboured for his own consumption and sold none of his produce or sold only enough to acquire the cash that king, lord, or landholder demanded of him. The artisan supplied only his local market. Difficulties of transportation forced each district to live off its own produce. Every region jealously guarded its grain crop, exported little, and lacked the means to import.

In large measure, the situation as yet was little changed. England still purchased no more than one-tenth of its wool. Central and eastern Europe lived in a virtually closed economy. Yet natural conditions dictated a certain economic interdependence. This was especially true of the grain trade; Turgot estimated that its volume ran to 25 or 30 million bushels. Spain, Portugal, Norway, and Sweden always bought grain, and Switzerland and Great Britain imported one-sixth of their domestic consumption. There was a regular demand for wood, resin, tars, and potash from Poland and Russia, for minerals and metallurgic products from Sweden and Germany. Wine, brandy, and salt came from southern Europe, soda and wool from Spain, alum and sulphur from Italy. Thus, the eastern, southern, and central portions of Europe supplied foodstuffs and raw materials, and the western areas furnished manufactured goods and colonial products in exchange.

The major avenues of inter-European trade were sea routes, benefiting chiefly the ports and merchant fleets of the North Sea, the English Channel, and the Atlantic. The English were the leading shippers, followed by the Dutch, the Hanseatics, and the Scandinavians. The Mediterranean ports of Marseille, Genoa, and Leghorn still played a role, but the most striking change was a surge of traffic upon the Baltic. This northern trade profited Denmark, ruler of the Oresund; became of vital importance to England's consumption and to her navy; and brought Prussia, Poland, Scandinavia, and Russia into the European economic circuit.

Commerce within states was relatively insignificant. Here, too, England took the lead, followed by France. Transportation by water was the only economical way to ship goods, but rivers were rarely navigable and canals were few, so land routes costing half as much again were generally employed. Highways in England, France, and the Netherlands were being improved, but elsewhere there were only more or less rocky trails which were unusable during the winter months. Mountain ranges such as the Alps did not yet have roads that could bear vehicles. Even the countries with the best roadways had neither main routes nor rural roads which could carry heavy traffic, and pack animals were still commonly used. In the South and East such difficulties grew more pronounced; whereas fairs were fading in western areas, they retained importance in the south, as at Beaucaire, were especially popular at Frankfurt and Leipzig, and farther east continued to play their medieval role. These conditions indicate that no state could have created a truly national market even if it had not already been divided by internal customs barriers—except for England—and manorial or royal toll houses.

Factors which had stimulated the transformation of Europe's economy over the past few centuries were still at work. The powerful states of Western Europe had begun to practise mercantilism as soon as they came into being, and eighteenth-century rulers abandoned none of the economic aspects of that policy: prohibition or strict control of imports; navigation acts and exclusive colonial rights; establishment of royal factories and monopolistic companies; privileges granted to private enterprises; controls exercised through the agency of gilds. In England and France there were always loopholes in these controls; gilds did not exist in the countryside and did not extend to all cities or to all trades. The mercantile system had undeniably protected nascent industries from a competition they could not have borne, particularly in the cases of textiles and luxury goods, and the policy had favoured accumulation of capital by reserving to nationals the profits accruing from freight service and colonial exploitation. Late in the eighteenth century criticism from economists began to undermine protectionist policies, but most of the enlightened despots supported them with a vigour befitting Colbert himself. Moreover, if liberty appealed to manufacturers and merchants, they had no intention of extending it to foreign competitors; they remained uncompromising protectionists. Commercial treaties of a liberal nature, such as that signed by Vergennes and Pitt in 1786 or those granted by Catherine the Great to her Black Sea ports, were the exception rather than the rule.

Luxury industries were aided by purchases from princes and courtiers, who set the style for the upper classes; metallurgical industries, shipyards, and textile and tanning factories were aided even more by government orders that resulted from expansion of the armed forces. And, finally, by farming out indirect taxes, by giving commissaries charge of certain public services, and especially by granting them responsibility for supplying the armies out of their own advances, by borrowing with loans granted in perpetuity, by issuing life, or, more often, short-term annuities, governments guaranteed the increasing prosperity of financiers and bankers. The productive activity of these men affected the central treasuries of almost all states.

Furthermore, colonial exploitation regained the importance it had held in the sixteenth century. Once again bullion poured into the Old World, reaching an unprecedented level after 1780. During the eighteenth century 57,000 metric tons of silver and 1,900 of gold were extracted; of these totals, 17,500 tons (30 per cent) and 356 tons (19 per cent), respectively, were mined in the last two decades of the century. Gold was at a premium; in England silver was used only for small change after 1774, and Calonne had to recoin the louis in 1785 to reduce its weight. Latin America supplied more than nine-tenths of the metal for this currency, but Spain and Portugal used it to pay for imports, and it thus passed into English, Dutch, and French circulation. From there a part reached Asia; luxury expenses and hoarding kept another portion in Europe. France's coin circulation may have ranged from 2 to 3 billion livres. Holland's *per capita* coin circulation is considered to have been greater; that of England, now estimated to have been less than a billion, was smaller; and in both countries there was also paper money issued by banks. With an abundant supply of money, financiers had funds at their disposal. They unfortunately followed tradition in offering indebted governments the option on this capital, but some part of it did go into production. Amsterdam was the financial centre of the world. Although its bank was jeopardized by advances to the India Company and to the city, its financiers were still able to provide credit to other states. It was said that they could lend 14 million florins annually and that their investments reached 1 billion. Genoa, Geneva, and Bern also placed funds abroad; London and Paris were more often borrowers. Bankers of these cities maintained close contact. Always on the lookout for advantageous speculation, they built up a network of international finance which ignored national boundaries. Among them were Baring at London, Hope and Labouchère at

Amsterdam, Parish at Hamburg, Rothschild and Bethmann at Frankfurt, and the foreigners—mostly Swiss and usually Protestant—who had colonized Paris. The exchange of each city was the gathering place for the money handlers. Dealings in futures had long been practised at both Amsterdam and London.

The increase in specie, boosted somewhat by fiduciary issue in England, by the paper currency of several continental states, by a certain amount of bank credit, by circulation of commercial bills of exchange, resulted in a steady rise in prices. A long-term upward movement which began about 1730 and lasted until 1820 replaced stagnation. Despite cyclical fluctuations, a rise of this nature encouraged investment with the allure of unearned income. An increase in population, marked after 1760, acted as a rejuvenating force by augmenting both consumption and the labour force, but the rise in prices remained a major stimulant to the European economy.

Commercial dealings with overseas territories caused a significant expansion in Western trade. On the eve of the French Revolution commerce with their colonies represented 40 per cent of the trade of France and of England. Both countries fed many colonial products into their exported goods, and because Spain and Portugal purchased those goods, France and England to a certain extent had at their disposal, indirectly, Spanish and Portuguese possessions. In addition, the French and British traded illegally with Spanish America and Brazil. Produce extracted from plantations owned by Europeans and the various profits accruing from colonial development also figured in Europe's commercial wealth. In 1798 Pitt valued revenue from the American plantations at 4 million pounds sterling and income from the English in Asia at 1 million. The slave trade too brought profits: in 1780 it was estimated that the slave traders of Liverpool earned 300,000 pounds each year; in the decade between 1783 and 1793 they outfitted between 110 and 120 vessels and sold 300,000 slaves for a total of over 15 million pounds.

This new money, concentrated in the hands of relatively few individuals, was spent for luxury items, lent to royal treasuries, invested in land, or hoarded. Nevertheless, a significant part was undoubtedly used to finance enterprises. In regard to technical progress, perhaps the most important stimulus was the introduction of cotton into European industry. From it was manufactured not only printed cloth—the first English machines were put to work spinning and then weaving cotton textiles.

It was maritime commerce which, by the boldness and risks it involved, had produced the first economic innovators. Trade from market to market and then finance in the service of the state were later associated with it. A mentality foreign to the conventional economy inspired these traders. Their attitude, characterized by a hazardous quest for profit, transformed the warring spirit into a ruthless determination to vanquish competitors and made speculation the mainspring of their activity. With them appeared certain characteristics of what we call capitalism—concentration of capital and of business concerns so that exploitation could be rationalized, a development that gave this economic technique cardinal importance in the rise of European civilization. By the end of the eighteenth century domestic trade and even financial transactions were less risky, but maritime commerce was still subject to the hazards of fortune—in France, funds invested in ocean trade were called loans 'for the great venture'. In recompense, these investments built up huge fortunes. Rationalization of business procedures had long been evident in methods of financial exchange, in use of commercial notes and deposit banks, in development of individual enterprises—firms or business associations—through adoption of double-entry book-keeping, made possible by the use of balance sheets. Monopoly companies introduced another improvement by specializing management, employing technicians rather than shareholders. But this process was in its early stages, and functions were still mixed—the shipowner was also a merchant, the merchant was also a shipper, both were commission agents, underwriters, bankers. Business methods were perfected in slow stages. The exchange was little more than a convenient meeting-place; trading in futures was rare. Few business houses employed commercial travellers, and the itinerant merchants who went from fair to fair as hawkers still played an important role, less to cover the markets than to deal with retailers as small-scale wholesalers. Many of the retailers themselves, such as those called *merciers* in France, did not specialize in any one item; moreover, in various regions—even in England—villagers supplied their needs by patronizing occasional pedlars.

Commercial capitalism, the master of distant markets, had soon begun to exploit the artisanry and to develop a rural industry which paid low wages and did not have strict regulations. The importation of cotton stimulated these home industries through all Western Europe. Merchants played a varying part in domestic production: some only picked up the finished goods; more frequently they rationalized productive methods by supplying raw materials and equipment, establishing standards, and themselves supervising the preparing and dyeing of cloth. They enlarged the peasant labour force through the offer of extra wages, taught new methods, and lengthened the work day. Women and children were herded into work brigades long before the advent of the factory. Often, what was called the manufactory of a town meant only the aggregate of resident workers employed in the urban centre or surrounding areas. The term acquired another meaning as some or all labourers were later gathered in one workshop and were sometimes forced to live in neighbouring buildings. Production of goods requiring costly equipment did not suit individual craftsmanship: mines, foundries, forges, glass and crystal works, earthenware and porcelain manufactories, paper works, silk winderies, breweries, and distilleries had long gathered the workers under the immediate supervision of proprietors. This system was the most practicable one for new industries such as those producing printed cloth. But rarely was the number of workers thus employed large.

The rise of commerce and industry did not overshadow agriculture as the mainstay of the economy. Everyone was in one way or another involved with land: the individual, rich or poor, who aspired to become a man of property; the statesman who knew that population increase depended upon more food and hence meant more taxpayers and prospective public servants. Yet mercantilism often sacrificed agriculture to industry by curtailing export of raw materials; and administrators hesitated to abandon trade controls despite strong criticism from economists and landed aristocrats. A free grain trade meant high bread prices and would cause starvation and riots. The farmer therefore was forbidden to sell his produce on the spot; instead he had to deliver it to the local market, where consumer pressure or, failing that, the municipality, kept prices down. Domestic trade employing sea routes was controlled by the *acquit à caution*, which required the shipper to furnish proof that the cargo was unloaded in a national port. Land shipments ran afoul of suspicions from the authorities and popular hostility. Shipments abroad were strictly prohibited. The state was reluctant to allow unregulated cultivation because almost all peasants remained devoted to traditional controls.

The economy of continental Europe thus remained essentially what it had been for centuries. Only in Flanders was intensive cultivation and the stabling of livestock commonly practised—which was made possible by abandoning the tradition of permitting the ground to lie fallow and instead using this land for fodder and oleaginous crops. Elsewhere in Europe extensive cultivation was relied on to increase production: new land was drained and cleared. In mountainous areas and all regions that, lacking lime in the subsoil, were wastelands, crops were raised in strips, fenced against the cattle who grazed over vast common lands. The commons were seeded only rarely, in patches where weeds had been burned off. In the fertile plains village lands were split up into separate fields, which lay fallow one out of every three years in northern Europe, one out of two in the South. Each farmer had at his disposal scattered strips of land within the fields. The strips were elongated and parallel in the North, of irregular shape elsewhere. The ground lay fallow because there was little manure; the peasants fed only a few beasts in stables during the winter because there was little hay; the animals were expected to graze in fallow fields, common lands, and forests the rest of the time. Free pasturage required open fields: enclosures were forbidden altogether in the North and frowned upon elsewhere unless there were large expanses of uncultivated land, as in western France. Free pasturage lost its importance only in the Mediterranean regions, where the few unproductive, small plots, partly irrigated or terraced, were planted indiscriminately in vines and fruit and olive trees.

The peasant was burdened with obligations and either did not possess the means to introduce new methods or else used his savings only to buy another plot. He was usually uneducated and clung to the security of traditional routine. He stubbornly defended the right of free pasturage, without which, he declared, he could not raise his livestock. Along with the right to use forests for building materials and fuel, free pasturage ranked first among the collective rights required for his livelihood.

These are the general characteristics of Europe's economy. Yet the eighteenth century witnessed decisive economic events. The development of a banking organization, of new business methods, of machines and mechanized power, was to entail a radical change in production, replacing commercial capitalism with industrial capitalism as the driving force within the economy. Similarly, aspects of modern agriculture were beginning to appear.

These innovations were at work in England, a nation which outstripped the rest of the Western world while its continental neighbours were only awakening to new developments, or, in central and eastern areas, were unaware of any changes.

## THE ECONOMIC REVOLUTION IN ENGLAND

Since the end of the seventeenth century economic progress had given England a clear lead. During the eighteenth, its ships tripled in number and the tonnage they carried quadrupled. In 1788 it outfitted 9,630 vessels, carrying a total of 1,453,000 tons; in 1790 three times as many ships passed through its ports as in 1714. Foreign trade rose from 6 million pounds in exports and the same in imports at the beginning of the eighteenth century to 19 million pounds for imports and 20 for exports on the eve of the French Revolution. Domestic trade was facilitated by coastal shipping, since the sea was never far from any British town. Geography also encouraged the construction of interconnected canals, and roads were improved with Macadam's process. Soft coal came into more extensive use at an earlier date than on the continent. As early as the fifteenth century commercial capitalism, not satisfied to use artisans of the towns, had begun to develop rural industries.

It is estimated that between 1740 and 1800 personal capital increased 500 per cent in Great Britain. Exportation, the slave trade, overseas plantations, freight services, and insurance brought in enough money to put the nation on a virtual gold standard during the last quarter of the eighteenth century. In 1694, however, business and the state, acting in concert, had founded the Bank of England upon entirely new principles: issue of bank-notes backed by cash on hand, and discounting of commercial notes. In 1789, 10–11 million pounds circulated in the form of bank-notes. Only 1 million at most were exchanged in the provinces, yet Scotland had had its own bank of issue since 1695, and another was established at Dublin in 1783. In addition, there were about sixty private banks in London, nearly three hundred outside the city, and others in Scotland and Ireland that all issued notes on their own authority. The Bank of England, like the financiers on the continent, bowed to a certain extent before needs of the state treasury, accepting exchequer bills and cash vouchers from the ministers. But the Bank also used its own special issue in discounting bills of exchange and thus offered short-term credit to companies. It dealt directly only with citizens of London, but by opening accounts for some private banks, which were adopting the practice of discounting, the Bank of London became a superbank.

The industrial revolution also confirmed Britain's economic superiority. Metallurgy was transformed with the substitution of coal for wood as fuel: puddling furnaces were introduced in 1783, rolling mills in 1784. An increasing number of machine tools generalized use of iron, which came to be employed in construction of barges and bridges. The fame of Birmingham hardwares spread. The engineering profession assumed prestige in public eyes, as Maudslay later illustrated. Changes in the cotton industry brought even greater fame: the jenny, the water frame, and, after 1780, Crompton's mule, mechanized spinning. Cartwright's invention of the power loom promised a similar revolution in weaving. Improvements were being introduced into pottery manufacture and dyeing as well. Watt's steam engine, perfected between 1764 and 1789, provided a source of power of unsurpassed importance.

Economic controls relaxed, and businessmen attacked the monopoly held by the British East India Company. Yet mercantilism by no means lost all its rights: customs protection, exclusive colonial rights, and navigation acts remained as a defence against foreign competition. On the other hand, agriculture freed itself from tradition and began to modernize as a result of consolidating open-field strips into compact holdings and dividing up the commons. This permitted enclosures and eliminated free pasturage. Enclosures had existed for some time, but now the gentry, masters of the country since the Glorious Revolution, found themselves in a position to enclose on a grand scale. Parliament regularized the process in 1780. Scottish lords began to follow suit in the Highlands. A number of enlightened farmers possessing extensive lands and sufficient capital suppressed the practice of fallow fields, developed fodder crops, and increased their livestock by stabling the animals during the winter and applying selective breeding. The reputation of British herds spread. Following 1688 the great landowners had protected grains by inaugurating a system of corn laws which flouted tradition in allowing exports to continue and in prohibiting imports whenever their domestic price did not exceed a level considered profitable.

The deep penetration of new techniques advanced at a slower rate than has long been believed. Enclosures, perhaps the most advanced of these techniques, let landholders remain in many regions. One cotton spinning factory employed the steam engine; in 1788 twenty-six furnaces, producing one-fifth of the nation's cast iron, still used wood for fuel. Cartwright's method was not used for weaving cotton fabrics; the woollen industry had not changed. With the exception of distilling and brewing industries, handicrafts prevailed in London. Even with progress in banking methods England could finance enterprises only to a limited degree, and concentration of industry on any large scale was therefore difficult. The joint-stock company, subject to Parliamentary authorization, had not adjusted to a new era.

In transportation there was an urgent need to revolutionize methods by adopting the steam engine for power. Shipbuilding was undergoing technical improvement, and after 1780 vessels were covered with copper. But they were built of wood and their number and dimension depended on the timber supply—it took 4,000 oak trees to build one large vessel—and on the size of trees—out of 10,000, only one might provide a suitable mast. Most ships were consequently built to carry less than 100 tons; only the East India Company owned a few with more than 800 tons capacity. The vessels could at best travel a slow and irregular course with their clumsy sails. Stagecoaches and diligences had been somewhat modernized, but even the stoutest could carry no more than 1,500 pounds and needed four horses to do so. The transportation industry employed an enormous labour force, and mechanization threatened congestion and unemployment.

A new economic era was none the less heralded. By 1789 England no longer fed its expanded and partly industrialized population from its own resources. Significantly, the depression of 1789 was attributed to over-extension of credit and to clumsy efforts at mechanization, as well as to a bad harvest. When the Bank of England's discount fell from 58 million pounds in 1788 to 35 million the next year blame fell upon private banks for making advances without thought for the future, thus generating overproduction, and upon the over-abundance of cotton, since not all could be absorbed by the unmechanized weaving industry. It was also observed that war in Eastern Europe shut off the markets and that because England had not widened those markets paralysis gripped the economy. During the Revolutionary and Napoleonic period Great Britain clearly asserted its economic supremacy: it was able to finance coalitions, and, ruling the seas, could open up new outlets for its industry when the continent was blockaded.

## THE BACKWARDNESS OF CONTINENTAL EUROPE

The states of Western Europe lagged noticeably behind Britain, not excluding France, which nevertheless led the rest. Stagnation increased proportionately as one travelled eastward.

Europe's first banks had been established in Italy and then in Holland—at Genoa, Venice, and Amsterdam. But these were still little more than deposit houses: their certificates of payment, although transferable, could not compare to bank-notes; and they did not practise commercial discounting. France alone had founded a Bank of Discount in 1776, authorized by the state to issue notes which could be exchanged for bills drawn upon clients by suppliers. These notes, however, circulated only in the Paris area. There were few private banks, and many of the important cities, such as Orléans, had none at all. Those in existence did not usually issue fiduciary currency upon their own authority. In France an abundant money supply was available only at Paris, where tax collections accumulated; in the provinces credit was rarely offered, and then only at high rates. In Italy endorsement of commercial bills was not practised. Entrepreneurs generally used personal capital drawn from family and friends and mortgaged real property to obtain necessary funds. They had to endure long delays from their buyers, even when the purchaser was wealthy, and so resorted to accommodation bills. The law recognized only 'general companies'— i.e., firms or other collective organizations—and sleeping partnerships. State authorization was needed to establish a joint-stock company. Stocks were registered, or at least could not be transferred without the company's consent. Sleeping partners and shareholders lacked the legal protection of limited liability. French jurisprudence, still in an indecisive stage, tended only to restrict the shareholder's contribution to the company's assets. In contrast with England, continental Europe lacked a banking apparatus that could accumulate savings and use them to finance new companies.

Amsterdam, Hamburg, and Lisbon were regarded by the British as important centres—since the Treaty of Methuen Portugal had been virtually an English colony, and Lisbon's exchange had figured prominently at London—yet the only country to offer what the English considered significant competition in the area of trade was France. Traffic from France alone could stand comparison with that of Britain: it surpassed one billion livres on the eve of the Revolution. True, its balance was unfavourable—542 million livres in exports and 611 million in imports—but over 200 million of the imports were brought in from the colonies. The merchant marine, in contrast, was relatively small, even with two thousand ocean-going ships. Communications within the country were still in a backward state. The only serviceable canals were those of Flanders and the southern region; three others, in Picardy and Burgundy, still had to be completed. Rivers were little used—two hundred ships a year sailed through Château-Thierry, four hundred through Mantes. The state was making a great effort to construct a network of royal roads under the direction of trained engineers from the ministry of roads and bridges, using *corvée* labour, but this was still far from complete, and no work was being done on either the connecting or local roads. Internal customs barriers and tolls exacerbated regional particularism. Only recently had grain been shipped from province to province, and almost all areas continued to raise their own grapes. The capital city of the kingdom exported few of its goods to the provinces, and of the 75,000 tons it shipped, none went to southern France.

Business, particularly maritime commerce, was traditionally of primary importance to the French economy. Marseille continued to thrive; Nantes gained a prominent position during the eighteenth century, Bordeaux in the latter decades of that period. Several industries, particularly sugar refining, brought new wealth to the ports. Finance in the service of the king had always been responsible for the accumulation of large fortunes. Commercial capitalism had begun to expand, employing the artisanry. As early as the sixteenth century in the silk centre of Lyon the 'manufacturer' had become a businessman who imported silk and exported finished goods, employing the local silk weavers as his salaried home workers. Domestic industry spread and was given official authorization by the king's council in 1762. Many provinces benefited from it: Flanders produced linen cloth, wool, and cottons; Cambrésis, Hainaut, and Vermandois, linen and batiste; upper Normandy the cotton print of Rouen as well as wool; Maine and Brittany, linen; Champagne and Orléans specialized in knitted goods, Languedoc in cloth. There were also factories in the true sense of the term. Some were founded by the king for production of luxury goods; others manufactured munitions, anchors, and cannons for the navy, guns and sidearms for the army. In some cases individual names were associated with particular industries—the ironworks of Creusot, and of the Périers at Chaillot; the textile factories and printed cloth manufactories of Alsace and of Jouy-en-Josas, where Oberkampf set up his industry: the chemical works of Chaptal at Montpellier. The administration leaned towards less economic control, but approached the issue in an indecisive fashion. Turgot suppressed the gilds; his successors re-established them, after introducing certain reforms. Businessmen grew more insistent upon exclusive colonial rights and customs protection as the threat of modernized production from England increased. The liberal treaty of 1786 provoked countless protests.

The French did not lack an inventive spirit. Berthollet transformed the bleaching process in 1785; the Montgolfiers had launched a balloon. Industrialists were interested in new machinery, and a few Englishmen provided workers for cotton. Yet in 1789 France had only an estimated 900 spinning jennies, as compared to 20,000 in Great Britain. The Périers built a few steam engines, but they were as yet used only in the mines of Anzin, Aniche, or Creusot. Metallurgy had undergone little change and, dependent upon wood for fuel, remained widely scattered.

Agricultural production in France slowly continued to improve. Corn had transformed it in the south-west, vineyards spread throughout the nation, potatoes and fodder crops were cultivated. The government endeavoured to improve the breeding of stock, and its agricultural associations lavished advice upon farmers. Yet traditions persisted. Special efforts were made to increase grain production in particular, but instead of practising intensive cultivation the grain growers usually chose to clear new land, often indiscriminately. The aristocracy inclined to follow the example set in England, as the physiocrats advised, but in this respect, too, the administration hesitated. Louis XV was content to authorize the enclosure and partitioning of communal lands in a few provinces, with mild success. Similar vacillations marked government policy towards the grain trade: internal restrictions were abolished by Bertin and then by Turgot, only to reappear later.

France remained a nation of agriculture and of handicrafts. The development of capitalism and of economic freedom met strong resistance on French soil, a fact which was to be of major importance during the Revolution: within the Third Estate, disagreement broke out between the upper bourgeoisie and the lower classes; the controlled economy of the Committee of Public Safety was thwarted by inadequate transportation and scattered sources of production; a nation still deeply attached to traditional economic methods did not think its neighbour, 'modern Carthage' whose power rested on credit and a thriving export trade, was invincible.

The countries bordering on France had similar economic histories but had not kept pace with the French because, with the exception of Holland, they did not profit as much from territories overseas. Nevertheless, Spain, and Catalonia in particular, seemed to be realizing some progress after Charles III authorized several ports to trade directly with the colonies and strengthened customs protection. The rise of rural industry, and particularly the production of cotton goods, brought new life to several regions—Switzerland, the Black Forest, Saxony, northern Italy—but mechanization lagged. Switzerland was beginning to use the spinning jenny, and it was adopted at Chemnitz in 1788. The coke furnace appeared in the Ruhr.

With the exception of regions bordering on the Baltic, Central and Eastern Europe did not participate extensively in international trade. Commercial capitalism took root only in a few port towns and in even fewer interior cities, mainly for the purpose of exporting raw materials. Enlightened despots practised a kind of borrowed Colbertism with promising but modest results, and they encouraged—or founded, as the situation required—factories. The mining and metallurgical industries of Silesia and the Urals were created and nurtured in this way. In some areas trade had subjugated artisans, such as the weavers of Silesia. Home industries developed in the Bohemian countryside, but Prussia's government proscribed them, finding that cities lent themselves better to the collection of taxes. Agriculture was little changed. A few men praised the English techniques—Thaër in Germany, for example, and Kraus at Königsberg—but they had few followers. Expansion of Baltic commerce encouraged grain production in surrounding areas. To increase produce landlords evicted tenants and enlarged the manorial domain to practise extensive cultivation with *corvée* labour. Governments, however, did not always leave them free to act: Prussian kings laid some limitation upon peasant dues; only Denmark consented to enclosures in Schleswig and Holstein, benefiting the squires.

By the end of the eighteenth century the economic revolution inaugurated by Great Britain seemed to confirm Europe's supremacy, although an observer fifty years earlier might well have been dubious. He might have noted that the wood supply was diminishing while industrial production increased but little, that agriculture appeared incapable of supporting the labour force; and that if the West did not succeed in supplying its overseas territories, colonial exploitation might soon exhaust them. Europe, it had seemed, might suffer the same fate as Rome, whose purely commercial and financial capitalism had ultimately ruined its conquered territories. Now, however, optimism was justified. Wood was being replaced by coal and iron, the steam engine and power-driven machinery were augmenting production, and Europe's agriculture fed its labouring population. The continent had not yet shifted to a new economy, but this was only a matter of time—provided that peace continued.

## THE ENRICHMENT OF EUROPE

In any case Europe was growing increasingly wealthy, especially in the West, as was to be expected.[1] The precise rate of enrichment is not known. It is believed that the national income of England and of France had more than doubled during the eighteenth century. These nations were able to raise taxes and borrow money. While England's national debt rose from 16 million pounds in 1701 to 257 million in 1784, that of France, reduced to 1,700 million livres in 1721, rose to 4.5 billion in 1789. Ease of material existence and refinement in human relations reached new and higher levels, although, naturally, improvements affected the upper classes most of all.

Ostentation has never been confined to any particular period, but an outstanding trait of the eighteenth century was the pursuit of well-being and of pleasure, enhanced and moderated by a more refined comprehension. To huge livingrooms intended for pomp and display were added comfortably furnished apartments that could be easily heated and were preferred for daily living. Styles of furniture changed accordingly—proportions were modified, curves replaced rigid lines, seats were padded; comfort and attraction were enhanced by varied lines and delicate ornamentation. Use of exotic materials such as mahogany spread; Alexandrian décor followed the discovery of Pompeii. Manners grew more polished in salon society, where gallantry tried its skill at respecting decorum within the confines of a clever remark.

In the cafés of Paris a more mobile, liberal, and varied society developed. A spreading thirst for knowledge led to more and more

[1] According to a new method of calculating imports, exports, and re-exports, worked out by A. H. Imlah ('Real Values in British Foreign Trade', *Journal of Economic History*, VIII [1948], 133–52), Britain did not grow rich from its balance of trade. Its balance of payments was, nevertheless, favourable, since abundant capital was available for investment in the economy, especially in industry, and was used to underwrite loans asked by the government. Freight service, insurance, and commissions undeniably contributed to exports. But during this period England did not furnish capital to continental Europe. On the contrary, the Dutch and Genevans had large investments in England, which weakened the balance of payments. It can therefore be concluded that Imlah's figures prove the essential importance of revenue from overseas territories—from the slave trade, funds tied up in plantations, salaries and pensions of the India Company agents, individual speculations by colonial traders. This was undoubtedly true not only of England but, to a varying degree, of the other colonial powers.

academies, reading rooms, lectures, and courses. Sentiment and sensitivity, charity and philanthropy lent new aspects to the enjoyment of life. Talleyrand turned the phrase, but many others, less fashionable than he, were to look back nostalgically upon the *douceur de vivre* of pre-Revolutionary life.

The new wealth filtered down to the artisans, to shopkeepers, and to well-to-do peasants. This was evident in a greater consumption of certain commodities. Tea-drinking, for instance, was becoming the custom in England. In 1784, 8.5 million pounds of tea, exclusive of contraband, were imported; and when Pitt lowered the customs duty this figure jumped to 12 million pounds two years later. Coffee enjoyed the same success in France. Sugar became a popular commodity; the English are said to have consumed ten times more than the French. Chocolate and tobacco, beer, wine, and brandy were articles in popular demand.

The rise in population is the most noticeable fact concerning the condition of the wage-earning classes, and the rate of increase continued to rise during the last decades of the century. France gained 3 million inhabitants after the Seven Years War. Britain grew from a nation of 5.5 million to one of 9 million people in the eighteenth century; Austria increased from 20 to 27 million, Spain from 5 to 10 million, Italy from 11 to 18. Fewer famines, plus the additional resources offered by industrial progress, lowered the mortality rate.

There are, of course, many qualifications necessary. In Central and Eastern Europe aristocrats continued to inflict physical punishment on their 'dependents'. In Western Europe aristocratic manners were growing more refined, but not necessarily more moral. The nobility thought itself born to live on a plane above the common man and too frequently displayed its extravagant and libertine nature. Among the lower classes, poverty and ignorance often encouraged drunkenness and violence. The petty bourgeoisie, the artisanry, and the wealthier peasantry were the most attached to restrained conduct, but were not exempt from crudeness and cruelty.

It is none the less true that Europe's enrichment was the basis of an optimism whose intellectual expression was the idea of progress and which encouraged the men of that era confidently and boldly to undertake the reforms that concomitant changes in social and intellectual life seemed to demand.

# 3

## EUROPEAN SOCIETY

The social structure on the European continent still bore an aristocratic imprint, the legacy of an era when, because land was virtually the sole source of wealth, those who owned it assumed all rights over those who tilled it. Priests and nobles had become royal subjects, but they had not lost their privileges. The state had assumed most of the lords' sovereign powers but left them more or less extensive authority over their own peasants. With the exception of certain regions, such as Sweden and Friesland, where peasants were classed separately, almost the whole population was lumped into a third 'order', called in France the Third Estate. Aristocratic prerogatives condemned this order to remain eternally in its original state of inferiority.

The social hierarchy was divided not only into 'orders', 'estates', or *Stände*. Because of financial or political interests the state was always willing to grant 'franchises' or 'liberties'—that is, privileges—to provinces or towns and even to certain groups within each order. By thus pursuing a policy of divide and rule, the state maintained a corporate structure with the governing principle from top to bottom resting on inequality of rights.

Throughout Western Europe, and especially in France, this ordering of society was being challenged by a long-term change which increased the importance of mobile wealth and of the bourgeoisie, emancipated the lower classes, and highlighted the leading role of productive labour, inventive intelligence, and scientific knowledge.

Socially, as in other ways, Britain differed from the continent. Partly because of its insularity, historical events of the past centuries gave British society certain unique characteristics which a burgeoning economy promised to intensify.

## THE CLERGY

Traditionally, since divine right made throne and altar mutually dependent, the prince imposed his religion on his subjects. The established church alone was privileged to conduct public worship. It kept the official registers of births, marriages, and deaths; it controlled education and poor relief and censored intellectual activity. In addition to the influence it derived from coercion and faith, it possessed land and collected the tithe. Its clergy constituted not only the foremost of the orders but also the corporate body which was most solidly united by a hierarchical organization and rigid discipline and most firmly administered through its own assemblies and courts.

Yet wherever the Reformation had triumphed, church supremacy had been broken. The ruler of a Protestant state, primate of his church, considered ecclesiastical ministers his auxiliaries. Even in England, where bishops sat in Parliament, the Established Church no longer met in convocation. In Protestant countries church property had been partly secularized and monastic orders had been entirely suppressed. An attitude of free thought fostered a multitude of sects, which were tolerated, although there was not complete freedom of conscience: dissenters were deprived of certain rights; Catholics were often subject to stringent regulation; society comprised Christians alone, the Jew being considered an outsider and the atheist as someone altogether excluded from social relations. Protestant ministers were educated at the universities and absorbed rationalist thought. This development in turn provoked the opposition of mystics, of 'awakenings', of fanaticism, but it also had several advantages. Because there was no universal head of the Protestant church, religious faith fused with a nascent national spirit in each reformed state; and because Protestantism went so far as to change dogmas into symbols it adapted itself to currents of ideas. Rarely did the Protestant church enter into conflict with the state, and its moral influence over society remained. In Russia the czar headed the Orthodox Church, and Catherine the Great had secularized much of the Church's property. The Russian empire, embracing a great many diverse peoples, allowed them to practise various faiths, confining its activities to the Orthodox, who were prohibited from changing their religion or stumbling into the pitfall of heresy.

The situation differed in the states that had remained Catholic. There the Church retained its wealth, privileges, and independent administration. The clergy of France consented to grant the king only a 'free gift' (*don gratuit*), for which it collected the money itself. In Germany the archbishops, electors, some bishops, and prelates were temporal rulers, as was the pope in Italy. The principle of doctrinal unity remained; recourse to pontifical authority was a supreme defence against the state, as the French revolutionaries were to learn.

Many observers, however, thought that the decline of the Catholic Church presaged its disappearance. Papal authority was waning. The Bourbons had forced the pope to suppress the Society of Jesus; Gallicanism forbade the pontiff to encroach upon temporal power and limited his authority over ecclesiastical concerns, to the profit of France's ruler. Joseph II regulated church administration in minute detail without encountering a break with Pius VI. In point of fact intolerance was weakening, and outside Spain the Inquisition had little effect. The prevailing temper inclined to regard priests as civil servants entrusted with moral guidance. Some wished to deprive the clergy of its educational and welfare activities so they could be modernized. Many clerics, the monastics in particular, were looked upon with hostility.

Internal conflict also seemed to be sapping the vitality of the Church. Bishops practised various brands of Gallicanism, defending their independence against the Holy See. Febronianism in Germany led to similarly independent action, and not without success, as the episcopate had shown in its recent *Punktation* of Ems. In Italy the synod of Pistoia followed this trend under the guidance of Bishop Ricci. What was known as *richérisme*[1] left its traces among parish priests. In return

---

[1] After the French theologian, Edmond Richer (1560–1631), a spokesman for Gallicanism who placed the authority of church councils above that of the pope. (Translator's note.)

the ultramontanes attacked these deviations as Jansenist in motive, thus implying that doctrinal unity was in no better state than discipline.

In no country did the clergy constitute more than a small minority of the total population. In France it is usually estimated at approximately 130,000 members, of which roughly half were entrusted with secular functions and half were members of various orders. The wealth of the Catholic clergy was a liability to its social importance, compromising both the influence and the cohesion of the Church. By engaging in a struggle with royal authority the pope risked loss of his territorial possessions. Nobles disposed of their children by setting them up in bishoprics, chapters, and abbeys, while the lower clergy and the faithful complained that Church revenue was diverted before reaching its proper destination.

The clergy was an order, not a class, and included nobles as well as commoners. The true aristocracy was the nobility.

## THE NOBILITY

The nobility of continental Europe constituted an order and often, but not in France, a corporate body as well. Its members were registered; its leaders forestalled derogation from noble rank and defended aristocratic privileges. Fiefs still existed, and the hierarchy among them from vassals to suzerains was maintained through the practice of obtaining the lord's consent (*aveu*), submitting an inventory, and paying a fee each time a fief changed hands. In states where the king authorized commoners to acquire fiefs, payment of a special tax, known in France as the *franc-fief*, came into use. The nobility preserved its customary laws, chief among them the law of primogeniture. There were numerous survivals of the authority commanded by the lord of the manor: manorial courts; village surveillance; honorific prerogatives; monopolies, including hunting rights and the rights, known as *banalités*, to maintain a mill, oven, or wine-press; the right to exact certain taxes and labour services (*corvées personnelles*); serfdom—especially in Central and Eastern Europe; and, finally, eminent ownership of the soil, which justified collection of dues from landholders. The lord also retained a portion of land for his own use, either leasing it or cultivating it for himself.

Nobility was hereditary. In principle it could be conferred only by birth, and noble blood was to be kept free from contamination through misalliance. The aristocrat considered himself racially distinct from the 'ignoble' commoner. His manner of living was regarded as an illustration of his dignity. He wore the sword; his profession was that of bearing arms. Born to serve as counsellor to the king, he consented to serve as minister, diplomat, governor, or provincial administrator. In Russia Peter the Great had compelled his aristocracy to serve him, basing noble rank upon a hierarchy of functions. Church office was also open to the noble, but he would derogate if he accepted a menial position or engaged in commerce. Colbert had opened maritime trade to the nobility, with little success. A changing economy which associated power with money had injured the feudal nobility. War no longer offered booty or ransom and it exhausted the nobleman's patrimony, already eaten away by rising prices, increasing extravagance, and division of lands through inheritance. As a result, great disparities in wealth and in manner of living had developed within the nobility. But as members of the aristocracy fell behind, their places in the ranks were filled by members of the bourgeoisie.

The ruler of a state had long ago assumed the right to ennoble his servants. To increase his revenue he sold certain administrative, judicial, financial, and military positions, and he added nobility to certain offices to raise their price. Venality in office, unusually widespread in France, there created a nobility of the robe, an administrative or municipal nobility whose titles were either hereditary or personal, the latter sometimes being inherited under specific conditions. These nobles, united by marriage and professional solidarity, formed a separate oligarchy. Their wealth and influence gave the nobility new force. They eagerly espoused aristocratic manners, affecting snobbery and disdaining the excluded; in turn they changed the noble mentality, making it more bourgeois. The accepted aristocratic profession was still that of bearing arms, but nobles fought only when summoned by the king, and they went to war more from duty than from taste for combat.

This change was less marked as one advanced eastward in Europe. There, ennoblement was less frequent and venality in office nonexistent; as a result the nobility was more cohesive. The extent of power and political influence wielded by nobles varied from state to state. The bourgeoisie counted for little in Central and Eastern Europe, where the aristocracy vied with monarchical power above all. But in the West, particularly in France, the nobility competed with both royal authority and the bourgeoisie, nourishing a strong resentment against the throne that had relegated it to an inferior position and jealously guarding its separate existence against the encroaching ascendancy of the middle class.

The nobility, like the clergy, constituted no more than a small part of the population, but estimates of its size vary more than do those of the clergy. Sieyes listed 110,000 nobles in France, but he probably included only heads of families and he definitely excluded those ennobled personally.

## THE BOURGEOISIE

The bourgeoisie formed neither an order nor a corporate body, but was the richest and most capable part of what France termed the Third Estate. These men had long been prominent in the United Provinces; economic changes had made them singularly powerful in France, much less so in Italy and Spain, and in Central and Eastern Europe of little influence. At base they were recruited from the artisans and the peasants employed in trades; some had risen to affluent positions by means of hard work and frugality, but for the most part they had found success through the favourable odds offered by commercial speculation, no matter how modest the activity: the middleman was always able to acquire wealth with greater ease and speed than was the producer.

The composition of this class was anything but homogeneous. Those who considered themselves the true bourgeoisie were a small number of commoners who had enough resources to dispense with manual labour and to live 'nobly off their possessions', that is, principally off revenues from land, ground rent, and, less frequently, transferable securities. The bourgeois condescended, not without reservations, to associate with members of two 'labouring' groups, provided that those members were wealthy, did not work with their hands (without exception), and held only supervisory or authoritative positions.

The first of these two groups was the civil service of the throne, the most coherent, stable, and best-educated body in the nation. Its members were more numerous and influential in France, where 'officers' (of the crown) owned their positions and were consequently not dependent upon royal power, and where, jealous of their prerogatives, they clustered together according to profession, in the courts, finance offices, and fiscal districts. Since some 'officers' acquired patents of nobility, the bourgeoisie in this instance was on good terms with nobles of the robe and of government service. Lawyers of varying positions—notaries, *procureurs*, bailiffs—were also connected with administrative offices and also purchased their offices; like the *avocats*, they formed a corporate body. This administrative bourgeoisie formed a sort of intermediary class through which social advancement, assured by money, had always been possible. Members of other liberal professions rarely entered this class. Its ranks included only a handful of doctors, scholars, writers, or artists who had distinguished themselves personally, and then only if their income made them worthy of consideration. If they lacked financial means the salons were open to them, in France at least, but not as equals.

The other group, less respected but often more wealthy, included financiers and directors of the economy. Of the financiers, those who served the state—farmers-general in France, commissaries, *faiseurs de service*[1] had considerable prestige. A few sooner or later moved up into the nobility. Necker, although a foreigner and a Protestant, rose to be a minister. Shipowners, merchants, and manufacturers were noted more for their numbers than for their influence. They joined corporate groups such as chambers of commerce or commercial tribunals in some towns; manufacturers sometimes enrolled in trade gilds.

This portion of the middle class under the Old Regime formed what we term the upper bourgeoisie. Like the aristocracy, it was small, but its corporate organization fostered the same exclusiveness it resented in the nobility. From one group to another, wrote Cournot, 'a cascade of scorn' forestalled solidarity. The traditional aspiration of these bourgeois was to insinuate themselves one by one into the ranks of their superiors. Nevertheless, in France their rise had been such that they

---

[1] Businessmen who supplied the state with goods or advanced it money. (Translator's note.)

were starting to be ranked by the government, along with those nobles who had managed to retain their wealth, as 'notables'. This was a social category based on money and transcending the legal classification of orders or corporate bodies. It was the embryo of the modern bourgeoisie.

Future events decreed varying fates for these bourgeois groups. Like the aristocracy, the true bourgeoisie of the Old Regime, those who lived like nobles, were to suffer from the Revolution. The 'officers' and members of the liberal professions had furnished since the sixteenth century most of the leaders in science and enlightened philosophy, while their experience with public office and the management of their properties had familiarized them with the conduct of administration and the handling of individuals. It was they who laid the intellectual foundation of, and then guided, the Revolution. But, having through prudent management and investment in land built up sizeable fortunes, they were not always spared by the cataclysm. In any case they did not profit as much as the financiers and the businessmen. These, driven only by a blinding passion for profit and power, failed to comprehend anything higher than their class interest. They selfishly used new ideas and revolutionary changes only to serve the bourgeoisie, yet upon their taste for enterprise, speculation, and risk depended nothing less than the development of capitalism and the fate of their class.

What we call the middle class or the petty bourgeoisie was disdainfully referred to by notables as 'the people', a term which was to be applied to the same group, but in affectionate tones, by the revolutionary democrats. The bourgeois considered these persons inferior because they worked with their hands—upon occasion, at least—or had in any case probably begun their careers with manual labour. The highest stratum included those who had received special privileges or legal dispositions, who were connected with the liberal professions, or had an occupation of particular importance. Such were postmasters, contractors, booksellers, printers, apothecaries, and a very few surgeons (those who practised surgery were usually barbers, and therefore belonged to a lower level). Widely varying stations were assigned artisans and tradesmen, much more numerous, some of them organized in gilds having to do with food, clothing, shoes, hairdressing, house furnishings, and furniture. They were ranked according to their prosperity and especially according to the quality of their clientele. Step by step the level descended to shopkeepers, cobblers, tavern-keepers, and pedlars. Whatever his rank, the petty bourgeois was frequently irritated at the airs put on by the bourgeois properly speaking, yet in turn he looked down upon proletarians. Madame Lebas, daughter of Robespierre's host, the contractor Duplay, declared that her father would have compromised his dignity if he had admitted one of his servants—i.e., labourers—to the table.

This classification requires one important emendation. In the eighteenth century intellectual ability tended to compete with moneyed power and to compose a social hierarchy of its own. Professors, men of letters and journalists, scholars and artists, musicians and singers, actors and dancers lived apart from those assured of material security. They constituted a varied and unstable milieu, often poor, sometimes morally loose. The law clerks who formed the corporation of the *basoche*, office-workers, gild masters, and storekeepers considered themselves not far removed from the middle class by virtue of their manner of living and their exemption from manual labour; among them were to be found not a few individuals able to speak correctly and to write with ease. The impecunious 'men of talent'—the 'ambitious minority' mentioned later by Boissy d'Anglas—were understandably champions of equality of rights. A constant and ubiquitous source of ferment, they were to furnish an important part of the revolutionary leadership.

Finally, it should be noted that although birth, corporate status, profession, and sometimes talent influenced social classification, there existed, in addition, a subtle gradation relegating each man, from the wealthiest to the meanest, to his own niche. This gradation implied a marked division of labour and indicated both a widespread desire to move up the social ladder and an increasing individualism. This was less and less true as one moved into Central and Eastern Europe, but it characterized Western civilization in general. Another characteristic was the condition of the peasants.

## THE PEASANTRY

Serfdom still existed in regions of Western Europe. Its subjects were bound to the land, were strictly limited in rights of inheritance, were forbidden to draw up wills, were forced to bear the heaviest obligations. Ordinarily, however, peasants were free; and whether serfs or freemen, they could invoke the protection of royal courts. In the capacity of 'holders' (ténanciers) they held part of an estate's arable soil and occupied most of the rest as tenants (fermiers) or sharecroppers (métayers), since nobles, priests, or bourgeois rarely farmed their own land. Louis XVI freed French serfs from the droit de suite, by which a lord could claim his subject wherever he found him. About one-third of the land in France was held by peasants. The possessor of a free holding, which was hereditary and inalienable, could dispose of his land as he wished and had come to be regarded as an owner. The condition of the peasants in France varied from province to province, but seemed relatively favourable. Their situation was also good in neighbouring countries, the Netherlands especially, Catalonia and the Basque country, Piedmont, and the Rhineland. It was deplorable in Castile and Andalusia and in southern Italy, where the aristocracy left vast latifundia uncultivated.

Regardless of geographic position, the peasant was regarded by bourgeois, townsman, and noble as an ignorant and uncouth being, destined by nature and by tradition to support the upper classes, to contribute the greater share of revenue to the royal treasury, and to feed the urban population. All village inhabitants were subject to manorial authority and personal obligations. Those who held land on the manor domain paid real fees (fees which fell on the land): the payment (cens) owed the lord because he held the right of eminent property; a quitrent (rente) or a portion of the crop called in France the champart, terrage, or agrier; and the lods et ventes, which fell due upon transfer of property. On top of these, the tithe, levied by the clergy, was sometimes subinfeudated to lay lords and was almost always more onerous than manorial rights. The king added his taxes. In France at least royal taxes had become the heaviest burden borne by the peasantry: they were deplorably unequal owing to privileges and to administrative diversity and lack of statistics or land surveys. The taille was paid almost entirely by the rural population; the nobles contributed only a small portion of the capitation (a form of poll tax) and the twentieths (ving-tièmes); the bourgeoisie escaped with few tax obligations; the clergy offered only a contribution (the don gratuit). Nothing, however, was more hateful to the peasants than the salt tax (*gabelle*) and excises (*aides*). In addition to tax obligations, the countryside was made to support towns by supplying markets. Under this accumulation of obligations the peasant felt himself little more than the beast of burden he was.

The rural community was united against the landlords, tithe collectors, taxes, and also against the towns, but it, too, was marked with inner inequalities. The population of the countryside was dominated by a handful of village 'bosses', large farmers or peasant proprietors who gave work to others and monopolized local offices. Together with the few farmers who had enough land to support themselves, they formed a peasant bourgeoisie capable of selling some of their produce and practising new agricultural methods. Most peasants, however, did not have enough land even to eke out an existence. They were forced to seek extra wages as day labourers, to take up an additional trade, or to work in the rural industries run by merchants. Labouring to eat and not to sell, they were intent upon retaining agricultural controls, ardently defended collective rights, and protested the consolidation of plots to form large farms. Forced to buy a part of their grain store (all of it if they were wine-growers), they shared the viewpoint of urban consumers towards the grain trade. Finally, it is erroneous to speak of the peasants as if they were all owners or tenants. Those who had no land actually formed a rural proletariat. On the eve of the Revolution landless peasants constituted a majority of the agrarian population in some parts of France, and were more numerous in the Po valley, southern Italy, and Andalusia.

Despite these qualifications, Western Europe, already differentiated by its powerful bourgeoisie, contrasted even more sharply with Central and Eastern Europe as far as its peasantry was concerned. Between the Rhine and the Elbe—in Bohemia, Austria, and Prussia—rural conditions had been growing worse since the fifteenth century, particularly since the Thirty Years War, and serfdom was widespread. The peasant of the Prussian kingdom was not a *Leibeigene*, a serf in the Western sense, but he was an *Untertan*, bound to the soil and subject to the arbitrary will of the landlord, although in theory he was the king's subject and could appeal to royal justice. Except for bourgeois who had been granted concessions by the king, only a noble could hold a landed property. The aristocrat sometimes ceded holdings under a title that was uncertain, but he cultivated most of his land by means of obligatory service (the *corvée*), entirely arbitrary in practice, forced on the *Untertanen*, who according to the *Gesindedienst* were obligated to give their children to the lord as domestic servants. In Poland and Hungary the serf was even denied recourse to ordinary justice; in Russia, where he was little more than a slave, he could be sold apart from the land or deported to Siberia.

## BRITISH SOCIETY

Continental observers found certain aspects of society in Britain comparable to those of Western Europe, but the differences were more striking than the similarities. Characterized by unique traits for many centuries, British society developed along increasingly distinct lines as its economy expanded and changed.

The law of the land recognized no differences among subjects: taxes were levied without exemption, and public office was accessible without the privilege of birth. As a result, there was in principle no distinction of orders to form a rigid barrier between nobility and bourgeoisie. This was often true in practice as well as in theory. The hierarchy and obligations of fiefs no longer existed. The specifically military character of the nobility was fading. Of the manorial system there remained little more than land agreements incorporated into civil law and effaced, along with peasant holdings, by the enclosure movement. Knights from the shires had from the beginning sat with burgesses in the House of Commons. The terms nobility and privileges meant, in reality, lords and their prerogatives; moreover, sons of lords were classed, with squires of the gentry, as commoners. There was no such thing as derogation from class, which meant that there was no stricture upon entering business. Social classification rested essentially upon wealth.

A nobility of the robe had never appeared in England because royal officials were few in number, lords and squires controlled local administration and kept their landed property, and venality was practised only in the army. The bourgeoisie did not include crown officers and was not as tempted by ennoblement or by acquisition of land as was its counterpart in France. The British bourgeoisie was composed mainly of merchants, bankers, and manufacturers; it was interested primarily in enterprise, speculation, and profit. Characteristically, a man wealthy enough to live a life of leisure did not harbour any prejudice towards another who headed a business firm to become affluent in turn.

The peasants had long been freemen, and now enclosures were detaching them from the land. They had not entirely disappeared, but were yielding more and more to large farmers, becoming day labourers, entering rural industry, or emigrating to industrial centres.

Nevertheless, if the English considered themselves theoretically equal before the law, *habeas corpus* did not protect the unfortunate from impressment, a common means of finding sailors for His Majesty's Navy, and inequality existed in practice and in British customs. Landed property was controlled by several thousand families; lords and squires reigned in the shires and parishes, where traces of manorial domination still remained. A strong sense of community bound together those who were 'born' to exclude others from family and social relations and to secure honorific and munificent positions for themselves. They were governed by the same spirit of exclusiveness that prevailed on the continent.

## THE PROLETARIAT

The nobility and bourgeoisie of Europe shared the belief that proletarians were destined by Providence to engage in manual labour and were thereby relegated to an inferior level of civilization. Religious sentiment encouraged the practice of charity, and common sense advised that the masses be treated with discretion; in the eighteenth century a general refinement in manners encouraged philanthropy, while philosophy introduced the concept of social obligation. To the bourgeois Puritans of England, however, poverty was a sign of divine reprobation and contrasted sharply with the accumulation of riches granted the elect. As capitalism spread across the continent it carried the idea that to be poor was a just punishment for laziness and vice. In any case the upper classes nurtured repugnance and even scorn for those whom fortune spurned, and everyone lived in constant fear of individual crimes or collective revolt at the hands of 'the populace', 'the rabble'.

Apart from the many domestic servants, proletarians were spread throughout rural as well as urban areas. Field work, threshing, forestry, transportation, mining, quarrying, and rural industry meant that there were then many more workers in villages than there are today. The poorest were agricultural day labourers employed only in season. They were scattered through the towns as well, since master workmen laboured alone or took on only one or two helpers. The labour force was not rigidly specialized—most workers left the shops when there was work to be had in the fields—and was not concentrated in certain sections or in large factories. It lacked class spirit, if not always corporate solidarity. It was not clearly distinguished from the artisans in France, with whom it sided when the Revolution began. A rupture between bourgeoisie and nobility would have been less likely, one suspects, had not the events of 1789 preceded the rise of industrial capitalism and the appearance of a proletarian opposition.

Although economic development may have aided the condition of the proletariat by reducing the occurrence of famine, a growing population added to the unemployed and held wages down while food prices rose. Between 1730 and 1789 wages in France rose by more than 22 per cent, while grain prices increased 60 per cent. Economists explained that, in the nature of things, a worker's remuneration could never exceed his minimum requirement for existence and for procreation. Turgot was the author of this 'iron law of wages'. Resistance was, however, manifested by boycotts and strikes, sometimes by sabotage and violence; in some trades it was organized. During the eighteenth century unions appeared in English industry, even among the textile workers, and against them the Statute of Labourers was invoked to fix wages. The French *compagnonnages*, or journeymen's associations, were remarkably strong in the building trades and in a few others. They had set up a countrywide circuit and arranged for watchwords to be spread from town to town. These associations, however, were strictly corporative. They competed strongly with each other and sometimes engaged in bloody fights. Mutual-aid societies which could support strikers also formed. Yet on the continent as in England, many workers sought the intervention of public authorities, who on occasion acted as mediators to restore public order but were in general antagonistic towards the proletariat. What was termed in France a *coalition*, that is, any form of collective resistance, as well as *compagnonnages* or unions, were proscribed by the state and censured by the churches.

Indigents formed one-fifth of the French population, and their numbers swelled with each economic depression. Poor relief was notoriously deficient. In England and the Netherlands the parish was in theory obligated to care for its paupers by means of the poor tax, and in other regions of the continent a portion of the tithe was supposed to be used for the poor. In practice, there was no regular assistance offered the aged, the sick, or the widowed; the unemployed received no aid whatsoever. Begging was a scourge in some regions, and fruitless efforts were put forth to reduce the number of mendicants through confinement. Vagrancy resulted, often degenerating into brigandage. Swarms of men wandered about in search of work, and smugglers took advantage of internal customs barriers to ply their trade. When crops failed and the inevitable industrial depression followed, workmen, sharecroppers, and holders of land were all reduced to begging. Fear of brigands spread through the country. The upper classes and the public authorities tried to pacify the poor by opening up labour centres and distributing food, but their main concern was to protect themselves from rioting and pillaging at the hands of hysterical mobs. This fear, easily converted into a 'great fear' marked by terror and panic, was shared by the lower and upper bourgeoisie. It was a source of unrest tending towards disintegration of the Third Estate; outside France it was to work against the spread of the Revolution.

# 4

## EUROPEAN THOUGHT

Intellectual changes did not keep pace with economic and social alterations: for most Europeans daily life did not change at a rate permitting much modification of thought. The temper of the bourgeoisie, however, in harmony with the unique mode of its activity, had differed since the beginning from that of the warrior or the priest. As commercial, financial, and industrial capitalism accented its progress and undermined medieval economy and society, bourgeois aspirations broke sharply with traditional ideas. Experimental rationalism had laid the foundations of modern science and in the eighteenth century promised to embrace all man's activity. It armed the bourgeoisie with a new philosophy which, especially in France, encouraged class consciousness and a bold inventive spirit. On the eve of the French Revolution the leaders of the Enlightenment were dead, but their thought survived intact. Their intellectual legacy remained unusually complex, and, in addition, the Old Regime did not lack defenders. European thought of this period therefore offers a picture of diversity and dynamism, at least in the three countries which testified best to its vitality: England, Germany, and France.

## THE MIND OF THE PAST AND THE AWAKENING
## OF THE MODERN MIND

In the old economy production was severely limited. The producer, afflicted by scarcity, pestilence, war, and the exactions of his masters, sought assistance and protection in close communities—family, neighbourhood, trade, parish. He sought security by restricting competition with controls, balancing the just price against wages to protect the right of each man to earn a living. He worked for subsistence: goods and commodities were valued only for their use. Since frugality promised little reward, expenditure of unnecessary energy seemed fruitless. The profit motive had led artisans and merchants to the idea of the value of exchange and to speculation, but most of them retained much of the medieval attitude well into the eighteenth century. Content to accumulate earnings slowly, scorning advertisement, they waited for clients to approach them, sold little and at high prices, and did not seek to stimulate circulation of capital. Their highest aspiration was to acquire land and live out their lives as *rentiers*. The bourgeoisie had long before visualized an order which would replace the anarchy of feudal wars and monarchical despotism. The businessman therefore extended to government the same method which brought order to his store and to his accounts; the judge and civil servant protected the dignity and value of their professions by seeking to make law prevail over violence and caprice. Society was none the less static and offered little hope of success in this life, making thoughts of life after death particularly alluring. The social and political structure, authoritarian and intolerant, aristocratic and hierarchical, corresponded to an inherent sense of inferiority in its subjects, reinforcing the respect and resignation imposed by force and commanded by religion.

In their relations with the lower classes, clerics remained a bulwark of tradition at the end of the eighteenth century, even though some had absorbed new ideas. In Protestant countries mysticism had caused a reawakening of religious fervour. Methodism spread throughout England, while other sects grew more active; the Anglican Church itself was an 'evangelical' body. The continued vitality of Pietism in Germany affected even Kant and Herder, disciple of Hamann. More significant, however, because its import extended beyond this period, appears the persistence of unorthodox religiosity. Among its many manifestations were magic, astrology, cabalism, and alchemy, now joined by speculative interpretations and quack exploitation of such scientific discoveries as magnetism and the flow of electricity. Pasquales and Saint-Martin had succeeded Swedenborg; the Rosicrucians in Germany and many of the Masonic lodges espoused these obscure and tenuous doctrines. In France, Alsace and Lyon provided followers for abstruse theories, which were the source of Blake's artistic inspiration and which Cagliostro and Mesmer imparted to masses of people. The lower classes, particularly the rural population, continued to hold superstitious beliefs concerning sorcery and the coming of the millennium. The power of magic was still strong.

But other currents of belief, long present in European thought, were now gaining influence. The increase of wealth, swelling private incomes, broadened interests and stimulated the desire to satisfy new tastes. Individualism chafed at restrictions: the contagious example of material success encouraged all those who judged themselves capable of enjoying the rewards offered during this life. The family disintegrated as each child demanded his rightful inheritance, and conventional standards of conduct were challenged and evaded. Urbanization acted as a catalyst—life in the city undermined social restraints, placing a greater part of existence outside traditional groups; ultimately, the community could classify its members solely on the basis of residence. Personal mobility was even stronger in effect: it responded to the call of opportunities presented by new lands overseas, expanding industry, and improved communications. Foreigners and Jews stimulated new ideas and modes of thought throughout Europe. Capitalism transferred warriors' traits to the bourgeois by appealing to a taste for adventure and risk, enterprise and competition. It also hastened social differentiation, enriching some and impoverishing others. It created a dynamic and unstable society in which power, based on money and always threatened with sudden destruction, could inspire only transitory respect. It added glamour to this life and obscured the afterlife. It reduced the importance of personal ties which bound the individual entirely and emphasized contractual relations dealing with objects and thus limiting obligations. Associations of family and friends gave way to the associations of business partners and joint-stock companies; the traditional market yielded to sales based on samples; bargaining surrendered to the fixed or quoted price. A paternal system governing serf and labourer and requiring service was replaced by a system in which labour was hired on a short-term basis, involving a profitable expenditure of effort in return for a stipulated wage.

In a hundred different ways the individual who had lain dormant beneath feudal, despotic, and corporate restrictions was awakening to independence and dreaming of freedom. The *philosophes* found an audience well prepared to hear their arguments.

## SCIENTIFIC RATIONALISM

A change in the nature of rationalism became evident in the first half of the seventeenth century through revolutionary advances in physics and mechanics in conjunction with those of technique. Descartes developed this new aspect into a method of research, and the achievements of Newton and Locke subsequently emphasized the importance of that change. It replaced a magical explanation of the universe with the theory that matter is governed by a deterministic scheme having inviolable rules that the human mind can discover, provided that the conclusions reached through deduction from these rules are regarded as hypotheses to be verified by observation and experiment. Based upon the reciprocal action of human reason and natural phenomena, science became what it is today, a concrete understanding of the perceptible world, expressed essentially in mathematical formulas; as various fields of science approached a basic unity the supreme scientific goal would be to reduce the world to a series of equations.

Scientific progress fired men's imaginations. In France the brilliant contributions made by Lagrange to mathematics were followed by those of Legendre and Laplace. The German-born Herschel had discovered Uranus and catalogued the stars. Physicists, led by Coulomb, pursued their studies of magnetism and electricity. After Galvani's experiment of 1786 at Bologna, Volta, who had already earned a reputation, was on the verge of discovering the electric current. Lavoisier founded modern chemistry and by explaining the respiratory system inaugurated physiology. Natural history and geology, less advanced although Buffon commanded universal respect, remained descriptive but attempted to establish rational methods of classification. Adanson succeeded in doing this for botany. The natural sciences attracted public attention because they inspired practical applications such as Franklin's lightning rod, Jenner's method of vaccination, and the Montgolfiers' balloon, or else, as Berthollet demonstrated in France, they began to renovate industry. The cumulative progress of experimental science opened up seemingly unlimited perspectives. Through it man could learn to manipulate natural phenomena to his advantage; he was evidently approaching the period when, as Descartes prophesied, 'we will enjoy without travail the fruits of the earth and all the conveniences to be found there'.

Descartes the metaphysician held that reason was an inherent gift of God. Abstaining from any incursion into politics and economics, disdaining history, he did not consider the study of man in society an empirical science. But thinkers of the eighteenth century enlarged the subject matter of rationalism, inaugurating what since have been called the 'human sciences'. Locke, a physician, discarded the notion of innate ideas and explained the operations of the mind in terms of sense impression. His theory of sense data, introduced to the continent by Voltaire and developed by Condillac, led to an experimental psychology. The most venturesome—Helvétius, Holbach, and Bentham—secularized ethics and made it a 'science of mores' by basing it on individual interest and social utility. The study of history had long been marked by efforts to utilize philological criticism and definite standards of scholarship to test evidence, but even though such efforts persisted, historical writing in the eighteenth century did not yet profit from them as one might desire. Voltaire did at least shift the focus of history from the vicissitudes of empires to the progress of civilization and the evolution of societies—subjects which harmonized with the interests of the bourgeoisie. This new history, together with the triumph of constitutional government in England and an interest in exotic subjects awakened by the accounts of missionaries and travellers, encouraged a comparative method of social study; *The Spirit of Laws* and *An Essay on the Customs and Spirit of Nations* made use of comparisons and thereby announced the birth of sociology. Economic history was scarcely even labelled, but public officials, recognizing the value of statistics, were beginning to gather figures. Without waiting for statistical evidence the physiocrats, and then Adam Smith, claimed to be founding a science of economics through observation of contemporary conditions.

Calling itself scientific and utilitarian, claiming as its domain the perceptible world and human activity, rationalism discarded metaphysics, which rationalists thought could offer only unverifiable hypotheses. In *The Critique of Pure Reason* (1781) Kant declared the 'thing in itself' unknowable; later, Laplace wrote that 'primary causes and the intrinsic nature of things will remain eternally unknown to us'. Rationalism therefore inclined to develop into a materialist philosophy—but the general public did not agree.

## DEISM AND NATURAL LAW

Sensationalism had not turned Locke away from 'natural religion', and most of the *philosophes* remained loyal to his deism. They justified it by comparative studies showing that the principles of deism were to be found buried beneath the particular and contingent dogmas of all religions. Universal agreement testified to the existence of a Supreme Being, the 'grand architect of the universe', and proved both that the soul was immortal and that punishment in the afterlife was necessary. The interests of the ruling classes conferred special value to these speculative ideas as appropriate instruments to assure popular submission: moral principles might be merely utilitarian or represent only social conventions; they were none the less to be obeyed, and in obeying them man was both free and responsible. Then came Rousseau, who gave sentiment primacy but did not repudiate reason. Through love of his fellows the 'sensitive' man would attain true, altruistic morality; his conscience, the 'immortal and heavenly voice', would penetrate the phenomenal world to reveal the most important truths, those illuminating his destiny. In 1788 Kant rebuilt metaphysics upon the rock of moral conscience. In addition, Jacobi in Germany, Hemsterhuis in Holland, and Reid in Scotland continued to philosophize in the traditional mode.

The new rationalists did not wish simply to comprehend the world; they wanted to change it, and thus upheld a spirit of reform. With greater consequence, they invoked natural law. This concept dated back to the Stoics, had reappeared in medieval theology, was later overshadowed by absolutism on the continent but was preserved by the Calvinists. Locke drew upon it to justify the revolution of 1688: society, founded to protect the individual, was based upon an original contract freely concluded among its citizens; similarly, governmental authority rested upon a contract between the sovereign people and their delegates, who had authority only to protect the inalienable rights conferred upon man by God. The Americans and the French later proclaimed the natural rights of man in the presence of the Supreme Being. Natural law perpetuated the universalism of classic and Christian thought by omitting distinction between the different branches of human kind.

In these different ways the rationalists retained many more ties with idealist philosophy than their attacks on the Cartesian metaphysic would imply. In this they reflected the traditional humanism they had imbibed in school. Their knowledge of science was usually quite superficial. Their education reinforced the class or professional prejudices that led them to consider material production inferior. Although the writing of the physiocrats influenced French thinkers, and although the Encyclopaedists were the first to assign importance to trades and tools, it cannot be said that any of these men formulated a synthetic theory encompassing technical improvements, changes in society and customs, extension of knowledge, liberation of the individual and of thought. Since natural science had not yet introduced the concept of evolution, the rationalists did not attempt to offer organic theories to explain the vicissitudes in that march of progress they believed could be detected through human history. Or else, as spokesmen of the bourgeoisie, they attributed such reversals entirely to intolerance, feudalism, or the despotism they hoped to eradicate for ever. They thought that once freedom from tyranny was achieved, social and political order would be established upon a rational and permanent basis. Within this framework progress would continue, but as a function of individual effort. Like all ascendant classes, the bourgeoisie implicitly closed the last chapter of history with the date of its own triumph.

Certain adversaries of the reformers claimed that they, also having studied history empirically, had found that man could not hope to realize concerted progress. Guided, like those whom they attacked, by irrational preferences, they were inclined to preserve existing institutions, which they thought were either providentially ordained or born of man's common experience. Early in the eighteenth century Vico, opposed to Cartesianism inasmuch as he was a Catholic, described history as an unending repetition of empires which, like living bodies, rose, flourished, and declined, to be replaced by successors according to the unintelligible design of Providence. Lessing discovered a continuous process of revelation in religious development. Beginning in 1784, Herder expounded his *Ideas on the Philosophy of History*: nature, in an eternal state of 'becoming' perceptible only through intuition, creates societies whose members are incorporated like cells in a living organism, powerless to will their fate.

In each of the three countries whose intellectual life was most brilliant, economic, social, and political conditions indicated which of these attitudes was to prevail.

## ENGLAND AND GERMANY

Roger Bacon in the thirteenth century, the Ockhamites in the fourteenth, and Francis Bacon, who set down its precepts before Descartes, testify to the importance that experimental research evidently had long commanded in English thought. On the other hand, the British were not concerned with formulating a philosophy which would demonstrate the unity of knowledge and justify absolute statements. Hume even deduced from sense-data associations that rational principles, inculcated in man through daily experience, could lead only to approximate and provisional generalizations. As a result, the value of scientific rationalism was limited to the fruitful results of its empiricism, and in fact that term is often used to distinguish it from purely deductive rationalism. This attitude was undoubtedly reinforced by the vitality of technical inventiveness in Great Britain during the eighteenth century. When Adam Smith undertook the study of political economy he was less tendentious than the physiocrats.

Few Britons were disturbed by the difficulty of reconciling scientific rationalism, metaphysics, and revealed religion. Since a large part of the English bourgeoisie adhered to one or another of the Calvinist sects, general interest advised members of the Established Church to follow an opportunistic course, and historical circumstances worked in the same direction. When the Stuarts were expelled for Catholicism, their co-religionists were denied certain privileges, but among Protestants Locke advised tolerance. Dissenters did not have complete freedom, yet their life was not unbearable. Early in the eighteenth century a few deists gave concern to the clergy of several churches; on the eve of the Revolution, Gibbon was no less hostile to Christianity than Voltaire when he attributed the fall of the Roman Empire to Christianity. The English rationalists had nevertheless soon ceased giving the impression that they wished to undermine Christian beliefs, while Anglicans such as Paley grew more latitudinarian, endeavouring to prove that their dogmas were consonant with reason. Members of the upper classes agreed that religion served a useful goal in enforcing social and political conformity; the Methodist revival of fideism was thought beneficial in that it sobered the populace.

In politics, too, the English were always more inclined to invoke precedent than principle. Natural law was none the less a familiar concept: Hobbes had used it and the social contract to justify absolutism, declaring that the people had irrevocably surrendered their sovereignty to the king. Locke justified constitutionalism and individual rights by a converse interpretation of the law of nature. The Whigs thereby seemed to be developing into doctrinaires; later, however, the oligarchy of nobles and upper bourgeoisie which controlled the state grew alarmed at nascent agitation for electoral reform, which would have compromised its rule, and Locke lost stature. As Burke was to demonstrate, England's rulers returned to the empirical view that their constitution was an evolutionary product peculiar to the British and unrelated to any rational presupposition.

The continent did not until later take notice of these developments in British thought. Montesquieu and Voltaire each chose England as his exemplary model, and in 1771 Delolme, a citizen of Geneva, extolled the island's incomparable merits. British Freemasonry, respectful of the Established Church and of the sovereign whom it accepted as its head, spread through many countries, disseminating its ideas of tolerance, freedom of the individual, and representative government. Only at the end of the Old Regime did England cease to represent the mother of liberty in the eyes of egalitarian Frenchmen.

Rationalism had been introduced to Protestant Germany through the teachings of August Wolf, at Halle, who was influenced by Leibniz rather than Descartes. Contact with England was maintained through the University of Göttingen in Hanover, which belonged to the British sovereign, and through Hamburg. As in England, Protestantism in Germany was represented by diverse sects, fewer in number owing to the dominance of Lutheranism over Calvinism, yet enough to encourage a policy of tolerance. Frederick the Great of Prussia even permitted speculative philosophy to develop with relative freedom. The German rationalists more often than their British counterparts refrained from attacking revealed religion, which was vulnerable to Biblical criticism; and in return ministers boldly introduced rationalist ideas into their doctrines. In scientific research, technical progress, and economic growth, Germany lagged far behind Britain; on this part of the continent rationalism remained far more deductive and abstract than experimental. The *Aufklärung*, whose stronghold was Prussia, asserted a preference for utilitarianism, a quality especially appealing to the enlightened despots and acceptable to royal administrators. In this form the *Aufklärung* penetrated Catholic regions, even Bavaria and Austria, and won over some Catholic clergymen. Yet it never influenced more than a handful of bureaucrats and intellectuals. Pietist mysticism still had deep roots. Rousseau had notable influence; the *Sturm und Drang* of literary circles represented anarchic preromanticism. Beyond Kant, German philosophy soon inclined towards transcendental idealism.

Absolute princely powers and surviving feudalism sharply distinguished Germany from England; the weakness of its bourgeoisie contrasted it in the same way with France. Leaders of the *Aufklärung* never criticized privileges strongly and rarely did they attack the practice of serfdom. They relied on the enlightened despots to enact concrete reforms and justified their enfeebling caution by declaring that progress depended upon improvement of individuals and not of institutions.

## FRANCE

Rationalists in Catholic states were exposed to far more serious dangers than in Protestant countries. Spain and Portugal were especially hostile, and Olavide had to flee his native land. The Church of Rome was the heart of resistance. Yet intellectual activity in Italy revived, heralding the *Risorgimento*; Beccaria is one illustration of the age of Enlightenment. It was in France, however, that the *philosophes* boldly attacked intolerance and Catholic censorship. Because the French clergy depended upon the temporal ruler for authority and the governing classes for membership, *philosophes* spiritedly and unmercifully ridiculed the Church's privileges, decadence, and even its dogmas. The ranks of Voltairians swelled and respect vanished. Assailants of the Church in France benefited from the events that had already weakened it: quarrels between Jansenists and Jesuits, Gallicans and Ultramontanes, the disastrous consequences of the revocation of the Edict of Nantes, and the indifferent attitude of Protestants, who were forcibly converted. They profited from the vogue for Freemasonry, too, because it recommended tolerance and natural religion. The pope condemned it, in vain: the king, failing to issue his necessary sanction of the bull, gave the impression that he was content to see great lords join the lodges. A number of priests, both lay and monastic, were Masons. Under Diderot's editorship the Encyclopaedia assembled rationalist philosophers into a sort of party whose manifesto was d'Alembert's *Preliminary Discourse*. It influenced the mentality to the extent that Necker, a Protestant, was appointed minister during the reign of Louis XVI, and although means of repression still existed, they were rarely used. The temporal ruler lost interest in attendance at Mass and Easter communion. Clerical courts often failed to prosecute offenders.

Even though they placed man within the natural scheme, most *philosophes* did not necessarily bind him to determinism. Diderot favoured a deterministic view more than did Voltaire, who never overcame his hesitations on the issue, but this aspect of Diderot's thought was expressed largely in his posthumous publications. Neither did they adhere to atomistic materialism, a traditional aspect of metaphysics defended by Helvétius, Holbach, and La Mettrie. As elsewhere, their preoccupation with ethical conformity led them to advocate natural religion—in Voltaire's words, 'If God did not exist, he would have to be invented.' It is true that people opposed the natural appetites to asceticism, the innate goodness of man to original sin, that they attributed to society the corruption which changed him and praised the qualities of the noble savage. But it is not certain that they had many illusions concerning the virtues of primitive man. In any case the propertied classes deemed it more prudent to keep their unbelief to themselves and to refrain from attacking the 'superstition' of the masses they dreaded. It was also Voltaire who wrote: 'The people must have a religion.'

Rousseau's outpourings relieved the dryness of this utilitarian deism. A new term, 'charity', was coined to describe the means enabling the 'sensitive' man to find contentment. This reversal in thought rendered even Catholicism the service of spreading a sentimental religiosity which was evident among many revolutionaries, Madame Roland, for example, and which later contributed to the success of Chateaubriand. Religious conformity did not disappear and many looked upon it as more than formality; orthodox publications were more popular than their mediocrity would lead one to believe. But even though Catholic faith was strong in western France, in the northern and eastern border regions, and in the mountainous areas, religious practice was declining in many towns and even in some rural sections—around Paris, in Champagne, central France, the Mâconnais—for when the Revolution suppressed religious coercion, public worship declined in these areas. Morals grew neither worse nor better because of this change of attitude: the dissolute practices of part of the nobility and of wealthy bourgeois should not reflect on the eighteenth century, since they were no worse than before. Moreover, neither utilitarianism nor sentiment erased the traditional French respect for a Cartesian and Cornelian ethical code, reinforced in schools by the study of classical texts, especially those of Plutarch.

It was also France which witnessed the most vehement attacks on privileges, feudal survivals, the imperfections and arbitrary nature of monarchical administration. The *philosophes* also proved themselves united in their appeal to natural law and in maintaining that reason should play an autonomous role in initiating reform. 'Man is born free, and everywhere he is in chains,' were the opening words of Rousseau's *Social Contract*. Even Montesquieu, whose theory of climates seemed to inaugurate deterministic sociology, wrote in the early part of *The Spirit of Laws*: 'A primitive reason exists . . . intelligent beings are capable of having laws that they have themselves made. To say that there is nothing just or injust save that commanded or forbidden by existing laws is to say that before the circle was drawn not all its radii were equal.'

The *philosophes* defended the whole Third Estate on certain issues, such as unequal taxation and manorial rights; but, undeniably, they rendered particular service to the bourgeoisie. When the bourgeois of France assumed rule of the nation they would introduce financial order and subordinate politics to productive prosperity. They would free the economy of its fetters: serfdom, which impeded recruitment of a labour force; ecclesiastical mortmain and nobiliary rights of inheritance, which interfered with free circulation of goods—and a high volume of trade was necessary to satisfy that thirst for profit viewed by economists as the basic stimulant to work and to enterprise. They would end inequality of obligations, which reduced purchasing power and popular savings; they would abolish customs barriers and varying weights and measures, which hindered formation of a national market, and would do away with intolerance, which prevented scientific research. This does not mean that these reforms aroused enough enthusiasm to rank first in the mind of the French bourgeoisie, which would imply that businessmen were the prime movers of the Revolution. Much more effective were rule of law and equality of rights, which appealed to the dignity of man as much as to his material interests. Government officers and lawyers, relatively independent and possessing some leisure, were professionally dedicated, as much from self-interest as from cultural background, to make law prevail over violence and caprice. They, the traditional bourgeoisie of the Old Regime, were in this respect the moulders of public opinion.

That bourgeoisie pinned all its hopes on the king; its interpreters, the *philosophes*, for the most part placed their trust in the enlightened despotism they praised in continental rulers. Rousseau, it is true, seemed to style himself the apostle of democracy and republicanism. But the *New Heloise* and *Émile* had a much wider reading public than did the *Social Contract*. Moreover, because he defined the general will as a disinterested one, democracy could exist only under the aegis of virtue, and his political discussions centred on direct popular government, which necessarily limited the republic to a small state. Mably gained much of his reputation after 1789, and the authors who were inspired by Rousseau's invectives against private and hereditary property had still less influence. The same was true of those who followed the tradition of a moral, ascetic communism, dating back to antiquity. The general public found these ideas utopian and considered representative institutions a necessary safeguard lest royal power degenerate into tyranny.

Offensive action against the throne came not from the bourgeoisie but from the aristocracy. The nobility had not been unaffected by bourgeois spokesmen: civil liberty would protect it from royal despotism, which occasionally became oppressive; economic freedom would increase the income it drew from large estates. Political liberty was especially appealing—the aristocracy had its own lawyers; the most distinguished of them, Montesquieu, advocated separation of powers to guarantee civil liberty. Separation meant that power should be distributed among the intermediary, privileged bodies—the nobility, parlements, the officials protected by venality, and even the clergy. Invoking a half-mythical history, Montesquieu traced aristocratic prominence and manorial rights back to the Germanic conquest, when nobles had forcefully imposed their authority upon degenerate Gallo-Romans. The parlements attributed their origins to Frankish assemblies, guardians of the 'fundamental laws' and of the ancient constitution which had subsequently been effaced by royal usurpation. The aristocrats expected political liberty to give them a dominant role in government and complete responsibility over provincial administration. Nobles and bourgeois were united in demanding liberty, but found themselves irreparably divided over equality of rights.

## ARTS AND LETTERS

New ideas, like economic and social developments, influenced art and literature. They brought success to the philosophic tale and to the recent plays of Beaumarchais. They gave popularity to the novel—considered by classicism to be unworthy of formal rules—and brought forth bourgeois drama as well as the paintings of Greuze. Within the salons light poetry was polished to perfection. The search for comfort led architects to subdue ostentatious ornamentation and painters and decorators to bow before a taste for erotic Epicureanism and exotic motifs. Engraving methods and pastel techniques were refined. Realism continued to dominate portraiture, landscapes, and paintings of animals. English painters remained apart from the academic tradition and were preparing to modernize landscape painting.

The reaction to rationalism heralded a more profound change in European culture. Doctor Johnson was the last representative of classicism in England. Young's *Night Thoughts*, Richardson's and Sterne's novels, inaugurated a renaissance of sentiment. In Germany the genius of Goethe and Schiller lent brilliance to the *Sturm und Drang* movement, which repudiated standards imposed by the prestige of the French writers. Rousseau's influence spread the preromantic spirit through Europe. Critics reproached both classicism and rationalism for failing to stimulate the imagination, for prohibiting introspection, for scorning the dark and the mysterious, for requiring man to think in terms of utility and ciphers. Popular taste turned to the natural display of English gardens, to mountain-tops and sea-scapes, night vigils and starlit reverie. Melancholy and tears, despair and horror, meditation and reflection on ancient ruins, passion and enthusiasm shook the boredom of ordered life. Germanic Europe searched for inspiration in everything of the past that was foreign to the classical Renaisance—in Dante and Shakespeare, medievalism, the self-styled Ossian, the Bible, Persian and Hindu civilization. Music used new instruments, among them the piano; in Germany the genius of Gluck, Haydn, and Mozart encouraged romantic expression through the symphony, the sonata, the opera. France felt the effects: English and German literature was read; Ducis translated Shakespeare. The writings of the comte de Tressan foreshadowed the 'troubadour' genre. In 1787 Bernardin de Saint-Pierre earned celebrity with *Paul et Virginie*. The idyll and the elegy became popular. But composers preferred entertaining, light operas studded with ariettas. In Paris, as in Vienna, the Italian *bel canto* was a favourite form.

The authority of classicism remained, none the less, even if its vitality had been sapped. Classical standards were consecrated in school and academy; authors such as Alfieri continued to write tragedies, although that form, along with epic and lyric poetry and even the recently fashionable descriptive poem, no longer found popular favour. In the freer drama, Goldoni, Sheridan, and Sedaine had more success. Art, too, continued to respect traditional canons, taught in France by the

Académie des Beaux Arts and by the École de Rome and sustained in England by the reputation of Wren. Architects and many sculptors observed the rules of classicism. Official honour was still given to paintings portraying great moments of history.

The interest in antiquity which was originally stirred by discovery of Pompeii and was later encouraged by the archaeological studies of Winckelmann in Germany, Caylus in France, and Flaxman in England, helped make classicism somewhat fashionable again. Barthélemy's *Voyage du jeune Anacharsis* was widely acclaimed upon its publication in 1787. Many Germans, notably Goethe and Schiller, were preoccupied with classical civilization, although French literature remained free from its influences—not until later did André Chénier introduce Hellenism into his poetry. The contrary was true of French art: neoclassic architecture grew more austere; David transformed painting; colour gave way to design, the live model to classical formulas. Other artistic currents were nevertheless influential. Fragonard and Houdon cannot be isolated from the talented group of eighteenth-century artists who enriched classical training with their expressions of individuality. Decorative art appropriated the Alexandrian motifs found at Pompeii and mixed them with Egyptian or allegedly Etruscan forms, making the style of Louis XVI more ornate without destroying its charm. David's paintings extolled civic virtue, as in the 'Oath of the Horatii' of 1784, and freshened memories of the Stoic morality demonstrated by Plutarch's heroes, heralding the revolutionary spirit. Public oratory and elaborate national celebrations would soon prove that classical forms were not necessarily bound to social and political conservatism. The wide range of expression in artistic life reflected increasing individualism in society. French youth, led by David, aspired to free itself from the onus of academies which absolute monarchy had imposed on it.

## COSMOPOLITANISM AND NATIONALITIES

European intellectual life had several centres. France was rivalled by England, Italy, and, more recently, Germany. New philosophical currents which marked the eighteenth century had been stirred by England, and Britain's intellectual role grew progressively stronger as its maritime and economic leadership asserted itself. The English aristocracy and upper bourgeoisie, considering that the British political system reconciled their interests with liberty, found their own influence more wholesome than French intellectual daring. Yet French thought benefited not only from inventiveness but from the brilliance and renown that Louis XIV had given the language and civilization of his kingdom. Bourbon political power was curbed in the eighteenth century, but every minor prince of Europe dreamed of Versailles, and French was becoming an international language. The reputation of French arts and letters was now equalled by that of 'philosophy' and the extravagant sophistication of Paris and Versailles. It was possible to speak of 'French Europe in the age of Enlightenment'.[1]

Cultivated circles were convinced that a community of European civilization was emerging. Europe was an entity to the inhabitants of overseas territories already conquered or threatened with invasion, and European culture seemed to possess an internal unity. Although political rivalries continued to divide the continent, it was remarked that public law tended to alleviate conflict through the notion of balance of power. A policy of equilibrium guided Vergennes after 1783, and Pitt seemed to agree, in the interests of peace. Warfare had become more humane in comparison with previous centuries: armies were provided with supplies and not expected to live off the country: officers, grown more humanitarian and 'sensitive', spared the civilian populace. Foreign policy was considered to be the business of statesmen, and theoreticians denied national self-interest. German writers even thought their homeland superior to any other because, in the absence of political and military unity, militant patriotism was yet unknown to it.

European unity was, however, only an illusion. Cosmopolitanism was in reality nothing more than an aristocratic and bourgeois veneer, a modish idea in intellectual circles. Mobility was still too restricted to dislodge the particularism of different European groups. Only in the minds of a few financiers or farsighted speculators, such as Talleyrand, did cosmopolitanism harmonize with the idea of an economic development that frontiers could only impede. These men were ahead of

---

[1] From the book *L'Europe française au siècle des lumières* (1938), by Louis Réau. (Translator's note.)

their time: capitalism had not yet created sufficient interdependence among states to discredit mercantilism, even in England.

What we see instead is that Europe was on the verge of transition from dynastic states to national communities. The ideology of this transformation lay in Herder's organic theories and in French voluntarism. It had already occurred in England, whose sense of community was enhanced by its size and insularity, even in Great Britain as a whole; it was well advanced in Holland and Scandinavia, in Switzerland and Spain, and especially in France, where the Revolution would not have been possible without it. In Germany and Italy a literary renaissance independent of French influence foreshadowed a political movement for unification. In Hungary the persistence of a national sense, of Slavic languages, and of the Greek Orthodox religion undermined the multi-national Habsburg empire. Successive partitions of Poland served to arouse its national consciousness. Autonomous Christian communities within the Ottoman empire were extremely antagonistic towards the Turks. What prevented full expression of nationalities was the dynastic nature of their governments, a survival of the medieval state structure. Despite advances of monarchical centralization, this structure continued to support provincial and municipal particularism and, above all, a social hierarchy based on privilege. The French Revolution was to weaken or destroy these obstacles, but, contrary to revolutionary aspirations, cosmopolitanism was simultaneously to recede rather than spread to the masses of Europe.

# 5

## THE STATES AND
## SOCIAL CONFLICTS

Absolutism still reigned over most of the continent although in modified forms, and *philosophes* heaped praise upon the 'enlightened despotism' practised by monarchs who, they believed, were affected by philosophic propaganda. Nevertheless—and all together—the aristocracy criticized royalty for having displaced nobles; the bourgeoisie was annoyed at being denied a position in government; and rivalry between the two classes was intensified. France was not the first to settle this three-cornered conflict by revolution. A brief glance at enlightened despotism and the solutions adopted in Great Britain and the United States will aid our understanding of the place the French Revolution was to assume in world history.

### ENLIGHTENED DESPOTISM

Continental monarchs continued to rule by divine right and with theoretically absolute powers. In practice, their authority was restricted, more in Western Europe than in other regions, by privileges, by whatever degree of independence the provincial assemblies and municipalities still enjoyed, and by the barriers against centralization resulting not only from difficulties in communication but also from the disorganized complexity of an administrative system that had developed little by little, under the pressure of events and without any master plan. Economic and intellectual changes were, at the end of the eighteenth century, subduing manners, and in Western states arbitrary power was diminishing. Royal subjects in the West distinguished despotism from monarchy in that monarchs respected the laws they had made. And in practice, unless a ruler considered his authority endangered, or yielded to caprice, or let the bureaucracy abuse its powers, secular courts protected the individual and his property.

On the other hand, during the seventeenth century, rulers in France, concerned with developing state power, responded as the Tudors had earlier and adopted a mercantilist policy that encouraged the growth of capitalism. In so far as Louis XIV gave Colbert a free hand, the monarchy during his reign, already bourgeois in character, roughly sketched what was later to be called enlightened despotism. This aspect became more pronounced when Louis curbed lords and crown officers in favour of royal intendants and, towards the end of his reign, forced the nobility to pay the *capitation* and the tithe. During the eighteenth century new ideas influenced certain ministers and a number of administrators. Intolerance became less militant; economic controls relaxed; in Spain, Charles III relinquished his monopoly on colonial trade. Domestic trade in grains was authorized more often than not. The king of Sardinia took the lead among reformers and decreed that rural communities could, collectively, redeem manorial dues. Finally, Catholic monarchs, intent upon ruling their clergies and limiting papal power in all matters that did not strictly involve dogma, practised a Caesaro-Papism of their own making. Suppression of the Society of Jesus and the declining influence of Rome encouraged partisans of enlightened policies.

Social conflicts, however, were unresolved. The achievements of enlightened despotism in Prussia and Russia were elaborately praised, yet few took time to reflect that in both countries the main issue was not modernization of society or even improvement of state power, but creation of the state itself.

In these two states, where part of the land was deserted and uncultivated, retarded conditions together with the driving ambitions of state rulers to enlarge central power were enough to determine policy. Religious toleration, indispensable to attract those seeking asylum from other states, had always distinguished Russia and Prussia, but their rulers borrowed heavily from Holland, England, France, and, through the agency of Habsburg institutions, from Spain. Moreover, Frederick the Great and his bureaucrats were French in culture and the czars put their nobles through the schools of traditional monarchies. Their enlightened despotism meant that Western institutions, economic policies, and civilization were extended eastward. They endeavoured to build a centralized, bureaucratic administration; they colonized their lands, practised rigorous mercantilism, and while receiving praise from the *philosophes*—achieved their goals—to fill the treasury, enlarge the army, and conquer new territory. No one realized that these rapid and incomplete reforms were tenuous at best, since the new regime was entrusted to bureaucrats who obeyed passively, as required of indifferent or rebellious subjects. The whole structure was threatened with collapse as soon as the strong personality that presided at its birth passed away. Prussia was soon to furnish proof: already Frederick William II, who succeeded Frederick the Great in 1786, had revealed his incompetence. In any case it was evident that economic reforms, which were intended to increase exports rather than raise the level of domestic consumption, benefited the state, the great land-owners, and the bourgeoisie, but did not aid the rest of the population. Taxes grew heavier; poverty, unemployment, and begging were no less severe in Prussia than in the countries of Western Europe.

A few princes of Germany deserved praise from men of the *Aufklärung*—Leopold of Anhalt because he patronized Basedow; Charles Augustus, who made Weimar an intellectual centre; the margrave of Baden, who suppressed serfdom. Others were distinguished only as tyrants—the elector of Hesse had sold his soldiers to England; when the Landtag thwarted Charles Eugene of Württemberg he imprisoned Moser and Schubart.

Austria in particular imitated the policies of Frederick the Great. After her military defeat Maria Theresa began to reorganize her state on the Prussian model, but with restraint and moderation. In contrast, upon the death of his mother in 1780 Joseph II plunged into reform with the commanding energy and impatient activity of a man who did not spare himself. His achievement as a whole is sufficiently original and consistent to make it difficult to explain solely on the grounds of his determination to acquire power and his desire to better a rival— perhaps he was inspired by doctrine. And yet, if the *Kameralisten*, the bureaucrats who served him, were genuine enthusiasts of the *Aufklärung*, it cannot be denied that he himself scorned and distrusted the *philosophes*, especially Voltaire, and that, remaining a faithful Catholic, he did not allow his subjects to change their faith. But he practised tolerance to the extent of making public office accessible to all Christians; he bettered the conditions of Jews and, more remarkable still, instituted civil marriage. If one insists that his reforms owed nothing to the influence of contemporary ideas it must be conceded that few sovereigns stamped their administrations with a more forceful imprint. Unfortunately, his kingdom offered the most unfavourable conditions imaginable: his possessions included regions varying as sharply in language, culture, economic development, social structure, and historic institutions as Belgium and Lombardy, the German provinces and Bohemia, Galicia and Hungary. Upon them all Joseph imposed his absolute authority and a fairly uniform administration that usurped the autonomy of local assemblies and traditional institutions. In most provinces he stipulated that his officials know German. At the same time he far surpassed the Caesaro-Papism of other Catholic rulers in reforming the ecclesiastic organization from top to bottom, confiscating the property of the secular clergy, whose members became salaried bureaucrats, and suppressing a number of monasteries, while disregarding the pope. Discontent with decrees from Vienna was already evident in Bohemia and even in the German provinces. In Belgium a strong opposition formed under clerical leadership. The kingdom of Hungary did not belong to the Holy Roman Empire and was bound to Austria only by a personal union. Its constitution and administration, still medieval in form, accorded power to the nobility. There, reaction was powerful. When he ultimately attacked the manorial lords Joseph provoked the Magyar aristocracy to active rebellion.

In developing their economies the enlightened despots of Prussia and Russia followed the course of the traditional monarchies, rendering the Old Regime bourgeois in character. One major difference, however, distinguished them from their models. The kings of Western

Europe did not make their bourgeoisie legally equal to the nobility, but neither did they prevent its members from acquiring lands, fiefs, or manors; in France the bourgeois could even buy his way into the nobility. In the West nobles were granted many privileges, but their submission was not bought at the price of complete aristocratic control over the peasants, and all subjects, including serfs, could appeal to royal courts in practice as well as in theory. In Prussia and especially in Russia, where palace revolutions were not uncommon, the sovereign dreaded the aristocracy but realized that its services were indispensable. Rulers handled the bourgeoisie with discretion, reserving to it positions in commerce and the liberal professions and helping it establish industry. Catherine granted it corporative autonomy and exempted it from military service. Frederick recruited its members for the army and administration. But no bourgeois was permitted to acquire land without royal authorization, and although ennoblement was possible, it was rarely granted because venality in office did not exist.

High official and administrative positions were filled by the nobility, and aristocrats monopolized landed property. Catherine's charter of 1785 granted them their own courts and grouped them in a caste under the supervision of dignitaries whom they designated themselves. In Prussia they controlled the provincial estates and appointed the *Landrath* for the circle. The king had set up a mortgage bank exclusively for their use. In both countries the most incriminating evidence of collusion between throne and nobility was subjection by the aristocracy of the rural masses. Frederick the Great may have favoured abolition of the *Leibeigenschaft* along with limitation and commutation of labour service and the fees owed by the *Untertan*, but he brooked no interference with affairs in the *Gut*, where the Junker retained arbitrary authority and even levied the king's land tax. Catherine extended serfdom to the Ukraine and distributed among her favourites untold numbers of peasants taken from the imperial domain and from secularized Church lands. The Russian noble, who sent his own serfs to fill the army's quota of recruits, had even greater discretionary power than his Prussian counterpart.

The experiences of Denmark, Poland, and Sweden served to commend the prudent attitude which Catherine and Frederick had adopted towards their aristocracies. At Copenhagen Struensee established an absolutist system only to lose his life; Bernstorff succeeded him and governed with consent of the nobility, abolishing serfdom but initiating an enclosure movement like that of England. In Sweden, where the peasants were free, conflict between Gustavus III and his nobles remained political, but in 1772 the king regained his power only through a *coup d'état* and in 1789 was weighing the necessity of a second such move. Poland offered a particularly instructive example, not in the oppression of its peasants, which scarcely troubled other rulers, but in the feudal anarchy that reigned there, serving as a reminder that Poland's neighbours had once before utilized that circumstance to partition the Republic.

Far from granting free rein to innovators, certain princes were alarmed by the decline of traditional ideas especially evident in Germany among the clergy, bourgeoisie, and even the nobility. Although Freemasonry, under the control of Ferdinand of Brunswick, was loyal to the crown, its more impatient members were annoyed at its lenience, especially in Bavaria, where Jesuit influence persisted. In 1776 Weishaupt founded the order of the Illuminati at Ingolstadt and, with the assistance of Knigge, a Hanoverian, organized it into a disciplined hierarchy. At a convocation of Freemasons held in 1782 at the monastery of Wilhemsbad, near Hanau, they tried unsuccessfully to win over the lodges. They did, however, draw more than two thousand disciples from members of the liberal professions, government officials, and the gentry in southern Germany and Vienna. Their followers bitterly criticized established powers and the social structure, but there is no evidence that they envisaged revolutionary action. Like the *philosophes*, they hoped to influence governments by gaining many members among administrative personnel. Austria was then planning to annex the Bavarian Electorate, and the Illuminati were denounced as agents of Vienna. The order was suppressed in 1785. Supporters of the Jesuits unleashed a campaign against free thought. Weishaupt fled; his followers were harried and after 1787 were subject to criminal prosecution.

At the same time the Rosicrucians were urging government action against the *Aufklärung*, and with the death of Frederick the Great in 1786 they gained a dominant position within the kingdom, because Frederick William II, nephew and successor of the great king, was one of their affiliates. Wöllner and Bischoffswerder were able to advance professionally, Wöllner as minister of justice and head of the *Geistes-departement*, Bischoffswerder as adjutant-general on the king's military staff. Frederick William could set no personal example of piety, being a bigamist, but he endeavoured to bring ministers and teachers back to orthodoxy. The 'religious edict' marked the beginning of an era of administrative harassment for them—candidates had to pass religious tests; textbook inspection and censorship grew severe. Reaction reached Saxony and Hanover.

Joseph II not only refused to join reaction but even failed to evaluate the circumspect approach which his powerful neighbours adopted towards their aristocracies. His subsequent failures recommended a policy of caution in dealing with the nobility. Attacking the manorial system, he abolished serfdom and offered the *Untertan* protection of royal tribunals. He ordered manorial fees and labour services to be set at a fixed rate, authorized their commutation into cash, then made such commutation obligatory. Finally, in 1789, he linked these changes to reform of land taxes and ordered an official survey: 70 per cent of the income from land was to remain with the landholder and 12⅓ per cent was to go to the state, leaving the landlord the remainder, 17⅔ per cent. A league of opposition, chiefly in Hungary, rose against him, and together with a costly and unsuccessful war begun against the Turks in 1787 it provoked the disintegration of his monarchy.

His setbacks, in conjunction with the success of Frederick the Great and Catherine, demonstrated that in Eastern Europe enlightened despotism could succeed only by coming to terms with the aristocracy at the expense of the Third Estate. The nobility had already grown docile—even apathetic in Italy and Spain—and would remain quiet as long as the social hierarchy was not seriously threatened. But the aristocracy of both Eastern and Western Europe would countenance no measure entailing abolition of privileges.

## GREAT BRITAIN

England's development brought into light the backwardness of the continent. The rise of the British bourgeoisie, favoured by economic progress in which the nobility played a role, had provoked the first two modern revolutions in the guise of a struggle between Anglicans and Calvinists and against Catholicism. These revolutions ended in compromises which lasted into the nineteenth century. On the one hand, the aristocracy and upper bourgeoisie reached an agreement permitting them to dominate society and control the government; on the other, the throne was forced to recognize, definitively, the principles of constitutionalism. Freedom of the individual and equality before law were guaranteed in theory, at least according to the interpretation given them by the upper classes, which meant that in practice they were infrequently realized. The king shared his powers with Parliament—that is, with the aristocracy of the House of Lords. With the aid of an electoral system supported by disorder and corruption, the upper chamber maintained some measure of control over membership of the House of Commons by respecting the interests of the wealthy notables and astutely yielding, from time to time, one of its 'pocket' or 'rotten' boroughs to some able man— such as the younger Pitt—who had distinguished himself at the universities.

The government's chief guarantee of a docile majority, however, lay in the exercise of royal 'prerogatives'—control over certain boroughs; distribution of sinecures, 'honours', and pensions; letting of government contracts. During the reigns of the first two Hanoverians the Tories were distrusted for Jacobite sympathies and the gentry harried the new dynasty. George I and George II therefore had to help the Whigs take government leadership and chose ministers from their ranks. The parliamentary system which thus took form meant that actual power resided in a homogeneous cabinet representing, and changing with, the majority. As memories of the Stuarts faded, however, George III thought himself capable of using his prerogatives to reassert control over the government. Beginning in 1784, Pitt, having broken with the Whigs, dominated Parliament in concert with the king. Because he and George agreed to confer the majority on the 'New Tories', Pitt acquired a reputation for having consolidated the parliamentary system. Actually, since he controlled no more than a small number of personal followers, he allowed the king to reject whatever reforms failed to meet royal approval. Hungry for power and convinced, as was his father before him, that he was responsible for the power and prosperity of his country, Pitt was willing to accept the disappointments dealt him by his sovereign.

This did not affect the social compromise, which dominated the period. The aristocracy sat in government and Parliament; its members controlled local administration as justices of the peace within the shires and as gentry in the parishes. It legislated according to its own interests, as the corn laws and enclosure acts clearly show. The upper bourgeoisie took its share: it watched over customs protection, navigation acts, colonial monopolies, and laws ensuring control of the labour force. Its income was swelled by interest on the huge public debt, by military contracts, and by the booty wrung from nabobs in India. The elder Pitt acted as the agent of these two associated groups in founding the British empire. His son, patiently repairing the misfortunes of war in America, could legitimately claim that he acted in the same capacity. He restored finances by requiring modest sacrifices of private fortunes, by reorganizing the treasury, and by paying off the debt. If peace seemed a pre-requisite to these ambitions, he none the less rebuilt the war fleet and watched for opportunities to strengthen his country's diplomatic position.

There were, however, threatening clouds on the horizon. Money ruled with unprecedented authority. Bribery was rampant; seats in Parliament were often sought only to enlarge profitable activity. Venality, co-optation, and nepotism corrupted the civil service, already weakened through aristocratic dominance. The Test Act was enforced against dissenters, and special laws restricting Catholics remained in force. The habits of the oligarchy shocked Puritans, who were gaining new strength in a religious revival. Many wanted to cleanse public office. Beneficence and social utility joined with a sense of charity to plead for poor relief, popular education, a better penal system. One group demanded abolition of the slave trade.

In addition, the Irish situation continued to cause concern. Most of Ireland's inhabitants, still Catholic, were angered by obligations to pay tithes and parish taxes in support of the Established Church when they were denied the right to vote. Irish Protestants joined them in protesting economic injury caused by the closing of English markets to Irish products. Grattan, Irish Protestant leader, wanted the Dublin Parliament to have legislative autonomy. Exploited by middlemen, poverty-stricken landholders were driven to take revenge by committing agrarian crimes which inspired constant insecurity and fear in the populace. Many began to emigrate to the United States. During the American wars the Irish were allowed to arm themselves as volunteers to ward off possible invasion by the French. This precedent could easily be exploited.

Yet little could be expected of the British Parliament in the absence of electoral reform. The Whigs, driven from power, under the leadership of Fox, Sheridan, and Burke were forming the first opposition party, one that possessed little cohesion but nevertheless directed systematic criticism towards the government, thereby fulfilling a basic requirement of parliamentary government. They attacked royal patronage and recommended 'economical' reforms—that is, suppression of sinecures and other abuses. They realized that electoral reform was essential, but, having themselves profited from the system, were in no hurry. Fox chose to pin his hopes of regaining power upon the accession of his friend the Prince of Wales.

More alarming was the development of democratic agitation within the petty bourgeoisie. Active after 1760, under the direction of Wilkes, the movement as yet had not gained proletarian support, and for the moment was inactive. The French Revolution was to awaken it.

Meanwhile, the chief threat to the existing regime lay in a possible rupture between aristocracy and business bourgeoisie. The capitalists did not command as much influence within the state as they thought they deserved, and industrialization threatened some day to turn manufacturer against landowner. Pitt was cognizant of these difficulties and hoped to alleviate them in part by emancipating dissenters and Catholics, by abolishing the slave trade, opening England's markets to Ireland, and instituting modest electoral reform. The king accepted none of his proposals. Pitt succeeded only in lightening customs duties and in signing a commercial treaty with France. Yet nothing discouraged the discontented from hoping that, through the agency of the nation's constitutional and representative institutions, the oligarchy would in time surrender peacefully.

The compromises which British leaders, acting with the realistic opportunism of businessmen, had imposed upon revolutionary foundations won them admirers. The French bourgeoisie of 1789 was particularly struck by the fact that in Britain no one liked to speak of equality; in fact, the governing classes thought civil and political rights should be distributed according to birth and wealth and considered equality of rights nothing more than an engine of war destined to upset the social hierarchy to the advantage of the lower classes. The upper bourgeoisie, partnered with the aristocracy, saw no reason to publicize egalitarian principles. This was not true in France.

## THE UNITED PROVINCES AND CONTINENTAL PATRICIATES

There were on the continent a few small states that invited comparison with England. They differed chiefly in the subordinate position of their military nobility and in the bourgeois origins, usually distant, of their governing oligarchies, whose members withheld authority from those who had only recently climbed the social ladder.

The Dutch United Provinces was a republican federation of autonomous states joined with certain subject territories. It commanded a reputation as the most liberal country and held a prominent place in the history of civilization. In the seventeenth century Holland had ranked among the leaders of Europe's economic expansion. Since then the nobility had continued to lose power, although it still enjoyed some measure of seigneurial authority, particularly in eastern regions. The Prince of Orange, William V, whose mother was English and whose brother-in-law was king of Prussia, preserved his stadholderate by armed force and was suspected of royalist aspirations, but the upper bourgeoisie was still master of the state, of the India Company, and of the Bank of Amsterdam. Yet decline was evident. England had usurped primacy on the seas and in Asia. Lacking coal and raw materials, industry failed to expand; capital instead was used to finance Europe's great powers. The Dutch bourgeoisie, living on unearned income, was losing its vitality. Nepotism and co-optation concentrated public office in the hands of a few families. The upper bourgeoisie was developing into a patriciate determined to conserve its monopoly upon public life and riddled with corruption. Some of those it held back formed a Patriot party, which wanted to change the political balance and assume power, give the government new life, and make the federation a unitary republic. The wars in America had recently demonstrated the government's weakness, and the bank was jeopardized by its advances to the India Company and to the city of Amsterdam. But the reformers obtained none of their goals. Moreover, they distrusted the proletariat, which had always supported the Orange faction out of resentment towards the bourgeoisie.

Switzerland was not a state but a confederation of independent cantons, some controlling dependent territories of their own, united only by the need for mutual defence. Some nobles remained, but manorial rights were less burdensome than the tithe, most of which had passed to the hands of the ruling Protestants. Each canton was ruled by an oligarchy, whose members in Bern, Zurich, and Basel disposed of sizeable fortunes. Several bourgeois families had acquired wealth through dealings in transportation, home industry, and foreign loans. Denied governmental power, they longed for national unity and political reform. This conflict issued in revolution at Geneva, a foreign republic allied to the Confederation. There the patriciate of Negatives was deposed in 1782 by the party of Representatives, bourgeois who would have sat in the general assemblies had they ever been convened, and by the Natives, who possessed no political rights at all. Order was restored through the intervention of France and 'the gentlemen of Bern'; immigrants from Geneva and Switzerland were to play prominent roles when revolution convulsed Europe.

Patriciates ruled in Germany within the several urban republics directly under the emperor's authority. Except for the Hanseatic ports and Frankfurt, they led a life of stagnant obscurity. In Italy the patrician republics of Venice and Genoa had reached a more advanced stage of development: their ruling families, possessing fortunes derived from commerce and finance, adopted titles of nobility. At Venice they registered their members in a Golden Book and made succession hereditary within a caste system. Their absolutist police state enjoyed legitimate fame.

These states shared several traits. Either their geographic position had prevented them from participating in Europe's expansion overseas or their limited area and population had kept that participation to a minimum; and for want of natural resources none could advance beyond the commercial stage of capitalism. The patriciates, ingrown and stultified, remained in power because they denied authority to the bourgeoisie which was itself very weak; it found neither exemplary model nor alliance in the remnants of military nobility, and it nourished as strong a distrust of lower classes as did the bourgeoisie elsewhere.

## THE AMERICAN REVOLUTION

The Anglo-Saxons in America offered an example that suggested another kind of development. In their struggle against the mother country the 'insurgents' employed not only the arguments of traditional liberties but also appeals to natural law, which remained alive in Puritan thought. They gave voice to the rights of man and the citizen in their declarations of universal principles and they erected a republic in the name of the sovereign people.

This upheaval profoundly affected the European world. A victorious rebellion stirred romantic enthusiasm and, as could be expected, shook the principle of submission to an established order. Its consequences were extremely varied. Ireland profited from the anxieties which beset the British government, because, after allowing the Irish volunteers to arm as a measure of defence against possible invasion, Britain thought it had to assure their allegiance by giving them access to colonial markets, authorizing them to export woollens and several manufactured products, and relaxing special measures against Catholics. The first secession from an overseas empire encouraged colonials across the globe to demand some measure of autonomy, if not independence. Revolution in America aroused the democrats in England; Thomas Paine crossed the Atlantic to join the insurgent cause. The American Revolution thus heralded a revival of democratic propaganda which events in France were soon to amplify.

Upon the continent, all who shared the ideals of the Enlightenment were roused. Benjamin Franklin's unprecedented popularity testifies to this. As the son of a chandler who served as a printer's apprentice and acquired wealth as a bookseller and trader, who had risen to prominence in the middle class, played an important role in journalism and Freemasonry and ultimately in politics and diplomacy, he symbolized the new order. Memories of the Seven Years War played a large part in

France's desire to aid the rebellious colonies against England, but many officers who fought for the insurgent cause, most of them gentlemen, first among them Lafayette, received a political education which destined them to form the nucleus of a liberal nobility during the impending crisis in their homeland. Many of the French revolutionaries, such as Condorcet, derived not a few of their proposals from the new American republic.

In the United States, as in England during 1688, the Revolution's success was based upon compromise between a landed aristocracy and an upper bourgeoisie of financiers, merchants, shipowners, and manufacturers. There were major differences as well: unlike England, the colonies had never known a House of Lords and preserved no hereditary political authority after rejecting the monarch; when the gentry, including George Washington, lost its privileges, the sole defining characteristic of its members was the predominance of land in their patrimony. In this society, where wealth more clearly determined hierarchy than in the Old World, the ruling classes were occupied with essentially the same issue faced by Great Britain's governors: to discover whether or not the republic would evolve into a democracy. However, it was the aftermath of war rather than concern with the future which placed the Revolution's leaders in a defensive position, for their material interests had been damaged by hostilities. The various states and the confederate Congress had issued paper money and contracted loans, both of which were assessed at a very low value, and private creditors faced reimbursement in deflated currency. War had crippled navigation, commerce, and industry; peace threatened to bring formidable British competition.

The lower classes had participated in the struggle against Britain, and agitation—particularly among small landowners and farmers, who, being debtors, profited from inflation—did not cease with independence. Some resented the capitalist bourgeoisie and plantation owners; they especially hated speculators who bought up notes and titles to loans at depreciated prices and then acquired huge lots of available land to divide them up for quick resale. As happened afterwards in France, the American Revolution brought about a transfer of landed property confiscated from loyalist émigrés. In addition, the 'squatters' were penetrating as far as the Ohio plains. In 1787 Congress passed an ordinance regulating the acquisition of north-western territory, and businessmen even tried to attract European investment in such land. Finally, the spirit of the Revolution challenged slavery. Several states abolished the trade altogether and indicated their willingness to abolish the practice as well.

Each of the thirteen states was in principle independent. It was not clear at first whether the union, like the Swiss Confederation in Europe, was to care only for matters of common defence. Federal power did not have authority to end inflation or stabilize the value of currency, to consolidate the debt and pay off its interest, to establish a tariff, or to maintain an armed force capable of protecting the new republic and the propertied classes. Those who seized the initiative by urging in 1787 adoption of the constitution, which founded the United States government, regardless of the significance of their action in terms of future events and the praise they justly deserve, were not motivated solely by the desire to found a nation. Class interest, even personal interest, guided them in part. Washington himself was one of the richest landowners of the republic. Robert Morris was a ranking speculator, and Benjamin Franklin did not disdain profit. Although in retrospect it seems that Hamilton, who died a poor man, merited less than any other the cruel attacks upon his eminent role, his policy undeniably favoured the rise of commercial and industrial capitalism. Great landowners nevertheless agreed to support the projected union so that effective federal power would protect them in the event of a slave revolt and on conditon that the slave question be left to the discretion of each state. Voting rights and eligibility were made dependent upon property qualifications. In an immense country unevenly populated and lacking adequate roads, the popular masses had not the means to organize themselves against a rich and cultivated minority. The urban proletariat was either indifferent or inclined to follow employers. Opposition was strong only among the rural inhabitants and disbanded soldiers who had been paid in depreciated currency.

The nation's leaders, masters at the constitutional convention in Philadelphia, recognized popular sovereignty but left untouched the electoral system of each state, and concentrated upon balancing federal powers to prevent any action capable of compromising state authority. The Senate and House of Representatives which were elected shortly afterwards were only a continuation of the convention. When Washington became president in 1789 more than half of those who had drawn up the constitution entered his cabinet. As secretary of the treasury Hamilton could apply his policies: in 1790 and 1791 Congress refunded the foreign debt and assumed state debts, which doubled its financial burden; founded a national bank whose terms of capitalization were that it could offer loans up to 75 per cent of its total funds; enacted a tariff; sold public lands, which could also be paid for in part with loans; authorized the recruitment of land and naval forces; and, finally, increased the government's financial resources with a tax on alcohol which was aimed at farmers operating countless stills. In setting up a state apparatus, the forces of reaction served thus their own interests and did all they could to block the road to democracy. If Hamilton had had his way, those forces would have gone even farther, for he admired in particular the hereditary lords of the English constitution. John Adams thought that at least life governorships would be more reassuring. The Society of the Cincinnati, an organization of army officers, represented a previous and unsuccessful attempt to establish a hereditary aristocracy.

It seems dubious that the democrats of Europe knew the economic and social roots of this political life. But in comparison with the principles proclaimed at the dawn of the American Revolution, they found cause to criticize the Revolution's outcome. Freedom of conscience meant freedom of Christians. Negro slavery remained. As in England, revolutionary leaders did not insist upon equality of rights, doubtless because they thought that this went without saying in a country which recognized no legal privileges, but also because this principle could serve as a pretext for demands from the lower class. As an added measure of security they throttled the masses by denying them the right to vote.

## FRANCE

The French monarchy lay midway between British constitutionalism and continental despotism. It did not share its power with the aristocracy, as was the case in England, and neither did it abandon its peasants to the nobles, as did Russia and Prussia. It let the French nobility keep its privileges but it permitted ennoblement to flourish and the bourgeoisie to thrive.

Under Louis XIV the monarchy had become absolutistic, centralist, and bureaucratic. Its supremacy was to all appearances firmly established; the nobility's submission seemed final. In reality the eighteenth century was marked by aristocratic revival as well as the bourgeoisie's ascent. The nobility no longer thought of recouping power through armed force: it now challenged and undermined the king's rule with bourgeois methods, opposing him through sovereign courts and appeal to public opinion. Nobles of the sword, who despite their pretensions had in the recent or distant past been commoners, pushed ambitiously forward. 'Officers' of the crown raised a chorus of protest because intendants, directly appointed by the king, were gradually usurping local administration. Gentlemen allied with bishops controlled the existing provincial estates or, in regions where these assemblies had disappeared, aspired to reinstitute them. Successors of the Sun King had gradually ceased to distrust the aristocracy and let nobles fill positions of authority. Under Louis XVI, Saint-Simon could no longer have reproached his sovereign for surrounding himself only with 'base bourgeois'. Except for Necker, all the king's ministers were aloof aristocrats; and the intendants, of the same stripe, residing for years in their districts, marrying there and buying land, hobnobbed with the local gentry.

As elsewhere, the only effective feature of enlightened despotism in France was its often remarkable administrative staff. Attempts at structural reforms such as those tried by Machault, Maupeou, and Turgot failed before the resistance of aristocratic bodies—parlements, clerical assemblies, and provincial estates. Organs of government were little improved: Louis XVI ruled through virtually the same ministries and councils that Louis XIV had used. National unity undoubtedly continued to advance through development of communications and economic interchange, through instruction given in schools, through the attraction Paris exerted. But France was still divided into *pays d'élections*, where the intendant ruled over his district and feared only the parlement, and *pays d'états*, where he had to contend with provincial estates which increased their autonomy, especially in Brittany. Southern France practised Roman law, northern France its numerous local customs; the nobility had its own usages; the ecclesiastic courts followed canon law, and royal ordinances were superimposed upon this complicated legal structure. The forming of a national market was thwarted by internal customs barriers, tolls, and variations in the fiscal system. Weights and measures differed among regions and even among parishes. Administrative, judicial, financial, and religious districts were unequal in the extreme and overlapped, presenting a picture of chaos. Provinces and towns, often endowed with privileges which they regarded as bulwarks against absolutism, displayed entrenched particularism.

In a sense it was the historic mission of the Capetian dynasty to give the community that it had formed by consolidating Frankish lands under its sceptre, an administrative unity which would correspond to the community's awakening self-awareness, and which would, besides, not only aid the exercise of royal power but prove useful and suitable for the whole population. The king's officials would have welcomed unity because its realization would enhance their influence as well as the crown's; but for this reason they immediately encountered the impassioned resistance of the aristocracy. Fulfilment of the royal mission questioned the very basis of a social structure which was itself the negation of unity.

Should circumstances furnish an occasion, royal power, having grown lax, risked facing even bolder aristocratic opposition, and the bourgeoisie might lend its support to aristocratic demands. Nobles of the sword or of the robe who supported themselves with historical precedent, crown officers who were devoted to their professional tradition, lawyers and philosophers who invoked natural law and rationalist ideas—all, in the end, curbed the ruler's power through law and protected the individual against arbitrary action. Great landowners and bourgeois capitalists alike favoured economic freedom. Nor was there any obstacle in principle to many administrative reforms. Upon this common ground an alliance of notables similar to the coalition that had emerged victorious in England would be formed in France to impose a constitutional system and respect for liberty on the king. This did in fact appear later in the Dauphiné.

Yet the British solution entailed not only a compromise between king and notables but another between nobles and bourgeois. The

French aristocracy desired no such compact, except for a small number of nobles who concluded from the experiences of Great Britain and the United States that they would lose nothing. Gentlemen were not unaware of the power of money, and they realized that without ample funds birth could not guarantee a successful career. At court they curried royal favour; some became involved in important enterprises; Talleyrand dallied in speculation; large landowners profited when enclosures and division of communal lands were authorized in a few provinces; efforts were being made to extract more revenue from the peasants, efforts collectively known as the manorial reaction. But whereas some nobles were close to the upper bourgeoisie in business sense and way of living, others were unable to preserve their rank. Mirabeau dropped out of his class to live by his pen. Chateaubriand vaguely yearned for the innovations that later opened the doors to his ambition—'Arise, desired storms.' Most of the French nobility, possessing a military and feudal mentality, neither knew how to adapt themselves to a bourgeois order nor wished to do so, preferring to grow poor and even to live as impecunious squires rather than forfeit noble title. Their solution was to live in an attitude of exaggerated exclusiveness. They wanted their order to be a closed caste and venality in office to be suppressed so that the hobnobbing of baseborn with aristocracy would end. They wished all offices compatible with their dignity to be reserved to them. They wanted an increase of special schools for their sons and of noble ecclesiastical orders for their daughters. Several parlements had already refused to admit any more commoners, and the king, first gentleman in the kingdom, respected their feelings. Every bishop was a noble; after 1781 no one could become an officer, without rising through the ranks, unless he proved four quarterings of nobility. In this the French nobility resembled other continental aristocracies, overlooking the fact that the rival class it scorned resembled, in terms of power, the Anglo-Saxon bourgeoisie. 'The roads are blocked at every access,' wrote Barnave. Sieyes, canon of Chartres, stated that he would never attain the office of bishop. Since the doors were everywhere closed, the only course was to break them down. To defend its cause the bourgeoisie of France, in contrast with that of England and of the United States, was led to emphasize equality of rights. In the larger perspective of world history, this is the significant originality of the Revolution of 1789.

## RIVALRY OF STATES

By suppressing feudal anarchy the formation of large states had aided the advance of European civilization. But the will to power of the dynasts creating those states had from the beginning brought them into conflict. Regarding themselves as owners of land, they wished above all to enlarge their properties at the expense of their neighbours. Had anyone pointed out to them that with the abrupt collapse of the Old Regime in France not only was society's hierarchic structure and their own power to be shaken, but also that states were to be transformed into national communities, they would have replied that cataclysm in the Bourbon kingdom would prove advantageous by removing France from European politics, whose vicissitudes were at that moment absorbing their attention.

People were too accustomed to international complications to doubt that conflict would soon break out. In all likelihood England would seek revenge for its recent defeat. Despite the peaceable mien presented by Vergennes and apparently imitated by Pitt, a new show of arms between Great Britain and France was expected. France would be supported by its maritime allies, particularly Spain, concerned about its American possessions and bound to the Bourbons through their 'family compact'. It was recognized that the British foreign office in such cases was skilled in financing coalitions to split enemy ranks through continental hostilities. Since the sixteenth century armed struggles had raged in Italy and Germany: diplomats and military men considered Italy nothing more than a geographical name, and the Germanic Holy Roman Empire was heading towards ruin now that Prussia had become Austria's rival. France had long thwarted the Habsburgs in Germany, where it supported the various petty princes, and in Italy, where it helped Spain restore a prince to the Neapolitan throne and another to that of Parma. The alliance of 1756 between France and Austria had subdued the rivalry, but in France it was unpopular, and the French public regretted the fact that Belgium now was in Habsburg hands. Hostility towards the Austrian dynasty, traditional since the sixteenth century and still a force in French opinion, encouraged an interested sympathy for the states threatened by Austria, and especially for rulers in Germany. Some still supported a Prussian alliance, and Versailles was making an effort to sustain French influence in the Rhineland. Choiseul and then Vergennes had preserved the pact of 1756, but had limited its terms to maintenance of the *status quo*. At Teschen, Vergennes concluded an agreement with Catherine to prevent outbreak of war between Austria and Prussia over the question of Bavarian succession and also to place the Holy Roman Empire, in its form determined by the West-phalian treaties, under the joint protection of France and Russia. When Joseph had recently tried to open the Scheldt estuary, closed since 1648, Vergennes did not support him, instead acting as mediator between Austria and Holland. Nor did he back Joseph against Frederick the Great and the Princes' League, which opposed the plan to exchange Bavaria for the Austrian Netherlands. Peace might, then, continue to reign in the West.

It was from the East that conflict now threatened. Catherine and Joseph were studying the possibility of taking more territory from the Ottoman empire, and Prussia intended to benefit from any such move by demanding a second partition of Poland. Vergennes refused the offer of Egypt and Syria, but Pitt was alarmed by the prospect of Russian control over the Indian routes and by the possibility that the Eastern question might become a European issue capable of provoking general war. Moreover, the reforms launched so precipitately by Joseph exposed his empire to internal decomposition should hostilities in the East prove disastrous. Internecine quarrels of unpredictable consequences might then break out in Europe.

Politically there was no Europe, any more than there was an Italy or a Germany. Its members were as incapable of uniting in the interests of domestic peace as they were of joining forces to subdue peoples over-seas. Even revolutions appeared to European sovereigns as nothing more than opportunities to fish in troubled waters. The revolutionary changes achieved in Anglo-Saxon regions had in part owed their suc-cess to this international anarchy. The French Revolution, as well, would profit from it.

# Part II

The Advent of the Bourgeoisie
in France

# 6

---

# THE ARISTOCRATIC
# REVOLUTION, 1787–1788

The French Revolution was started and led to victory in its first phase by the aristocracy. This fact is of primary importance, but for differing reasons both the Third Estate and the aristocracy took pains to thrust it into the background. The immediate cause of the Revolution was a financial crisis originating with the war in America. Necker had financed the war by borrowing, and his successor, Calonne, had used the same method to pay off arrears. The deficit grew to such proportions that on August 20, 1786, Calonne sent Louis XVI a note declaring state reform imperative.

## CALONNE AND THE NOTABLES

The fiscal administration was so confused that the situation can be described only roughly. A statement of financial expectations drawn up in March, 1788, the first—and last—budget of the Old Regime, estimated expenditures at 629 million livres and receipts at 503 million, leaving a deficit of 126 million, or 20 per cent. Contemporaries attributed the deficit to court wastefulness and financiers' profits. Some economies could be and were made, but servicing the debt alone required 318 million, more than half of expenditures. The government could have reduced expenses only by repudiating the debt; raising taxes seemed out of the question, as taxes were already considered too high. At any rate there was one resource left. Certain provinces paid very little in taxes; the bourgeoisie less than the peasantry, the nobility and clergy least of all. From a technical point of view, the crisis could be easily resolved: equality of taxation would provide enough funds.

Calonne did not prove bold enough for fiscal equality, but he at least proposed to extend the salt and tobacco monopolies through the whole kingdom and to replace the *capitation* and twentieths by a direct land tax, a 'territorial subvention', to be levied without exception upon all landowners. At the same time he planned to stimulate economic activity and consequently swell treasury receipts by freeing the grain trade from all controls, by abolishing internal customs barriers, and by suppressing certain indirect taxes. Going even further, he intended to give responsibility for apportioning taxes to provincial assemblies elected by landowners without distinction as to order, and to relieve the clergy of its own debt by selling the Church's manorial rights. Financial stability would strengthen royal power, reducing opposition from the parlements to insignificance. Unity of the kingdom would be advanced. The bourgeoisie would be permitted to take part in government administration.

Although the sacrifices required of privileged groups were modest—they would still be exempt from the *taille* and from the tax which Calonne proposed to substitute for road-service obligations (the *corvée des routes*)—he entertained no illusions as to how the parlements would receive his plans. He might have attacked them openly had he been able to count upon the king's support, but the fate of Turgot and Necker gave him no encouragement. Moreover, although royalty still carried prestige, Louis personally had none. He was devoted to the hunt and liked to work with his hands; he drank and ate to excess; he liked neither high society, gambling, nor dancing; he was the laughing-stock of his courtiers; and rumours of the queen's conduct made him appear ridiculous. Marie Antoinette had gained the reputation of a Messalina and had lost face in the Diamond Necklace Affair of 1785. Calonne was therefore resigned to practise indirect methods. He thought out a plan to convoke an assembly of notables consisting primarily of various noble elements. By selecting them himself and banking on administrative influence plus respect due the king, he expected that they would prove amenable and that their acquiescence would in turn impress the parlements. But the calling of an assembly was an initial surrender: the king was consulting his aristocracy rather than notifying it of his will.

When they convened on February 22, 1787, the notables were angered by the proposal to elect provincial assemblies without distinction as to order, by the restriction of their powers, and by the attack on the clergy's manorial rights. As could be expected, they censured the direct land tax and asked that they first be given a treasury report. They declared themselves desirous of contributing to the welfare of the state—but they intended to dictate their own terms. Louis saw that Calonne would get nowhere with the assembly, and dismissed him on April 8.

## BRIENNE AND THE PARLEMENTS

At the head of those who opposed Calonne stood Loménie de Brienne, archbishop of Toulouse, who wanted to become minister and did so without delay. To soothe the notables he submitted the treasury accounts to them, promised to retain the three orders in the provincial assemblies and to leave the clergy's manorial rights alone. But he took over the plan for a territorial subvention and to it added an increase of the stamp duty. The notables replied that it was not within their power to consent to taxes, an allusion to the Estates-General. On May 25 their assembly was dissolved. Calonne's device had failed; it was obvious that Brienne had next to proceed to the parlements.

The Parlement of Paris made no protest over registering freedom of the grain trade, commutation of the *corvée des routes*, and institution of provincial assemblies. But it drafted remonstrances against the stamp tax and rejected the territorial subvention, openly referring this to an Estates-General. A *lit de justice* was held on August 6; the parlement declared it null and void, then started proceedings against Calonne, who fled to England. On August 14 the magistrates were exiled to Troyes. Other sovereign courts supported them. Brienne quickly retreated, and on September 19 the reinstated parlement recorded restoration of the old taxes.

Brienne fell back on loans, but the same problem faced him: he had to have consent of the parlements to borrow. A few members agreed to negotiate and did not hesitate to set their decisive condition—that the government should promise to convoke the Estates-General. Brienne asked for 120 million livres to be raised over a five-year period, at the end of which—in 1792—the Estates-General would be convened. But, uncertain of a majority, he suddenly had an edict presented by the king himself on November 18 in a 'royal session', that is, a *lit de justice* in which traditional ceremonies of convocation had not been observed. The duc d'Orléans protested and the registering of the edict was declared void. Louis retaliated by exiling the duke and two councillors. The parlement came to their defence, condemning *lettres de cachet* and demanding that royal subjects be given personal freedom. To ward off an attack by force, on May 3, 1788, it published a declaration of fundamental laws of the kingdom, stating that the monarchy was hereditary, that the right to vote subsidies belonged to the Estates-General, that Frenchmen could not be arbitrarily arrested and detained, that their judges were irremovable, the customs and privileges of provinces inviolable.

The government had evidently resolved to imitate Maupeou. On May 5 armed soldiers took up posts around the Palais de Justice until two members of the parlement who had been placed under arrest gave themselves up. On May 8 Louis succeeded in registering six edicts drawn up by Lamoignon, keeper of the seals. According to them the power of registration was transferred to a 'plenary court' composed of princes and crown officers, and at the same time the judiciary was reformed at the expense of the parlements—without, however, abolishing venality. The *question préalable*—torture preceding the execution of criminals—was abolished (the *question préparatoire*, used to extract evidence during a judicial inquiry, had ended in 1780). Last of all, a fresh blow was dealt the aristocracy: a litigant could now refuse to accept the ruling of a manorial court by referring his case to royal tribunals.

This time resistance was more widespread and more violent. The provincial parlements and most of the lower tribunals protested. The assembly of the clergy, already annoyed by a recent edict granting

Protestants a civil status, criticized the reforms and offered only a small contribution as its 'free gift'. Riots broke out in Paris and several other cities. On June 7 the citizens of Grenoble rose and rained missiles upon the garrison from the rooftops in what was known as the 'Day of Tiles'. The provincial assemblies set up at the end of 1787 satisfied no one; several provinces clamoured for their old estates vested with the right to vote taxes. In the Dauphiné nobility and bourgeoisie met together at the château of Vizille on July 21, 1788, to convoke the estates on their own authority. Brienne gave way.

The treasury was now empty. Pensions had had to be cut. Stock-holders received nothing and notes from the Bank of Discount were made legal tender. Having no money, Louis had to leave it to the Prussians to invade Holland and support the Stadholder against his burghers. The Stadholder broke his alliance with France and joined with the English. Brienne yielded again, this occasion being the last: the Estates were to convene on May 1, 1789. He resigned on August 24, 1788. The king recalled Necker, whose first act was to dismiss Lamoi-gnon and reinstate the Parlement of Paris. On September 23 the parle-ment hastened to stipulate that the Estates-General would consist of three orders, as in 1614. Each order would have the same number of representatives, would make its decisions separately, and would have a veto over the others. The nobility and clergy were made masters of the assembly. This was the aristocracy's victory.

During these events privileged groups—especially those in Brittany—had acted together in forming propaganda and resistance organizations to protest royal authority; they had intimidated and sometimes won over the intendants and army leaders; occasionally they had roused sharecroppers and domestics. These revolutionary prece-dents were not to be forgotten. The parlements above all had taught a lesson: the Third Estate would duplicate their tactics when the Estates-General met. They had even presumed to indict a minister, making Calonne the first émigré.

# 7

## THE BOURGEOIS REVOLUTION

To annoy the ministers a number of commoners, notably lawyers, had favoured the revolt of the nobility. Many others, such as the Rolands, expecting nothing, remained neutral. The summer of 1788 brought no evidence that bourgeois would take part in events. But news that an Estates-General was to be convened sent a tremor of excitement through the bourgeoisie: the king was authorizing them to plead their case. In this early stage accord with the aristocracy was not out of the question: the example set by the Dauphiné, where nobles granted commoners vote by head and equality of taxation, was welcomed enthusiastically. The atmosphere changed abruptly when the Parlement of Paris showed its true colours on September 23. Suddenly the popularity of the magistrates vanished. A clamour arose throughout the kingdom. 'Public debate has assumed a different character,' Mallet du Pan stated in January of 1789. 'King, despotism, and constitution have become only secondary questions. Now it is war between the Third Estate and the other two orders.'

### FORMATION OF THE PATRIOT PARTY

The rupture was still not complete. Some of the liberal great lords joined the upper bourgeoisie to form the 'National', or 'Patriot', party.

The 'Committee of Thirty', which seems to have exerted considerable influence within the party, counted among its members the duc de La Rochefoucauld-Liancourt, the marquis de Lafayette, and the marquis de Condorcet, along with Talleyrand, bishop of Autun, and the abbé Sieyes. Mirabeau also appeared at its meetings. Sieyes and Mirabeau were in contact with the duc d'Orléans, who had at his disposal a large sum of money and who wielded unquestionable influence within his extensive appanage. Personal connections as well as bonds created by the many associations that had sprung up in the eighteenth century—academies, agricultural societies, philanthropic groups, reading circles, Masonic lodges—were utilized in the provinces as in Paris. Some have attributed to the Masonic Grand Orient, whose grand master was the duc d'Orléans, a decisive role. But the duc de Luxembourg, its administrator-general, remained devoted to the aristocratic cause, and the lodges were full of nobles. It is difficult to imagine that Masonry could have sided with the Third Estate without being split by conflicts, of which we have no evidence.

Although propaganda of the Patriots provoked counterarguments, the government raised no objection to controversy: the king had invited his subjects to air their thoughts and viewpoints concerning the Estates-General. Under pretext of replying to his appeal, a flood of pamphlets appeared, and their authors slipped into them whatever they wanted to say. The Patriots none the less used brochures with cautious skill—they limited themselves to requesting as many representatives for the Third Estate as for the nobility and clergy combined, invoking the example of the provincial assemblies and the Estates of the Dauphiné. The order of the day was to overwhelm the government with petitions, for which the municipalities assumed, willingly or not, full responsibility. Actually, all were counting on Necker.

## NECKER AND THE DOUBLING OF THE THIRD ESTATE

The minister of finance took care of the most urgent fiscal needs by drawing upon the Bank of Discount and by granting financiers, as security for their advances, 'anticipations' on future tax receipts. He did this only to gain time until the Estates assembled, since he expected them to abolish fiscal privileges. If the nobility dominated the Estates the government would be at its mercy. Necker was therefore inclined to favour the Third Estate without being under its power. By doubling that order, and by limiting the vote by head to financial questions, all could be reconciled: equality of taxation would be adopted, while constitutional reform would bring conflict and require arbitration by the king. There can be no doubt about Necker's own view concerning the type of government to be instituted. He admired the British system—a House of Lords would soothe the aristocracy; admission to public office regardless of distinction by birth would satisfy the bourgeoisie.

He had no intention of revealing these plans. As an upstart financier, a foreigner, a Protestant, he had always been suspect in the eyes of the aristocracy, the court, and the king. Several of his colleagues—especially Barentin, the new keeper of the seals—opposed him. Determined above all else to preserve his power, he advanced with measured step. Like Calonne he hoped to persuade the notables to approve doubling of the Third. To this end he again convened them on November 6, 1788, but they disappointed him. On December 12 the royal princes sent Louis an entreaty which, by virtue of its clarity and moving tone, can be considered the manifesto of the aristocracy.

> The State is in danger . . . a revolution of governmental principles is brewing . . . soon the rights of property will be attacked, inequality of wealth will be presented as an object of reform: already the suppression of feudal rights has been proposed. . . . Could Your Majesty resolve to sacrifice, to humiliate, his brave, his ancient, his respectable nobility?. . . Let the Third Estate cease attacking the rights of the first two orders . . . let it confine itself to asking a reduction of the taxes with which it is perhaps overburdened; then the first two orders, recognizing in the third citizens dear to them, may renounce in the generosity of their feelings, the prerogatives relating to pecuniary matters, and consent to bear public obligations in the most perfect equality.

But Necker went further and with the support of a few colleagues won the day—probably because Brienne's fall had displeased the queen and the nobility's rebellion had antagonized the king. An 'Order of the Council' of December 27 granted doubling of the Third Estate. Louis

XVI has since been criticized for not specifying the voting method at that time. This reproach is groundless, for in his report Necker mentioned that voting by order was to be the rule. But the decree failed to record this, and the minister had already hinted that the Estates-General might consider it appropriate to vote by head on tax questions.

The Third Estate cried victory and affected to consider the vote by head won. The nobility denied this interpretation and in Poitou, Franche-Comté, and Provence violently protested the doubling which had given rise to that conclusion. In Brittany class struggle degenerated into civil war; at Rennes fights broke out at the end of January, 1789. The Third Estate, annoyed, moved towards radical solutions. In a famous pamphlet issued in February, 'What Is the Third Estate?' Sieyes described with cool rancour the hatred and scorn inspired in him by the nobility: 'This class is assuredly foreign to the nation because of its do-nothing idleness.' At the same time Mirabeau, in a speech which he had planned to deliver to the Estates of Provence, praised Marius 'for having exterminated the aristocracy and the nobility in Rome'. Fearful words, heralding civil war.

## THE ELECTIONS AND THE *CAHIERS*

The electoral rules could have handicapped the bourgeoisie either by giving existing provincial estates the right to appoint deputies or by reserving a proportion of seats in the Third Estate to provincial delegates. Some of the nobles recommended these devices; Necker brushed them aside.

The method of election varied considerably, but the ruling of January 24, 1789, generally prevailed. It designated bailiwicks (*bailliages*) and seneschalsies (*senéchaussées*) as electoral districts, even though these judicial areas were unevenly populated and differed widely in size. Contrary to precedent, whether or not he possessed a fief every noble was summoned to appear in the assembly of his order, but those ennobled by personal title only were relegated to the Third Estate—an error, for it wounded their pride. To elect clerical deputies, all parish priests met with the bishops, whereas monks and canons were merely allowed to send representatives. Most parish priests were of the Third Estate and, commanding a majority, often neglected to elect their aristocratic bishops as delegates. The electors who chose the Third Estate's deputies assembled in bailiwick meetings after themselves being named by tax-paying heads of families within villages and parishes. They were elected directly in the villages, by two stages in the large towns. In each of the small bailiwicks designated 'secondary' electoral districts the meeting was allowed only to draw up a *cahier de doléances*, or list of grievances, and send one-quarter of its members to the assembly in the 'principal' bailiwick to which it was attached. Peasants outnumbered all others at these meetings, but, lacking education, were incapable of expressing their opinions and were all the more intimidated because the meetings began with discussion of what should be included in the *cahiers*. They almost invariably elected bourgeois deputies.

Among the representatives elected by clergy and nobility were able men who opposed reform, such as Cazalès and the abbé Maury, but owing to circumstances only the liberals—Duport, Alexandre de Lameth, and notably Lafayette—took a leading role. Deputies of the Third Estate were for the most part mature, often rich or well-to-do, educated, industrious, and honest men. Sometimes they had received special distinction—Bailly and Target were members of the Académie Française—but more often they had earned a reputation in their particular province. Mounier and Barnave were well known in the Dauphiné, Lanjuinais and Le Chapelier in Brittany, Thouret and Buzot in Normandy, Merlin de Douai in Flanders, Robespierre in Artois. A telling characteristic of the bourgeoisie was that it had long idolized the marquis de Lafayette, noble deputy from Riom, and that the most celebrated of its own deputies, Sieyes and Mirabeau, came from the privileged classes. This foretells what position the nobility could have assumed in a reformed society by siding with the bourgeoisie.

Sieyes and Mirabeau were both from Provence. Sieyes, the son of a notary in Fréjus, had become canon of Chartres and was elected deputy from Paris. He guided the Third Estate during the early weeks. His pamphlets earned him a reputation as an oracle. It was he who developed the theory of 'constituent power', declaring that sovereignty resided in the nation alone and that representatives of the nation were to be invested with dictatorial power until a constitution could be written and put into effect. He was the loyal interpreter of the bourgeoisie and later made the significant distinction between 'active' and 'passive' citizens. But, lacking application or special talent as an orator, he quickly shut himself off in isolation. Mirabeau, on the other hand, possessed the realistic foresight of a statesman, knew how to handle men, and was unexcelled in eloquent oratory. Unfortunately his scandalous youth and cynical venality made it impossible to respect him; no one doubted that the court could buy him at will. Neither he nor Sieyes could direct the Third Estate. Its work remained a collective achievement.

Necker could have exerted considerable influence over the drafting of the *cahiers de doléances*. Malouet, an official in the naval ministry and a deputy of the Third Estate from Riom, pointed out to him that he must draw up a royal programme to guide public opinion, impress the nobility, and—most important—restrain the enthusiasm of the Third Estate. Necker very likely sensed the wisdom of this suggestion, but he had already been soundly criticized for permitting the doubling and was now inclined to consider his moves carefully. He rejected this additional risk, content with having persuaded the king to remain neutral.

The bourgeois were therefore free to participate in drafting lists of grievances from the parishes. Some model *cahiers* were sent out from Paris or were drawn up regionally; lawyers and parish priests sometimes set pen to paper for the cause. A number of *cahiers* were nevertheless original: indifferent to constitutional reform, they were content to criticize the overwhelming burdens laid upon the populace. But these should not necessarily be taken as an accurate reflection of what the lower classes felt most deeply, for in the presence of a manorial judge peasants were not always likely to say what they thought. Moreover, the proletarians rarely participated in deliberations. Grievances sent out from the bailiwicks are even less representative, since bourgeois members simply eliminated from the original lists those demands which displeased or did not interest them. The popular classes of town and countryside were concerned not only with attaining fiscal equality and tax reduction, but with suppressing the tithe, manorial rights, and seigneurial authority, with gaining observance of collective usage, regulating the grain market, and instituting controls to curb capitalist expansion. The people threatened aristocratic property along with aristocratic privileges, and bourgeois aspirations as well. But since the populace did not have access to the Estates-General, king, aristocrats and bourgeois were left alone to settle their triangular conflict.

In their *cahiers* the nobles and bourgeois were of one accord in expressing devotion to the monarchy, but they also agreed upon the need to replace absolutism with rule of law accepted by representatives of the nation; with reasonable freedom of the press and guarantees of personal liberty against arbitrary administrative and judicial ruling; with reform of various branches of the administration, including ecclesiastic reorganization. To the desire for national unity was joined a keen desire for regional and communal autonomy which would end ministerial despotism by loosening the grip of a centralized administration. Both classes agreed to religious toleration, but secularization of the state stopped at this point: they wished to leave the privilege of public worship to the Catholic Church and did not consider abolishing religious instruction or Church poor relief, nor did they deny clerics the right to register births, marriages, and deaths. The clergy was not satisfied with this much: it would not allow criticism of its doctrines through the press or equal treatment for heretics and true believers. Even a recent edict granting legal status to Protestants had provoked protest. Except for these qualifications, not inconsiderable in themselves, the clergy agreed with the other two orders. More or less generally conceived, liberty was a national desire.

Class conflict was none the less evident. The privileged classes resigned themselves to financial sacrifices—with strong reservations as to the extent and method of contributions demanded of them—but they were generally opposed to the vote by head and expressly stipulated that the orders be preserved and honorific prerogatives and manorial rights be retained, whereas for the Third Estate equality of rights was inseparable from liberty.

But this did not mean that royal arbitration was destined to fail. No one challenged the king's right to approve legislation or the need to leave executive power intact. By renouncing the exercise of arbitrary will and by governing in accord with the Estates-General, the Capetian dynasty would only emphasize its national character; royal authority would not be lessened if reformed. There were many men among the aristocracy and bourgeoisie who, whether they actively desired it or not, might have leaned towards compromise. Among the nobles obedience to the princely will might have quelled opposition. Such bourgeois as Malouet and Mounier wanted above all to end despotism and judged that wrangling among the orders would perpetuate it. With little concern for the peasants, they were willing to respect the manorial authority and honorific primacy of the noble. Among each of the orders fear of civil war, already perceptible, secretly pleaded for conciliation.

A great king or a great minister might have taken the initiative towards a settlement. But Louis XVI was not Henry IV; Necker was clearsighted, but his background paralysed him. The nation was left to itself.

## THE VICTORY OF THE BOURGEOISIE

Far from thinking of compromise, the court tried to get rid of Necker. The Parlement of Paris, repentant, gladly offered its assistance. In April rumour had it that a new cabinet would be formed and would promptly adjourn the Estates-General *sine die*. The issue of verifying powers aroused contention among the ministers: Barentin held that precedent accorded power of verification to the Council of State; Necker objected. Louis ended by supporting Necker, thereby averting a palace revolution but leaving the question of who was qualified to verify powers undecided. This conflict probably accounts for the postponement of the opening of the Estates from April 27 to May 5.

Prudence advised that the deputies should assemble far from Paris, but Versailles was the preferred choice—by the king so he could hunt; by the queen and her entourage for their own pleasures. The court also acted unwisely in clinging to a protocol that humiliated the Third Estate. Each order was assigned a particular dress, and they were segregated for presentation to the king on May 2. In the procession of the Holy Ghost, on May 4, they paraded in separate groups from Notre Dame to Saint Louis. Representatives of the Third, dressed in black, were indistinguishable except for the commanding ugliness of Mirabeau, but were applauded confidently by an immense crowd. The nobles were decked and plumed. The dark mass of parish priests came next, then the king's musicians, then bishops dressed in dazzling robes.

This war of ceremony lasted until July 14: in royal sessions the Third affected to wear hats, as did the privileged orders; Bailly gave notice that deputations he led to the king would not kneel before the royal presence.

The Hôtel des Menus-Plaisirs on the Avenue de Paris, actually an ordinary storehouse, had been prepared for the meetings of clergy and nobility. Behind it, on the Rue des Chantiers, a room built for the notables was enlarged and redecorated for plenary sessions, which were presided over by the king. But because nothing else was large enough to hold the Third Estate, this 'national hall' was turned over to it on ordinary occasions. Spectators sat on the speakers' platforms, thronged in and out, and were allowed to join in discussions, a habit which persisted until the end of the Convention. This careless arrangement increased the importance of the Third Estate and subjected the more timid to pressures of intransigent and rash opinions.

Louis opened the meeting on May 5. His brief address was applauded. Barentin, who could not be heard, followed. Then Necker, with the aid of an acting official who relieved him from time to time, harangued the anxious deputies. His listeners were soon disappointed and seriously annoyed. For three hours the minister of finance explained the detailed situation of the Treasury and the proposed improvements, made no allusion to constitutional reform, expressed confidence in the generosity of the privileged classes, then repeated the method of voting which had been announced in December. On the following day the nobility and clergy began to verify their powers separately. The Third Estate refused to follow suit. The Estates-General was paralysed.

Deputies from Brittany and the Dauphiné favoured outright refusal to vote by order, but that would have been an infringement of legality, and the politicians did not want to take chances so early in the game. The representatives were not yet familiar with one another, and no one knew how far each would agree to advance. Some found the ardour of the Bretons alarming. A delaying tactic was necessary, and Necker's refusal to grant the Council of State power of verification provided an escape. The Third Estate alleged that each order had to establish whether the two other orders were legally constituted, and that powers should therefore be inspected in common session. During this stalemate the Third refused to constitute itself as a separate order: no minutes were taken, no rules established; not even a steering committee was set up. They consented only to choose a 'dean', who after June 3 was Bailly. At the beginning the Third had taken the name Commons (*communes*) for itself. Although no one other than a few of the more erudite knew exactly what the medieval communes were, the word evoked a vague memory of popular resistance to feudal lords, an idea strengthened by what knowledge they had of English history. To the Third Estate the name meant refusal to recognize a social hierarchy that had relegated it to third rank.

This attitude had its drawbacks. The people were told that the Third Estate was responsible for delaying the abolition of fiscal privileges. When Malouet tried to negotiate by offering to guarantee the rights and property of the aristocracy he was roundly criticized. Everyone, however, sensed the need for some new tactical issue; and it was the clergy which furnished them with just that. The nobility, in no way perturbed, on May 11 announced itself constituted as a separate order. Because a large proportion of the parish priests supported the Commons, the clergy instead proposed that designated members of the three orders meet in conference. To humour the other order, the Third Estate agreed. But the discussions of May 23 and 25 came to nothing: the nobles retreated behind precedents which the Third Estate either challenged or fought with arguments of reason and natural right. They next tried to get the clergy to agree that the three orders should be fused. The bishops sensed imminent defection from the parish priests and asked the king to intervene. On May 28 Louis asked that the conferences be resumed in the presence of his ministers, and on June 4 Necker drafted a conciliatory proposal: each order should first verify the powers of its own members, then announce the results to the others and consider any objections that were raised. If no agreement could be reached, the king was to deliver a final decision. Once more the Third found itself in a difficult position. This time it was the nobility that came to its rescue by rejecting royal arbitration except for the 'complete' delegations—those which, as in the Dauphiné and in several bailiwicks, had been chosen in common by the three orders. This was the signal for revolutionary action.

On June 10 the Third Estate followed a proposal from Sieyes and invited the privileged members to join it. Those who did not appear to answer a roll call would be considered to have defaulted. The roll was begun on June 12 and finished on the 14th: several parish priests had responded, but not one noble. After two days' debate the Third Estate on June 17 conferred the title 'National Assembly' upon the combined and enrolled orders. It immediately arrogated to itself the power to consent to taxation, confirming existing taxes provisionally. Had sovereignty passed to the nation? Not exactly. On June 20 Bailly acknowledged that these revolutionary resolutions required the king's approval.

Louis had no intention of approving them. The Dauphin had died on June 4, and the king had withdrawn to Marly, where the queen and royal princes instructed him. The nobility finally abdicated in favour of the throne and begged the king to make the Third Estate return to the path of duty. On June 19 the majority of the clergy declared itself in favour of fusing the three orders. The bishops hastily called for assistance. Royal ministers and even Necker agreed that intervention was necessary. The Council of State announced that a royal session would be held on June 22. But what would the king declare then? With the support of Montmorin and Saint-Priest, Necker hoped to manage the Commons by simply ignoring their decrees rather than by overriding them. At last he came out into the open, proposing to establish equality of taxation, to admit all Frenchmen to public office, and to authorize the vote by head in constituting future Estates-General, stipulating that the king would agree to this only if the Estates met as two houses and if he were granted full executive power with a legislative veto. Necker protected aristocratic prerogatives and property with the vote by order, but Barentin objected: did this mean they were to adopt the British system of government? Louis hesitated, postponing the decision. The royal session was put off until June 23.

On June 20 the Third Estate discovered its hall closed without notice or warning. It finally found asylum in a neighbouring tennis court, where, because there was talk of retiring to Paris and seeking the protection of the people, Mounier stepped in and proposed the famous oath, that they remain united until a constitution was established. A threatened *lit de justice* had provoked enough indignation to incite the deputies, with few exceptions, to sign the oath. The Third

Estate, like the Parlement of Paris, rebelled in advance against the royal will.

On June 21 Louis admitted his brothers to the Council and, finally, withdrew his support from Necker, whose programme was defeated the next day. On the 23rd an impressive show of armed force surrounded the Hôtel des Menus-Plaisirs, from which the public was excluded. Received in silence, Louis had Barentin read two declarations of capital interest in that they revealed quite clearly what was at stake in the struggle. They granted the Estates-General power to consent to taxes and loans and to various budget allocations, including the funds set aside for upkeep of the court. Personal liberty and freedom of the press would be guaranteed; decentralization would be carried out through the provincial estates; an extensive programme of reforms would be studied by the Estates-General. In sum, the proposals meant that a constitutional system, civil liberty, and achievement of national unity were to be the common inheritance of monarch and nation. Louis made an exception only for the clergy: its special consent was required for everything touching upon ecclesiastic organization and religious matters. Furthermore, he appeared as arbiter among the orders—if the Third Estate's decrees were overridden, so were the binding mandates that the privileged orders had invoked to compel voting by order and to postpone equality of taxation. Verification of powers would follow the system proposed on June 4. The orders were authorized to meet together to deliberate matters of general interest. The king strongly hoped that the clergy and nobility would agree to assume their share of public burdens.

But Louis failed to impose equal taxation and remained silent upon the question of admittance to public office; he expressly retained the orders and excluded vote by head from such matters as organization of future Estates-General, the manorial system, and honorific privileges. The throne thereby committed itself to preservation of the traditional social hierarchy and aristocratic pre-eminence. As a result of this decision, the Revolution was to mean conquest of equality of rights.

The king concluded by ordering the Estates to separate into orders and by giving them to understand that he would dissolve the assembly if its members did not obey. He then departed, followed by the nobility and most of the clergy. The Third Estate did not stir. Brezé, grand master of ceremonies, repeated his sovereign's command, to which Bailly replied: 'The assembled nation cannot receive orders.' Sieyes declared: 'You are today what you were yesterday.' Ignoring, as the Parlement of Paris had done previously, the existence of a royal session, the Third Estate confirmed its own decrees and declared its members inviolable. The expressive and significant statements made by Bailly and by Sieyes deserve to be those remembered by posterity, but Mirabeau's epigraph has proved more popular: 'We will not stir from our seats unless forced by bayonets.' The Commons could not have carried out this challenge, but the court thought itself in no position to find out, as agitation had already reached menacing proportions. After this point, resistance to the Third Estate disintegrated: a majority of the clergy and forty-seven nobles joined the Commons; on June 27 the king asked the others to follow suit.

The legal, peaceful revolution of the bourgeoisie, achieved by lawyers who borrowed their methods from the Parlement of Paris, was to all appearances victorious. On July 7 the Assembly appointed a committee on the constitution and two days later Mounier delivered its first report. From that day, and for history, the Assembly was the Constituent Assembly. On July 11 Lafayette submitted his draft for a declaration of human rights.

## APPEAL TO ARMED FORCE

The Third Estate did not lose its composure. Dictatorship of the constituent power, advocated by Sieyes, was not instituted. Royal approval was still considered necessary. The modern idea that a constitution creates its own powers before it regulates them had not yet been formulated; instead, Louis XVI, invested with his own power rooted in history, would contract with the nation. On the other hand, although the Third Estate fused the three orders, it did not proclaim their disappearance within the nation, nor did it call for election of a new assembly: the bourgeoisie therefore did not aspire to class dictatorship. On the contrary, it seemed possible that a moderate majority would be formed: the clergy, the liberal nobility, and a segment of the Commons favoured a party of the middle. Most of the nobles, however, made it known that they by no means considered the matter settled, and when troops were seen thronging around Paris and Versailles the king was suspected of preparing a show of force. He had excuses: agitation was growing; hunger multiplied disturbances; at the end of June disorderly conduct of the French guards caused a riot in Paris.

The court had not yet fixed a plan of action. To draw one up, it had to get rid of Necker and his friends. The maréchal de Broglie and the baron de Breteuil had been called in. Wisdom commanded that a cabinet be formed secretly, ready to appear when sufficient forces were on hand. This was a game with fearful consequences. We can understand that the king regarded deputies of the Third Estate as rebels and that the nobility considered surrender a humiliation. But if a show of arms failed, the blood spilled would stain both king and aristocracy. Nevertheless, on July 11 Necker was hastily dismissed and banished from the kingdom; his friends were replaced by Breteuil and his cohorts. No further steps were taken. But the Assembly expected the worst, and the bourgeois revolution seemed lost. They were saved by popular force.

# 8

## THE POPULAR REVOLUTION

Resort to arms transformed the struggle of social orders into civil war which, abruptly changing the character of the Revolution, gave it a scope that far surpassed what the bourgeoisie had intended or expected. Popular intervention, which provoked the sudden collapse of the social system of the Old Regime, issued from progressive mobilization of the masses by the simultaneous influences of the economic crisis and the convocation of the Estates-General. These two causes fused to create a mentality of insurrection.

### THE ECONOMIC CRISIS

Following the Seven Years War, a surge in production after 1778 gave rise to what is known as the splendour of Louis XV. It was checked in France by difficulties rooted in agricultural fluctuations, a continual problem of the old economy. These setbacks became established in cyclical depressions and caused what their historian[1] called the decline of Louis XVI. First, unusually heavy grape harvests provoked a dreadful slump in the wine market. Prices fell by as much as 50 per cent. They rose somewhat after 1781 because of scarcity, but short supply then

[1] Camille Ernest Labrousse. (Translator's note.)

meant that the wine sector could not recoup its losses. Wine growing was still practised in almost every part of the kingdom and for many peasants was the most profitable market product. They suffered cruelly; those who were sharecroppers found their income reduced to nothing. Grain prices were the next to fall, remaining relatively low until 1787. Finally, a drought in 1785 killed off much of the livestock.

Rural inhabitants constituted the majority of consumers, and because their purchasing power was reduced industrial production was in turn threatened after 1786. Traditional interpretation has laid primary blame for industry's troubles upon the commercial treaty with Britain. Although this was not the most important cause, it certainly did obstruct industry temporarily, since production had to modernize if it was to withstand foreign competition. Unemployment spread. The countryside, where domestic industry had developed, suffered as much as the cities.

The lower classes therefore had no reserves left when they faced the brutal prospect of famine after grain crops failed in 1788. The price of bread rose steadily. At the beginning of July, 1789, a pound of bread sold for four sous in Paris—where the government nevertheless sold its imported grains at a loss—and twice as much in some provinces. At that time wage earners considered two sous per pound the highest price they could possibly pay and still subsist, for bread was their staple food and average daily consumption ranged from one and a half pounds per person to two or three for an adult manual labourer. Necker ordered large purchases from abroad, and, as usual, labour centres opened up, while measures were taken for distributing soup and rice. The previous winter had been severe, and the cruel effects of high prices did not lessen as the harvest season drew near. For over a half-century we have known, chiefly from the works of Jaurès, that the prosperity of the kingdom of France was responsible for the growing power of the bourgeoisie, and in this sense it is with reason that Michelet's interpretation has been attacked, for the Revolution broke out in a society in the midst of development, not one crippled and seemingly threatened with collapse by nature's Providential shortages. But the social importance of this enrichment should not deceive us. Since colonial profits were realized mainly through re-exportation, the nation's labour force did not benefit as much as we might think, and, while a long-term rise in prices swelled the income of large land-owners and bourgeoisie, wages failed to keep pace. We now know that production was dislocated and curtailed in the last decade before the Revolution, and we can justifiably state that the living standard of the masses was steadily declining. Famine, when it came, over-whelmed the populace.

'The people' (artisans, shopkeepers, hired help) as well as proletarians ('the populace'), peasants—small proprietors and sharecroppers who did not raise enough to support themselves or wine-growers who did not raise any grain—as well as townsmen unanimously agreed that the government and upper classes were responsible for these afflictions. Income declined but taxes did not. Tolls and duties on consumption became more hateful in times of high prices. If the wine market was restricted it was because excises limited consumption. There was no bread because Brienne removed controls on grain exports and shipments in 1787. True, Necker had stopped exports, subsidized imports, and reinstituted market sales. But he was too late. 'Hoarders' had gone to work. Anyone in authority, all government agents were suspected of participating in hoarding. The 'famine plot' was thought to be more than a myth. Tithe collectors and lords were just as odious—they were hoarders because their levies cut into a poor harvest and consumed the peasants' supplies. The final blow was that collectors and lords profited even more from the high prices that increased poverty. And, finally, the solidarity of the Third Estate was shaken: the grain merchant, the baker, and the miller were all threatened; the bourgeois, partisan of economic freedom, clashed with popular hostility towards capitalism, since the people by nature favoured requisitions and controls. In April Necker authorized requisitions to replenish the markets, but the intendants and municipal officials rarely used this power.

As the months of 1789 passed, riots kept the tired and frightened officials in a constant state of alert. On April 28 Parisian workers from the faubourg Saint-Antoine sacked the manufactories of Réveillon and Henriot. Throughout the kingdom markets were the scenes of disturbances. Grain shipments, forced by milling and transportation conditions to use roads and rivers in plain view of famished hordes, were sometimes halted. The army and constabulary exhausted themselves rushing from one place to another, but were not inclined to deal harshly towards rebels whose privations they shared and unconsciously began to feel a common sympathy with them. The armour of the Old Regime was rapidly disintegrating.

Agitation was especially pronounced in the countryside. There the tax burden was crushing; tithes and manorial dues drove the peasants to desperation. Sentiment in the peasant community was divided among journeymen, sharecroppers, small proprietors, and large-scale tenant farmers, but on all matters of taxation it was solidly opposed to royal authority and the aristocracy. Tremors of agrarian revolt could be felt well before July 14—in Provence at the end of March, around Gap in April, in Cambrésis and Picardy in May. Near Versailles and Paris game had been exterminated, forests cleaned out. Moreover, the people were afraid of each other because begging, a regional trouble, spread before their eyes. Many journeymen and small landowners became mendicants. The poor left their villages to crowd into towns or else became vagabonds, forming groups which coursed through the country. They invaded farms even at night, forced themselves in by the fear of burning and of attacks on livestock, trees, the crops that were just beginning to grow, or by threatening to pillage everything. Officials had their own reasons for worrying about the crops and let the villagers arm themselves for protection. As fear of brigandage spread, panics broke out. The slightest incident was enough to put a timid person to flight, convinced that brigands had arrived, sowing fear wherever he fled.

## THE 'GOOD NEWS' AND THE GREAT HOPE

But we cannot be sure that economic crisis would have driven the people to aid the bourgeoisie if the calling of the Estates-General had not deeply moved the populace. The goals appropriated by the bourgeois they elected scarcely concerned the lower classes, but an event so foreign was welcomed as 'a good piece of news' presaging a miraculous change in men's fates. It awoke hopes both dazzling and vague of a future when all would enjoy a better life—hopes shared by the bourgeoisie. This vision of the future united the heterogeneous elements of the Third Estate and became a dynamic source of revolutionary idealism. Among the common people it gave to the Revolution a character that can be called mythical, if myth is taken to mean a complex of ideas concerning the future which generate energy and initiative. In this sense the Revolution in its early stages can be compared to certain religious movements in nascent form, when the poor gladly discern a return to paradise on earth.

Arthur Young has recorded that on July 12, while walking up a hill near Les Islettes, in the Argonne Forest, he met a poor woman who described her misery to him. ' "Something was to be done by some great folk for such poor ones," but she did not know who nor how, "but God send us better, *car les tailles et les droits nous écrasent*" ' (for the *taille* and [manorial] rights are crushing us).

Since the king consulted his people, he pitied their plight. What could he do if not remove their burdens—taxes, tithes, fees? He would therefore be content if they went ahead and helped him: after the elections aristocratic cries of alarm arose on all sides, for the peasants openly declared that they would pay no more.

At the same time this great hope inflamed fearful passions, from which the bourgeoisie was not exempt. The revolutionary mentality was imbued with them; the history of the period bears their deep imprint.

## THE ARISTOCRATIC CONSPIRACY AND THE REVOLUTIONARY MENTALITY

The Third Estate was at once convinced that the nobles would stubbornly defend their privileges. This expectation, soon confirmed by aristocratic opposition to the doubling and then to the vote by head, aroused suspicions that with little difficulty hardened into convictions. The nobles would use any means to 'crush' the villagers; they would outwit their well-intentioned king to obtain dissolution of the Estates-General. They would take up arms, bar themselves in their châteaux, and enlist brigands to wage civil war just as the king's agents enlisted the poverty-stricken. Prisoners would be released and recruited. Nobles who had already hoarded grain to starve the Third Estate would willingly see the harvest ruined. Fear of the aristocracy was everywhere rapidly linked with fear of brigands, a connection that fused the results of the calling of the Estates with those of the economic crisis. Moreover, foreign powers would be called on to help. The comte d'Artois was going to emigrate and win over his father-in-law (the king of Sardinia), the Spanish and Neapolitan Bourbons, and the emperor, brother of the queen. France, like Holland, would be invaded by the Prussians. Collusion with foreign powers, which weighed heavily in the history of the Revolution, was assumed from the beginning, and in July an invasion was feared imminently. The whole Third Estate believed in an 'aristocratic conspiracy'.

The burden of royal centralization and the conflict of orders dominated the Third Estate's view of the crisis. Neglecting to accuse natural forces and incapable of analysing the total economic situation, the Third Estate laid responsibility upon royal power and the aristocracy. An incomplete picture perhaps, but not inexact. The freeing of the grain trade, which Brienne had decreed, did favour speculators; to the argument that this would increase production the people replied that it would profit the aristocracy and bourgeoisie first, while they had to bear the costs. Similarly, if the Third Estate falsely imputed Machiavellian qualities to the aristocracy, it was true that the court, in agreement with the nobles, thought to punish the deputies for their insubordination; and it was true that the aristocratic conspiracy, although denounced prematurely, was soon to become a reality. In any case the mind of the Third Estate is of capital interest in showing the historian that events have their immediate roots not in their antecedents but in the men who intervene by interpreting those events.

If aristocratic conspiracy and 'brigands' instilled many with enough fear to cause occasional panics, there were others who, although frightened, remained rational and faced danger resolutely. Consequently the labels 'fears' and 'Great Fear' unjustly imply that the whole Third Estate was struck dumb with terror. Actually the revolutionary mentality was capable of countering unrest with vigorous defensive reaction. The Third was kept informed by letters from its deputies and in turn encouraged its representatives with innumerable appeals. The bourgeoisie would gladly have pushed further: it wanted to take municipal control from the petty oligarchy made up of those who owned offices, many of whom had acquired noble titles. At Paris the electors who had chosen deputies organized a secret municipal council in the Hôtel de Ville at the end of June. Notables hoped to set up a 'national militia'. This was proposed by Parisian electors to the Constituent Assembly, but deputies did not dare authorize it. A double purpose lay behind the desire to organize a militia: to resist royal troops should the occasion rise, and to hold the people in check. Meanwhile efforts were made to win over the army, not without success, since lower-ranking officers had no hope of advancement and the soldiers, who had to pay for part of their subsistence, were affected by high prices. The French Guards fraternized with crowds at the Palais Royal; at the end of June the people freed prisoners at the Abbaye. Several men are known to have distributed money among the soldiers or to have paid the July insurgents. Beyond doubt the agents of the duc d'Orléans did as much.

Finally, along with the defensive reaction there existed a punitive will either to cripple the aristocratic conspiracy, hoarders, and all enemies of the people, or to punish those enemies. From July on this took the form of imprisonments, acts of brutality, and popular massacres.

These three aspects of the revolutionary mentality—fear, defensive reaction, and punitive will—together constitute one of the keys to the unfolding narrative of the French Revolution. The conspiracy was to all appearances halted by the end of 1789, and repression slackened. The plot later reappeared, cloaked with many of the characteristics given it in advance, and foreign powers came to its aid. The resulting defensive reaction first stimulated the volunteers who poured in and then was responsible for the mass levy. Punitive will provoked the massacres of 1792 and, when danger again loomed in 1793, the Convention warded off further perils only by setting up the Terror. Fear and its accompaniments died out only, and gradually, after the uncontested triumph of the Revolution.

## THE PARISIAN REVOLUTION

Against this background, Necker's dismissal was a torch set to a powder keg: it was taken as evidence that the aristocratic conspiracy had begun to act. News of the event circulated in Paris on Sunday, July 12. The weather was good and a crowd gathered at the Palais Royal, whose garden and arcades, recently opened by the duc d'Orléans, had become a centre of amusement. Groups clustered about extemporaneous orators; only one, Camille Desmoulins, do we know by name. Soon processions of demonstrators reached the boulevards, then the Rue Saint-Honoré. The cavalry undertook to make them disperse and charged the crowd at the Place Louis XV. The French Guards in return attacked the cavalry. The baron de Besenval, military commander, mustered his whole following on the Champ de Mars that evening.

The Parisians did not think of rallying to the aid of the Assembly; they saved it, but only indirectly. They were concerned with their own fate, convinced that their city, surrounded by royal troops and brigands, would first be bombarded from Montmartre and the Bastille and then would be pillaged. Panics erupted continually during these 'days', Act One of the Great Fear. The police were gone. Toll gates were burned. Saint-Lazare was sacked. Person and property were seemingly endangered. Fright hovered over the capital, abandoned to its own resources.

A defensive reaction followed immediately. Barricades arose in the streets, and gunsmiths' stores were wiped clean. The electors appointed a permanent committee and set up a militia. To arm their forces, they took 32,000 guns from the Invalides on the morning of July 14. In search of more, they went to the Bastille. Its governor, de Launey, parleyed. Commanding only a small garrison, he had ordered the outer courts evacuated. They were quickly filled by the crowd. Behind walls ninety feet high, surrounded by a water-filled ditch seventy-five feet wide, he had no cause to fear an attack. But he lost his nerve and opened fire. Several men fell; others drew back in disorder, crying treason, convinced that they had been permitted to advance only to offer better aim. Shots rang out from those who were armed, and battle was engaged, but on an entirely unequal basis: the assailants lost a hundred men, whereas one sole member of the garrison was hit. A census was later taken among the 'conquerors of the Bastille', so we know a good number of the attackers. All classes of society were represented among them, but most were artisans from the faubourg Saint-Antoine.

The tide of battle was still uncertain when the French and National

Guards arrived from the Hôtel de Ville. Led by a former non-commissioned officer named Hulin and by Lieutenant Élie, they entered the courtyard of the Bastille and under heavy fire aimed their cannons at the gate. De Launey took fright and offered to give himself up. Élie accepted, but the attackers protested—No surrender! Amid total confusion the governor had the drawbridge lowered, and the crowd rushed across into the fortress. Efforts to save most of the defenders were successful, but three officers and three men were massacred. De Launey was with difficulty led to the doors of the Hôtel de Ville, where he lost his life. Shortly after, Flesselles, provost of the merchants, was also killed. Their heads were paraded through the city on pikes.

Besenval ordered a retreat to Saint-Cloud. The electors took over municipal control, appointed Bailly mayor, and offered command of the National Guard to Lafayette, who soon afterwards gave the Guard a cockade of red and blue, the colours of Paris, between which he placed a white band, the king's colour. Through Lafayette the tricoloured flag, emblem of the Revolution, joined old France with the new.

No one considered the Bastille the stakes of the struggle, and at first no one thought that its fall would determine the outcome. Panics continued. But seizure of the Bastille, of mediocre importance in itself, broke the court's resistance. The forces Versailles had on hand were not enough to take Paris, especially since the loyalty of the troops was not certain. Louis hesitated. Would he try to flee? Against the urgings of the comte d'Artois he decided to give in. On July 15 he yielded to the Assembly and announced the dismissal of his troops. The next day he recalled Necker. On the 17th he went to Paris and accepted the cockade.

Few concluded from this that the aristocracy had laid down its arms, and wild rumours continued to circulate. The comte d'Artois and many others emigrated; according to one story an English squadron lay in wait off the coast of Brest. The permanent committee searched the edges of Paris for brigands. Finding only vagabonds, it sent them back where they had come from. The suburbs feared that they would be overrun with such wanderers, and panic spread. Bertier de Sauvigny, the intendant of Paris, his father in-law, Foullon de Doué, and Besenval himself were arrested. Massacres began again: on July 22 Sauvigny and

Doué were hanged at the Place de Grève; Necker returned just in time to save Besenval on July 30. These murders provoked strong protest, but now part of the bourgeoisie, roused by the obvious danger, joined the people in their fury—'Is this blood then so pure?' cried Barnave before the Constituent Assembly. Nevertheless, they could hardly deny that summary executions ought to cease. On July 23 a notary from the Rue de Richelieu proposed, in the name of his district, that a popular tribunal be set up; and on the 30th Bailly made a similar request. The Assembly paid no heed. Only in October did it institute prosecution for crimes of *lèse-nation*, to be handled by the Châtelet of Paris—an ordinary court. In July the Assembly did at least establish a 'committee of investigation', prototype of the Committee of General Security; and the municipality of Paris organized another which was the first revolutionary committee. While debating the issue of privacy of correspondence during the summer, deputies of all representation, from the marquis de Gouy d'Arsy and Target, member of the Académie Française, to Barnave and Robespierre, firmly maintained that one could not govern in time of war and revolution as in time of peace—in other words, that the rights they were proposing to grant to all citizens depended upon circumstances. This was to become the doctrine of the revolutionary government.

## THE MUNICIPAL REVOLUTION

In the provinces, too, Necker's dismissal provoked strong feeling and an immediate reaction. The populace was no longer content only to send addresses, now often menacing, to its representatives. In several towns the public coffers were broken open and arsenals or military storehouses looted. One committee undertook to set up a militia and issued an appeal to neighbouring communes, even to the peasants. The governor of Dijon was arrested; nobles and priests were confined to their dwellings—this was the first example of detention of suspects. At Rennes the townsmen persuaded the garrison to desert and then rose up. The military commander fled.

When news came of the fall of the Bastille and of the king's visit to Paris—an event celebrated in some places—the bourgeoisie took heart and laid hands on the instruments of control in almost every area. The 'municipal revolution', as it is known, was in most cases a peaceable one: the municipal councils of the Old Regime took on notables or stepped down for the electors. Very often they had to create, or permit the formation of, a permanent committee. It was charged initially with organization of the National Guard, but gradually absorbed the whole administrative apparatus. Nevertheless, the people, having taken part in bourgeois demonstrations, demanded that bread prices be lowered. If this was not soon granted riots broke out, the houses of officials and those known as hoarders were sacked, and often the former municipal councils were ousted.

The municipal revolution thus differed from place to place and was often arrested half way. In every instance, however, the only orders obeyed were those of the National Assembly. The king no longer commanded authority. Centralization, too, was weakened: each municipality wielded absolute power within its own confines and over surrounding districts as well. From August on, towns started to conclude mutual-assistance pacts, spontaneously transforming France into a federation of communes. Local autonomy opened the field of action to a small group of resolute men who, without waiting for instructions from Paris, passed what measures they considered necessary to secure public safety. This was a basic stimulant to revolutionary defence.

Yet the other side of the coin was immediately visible. The Constituent Assembly enjoyed a prestige accorded none of its successors, but the populace observed only such decrees as suited it. What did the people want above all else? Tax reform, abolition of indirect levies, institution of controls over the grain trade. Tax collection was suspended; the salt tax, excises, and municipal tolls were suppressed; exchange of grains was either forbidden or continually thwarted. Proclamations and decrees against this had no effect. At Paris the populace went even further. Within the districts—divisions established for elections to the Estates-General—assembled citizens, like the electors before them, claimed to supervise the municipal authority they set up to replace the electors. In their eyes national sovereignty entailed direct democracy, an idea that would remain dear to the sans-culottes.

## THE PEASANT REVOLUTION AND THE GREAT FEAR

The countryside had joined the towns, but revolution in Paris had even greater effect on rural areas. Agrarian revolt broke out in several regions. In the woodlands of Normandy, in the Hainaut and Upper Alsace, châteaux or abbeys were attacked by those seeking to burn archives and force surrender of manorial rights. In Franche-Comté and the Mâconnais peasants set fire to many châteaux, sometimes laying them waste. The bourgeoisie was not always spared: they, too, had to pay. In Alsace the Jews suffered. On the other hand, there was clear evidence of rural hostility towards a menacing capitalism whose instrument had become the manorial reaction: free pasturage was reclaimed, enclosures destroyed, forests invaded, commons taken back or demanded for the first time—the peasant revolution was a double-edged sword. Faced with this threat, the notables drew closer together. Urban militias were used to restore order. In the Mâconnais the bourgeoisie set up extraordinary tribunals beside the old provost courts, and thirty-three peasants were hanged. Revolt fired men's minds. Even more important, however, was a passive resistance which everywhere interfered with collection of the tithe or the *champart* demanded from crops harvested. Only those who wished to pay did so. The Great Fear gave irresistible force to this movement.

Events in Paris strengthened fear of the aristocratic conspiracy, of foreign invasion which could carry it out, of recruitment of brigands for its service. Brigands were the source of even greater fear now that the wheat was ripe, and Paris, along with other large towns, was expelling beggars and vagabonds. Grain riots and agrarian revolts heightened tension. So did forays by National Guards who left towns to pillage châteaux or demand grain. The Great Fear grew out of six localized incidents no different from those which had unloosed so many panics, but this time they set off currents which were fed along the way by new outbreaks acting as relay reinforcements. Some of these can be traced for hundreds of miles, with branches that covered entire provinces. This extraordinary diffusion in a chain reaction gives the Great Fear its distinctive character and illuminates the mentality that made it possible.

A 'disturbance' at Nantes alarmed Poitou. At Estrées-Saint-Denis, in the Beauvais, another spread fright in all directions. A third in southern Champagne sowed terror through the Gâtinais, Bourbonnais, and Burgundy. A fourth, originating near the Montmirail forest, close to La Ferté-Bernard, alerted Maine, Normandy, Anjou, and the Touraine. From the edge of the Chizé forest fear struck Angoulême, spread into Berry and the central mountains, alarmed Aquitaine as far as the Pyrenees. In the east, agrarian revolts in Franche-Comté and the Mâconnais drove fear to the shores of the Mediterranean.

Revolutionaries and aristocrats accused one another of having contrived the Great Fear. The enemies of the Revolution, charged the revolutionaries, sowed anarchy in an effort to paralyse the National Assembly. The bourgeoisie, replied the aristocrats, alarmed the people to make them take up arms and rebel just when the lower classes desired to remain at peace. This last version met with success because the Great Fear provoked a defensive reaction which turned upon the aristocracy. Near Le Mans and in Vivarais three nobles were put to death, and peasants in the Dauphiné provided a formidable relay station for panic by burning châteaux.

It was therefore repeated afterwards that fear had broken out everywhere and at once, spread by mysterious messengers and engendering agrarian revolt. It did not, in fact, cover the whole kingdom: Brittany, Lorraine, lower Languedoc, among other areas, were unaffected. The Great Fear lasted from July 20 to August 6. Documents show that some propagated it in good faith, and one significant fact is that it never touched the districts which had previously witnessed insurrection. The *jacquerie* of the Dauphiné was the only such incident it provoked. If it encouraged the revolution of the peasants it did not cause it. They were already on their feet.

## THE NIGHT OF AUGUST 4 AND THE DECLARATION OF THE RIGHTS OF MAN AND THE CITIZEN

While popular revolution spread, the Assembly's debates dragged on ineffectively. Was this the appropriate moment to publish a declaration of rights? Would it not be better to postpone any such action until the constitution was drawn up, so that the two could be reconciled? Arguments of a general nature were voiced with no mention of the reasons behind opposing views: the existence of orders and the privileges, both of which would be suppressed by the principles to be proclaimed. Aristocrats therefore favoured postponement, hoping to preserve a few of their prerogatives, while the Patriots, growing impatient, accused the nobles of undue obstruction, and the more clairvoyant suspected that privileges held by provinces and towns gave the nobility secret supporters within the Third Estate. On the morning of August 4 the Assembly ruled that it would begin by voting the declaration. But its members could expect discussion to provoke new resistance.

On the other hand, the popular revolution had to be resolved. The Assembly, which it had saved, had no choice but to endorse it, yet order had to be re-established, since the people were quietly waiting for the reforms their representatives would deem appropriate. The bourgeoisie in all probability could control townsmen, but the peasants were a different matter. They were destroying the manorial regime without concerning themselves about the Assembly. What course should be taken? If it resorted to the army and provost courts, the Assembly would break with the people and place itself at the mercy of king and aristocracy. The alternative was to grant satisfaction to the rebels—but then how would the parish priests and liberal nobles react? And it was their support which had assured the Third Estate's victory.

The terms of the decision and the tactics to carry it out were decreed during the night of August 3–4 by a hundred deputies meeting at the Café Amaury as a 'Breton Club', which dated back to the end of April, when deputies from Brittany had, as soon as they arrived in town, adopted the custom of concerting their moves and had immediately opened their debates to colleagues from other provinces. They resolved to sway the Assembly by 'a kind of magic'. In matters involving the feudal system, the duc d'Aiguillon was to take the lead.

But on the evening of August 4 it was the vicomte de Noailles who made the first move, and there was no alternative but to support him. Without debate the Assembly enthusiastically adopted equality of taxation and redemption of all manorial rights except for those involving personal servitude—which were to be abolished without indemnification. Other proposals followed with the same success: equality of legal punishment, admission of all to public office, abolition of venality in office, conversion of the tithe into payments subject to redemption, freedom of worship, prohibition of plural holding of benefices, suppression of annates (the year's income owed the pope by a bishop upon investiture). Privileges of provinces and towns were offered as a last sacrifice. Nevertheless, the 'magic' had worked its powers.

These resolutions had to be written up formally, so the debate opened again the next day and lasted until August 11. The final decree began: 'The National Assembly destroys the feudal regime in its entirety.' This was far from exact: they retained the law of primogeniture and honorific prerogatives, while requirement of an indemnity promised a long life to manorial fees. The tithe was suppressed without indemnity, but, just as fees could be collected until the method of redemption was determined, the tithe could be exacted until a law on public worship was passed.

Despite these qualifications, on the night of August 4 the Assembly achieved in principle the legal unity of the nation. It destroyed the feudal system and aristocratic domination over rural areas; it launched fiscal and ecclesiastical reform. The way was paved for discussion of a declaration of rights. This started on August 20 and continued without intermission until the 26th. Proclaiming liberty, equality, and national sovereignty, the text was in effect the 'act of decease' of the Old Regime, which had been put to death by the popular revolution.

## THE OCTOBER DAYS

But the king did not approve the decree of August 5–11, nor did he sanction the declaration. Once again crisis opened. The Assembly held that the two texts were constitutional, and Mounier stated that because constituent power was sovereign, the constitution, 'anterior to the monarchy', did not require the king's consent. This thesis, which came from Sieyes, won the day. The constitution ceased to be a contract and assumed modern aspect.

A difference of opinion threatening to split open the Patriot party urged Louis to play for time. A few liberal nobles, parish priests, and some bourgeois holding either manorial rights or public office joined forces to halt the Revolution by coming to terms with king and aristocracy. To Louis they would grant an absolute veto—the legislative sanction which Necker had stipulated in June—and for the aristocracy they would create an upper house, which he had also mentioned before. This group comprised those called 'Anglomaniacs' or 'Monarchicals.' Among them were Lally-Tollendal, Clermont-Tonnerre, and Malouet, soon joined by Mounier, and supported by Mirabeau on the veto. Duport, Barnave, and Alexandre de Lameth—the 'triumvirate'—then assumed direction of the Patriot party. Victory was theirs: on September 10 bicameralism was rejected; on the following day a suspensive veto was granted the king in legislative matters, with the understanding—as was made clear to Necker—that Louis would in return tacitly renounce royal sanction of the constitution by approving the August decrees. The king did nothing. Finally, on October 1 the Assembly decided to present the decrees only for royal 'acceptance'. No headway was gained by this, as he could just as well refuse to 'accept' them as to approve them. There was nothing left but to apply pressure on him once more.

Agitation in Paris did not abate. Newspapers and pamphlets flooded the city. One of them, L'Ami du peuple, founded by Marat in September, bitterly criticized Bailly, Lafayette, and Necker. At the end of August an abortive march on Versailles was begun from the Palais Royal. Soon, however, there were indications that the aristocratic conspiracy was about to rear its head again: the king had recalled the Flanders Regiment, which arrived on September 23. Although Lafayette had made the National Guard an entirely bourgeois organization by eliminating popular elements, its presence, along with the hired companies he had formed, now admitted the possibility of a new 'day'. Neither the circumstances nor the terms are known, but it is probable that some sort of agreement between Parisian revolutionaries and Patriot deputies was concluded. Probably, too, Mirabeau entered the game on behalf of the duc d'Orléans. Regardless of what Lafayette said, it seems that neither he nor Bailly disapproved the plan, for they did nothing to stop it.

Political motives therefore seem to be at the bottom of the October Days, but, as in July, they would not have been as effective without economic unrest. Foreigners, nobles, and the wealthy dismissed their servants and fled from Paris. Money was hidden in some safe place or sent out of the country. Luxury industries were in danger of foundering. The number of unemployed had never been so great. Bread was still expensive, and sometimes could be obtained only with considerable difficulty. The wheat crop was good but had not been threshed; the markets were empty and shipments were held up. Mills were slowed by mild winds and low water levels. Scarcity was again attributed to a conspiracy: laying hands on the king appeared to be one remedy. Once again, economic and political crises merged their effects.

On October 1 the officers of the Royal Bodyguard held a banquet to fête their colleagues of the Flanders Regiment. Towards the end of the feast the royal family entered and was acclaimed. The guests grew more demonstrative, staging a show of hostility towards the nation and insulting the cockade. Like Necker's dismissal, news of this incident set off insurrection. On October 5 women from the faubourg Saint-Antoine and Les Halles gathered at the Hôtel de Ville to demand bread. This could not have been a matter of chance, but we have no knowledge of previous preparation. Neither Bailly nor Lafayette was present. The women put Maillard, one of the 'Bastille volunteers', at the head of their procession and set out for Versailles. Towards noon some members of the National Guard in turn assembled and told Lafayette, when he finally arrived, that they too wanted to leave for Versailles. Little by little the crowd grew larger and more threatening. The Commune finally ordered them to set out and sent two commissioners to join Lafayette. They were charged to bring the king back. The political aspect of the movement became obvious.

The Assembly had just made another request for Louis to accept the August decrees when the women appeared. Maillard asked that Paris be given supplies and that the Flanders Regiment be dismissed, but did not mention the king. As president of the Assembly, Mounier was sent to the palace. Called back from a hunt, Louis received the women goodnaturedly and promised to send food to Paris. One part of the crowd turned to go. Still unaware that National Guards were on the way, the court thought it had escaped a bad situation. When he was soon afterwards informed by a message from Lafayette, the king heeded Saint-Priest's advice and decided to leave for Rambouillet. Then he changed his mind. Thinking that they were probably coming to ask him to accept the decrees, he judged the crisis over when he then notified Mounier of his affirmative decision. But at eleven that evening Lafayette arrived with the commissioners of the Commune, who asked the king to come and take up residence in the capital. This was the first time the proposal had been advanced to Louis. He postponed the matter until the morrow. Acceptance of the decrees was the only substantial advantage the Assembly had gained from the day's events.

The next morning demonstrators entered the courtyard and were stopped by the bodyguard. A scuffle ensued. One worker and several guards were killed. The mob found its way to the queen's antechamber, but she escaped, fleeing to the king. The National Guards finally arrived and cleared out the palace. Lafayette appeared on the balcony with the royal family. They were hailed, but with cries of 'To Paris!' Louis gave in, and the Assembly declared it would follow him.

At one o'clock the bizarre procession set out. The National Guards first, with bread stuck on their bayonets; then wagons of wheat and flour garnished with leaves, followed by market porters and the women, sometimes sitting on horses or cannons; next the disarmed bodyguard, the Swiss, and the Flanders Regiment; the carriages bearing the king and his family with Lafayette riding beside the doors; carriages of one hundred deputies representing the Assembly; more National Guards; and finally, the crowd bringing up the rear. They forged ahead willy-nilly through the mud. It was raining, and day gave way to night at an early hour. Insensitive to the gloom, the people, appeased and confident for the moment, rejoiced in their victory. They had brought back 'the baker, the baker's wife, and the baker's boy'.

The king was welcomed by Bailly, who led him to the Hôtel de Ville; then he retired to the Tuileries. The Assembly did not leave Versailles until October 19. After sitting first in the archbishop's residence, on November 9 it was installed in a hastily redecorated riding school adjoining the Tuileries.

Along with the aristocracy a group of bourgeois were indignant that violence had been done the king. The Patriot party rid itself of the Monarchicals, who passed into the opposition. Mounier returned to the Dauphiné and soon afterwards emigrated. The general inclination was to believe that at least the October insurrection had saved and enlarged the revolution of the bourgeoisie and that the period of crisis was drawing to an end. Actually, the consequences of the popular revolution were to widen. The nobility was now struck in its material possessions and not only in its pride by suppression of orders and privileges. As a result, most nobles vowed inexpiable hatred of the

Revolution. The aristocratic conspiracy was to become a reality, leading to civil war and to an appeal for help from foreign powers. At the same time the Third Estate split: the petty bourgeoisie, if not the proletariat, would be excluded from political life only with strong protest, for now its members too had taken part in the struggle. In municipal councils and Parisian districts the democratic movement germinated. The Assembly enjoyed boundless respect. It alone was obeyed, but on condition that it agreed with public opinion. Now everyone refused to pay former taxes and fees. A decree had re-established freedom of the grain trade; no one obeyed it.

As Mirabeau told the bourgeois, they needed an energetic government to consolidate their accession. But because of his July attempt the king was suspect. During the following months he proclaimed his loyalty to the constitution, and the Assembly declared, in an effort to reassure the more timid, that it was sure of his allegiance. Yet doubt persisted. Distrusting Louis, the Constituent subordinated executive power to its committees and in effect exercised a dictatorship—without dictatorial efficiency, because ministers and their departments retained enough control to obstruct it behind the scenes. This was why Sieyes, Mirabeau, and many others considered getting the king to abdicate and replacing him with a regency, in the name of his son, which would secure the nation's confidence. But they failed, having at hand only Philippe d'Orléans—discredited, void of prestige and character. The Revolution reduced Louis XVI to impotence, but until 1793 it had no government.

# 9

## LAFAYETTE'S YEAR

The old regime was destroyed in principle, but most of its institutions and administrative staff remained until new laws should replace them. For long months the Constituent Assembly continued the foundation work it had begun in September. As they laboured, the members of the Assembly paid close attention to aristocratic intrigue and popular unrest. This period was well characterized by the popularity accorded Lafayette, idol of the partisans of this bourgeois revolution that had turned into a constitutional monarchy—Lafayette who, like those partisans, thought to reconcile opposing forces.

### LAFAYETTE AND THE PATRIOTS

Judging that he had saved the king and queen on October 6, Lafayette thereafter styled himself their mentor. To gain time the royal couple pretended to approve of the 'mayor of the palace', but privately they despised him. When the Favras plot to restore the king and suppress the Constituent with aid from abroad was revealed on February 4, 1790, Louis let himself be led to the Assembly, and there he swore loyalty to the constitution. The 'hero of two worlds' seduced the bourgeoisie with his chivalric generosity; the citizenry was overcome to have such a leader. As a great lord, magnanimous and liberal, he impressed the people; his ascendancy seemed to guarantee order. He aspired to be the George Washington of France, to rally king and nobility to the Revolution and the Assembly to a strong and energetic government. Filled with naïve optimism and, moreover, confident of his ability, he walked out on a tightrope. Jefferson, back in America, feared for Lafayette's future, while the new United States representative, Gouverneur Morris, sardonically predicted his downfall.

As a good 'American' Lafayette stated that his power was based upon popular will, but he manipulated that will with a sense of realism. A few newspapers—the *Moniteur*, Brissot's *Patriote français*, Condorcet's *Chronique de Paris*—yielded to his prestige. He was handicapped by lack of oratorical skill, but with the help of Sieyes set up for his followers a centre, the Society of '89, where plans could be concerted and specific measures decided. There deputies and journalists mingled with nobles and bankers. He did not disdain hired supporters: when the democrats grew vehement he put out inflammatory news-sheets and filled the Assembly galleries with a hired audience. But his main chance of success would have been to mould the Patriots into a disciplined group capable of controlling and speeding the Assembly's debates and to form their leaders into an active, stable cabinet. The Assembly's majority could not reach complete agreement on any single issue; revolutionary individualism rejected party discipline with horror. Nor could the deputies agree upon fixed rules to govern their business. Besides the obstructions continually placed in their path by the opposition and by circumstances, the urgent need to maintain contact with public opinion led to constant interruptions for hearing petitions and receiving hordes of delegations which filed up to the speaker's desk, facing the president.

The opportunity to form a new cabinet was at hand. With bankruptcy imminent, Necker's star was fading. The two loans he floated in August had failed, and the 'patriotic contribution' of September 29, calling for 25 per cent of each person's income, would not replenish the treasury for some time. Lafayette began to bargain with Duport, Lameth, and Mirabeau. He had got rid of the duc d'Orléans by sending him to London, and now intended to dispose of Mirabeau, reputed to be his accomplice, by offering him the post of ambassador to Constantinople. Far from swallowing the bait, the orator carried the debate into the Assembly on October 24. He argued that the only way to reconcile constitutionalism with an effective executive was to have the king select his ministers from the Assembly, thus guaranteeing co-operative confidence between the two powers. This was a defensible thesis, directed towards a parliamentary system and already practised in England. But it also set forth undisguised his ministerial ambitions. The Patriots thenceforth regarded him as more than suspect and, realizing that the lure of cabinet positions would encourage other deserters, proposed that deputies be prohibited from accepting ministerial posts. This measure was achieved on November 7. Lafayette's plan fell through; the ambitions of others were frustrated. With the comte de La Marck interceding for him, Mirabeau entered the pay of the court, and on May 10, 1790, sent the king and queen the first in a series of advisory notes, all of which went unheeded. At the beginning Louis paired Mirabeau with Lafayette in trying to have the right of declaring war or peace made a royal prerogative. Their partnership was of short duration: Mirabeau, who envied this simpleton Caesar (expressed in the pun 'Gilles-César'), began to disparage him to the royal couple and tried to weaken his popularity with the people. He advised Louis to set up an extensive organization for propaganda and bribery in order to form his own party, then to leave Paris, dissolve the Assembly, issue an appeal to the nation, and if necessary resort to civil war, but under no circumstances to go near the border or arouse the least suspicion of conspiring with foreign powers. The triumvirate of Duport, Barnave, and Lameth envied Lafayette no less, though there was basically nothing to distinguish their position from his. But, to annoy him, they sometimes went to extremes.

## PROGRESS OF THE REVOLUTION

The work of the Constituent Assembly gradually began to take shape. A decree of November 7 made it clear that social orders had ceased to exist, another, on February 28, 1790, that venality in office was abolished from the army and that any soldier could be promoted from the ranks. A third on September 23, 1790, reserved one-fourth of the sub-lieutenants' places for non-commissioned officers. In February of 1790 each commune elected its municipal council in accordance with the law of December 14, 1789: manorial authority over the villages was destroyed. From November to February new territorial divisions were drawn and the administration was reorganized; early in the summer councils and directories in departments and districts began to function. According to a decree of May 14, the sale of church lands was to begin, and in September the assignats became non-interest-bearing notes. On July 12 the Civil Constitution of the Clergy was voted, climaxing clerical legislation. Finally, on August 16, transformation of the judiciary was completed.

Meanwhile the Patriots improved their organization and expanded their propaganda. Many of them were members of the National Guard, more belonged to various clubs. In November of 1789 the Breton Club was reconstituted in Paris at the Saint-Honoré monastery of Dominicans, who were more popularly known as Jacobins, under the name Society of Friends of the Constitution. Following its example, such clubs sprang up in all towns and were soon affiliated with the mother society. The group known as 'Brothers and Friends' was composed of liberal nobles and affluent bourgeois who followed Lafayette and the Assembly. They were moderate, essentially cautious, but loyal to the Revolution. Their loyalty often caused strained relations with administrative bodies, for a number of official positions were quietly being filled by aristocrats or lukewarm partisans who often resented the fact that these clubs acted as watchdog committees and urged them to take action. The number of publications multiplied—Loustalot's *Révolution de Paris*, Camille Desmoulins's *Révolutions de France et de Brabant*, Gorsas' *Courrier*, Carra's *Annales*.

The chief success of Patriot activity was the formation of 'federations', or provincial leagues. These groups gave convincing evidence of the nation's adherence. The first dated from 1789: Valence formed one on November 29. More were organized in 1790, at Pontivy and Dole in February, at Lyon on May 30, at Strasbourg and Lille in June. All of them joined to celebrate a National Federation on July 14, 1790, an event which gave solemn and definitive expression to the unity of France. Lafayette appeared in all his glory and, after a Mass celebrated by Talleyrand at the Altar of the Fatherland, took an oath in the name of the people's army. The king was obliged to imitate his act. Unmindful of the showers which marked the occasion, the enthusiastic crowd showed its confidence by singing *Ça ira*.

There were, however, shadows marring the picture. It was obvious that the Third Estate's civic education was nonexistent, that its members were wedded to the benefits they anticipated from the Revolution but were not eager to expend the efforts it required; nine-tenths of the active citizens had not taken part in the elections, and the National Guards were rapidly tiring of service. Passive citizens were nevertheless bitter at being denied municipal office. Indifferent to universal suffrage, which Robespierre and a few democrats vainly defended, petty bourgeois and members of the liberal professions were annoyed with property qualifications that prevented them from holding elective office. Finally, the citizens interested in public life leaned towards direct democracy and harried their representatives. In Paris the districts opposed Bailly and Lafayette; the district of the Cordeliers Club, led by Danton, rose in rebellion to protect Marat from judicial prosecution in January of 1790. In June the Assembly reorganized the Paris administration, replacing the sixty districts with forty-eight 'sections'. The new divisions soon proved equally troublesome.

Nevertheless, the greatest source of concern was security of person and property. The Assembly had scarcely arrived in Paris when a baker was put to death near the archbishop's palace, where its sessions were held. The deputies were so alarmed by this that they immediately voted, on October 21, the famous Martial Law: in case of disturbance, municipalities were authorized to proclaim the law, hoist a red flag, issue three warnings, and then give the order to fire. But would the National Guard obey? Lafayette relied on them in Paris, not without delusion. He had reduced the Guard to 24,000 men, necessarily recruited from those who had money, because they were required to buy their own uniforms. He reinforced the Guard with hired companies to form a permanent body of 6,000 men drawn chiefly from the old French Guard. But outside Paris, and especially in the villages, the situation was different. Furthermore, there were not enough muskets: the minister of war, who would gladly have disarmed the people, as it is thought, declared his arsenals empty and cut back orders for supplies. Municipal authorities could request aid from the army, yet were reluctant to do so. The Right asked that the military be permitted to intervene whenever it saw fit, but the Assembly never consented to this—the implications were obvious. As to the provost courts, they had been suppressed in principle on October 9, 1789; the following March all prosecutions by them were forbidden.

Disturbances at market-places and interference with grain distribution continued. The excellent harvest of 1790 helped the situation in general, but did not bring relief to local crises. Agrarian revolt persisted. Some intimidated peasants paid their manorial fees, but redemption, confirmed by the law of March 15, 1790, caused unrest. *Jacqueries* broke out in the Quercy and Périgord regions in January and swept through upper Brittany, from Ploërmel to Redon. In May others plagued the Bourbonnais and surrounding areas. When the harvest came, peasants throughout the Gâtinais refused to pay the tithe and the *champart*. At the end of the year Quercy and Périgord again witnessed uprisings. Finding itself threatened with increasing violence, the aristocracy hardened its resistance. Retaliatory action led by the nobility and sometimes accompanied by bloodshed added to general disorder, bitterly intensifying class antagonism. Lafayette's cherished hope of compromise was becoming an illusion.

## THE ARISTOCRATIC CONSPIRACY

The Blacks (reactionary aristocrats) scorned the Monarchicals for having compacted with the Revolution. Of their orators, the abbé Maury confined his efforts to obstruction, and Cazalès, who was more shrewd, had a poor following. Of their journalists, Montjoie, Rivarol, and the abbé Royou in *L'Ami du roi* attacked all reforms, extolled the Old Regime, and disavowed even the aristocratic revolution; Suleau in the *Actes des apôtres* and the *Petit Gautier* expressed contempt for the Patriots and ridiculed *patrouillotisme* (playing on the words for patrol and patriot). In October and November of 1789 the Blacks tried to make use of the parlements and provincial estates of the Dauphiné and Cambrésis. They demanded new elections, and during the following spring the Third Estate accused royal commissioners charged with installing the new administrative staff of intending to carry out this plan. When Dom Gerle unsuccessfully proposed, on April 13, that Catholicism remain the state religion, a protest was drawn up and signed by 249 deputies. Among them was the comte de Virieu, president of the Assembly, who afterwards had to resign. Later in the year aristocrats discredited the assignats and tried to obstruct sale of Church lands. They told the impoverished that ruin of the privileged classes deprived the poor of work and alms. Throughout the nation counter-revolutionary clubs of 'friends of peace' sprang into being.

Some of the malcontents emigrated to find peaceful asylum, while others did so to arm themselves in preparation for foreign intervention. The comte d'Artois, at Turin, was soliciting aid for invasion from every possible source. Still others, in collusion with Artois, were fomenting civil war in the Midi. Their first plot, called the Languedoc Plan, included among its helpers Imbert-Colomès, former mayor of Lyon, Monnier de La Quarrée in the Comtat, Pascalis at Aix, Lieutaud, commander of the National Guard at Marseille, and Froment, from Nîmes, who wanted to pit Catholic workers against Protestant manufacturers. The conspiracy resulted not in war but in bloody fights at Montauban on May 10 and at Nîmes on June 13. Next came the Lyon Plan, since a riot in the city to protest toll collections on July 25 had given La Tour du Pin, minister of war, an excuse to send out loyal regiments under a trustworthy commander. The comte de Bussy was in charge of stirring up the Beaujolais; the brothers Allier were assigned the Gevaudan; and in August Malbos assembled the Catholics of Vivarais at Jalès. Nobles of Poitou and Auvergne formed leagues, or 'coalitions', which promised to march on Lyon, where the comte d'Artois hoped to meet them with Sardinian troops. They wanted the king to join them there.

After the October Days first Augeard and then Mahy de Favras, on behalf of Monsieur, the king's brother, had tried to arrange for Louis to flee. In 1790, as summer drew near, the royal family was permitted to move to the château at Saint-Cloud. Escape from it appeared possible, and the French Salon, a club of Blacks, proposed that it be carried out. In this connection the Lyon insurrection was fixed for December 10. But Louis rejected the plan as well as Mirabeau's proposal—in October he had begun his own preparations. The Patriots were on the alert: word of the king's departure was constantly being announced; in February, Favras had been convicted and hanged. A number of conspirators were arrested—Bonne de Savardin in April, Trouard de Riolles in July, Bussy in September. Finally in December, a police dragnet cleaned out Lyon.

The nobles of Auvergne who were already on their way to the city emigrated. Artois left Turin and after an interview with Leopold at Mantua (May, 1791) headed for Coblenz.

Alarms among the people led to new fears in Thiérache, Champagne, and Lorraine, particularly in the area of Varennes when, during July and August of 1790, it was rumoured that Austrian troops sent to Belgium were entering France. The masses remained prepared for a defensive reaction. Marat, in July, urged them to take the offensive. Punitive reaction at any rate was not absent: Pascalis was killed at Aix.

## DISINTEGRATION OF THE ARMY

Unfortunately for Lafayette, dissension reached the army. Some of the noble officers gave their entire allegiance to the Revolution, but the majority of them, at first reticent, became more openly hostile as the Constituent's reforms started to affect them. Their soldiers also split into opposing groups, some scorning the National Guard, 'blue porcelain that can't bear firing', others frequenting clubs and turning against their commanders. Agitation among sailors and ship-workers at the naval bases also began. The Patriots, extremely distrustful of aristocratic officers, who began to emigrate in large numbers, either criticized them or on occasion defended the rebellious soldiers. But, faced with a hostile Europe, the Assembly did not dare dismiss officers and start a military purge, as Robespierre demanded. Soldiers were recruited from the poor and were of little interest to the deputies; nor did the representatives accept the proposal of Dubois-Crancé that the royal army be made into a national military organization by means of the draft. The Assembly well knew what popular hostility the militia under the Old Regime had inspired. It seemed sufficient to raise pay and pass several administrative and disciplinary reforms.

The naval ports and garrisons mutinied one after another. To Lafayette, a professional soldier, discipline was a serious matter. By August of 1790 he wanted to put an end to all revolt: when the Nancy garrison rose up, he supported his colleague, the marquis de Bouillé, who subdued the rebels in a pitched battle, had several insurgents executed, and sent forty-one Swiss from Châteauvieux to the galleys. The Assembly at first approved his action. Lafayette had nevertheless stained his hands and injured his popularity. A few of the Patriots protested immediately, and soon most of the Constituent was bewildered to learn that at Nancy, Bouillé was treating all partisans of the Revolution as suspects. In October the baron de Menou proposed to indict the ministers. The Constituent limited its reproof to a declaration that the ministers, excepting Montmorin, no longer enjoyed the nation's confidence. They resigned; their successors seemed little better. The Civil Constitution of the Clergy was by this time threatening to open another schism, and Louis was appealing to foreign powers. The Revolution was headed towards a new eruption.

# 10

## THE WORK OF THE CONSTITUENT ASSEMBLY, 1789–1791

Edmund Burke, who was followed by Hippolyte Taine, criticized those who sat in the Constituent Assembly for disrupting French society in order to apply abstract principles divorced from reality. Whether the principles of 1789 embody universal values is not at issue here, but they released new energy and moulded a society which endured. And if the Assembly's members had read the *philosophes*, their educations neither obstructed nor weakened their grasp of events. Threatened with counter-revolution and outdistanced by the people, dealing cautiously with parish priests and Patriot nobles, with economic interests and especially with the colonials, the deputies never ceased to take account of circumstances. Indeed, it was for reflecting circumstances too closely that parts of their work were to prove ephemeral.

### THE PRINCIPLES OF 1789

With the Old Regime destroyed, the representatives were bent on making their victory legitimate: force had been put at the service of law. At the same time, Frenchmen would be instructed in the principles of the new order through a 'national catechism', as Barnave termed it. The Americans had taught them how to go about it, and the French in turn promulgated a Declaration of Rights. As we shall see, however, the Declaration was not the whole of their thought: we must look further, in their laws and in the preamble to the constitution of 1791.

They had the American bills of rights before them, and Lafayette submitted his draft to Jefferson, who was then representing the United States at Versailles. A literal comparison of texts, however, does not reveal the deeper kinship they bear. In affirming the dignity of the human person and the value of individual initiative, the declarations of both countries carry the imprint that Greek philosophy and Christianity stamped upon European thought. They appeal to the protection of the Supreme Being, and most of their drafters, believers in revealed religion or followers of spiritualistic metaphysics, regarded liberty as the result and guarantee of the soul's free will. To this interpretation, historic observation adds another: individualism symbolizes European man's impulse to surmount all obstacles and conquer the world, to master nature through knowledge and invention, ultimately to control his conduct, government, and society. In this sense the new principles defined an ideal—the earthly well-being of man become his own God, a condition slowly drawing near as a reward for centuries of striving.

The work of the Constituents none the less shows originality. They closely joined equality to liberty, and by bringing the resounding collapse of privileges and feudalism the popular revolution highlighted equality as the Anglo-Saxons had not done. The revolutionaries and even the bourgeoisie valued the attainment of equality above all else. In their eyes, the free man was independent of all his fellows except those invested by laws voluntarily approved by the community with power to command in the community's name. To the French peasant, disappearance of manorial dominance remained the primary result of the Revolution.

The principles of 1789 may thus be reduced to two. First, 'Men are born and remain free and equal in rights.' They are masters of their persons; they may exercise their physical and intellectual powers freely, provided they respect the liberty of others. They may speak and write, work and invent, acquire and possess. Law is the same for all.

Professions and public offices are open to everyone regardless of birth. Second, the state does not find its end in itself; its reason for being is to preserve the citizen's enjoyment of his rights. The sovereign is the citizenry, the nation, which delegates authority to a responsible government. If the state fails in its duty the citizens will resist oppression.

Like America's insurgents, the Constituents invoked natural right based on philosophic, non-temporal values, which required expression in universal terms. The general formulas they employed have been used by some as a pretext to represent them as ideologues lost in abstractions. The 'historical' character of the Declaration is none the less evident: under each article its authors—and their contemporaries—mentally placed concrete facts which had caused their sufferings. No man is to be arrested and detained without judicial order—that is to say, no more *lettres de cachet*, the king's administrative orders for arrest. Citizens are equal before the law—that is, privileges are abolished. Resistance to oppression is legitimate—thus, the insurrection of July 14 is justified. As Aulard has said, the Declaration was above all the 'death certificate' of the Old Regime.

The Assembly did not proclaim the principles in logical order or with equal emphasis. Freedom of the individual takes up three articles; freedom of conscience seems just as important to us, yet they were content with only a discreet allusion to religious tolerance, inserted out of respect for the Patriot priests. Gaps in the Declaration were equally conclusive. Should not property have been defined, the terms of its inheritance stipulated? It is only mentioned and not defined in Article 2. The question was not asked; the subject was not touched upon again until Article 17, added at the last moment, implicitly confirming redemption of manorial dues by requiring a just indemnity, to be previously determined, in cases of expropriation for reasons of public utility. Although economic freedom ranked first with the bourgeoisie, it was not proclaimed until 1791. This was because the Old Regime no longer threatened economic liberty and because the Third Estate was no longer united in its views towards gilds. The rights of assembly and petition were also omitted, and not until 1791 was a system of public education and poor relief promised. All that involved the future, not the past.

The principles proclaimed to condemn the Old Regime nevertheless announced a new order. There could be little debate over applying the principles to the old system, since everyone censured those circumstances towards which the principles were aimed. But the principles were vague concerning a new system, and as a result were subject to controversy. Certain deputies had argued that the Declaration should not be published until the constitution was drawn up so that the two could be reconciled. Others proposed that at least the Declaration should be expanded. Sieyes wanted to block the road to social equality by stipulating that equality did not extend to means. Abbé Grégoire wanted the duties of citizens to be listed along with their rights. These proposals were overruled by the majority, a fact which shows another aspect of the Declaration: in the minds of its authors, its meaning was not subject to debate. Warnings were considered groundless. It was the achievement of a victorious class, certain of its future, sure that the order it conceived was in accord with natural law or the rational will of God and would assure eternal well-being to humanity.

It is no less true that in decreeing liberty and equality of rights this class served its own interest and at the same time succeeded in attracting countless followers to the Revolution. By opening the gates to individual effort, to intelligence, to the spirit of enterprise, the bourgeoisie called upon the most capable to come forth from the mass and seize society's economic and political leadership. Stimulated by competition, the selective process would rescue society from the senility that inevitably accompanied hereditary succession. By extending to all the invitation for each to try his luck, the bourgeoisie awakened fresh hope, which generates energy. The Revolution's disruptive effects brought extraordinary force to such promises. A huge amount of land was put up for sale. Fiduciary currency multiplied assets and opened up wide horizons to speculation. Corporate ownership was abolished and perpetual leases ended; wealth was to be continually divided through equality of inheritances and suppression of the law of primogeniture, of entailed properties and trusts. In the future all goods would be available to those who had put forth the effort to acquire them. For the poor but educated, new prospects were unveiled with expanding public employment, periodic renewal of the political staff, development of journalism, advancement of learning, and promotion of machine industry. The appeal to personal initiative, issued in the face of a monarchical Europe incapable of throwing off the fetters that checked and discouraged social growth, was for the Revolution—as it was afterwards for modern society—an incomparable source of life and power. Managers, scholars, and generals defended the Revolution; in time it absorbed all who welcomed the chance to prove their talents and make a personal contribution.

The competitive unleashing of individualism involved certain inescapable results. The strong would thrust the weak aside—and in many cases the strong were the wealthy and their heirs. Equality of rights was proclaimed, and each man was left to find the means to enjoy those rights. Disenchantment was soon to set in. But concentrated capital did not yet govern the economy; not all those without inheritance at first despaired of the future. Further, the Third Estate's solidarity in face of the aristocracy entertained a sense of unity and fraternity that partly disguised the deeper antagonism of its classes. Liberty and equality thus worked irresistible charm upon imaginations. The French people believed that their existence would improve, that their children, if not they themselves, would live in more favourable circumstances; they even hoped that other peoples would live so, and all, becoming free and equal, would be for ever reconciled. Peace would then regenerate a world freed from oppression and poverty. The mythic character of the French Revolution unfolded. A cause so noble awoke an ardour that the need for sacrifice extinguished in many, but moved others to feats of heroism and spread through the world. Michel Beaupuy brought the good news to Wordsworth before setting out to combat tyrants, and the dream still glows in the verses of the *Prelude*. The Revolution yoked realistic energy to enthusiasm, a twofold strength that was the secret of its triumph. In every land it awakened the minds and stirred the souls of men who forthwith offered themselves as its publicists.

At least a part of the bourgeoisie shared these hopes. It did not look upon itself as a caste, and even believed that it had suppressed classes by destroying orders and opening its ranks to all. But it never lost sight of existent realities or of the pre-eminent position it planned to occupy. To make the rights of man its challenge to the Old Regime, it declared them natural and inalienable. Were they therefore anterior to society? Were they recognized in all men? Were they unaffected even by national sovereignty? Conflicting opinions were delivered on various occasions, and the debate was never resolved. But in practice the realistic mind applied principles according to circumstances, placed public safety first, and restricted the universal content of precepts announced. The Declaration noted that rights were governed by law; no matter how absolute they seemed, they became relative, since proclaiming them did not amount to codifying them, but expressed an ideal, a direction of intent whose scope was to be determined by circumstances and, inevitably, by the interests of the ruling class. There is abundant proof that the Constituents thought themselves free to apply their principles in varying ways, even to postpone the consequences or deny them altogether.

Where individual liberty was concerned, the Assembly showed its loyalty to the Declaration by reforming criminal procedure, one of its finest titles to honour. Arrest required judicial order unless a criminal was caught in the act. Within twenty-four hours the judge would call the accused before him and would advise him to seek or would assign him a lawyer, who would have free access to his client. Judges were deprived of the power to indict or to pronounce guilt; for these functions they were replaced by citizen juries. Written procedure, the former process according to which the court made its decision on the basis of material in a dossier, was replaced with public and free debate among prosecutor, witnesses, and the accused and his lawyer.

In religious toleration the Constituent went beyond the Declaration. On December 27, 1789, Protestants were given civic rights, which were granted one month later to Jews in southern France, and to those in eastern France only on September 27, 1791. Freedom of belief, however, did not triumph completely: the Church's register of births, marriages, and deaths was not replaced by a civil register, and public worship remained a Catholic monopoly. Because individualism distrusted associations, the corporative organization of society disappeared and most religious orders were dissolved. But, since counter-revolution threatened, political societies were allowed to flourish, their group petitions rarely being denied a hearing. Later, when the democrats began to alarm the Assembly, it adopted, shortly before breaking up, a law curbing the clubs. Economic freedom ultimately led to the suppression of trade gilds, but the bourgeoisie did not conceal the fact that it was aiming at journeymen's associations and strikes when it prohibited combinations (*coalitions*).

The Declaration was clearly stretched on two points: slavery and the electoral system. Not satisfied to limit freedom by law, the Constituents thought that man should enjoy liberty according to reason and with the guidance of 'virtue'—that is, civic spirit. Judged by this standard, a great many people seemed insufficiently mature to assume full rights; in these cases the interests of the new order together with those of the bourgeoisie led to denial or to limitation of rights. Serfdom was abolished in France without compensation, but slavery and the slave trade, essential to the maintenance of colonial plantations, remained. The deputies ended by abandoning determination of the political status of 'people of colour'—mulattoes and free Negroes—to the colonists, whose decision could be all too easily predicted.

The Declaration recognized for 'all' citizens the right to take part 'in person or through their representatives' in the making of laws. In person? The Constituent established a wholly representative system: national sovereignty was exercised only when elections were held, and thereafter the people's delegates wielded unlimited power. The constitution of 1791 was not even submitted to the people for ratification, and amendment, surrounded with detailed restrictions, could not be initiated by citizens. Did the deputies at least represent everyone? Not at all. Sieyes pointed out that both elector and elected carried out a function for which, as for any other function, they should qualify, and the bourgeoisie took care to conclude that qualification involved wealth, for if merit was not joined with money it could easily change into revolutionary ferment. The Assembly denied the vote to 'passive' citizens—domestic servants and all who did not pay taxes equivalent to at least three days' labour—and also excluded them from the National Guard. The views of 'active' citizens were filtered through two-stage elections, a procedure which gave the notables even more influence, since the 'electors', a smaller number of men chosen in the second stage, were eligible only if they paid taxes amounting to ten livres. Finally, to be eligible for the office of national deputy, the candidate had to pay taxes of one silver mark (about fifty-two livres) and hold landed property of some sort. There were even a few who wished to make the requirements more stringent by allowing a man to hold elective office only after he had held subordinate positions in government service.

To bend principles or to contradict them altogether, sometimes in an effort to fight the aristocracy and sometimes in an attempt to restrain or court the people, was to build a structure based on reality, not on abstraction. Other examples may be found in the pages that follow.

## ORGANIZATION OF THE GOVERNMENT

The Declaration stipulated that all those who governed were to receive their power 'expressly' from the nation and that they were in turn responsible to it. Undeniably, the modern idea of a constitution took form after the October Days. Louis had only to 'accept' the constitution which 'established' his powers. Before long he was referred to as 'first public official in the nation', a term used not to belittle him, since public official (*fonctionnaire*) referred only to a political representative of the people and not the salaried employees.[1] But even as a representative the king, despite the Declaration, held hereditary office, was responsible to no one, and was inviolable. No measures were taken to govern the case of high treason on his part; everyone considered that possible, but how could they admit it when agreement between king and Assembly was being celebrated? The Declaration had multiplied precautions against him: public officials were held responsible; the use of force was regulated by law; taxation was levied only with popular consent; executive, legislative, and judicial powers were separate and independent—at the risk of paralysing the government. Louis nevertheless retained significant prerogatives. A civil list of 25 million livres was placed at his disposal. He was granted diplomatic initiative and the right to appoint military leaders, ambassadors, and the six ministers according to his own choice. In defiance of separation of powers he was even given a suspensive veto to be valid for two legislatures (at least four years) over decisions of the Legislative Assembly.

---

[1] The distinction continued long afterwards: the characters in one of Balzac's novels, titled *Les employés*, consist solely of bureaucratic personnel within a ministry, including the ministerial chiefs.

Yet he was denied exercise of these wide powers. To issue an order he had to have the countersignature of a minister, who could be indicted by the Assembly and upon quitting office was required to give an account of his actions to the Assembly before he could leave Paris. The king in return had no hold over the Assembly. Permanent and inviolable, it could not be dissolved. Legislation could be initiated only by its members. The king could not veto fiscal laws, decrees of arraignment, or proclamations addressed by the Assembly to the nation. Only the Assembly had regulatory powers—that is, the power to interpret its decrees and to issue instructions about applying them. The parlements would no longer offer obstruction: courts were to obey the laws without debate, and there was no judicial body, as in the United States, to decide the constitutionality of a law. Like the purely representative system, subordination of the judiciary was to remain an unchanging principle of French public law.

The Legislative Assembly was thus made master of the state, and the Legislative Assembly was the French bourgeoisie. Despite exclusion of the estimated three million passive citizens, there remained four and a quarter million active citizens. Meeting in 'primary assemblies', they chose approximately 50,000 electors, who met in the main town of a district or, especially when selecting deputies, in the main town of a department. Everything was calculated to reserve seats to the notables. This constitutional monarchy was a bourgeois republic.

But it was a republic with no real government. The ministers could do nothing without the Assembly's confidence; yet this they were unable to obtain because the king's appointees were as suspect as the crown. Ministers were criticized in the Assembly, were summoned before it, were carefully watched by committees. The British Parliament did not appoint committees; the French Assembly multiplied its own. In addition, the Assembly received direct requests for instructions from administrative bodies and answered without consulting any minister. The administrative bodies themselves were so organized as to leave them no effective means of acting or even of obtaining compliance to their commands.

## ORGANIZATION OF THE ADMINISTRATION

The Constituent Assembly in effect completely decentralized the administration of France. It did so gladly, because this was a way to cut off one of the king's resources, but it also responded to the country's heartfelt wish. Provinces and local communities, long ruled by intendants, unanimously demanded the end of that form of royal authority. In the *cahiers* hostility towards central power had been expressed in terms of an often narrow particularism. As has been said before, this hostility profited from the municipal revolution and after the night of August 4 did not abate. If the French surrendered local privileges and supported national unity, it was because they considered themselves thenceforth free to govern themselves.

The decree of December 14, 1789, accordingly granted wide powers to municipalities. They were to levy and collect duties, to maintain public order with direction from the National Guard; they had the right to requisition troops and proclaim martial law. They had jurisdiction over petty offences, another contradiction of separation of powers. Nevertheless, they could not do without intermediary bodies between themselves and the central government, a necessity that the drafters of the *cahiers* had recognized in asking for provincial estates. France was divided into eighty-three departments, the departments into districts, the districts into cantons. The monarchy had already undertaken to break down the traditional framework of provincial life by creating fiscal districts called *généralités*; the new organization completed that task. The immediate goal, however, was less ambitious. As Thouret described the plan in his report to the Assembly, the French simply wanted clearly defined administrative units that would group villages under the authority of easily accessible main towns where markets already existed. As soon as the principle of national representation was established, new electoral constituencies had to be created, it being generally agreed that the former bailiwicks were inadequate. Deputies of each region worked together in drafting the electoral map. There is nothing more practical or down-to-earth than their discussions.

The decree of December 22, 1789, gave each department a general council, a directory or executive body, and a *procureur-général-syndic*. Each district was given a council, a directory, and a *procureur-syndic*. The *procureurs* were charged with overseeing application of laws and became, to all practical purposes, secretaries-general, office directors. The 'electors' chose all these administrators from their own numbers; these administrative bodies also belonged to the notables; and departments were often more moderate than districts. Municipalities, in contrast, frequently showed a stronger democratic spirit than even the National Assembly because the 'municipal body', consisting of the mayor and a number of officials, as well as the notables and the *procureur* who joined them to constitute the general council of the commune, were all appointed by active citizens there, who, since those able to pay taxes amounting to ten days' labour were hard to find in rural areas, often elected men from their own ranks despite the law. Even so, the poorer people were amazed to find that in the midst of revolutionary activity they were pushed aside—under the Old Regime they had at least taken part in local assemblies. On the other hand, during the Revolution communes were very active in public affairs, and this was one of the original features of the period.

The new organization provoked some dissatisfaction. Electoral meetings were held at relatively frequent intervals because half of the members of the administrative bodies had to stand for election every two years. The electoral meetings were time-consuming, and members had to be present to accept nomination. Most citizens lost interest. Even the 'electors' were not always pleased at having to finance the journey to a designated town and were reluctant to accept offices that required much time away from their own affairs. Many communes were too small to find competent municipal officials. Meetings had been postponed to a later date and then never held, and the formation of 'large communes', which would group several under one municipal council, was rejected because each group insisted on autonomy.

The new territorial boundaries were also the limits of administrative authority, notably court jurisdictions. Prone to litigation, the citizens of that period wanted their judges close at hand and also wanted a justice of the peace residing within the canton to handle civil trials. Districts, the next administrative level, were each given a court. Appeals were to be made from them to neighbouring district courts, because the Assembly, wishing to erase memories of the parlements, refused to create a superior jurisdiction. For criminal cases the municipality handled minor violations, justices of the peace more serious offences, and a departmental court felonies. There were two national tribunals, the Court of Appeals and the High Court. The commercial courts were preserved, but administrative disputes—which included those involving nationalized property and later the émigrés—were settled by district and departmental directories.

Venality in office was forbidden and litigants would not have tolerated royal appointment of justices from the Old Regime to the new courts. Judges were therefore elected, like administrators. The new judicial staff was usually well qualified: its members were chosen for six years and were eligible only if they had been professional lawyers for at least five years. Notaries were selected on the basis of competitive examinations. The profession of *procureurs*, henceforth called *avoués*, was opened to all, and the order of *avocats* disappeared. The nation might have wished to be more directly associated with the course of justice in the interest of equity, speed, and economy. The Constituent Assembly granted a jury composed of citizens only in criminal cases—in the district courts for indictment, in departmental criminal courts for deciding the offence. Civil matters could only be voluntarily arbitrated or sent to a family tribunal (*tribunal de famille*).[1] In the former case the district court had appellate jurisdiction; in the latter it ratified the decisions.

Central authority over administrative bodies was almost entirely eliminated. The most the king could do was to suspend them, and the Assembly could reinstate them. Separating civil and criminal justice from administrative functions was an important step, yet the office of the public prosecutor was indisputably weakened by being divided among four men of different backgrounds and allegiances: the police chief; the president of the district tribunal (who presided over the indictment jury); the prosecuting magistrate (*accusateur public*) of the criminal court (this office like the previous one, was elective); and the king's own commissioner, who represented the crown at each of these courts. Like the king, the Assembly had no effective means to force citizens into paying taxes or respecting the law. Elected bodies in some instances became counter-revolutionary and invoked against the

[1] These courts adjudicated disputes among family members. (Translator's note.)

Assembly the principle of resistance to oppression. Administrative decentralization would be a threat to the nation's existence if the revolutionary crisis should deepen. The state of mind which prompted decentralization and which decentralization in turn encouraged was, basically, federalist in tendency. Fortunately for the Revolution, there was also room for initiative actions by its defenders—for what has been called Jacobin federalism.

## FINANCES

The same principle of decentralization that favoured discord had an unfortunate influence on financial affairs. Now in arms, the people refused to pay indirect taxes and were slow in contributing the others, especially since the municipal councils did not care to force them. The Constituent has been criticized for approving abolition of indirect taxes, which alone could have filled the treasury promptly, and for undertaking to remodel other taxes. But it would have been just as difficult to collect the salt tax and the excises as to collect the tithe and manorial fees, and as for direct taxes, the previous ones could be levied only as a temporary measure, since their reform was one of the most urgent demands of the *cahiers*.

Land was the main source of wealth, and taxes upon it were the most important, being estimated to yield 240 million livres. In addition, the Constituent levied a tax on income and movable property (*contribution personnelle et mobilière*), estimated to provide 60 million livres, and a tax on commercial and industrial revenue, called the *patente*, which was proportional rather than fixed. In principle, these taxes were on real property and were assessed on external signs of wealth, but some taxation of office still existed in the tax on movable property. This reform provoked countless recriminations. The *cahiers* had asked for a land survey; the Constituent decreed that meanwhile tax registers would be based on the contributor's declarations. This produced results within the communes—the declarations provided a fairly equitable distribution of taxes, especially since privileged groups consented on this occasion to contribute their share. But the *cahiers* had also attacked extreme inequalities among provinces and local communities, and without a national land survey, how could taxes be equalized? For the time being

the Constituent and then the administrative bodies had to fix quotas
according to the total amount paid under the old tax system, with a few
corrections made by guesswork! Everyone had expected to pay less
than before; instead many communes paid just as much, others sometimes more. Paradoxically, the tax on movable property weighed most
heavily upon the peasants, while the town bourgeoisie still escaped
with lighter amounts. Disappointment with financial reform was a
grave setback to popular support of the Revolution.

Putting the new levies into operation required time, and rural municipalities had neither the desire to do it quickly nor the means to do it
well. The Constituent did not hurry. Old taxes lapsed on January 1,
1791, but the land tax was not established until November 23, 1790;
taxes on movable property followed at the beginning of 1791, the
patente on March 2. The 'patriotic contribution' requiring each person
to pay one-quarter of his income, levied in 1789 on the basis of declarations that long remained voluntary and unverified, could not furnish
receipts in the near future. The treasury therefore remained empty.
And, unfortunately, measures which even in normal circumstances had
been used to obtain money while taxes were collected now failed: the
two loans floated in August of 1789 were unsuccessful, and the
Assembly prohibited 'anticipations', which would have assured loans
from financiers. Under the Old Regime tax collectors had bought their
offices and had taken a certain percentage out of receipts. By substitut-
ing salaried collectors, the Assembly cut off an important source of
income—the advances on proceeds which former collectors had
granted the treasury in the form of what were called rescriptions,
discounted by bankers. Now there were new expenditures, required by
ecclesiastic pensions and maintenance of public worship. In addition,
besides its consolidated debt the Old Regime had left huge arrears. The
Assembly ordered payment of annuities (rentes) to begin again, and
within two years 370 million livres were paid out for this purpose. In
the same period the floating debt rose by one billion because of new
obligations: the clergy's debt had to be paid off, compensation had to
be given the officials who had owned their offices and had put up
money as security, and those who had collected tithes that were
subinfeudated—i.e., ceded to laymen for collection.

As early as October of 1789 the situation seemed desperate. Necker survived from day to day with advances from the Bank of Discount. Then the Bank, having in circulation 114 million livres in notes, of which 89 million were advanced to the state, declared itself out of funds. Resources had to be found if the Revolution was to be completed: under such circumstances paper money is the only resort. The Constituent at least saw a way to back its notes. Thus, financial crisis imposed two of the Assembly's most important measures: sale of Church property and issue of assignats.

The arguments for confiscation of Church lands were that because the clergy no longer formed a corporate body its properties had no master and therefore reverted to the state; that if the state took over the responsibilities of Church services, of education and poor relief, the wishes of the donors would be respected; and that—this was least subject to debate—general interest demanded that property in mortmain be put into circulation. On November 2 the estates of the Church were put 'at the nation's disposal'. This left unsettled the question of ownership, which lent itself to doctrinal objections from the clergy, and since a just salary was promised the parish clergy, a majority of its representatives voted for the decree. Necker proposed to make the Bank of Discount a national bank, but the Assembly did not intend to place the issue of paper currency at the king's disposition and on December 19 it created an 'extraordinary treasury' (*caisse de l'extraordinaire*) charged with selling Church and royal lands to the amount of 400 million livres in the form of assignats, or certificates recognizing indebtedness, bearing interest at 5 per cent. The notes were not accepted readily owing to the uncertainties which remained: the clergy still administered its properties; ecclesiastic reform had not yet begun; and it was not clear which lands would be offered to creditors. To remedy this situation the Constituent was led to suppress the regular clergy except for teaching or charity orders (February 13, 1790), to relieve the clergy of authority to administer its property (March 17), to set up a budget of public worship (April 17), and to decree the specific terms of sale (May 14). Thereafter it could order creditors to accept payment in assignats.

But it was obvious that ready money was needed, that certificates recognizing indebtedness would not meet the treasury's current needs. Debate began again in August, this time producing decisive results: the assignat was made a bank-note and its issue was raised to 1,200 million livres. Dupont de Nemours, Talleyrand, Lavoisier, and Condorcet predicted inflation and its ills. But political concern had joined financial necessity: whereas the first assignats would have transferred properties only to state creditors—financiers, contractors, former office-owners who had to be reimbursed—the new notes might be acquired by anyone. They were bought up rapidly, sometimes just to get rid of the paper, whose depreciation benefited the poor as well as the speculators. One could say that the more the operation was to succeed in this respect the more it was to fail from the financial point of view.

A decline in the value of the assignat was inevitable, especially at a time when the memory of John Law's bubble was still fresh and aristo-crats repeatedly announced that upon return to power they would not honour revolutionary currency. The Constituent made matters worse by authorizing business transactions in the paper money on May 17. The state itself bought notes to pay troops. Metallic currency was hid-den away. The Assembly, in order to discourage payment of wages in paper money, had refused to issue small denominations, and to make change private companies issued more and more notes on their own initiative (*billets de confiance*). Ultimately the Assembly had to permit, in a decree of 1791, assignats of five livres. As commodity costs began to rise, two separate prices, one in coin and one in paper, were generally recognized. Before long the higher cost of living would produce effects not unlike those of hunger, stirring up a populace grown for the moment relatively apathetic.

The Assembly's financial policy was dangerous because the issue of assignats served to make up the budget deficit and not merely to liquidate the debt, yet the idea behind it was not bad. Within several years, after tax collections had been re-established, the sale of national property together with government borrowing could reabsorb the inflation. Besides gaining time for the Revolution, the policy, as is customary at first, stimulated the economy, ended stagnation, and made new jobs available. French money depreciated in foreign exchange: at the beginning of 1790 100 livres on the London exchange were transacted at 90, and in May of 1791 had fallen to 73. Exporters who collected gold or silver abroad, and at home paid wages which rose slowly and by small amounts, found themselves in a favour-able position. It was the torrent of notes used to finance the war that killed the assignat. Since that time wars have undermined many other currencies, which, moreover, have not had the substantial backing of this one.

## ECONOMIC WORK OF THE CONSTITUENT ASSEMBLY: AGRARIAN REFORM

The Declaration of Rights failed to mention the economy. The neglect arose because the populace remained deeply attached to controls, while the bourgeoisie of lawyers distrusted financiers and had reservations about large-scale agriculture and big industry. Economic freedom advanced by degrees, to be sanctioned, finally, in the constitution of 1791 and the rural code of September 27.

Loans at interest had been legalized since October 12, 1789, but gilds and controls on manufactured goods were not suppressed until February 16, 1791. These measures gave free rein to the use of capital, of machinery, and of new processes, protected by authorization of patents on inventions. Full liberty of the grain trade, which Brienne had granted, was restored in August, 1789, with the exception of exports. Some of the monopolies were abolished, including that held by the state on tobacco, but the state kept its control of saltpetre, gunpowder, and coinage. The India Company lost its monopoly, and trade beyond the Cape of Good Hope was released from controls. Marseille was deprived of its privileges over trade with the Levant. Free ports retained their status until the Legislative Assembly placed them under ordinary law. A law of 1791 upheld the state's authority (adopted by the monarchy in 1744) to grant mining rights, except for the many surface mines.

On the other hand, unification of the national market was completed. With the 'rolling back of barriers'—i.e., transfer of customs points to political frontiers—provinces such as Alsace and Lorraine, known as 'foreign lands in effect' because they traded freely abroad, were absorbed into France's economy. Domestic traffic was relieved of tolls and of the checkpoints required for the salt tax and excises, which varied among regions, and the customs barriers dividing the Five Great Farms from 'provinces termed foreign' and the latter from 'foreign lands in effect' were abolished.

Protective measures against competition from abroad were continued. Manufacturers gladly would have welcomed repudiation of the 1786 treaty with England, but in its tariff of 1791 the Assembly adhered to moderate rates and prohibited only a few imports, such as thread, and the export of some raw materials.

Unbinding its fetters was not enough to transform production, and for that reason many have stated that the Revolution did not mark a decisive date in French economic history. In fact, it neither launched nor accelerated production, and later the war actually retarded it. The Constituent Assembly nevertheless paved the way for future events. We have no better testimony to the advent of the bourgeoisie than the first proclamation of economic freedom in Europe.

Although contemporaries could not foresee the scope of future economic development—triumph of machines, increasing concentration of capital—economic liberty met strong resistance. In some trades the law abolishing gilds led to more democratic practices—for instance, former wage earners opened their own workshops or stores with a minimal outlay—but many masters were seriously alarmed at being deprived of their monopoly. There was general hostility against free trade in grains, not only within the proletariat but among artisans as well, not only among townsmen but also among agrarian day-labourers and farmers who could not subsist on their crops. The assemblies did not succeed in enforcing the grain decree.

For their part, most of the peasants were alarmed: freedom of cultivation was returning to consecrate definitively the private ownership of land, abruptly completing the eighteenth-century legal evolution which had been removing qualifications to ownership—such as the obligation to rotate crops, let fields lie fallow, and refrain from enclosures. Thus, open pastures seemed doomed, and the rural code made no exception even for pastures that had been planted with grazing crops. Actually the Constituent took no steps to enforce abolition of open pastures: its members must have realized that in England consolidation of plots had been the necessary pre-requisite, yet they made no allusion to it. And although the Assembly permitted enclosures, to placate the rural population it stipulated that whoever did not allow anyone else's animals in his fields must refrain from sending his own stock into the pastures of others—a practice which until then had been provoking angry protests. The measure was to no avail. The peasantry was adamant in defending its collective rights, which were to remain long afterwards, for no one, not even Napoleon, dared to deprive the peasants of their authority over collective usages. But any hopes they may have had of seeing great farms broken up, sharecropping reformed, tenant farming regulated, vanished. The Constituent was insensitive to all such demands.

Furthermore, as in the case of tax reform, most peasants were deeply disappointed by the Assembly's method of suppressing manorial rights and selling national land. The Constituents had no qualms over abolishing the tithe outright, since they regarded it as either a tax or a property held by a corporate body, nor did they see any obstacles to suppressing the classification of land as 'noble' or 'non-noble' or to abolishing the hierarchy of fiefs and laws pertaining to it—notably the law of primogeniture—and the franc-fief paid by commoners holding 'noble' land. Nevertheless, they ordered transfer fees to be redeemed and thereby recognized eminent ownership on the part of the suzerain. Sacrifice of eminent ownership would in the deputies' view have set a damaging precedent with respect to private property in general. Similarly, when they definitely regulated (in the decree of March 15, 1790) the application of the decrees of August 5–11, 1789, concerning manorial rights, they followed the report of Merlin de Douai in classifying certain rights as usurped from the state or established by violent means; among them were honorific rights and manorial courts, hunting and fishing rights, the lord's exclusive right to maintain warrens and dovecotes, mills and wine-presses, to collect tolls and market fees, to demand personal taxes and labour obligations (the corvées), and particularly to hold serfs. All disappeared without indemnity. The partitioning of common lands, practised for the last thirty years despite the ordinance of 1667, was also abolished. Quite different was the Assembly's attitude towards the so-called 'real' fees associated with the holding of land, by far the heaviest. These included payments called the cens, quitrents, the champarts levied on part of the harvest, and transfer fees and other 'perquisites'. Considering these obligations to be part of an original contract between the lord as owner and the person to whom he ceded a holding, the Assembly decreed their redemption at a rate (fixed on May 3) amounting to twenty times the money fee, twenty-five times the fee in kind, and proportional to the 'perquisites' which were being abolished. This distinction of rights was dubious on legal as much as on historical grounds. In any case, the peasants maintained that if this principle were enunciated the lord must be required to produce his original title to the land, a title which usually had never existed or could not be found. Meanwhile the peasants paid neither redemption fees nor dues.

Moreover, the Constituent made abolition of the tithe a benefit to the owner rather than to the sharecropper or tenant, and when, later, the Legislative Assembly and Convention ended redemption of 'real' fees they followed the same principle. Suppression of the gentry's 'personal' rights was by comparison a poor consolation, and the peasant without land did not obtain his plot. Thus, distribution of nationalized lands, to the extent that it swelled the number of rural proprietors, would give the destruction of feudalism part of its social significance. And since the great majority of peasants had no land at all or not enough to earn a living, transfer of state land was of even greater importance: it could lessen the agrarian crisis. If the Assembly ceded land to rural communities for distribution or authorized the officials of the local town hall to divide the land into small plots and either rent them for a fixed annual sum or sell them without auction at a price based on the estimated value, then the poor day-labourer could acquire a plot and build his own cottage. Or might they not even give it to him for nothing?

This dream was incompatible with the state's financial needs and its creditors' interests, and the law of May 14, 1790 (made more stringent by another on November 2), dispelled such hopes. Leases were kept to avoid angering tenants; holdings were sold in a block, rather than being split up, at auctions held in main towns of districts. The Constituent nevertheless wanted a certain number of peasants to become landowners and thus tie them to the Revolution and to the bourgeois order. It therefore authorized payments to be spread out in twelve yearly instalments and allowed different sections of a field to be auctioned off separately if the proceeds exceeded a bid offered for the whole field—but this worked only if the peasants combined. Fortunately for them, many fields, especially those of the parish priest, were rented out in strips, and speculators often performed the service of dividing up lands for resale; and in some areas peasants combined to buy village land. The agrarian revolt thus ultimately attained its goal. From 1791 to 1793 the peasants of Cambrésis acquired ten times more land than did the bourgeois. The results were similar in the Laonnois and in the plains of Picardy. Peasants also gained a good deal in the Sénonais, in a part of Flanders and of Hainaut, and in the district of Saint-Gaudens.

Few detailed studies have yet been made, but there is little doubt that these regions were exceptional cases. On the whole the number of property holders rose a little; so did that of tenants, thanks to division of large estates. But sale by auction meant that farmers who were already well off acquired more land, whereas in most districts the majority of peasants and especially of day-labourers were pushed aside. The agrarian problem was not solved. No worse blow was dealt to revolutionary enthusiasm in the countryside.

The proletariat was given little attention except for the Le Chapelier law (June 14, 1791), which confirmed proscription of journeymen's associations and strikes. The Constituent thereby denied workers the means to protect their wages at the same time that it refused to control commodity prices. It continued to support labour centres, thus offering some form of temporary employment, but had no intention of recognizing a right of this nature. In May of 1791 the centres were closed. The only form of public aid offered was assistance to the disabled, which in practice amounted to very little. The field of public relief was not widened; instead, the disappearance of alms distributed by the clergy made conditions much worse. Wage earners and indigents drew no benefit from the Revolution. The Constituent at least promised to organize a national system of education, but for the moment Talleyrand's report was a dead letter. The democrats were skilled in exploiting the disillusionment of the masses. But so were the aristocrats, and with them the refractory priests.

## REFORM OF THE CLERGY

The clergy could hardly welcome the fact that its pre-eminence was undermined, since Catholic worship ceased to be the state religion and toleration was written into law, or that its independence was compromised, since its corporate status ended and secularization of Church lands reduced clerics to salaried civil servants. And yet the religious struggle, so favourable towards counter-revolution, was unforeseen by deputies in the Constituent Assembly. Nor did they want it: the idea of a lay state was unknown to men raised by priests and nurtured on an antiquity that knew no such concept. Far from planning to separate Church and state, they dreamed of bringing the two more closely together. The *philosophes* agreed, for the state could not function without religion, and in France religion could only be Roman Catholicism. True, they might have preferred a civic religion; true also that revolutionary idealism inclined to establish its own cult with an Altar of the Fatherland, celebrations, and symbols. But the people spontaneously associated these ceremonies with Catholic worship and Patriot priests justified the Rights of Man and the Citizen by quoting from Gospel. The Constituent realized that it needed an agent in each commune to explain its decrees to the uneducated masses and instruct them in obedience to the law. No one was better suited to this task than the parish priest. Moreover, many representatives sitting in the Constituent Assembly were not only believers but practised their faith regularly. The deputies therefore decreed that the Church should retain the privilege of conducting public worship and that its clergy alone should be supported by the nation. A civil register of births, deaths, and marriages was not substituted for Church records, and temporarily at least the Church continued to have sole rights to education and poor relief.

However, according to the famous statement of Camus, 'the Church is within the state, not the state within the Church'. And, he added, 'We certainly have the power to alter religion,' hastening to state, however, 'but we will not do so; to abandon the Church would be a criminal act.' The king's jurists had always taught that except for matters involving dogma the state had full authority to reform Church organization and discipline. Joseph II had exercised such authority, and in France the monarch had dealt severe blows to religious orders in the eighteenth century, at best recognizing that there were some matters of 'mixed' jurisdiction, with the extent never fully defined. That the Gallican Church had to be reformed, the clergy agreed. The greater its role in the new society, the less reason was there for letting the king choose bishops; and when the state undertook to support clerics after selling their properties it had to reduce their numbers for budgetary reasons. As early as August 12, 1789, the Constituent had appointed an Ecclesiastical Committee.

It was predicted that the Concordat would not survive. Already the decrees of August 5–11, 1789, had forbidden annates, dispensations from Rome, and plural holding of benefices. But no one was worried about a struggle with the papacy. Pius VI commanded little authority: he had not broken with Joseph or even with the schismatic Catherine when she disrupted the organization of Polish dioceses without consulting him. The French clergy was in part hostile towards the Concordat, and Gallicanism, which was not yet contrary to dogma, had not lost its strength.

The Constituent turned first upon the regular clergy, long disapproved by statesmen and economists. Its decadence—at least that displayed by the monks—was well known. On February 13, 1790, religious orders were suppressed. Members who so desired returned to secular life with a pension; others were sent to the few monasteries temporarily kept open. Charity and teaching orders were spared for the time being, but the prohibition upon taking of vows denied them new members.

In an atmosphere of calm, debate on reform of the secular clergy began on May 29, 1790. On July 12 the Civil Constitution of the Clergy was passed. Ecclesiastic organization was adapted to the administrative framework: each department had a bishop, each commune one or more local priests. They would be elected like other civil servants, and the priest would choose his curates. Deliberation among Church members was revived: provincial synods were authorized, and in place of the abolished cathedral chapters the bishop would be advised by a council whose decisions were binding. The pope would no longer be able to draw on France for money—his 'primacy' was recognized but not his 'jurisdiction'. The elected bishop would enter into communion with the pope, but could not ask for papal confirmation. He would be consecrated by the metropolitan bishop and would confirm his own priests.

The Gallicanism of jurists, however, differed profoundly from that of the French clergy. The national Church could defend its autonomy against the Roman curia, but did not propose to sacrifice it to the state.

And Rome was one recourse against state encroachment. In addition, the bishops did not like curtailment of their prerogatives. Those who sat in the Assembly entered no formal objection, but abstained when the vote was taken; many others were inclined to conciliation. However, Boisgelin, the archbishop of Aix, flatly declared that the reforms required canonical consecration—in other words, that the Church did not reject agreement with the state but challenged state supremacy over it. It remained to be seen whether the national council or the pope represented the Church. The bishops would gladly have met in synod, but the Constituent prevented them for fear that the bishops, all noblemen, would let the council turn into a war machine at the disposal of counter-revolution. In that case, stated Boisgelin, only the pope could 'baptize' the Civil Constitution. The Assembly did not want to ask this of him either, but it tacitly allowed the king and bishops to make the request. The Constituent and the French clergy thus placed themselves in the pope's hands, and conflict between them now depended on him. The decree being constitutional, it was understood that the king could not exercise his veto. He was asked to accept and not to approve it. Acting on the advice of Boisgelin and of Champion de Cicé, archbishop of Bordeaux and minister of justice, Louis gave his acceptance on July 22. On August 1 Cardinal Bernis, ambassador to Rome, received the order to obtain the pope's consent.

Pius VI had already indicated his antagonism. At the king's request during the previous year he had not protested suppression of annates, but now his authority was at stake. Further, Avignon had repudiated his sovereignty and asked, on June 11, to be joined with France. A gentleman, Pius was as jealous of his temporal power as of his spiritual prerogatives; the Declaration of the Rights of Man offended him, and he secretly condemned it on March 29. On July 10 he issued two other papal briefs declaring the Civil Constitution unacceptable, but the briefs arrived in Paris after the king had given his acceptance. The bishops who had advised Louis to consent did not abandon hope: they kept the briefs secret, and the pope did not divulge their existence. The Assembly and Montmorin, minister of foreign affairs, calculated that since Pius was counting on France to restore his authority over Avignon, he would eventually yield. But he was waiting for proposals to be made, and how could they advance any? The Assembly had postponed the debate on Avignon, but in any case there could be no question of supporting counter-revolution there. Meanwhile Bernis, in touch with the comte d'Artois, encouraged the pope to stiffen his resistance. Probably because of his fear that he would annoy the Gallicans, Pius did not hasten to make a public pronouncement and waited to learn the clergy's attitude.

Matters dragged on; the Constituent demanded that the constitution be promulgated. When a few bishops and local priests died, their replacements were elected. Protests arose. The pope's silence disturbed those favouring conciliation. When on October 30 the bishops in the Assembly published a declaration of principles, however, they did not condemn the Civil Constitution, limiting themselves to a request that the pope give his approval before the document be put into force. But since the clergy still kept the register of births, deaths, and marriages, curacies could not be left vacant. Under pressure from its administrative bodies, the Constituent finally took the bit in its teeth.

On November 27 it required all priests holding public office to take an oath adhering to the constitution of the kingdom and, consequently, to the Civil Constitution which was part of it. Those who refused the oath would be replaced in office and forbidden to administer the sacraments, although they would continue to receive a stipend. Approval of the decree was finally extracted from the king on December 26. The results astounded the deputies. The fact that some priests led scandalous lives and others quarrelled over benefices had led the Assembly to look down upon clerics, who, the Constituents thought, would acquiesce to protect their own interests. In fact, a total of seven bishops took the oath. Parish priests were generally divided half and half, but the proportion varied from region to region. For example, the 'juring', or 'constitutional', priests far outnumbered others in the south-west; yet only a few took the oath in Flanders, Artois, Alsace, and especially in western France. The number seems also to have depended upon an individual bishop's popularity and the attitude within his seminary, upon the remaining strength of quarrels among Gallicans, Jansenists, and Ultramontanes, and upon the lingering tradition of richérisme. Some departments earned the co-operation of former monks but could not form a new parish clergy. The danger of discontinuing services was frightening enough to leave non-jurors in office when others could not be found.

Nevertheless, Talleyrand, bishop of Autun, and Gobel, bishop of Lydda and future bishop of Paris, agreed to consecrate the elected bishops, and organization of the constitutional Church got under way. Then Pius broke silence. He officially damned both the principles of the Revolution and the Civil Constitution (March 11 and April 13, 1791), thereby completing the rupture between Rome and Paris, and in an act of incalculable importance the Church of Rome opposed its doctrine to the Declaration of the Rights of Man and Citizen.

Counter-revolutionary agitation was greatly stimulated. The non-jurors did their best to hold their congregations and administered the sacraments secretly. A few, such as the bishop of Langres, even asked that the registers be secularized in order to take them away from the constitutional clergy. Often the constitutional priests had to be installed by force, and they found themselves exposed to severe abuse. Peasants and workers, hitherto united, parted company: many did not wish to risk damnation by renouncing the 'good priests'. Yet they had no thought of reinstituting the tithe or manorial rights, even though they were induced to side with the aristocrats who led them in insurrection. The worst was that Louis ended by compromising himself. In February of 1791 his aunts emigrated, with some difficulty. When on April 18 he wanted to leave for Saint-Cloud after attending a Mass said by a non-juring priest on the preceding day, an angry crowd prevented him.

The revolutionaries treated the non-jurors as public enemies. From then on, some administrative bodies proposed to evict non-jurors from their parishes. The mob stepped in: at Paris in April some of the devout were whipped. The Assembly followed the department of Paris in trying to intervene by legalizing worship conducted by non-jurors: a decree on May 7 closed chapels and oratories where the constitution had been attacked, but also declared that non-juring priests could officiate in the same churches as their rivals. As might have been expected, this *simultaneum* aroused strong protest, while the non-jurors were still unsatisfied at being denied the right to administer sacraments or keep Church records. Jealous of their position, the constitutionalists grew militant, and many began to lean towards the Jacobins, who lent them support. Yet some Jacobins who wanted to see services conducted in French and priests allowed to marry thought the Civil Constitution too weak. The constitutional Church was no sooner born than its existence was endangered. Further, an anti-clerical group opposed to Christianity itself arose: after all, both juring and non-juring priests preached the same religion, which itself became suspect once part of the clergy had broken with the Revolution.

## THE COLONIES

The bourgeoisie never considered that its revolution could threaten colonial prosperity, one of the main sources of its power. Rivalry among the orders, privileges, and manorial rights had little importance in the overseas possessions; the colonies could therefore be expected to work with the mother country against administrative despotism. At first there were indications that they would draw closer to France. When the influential planters of Saint-Domingue were unable to obtain representation in the Estates-General they nominated their own deputies with consent of the plantation owners residing in Paris. The Constituent seated six of them, then accepted representatives from other colonies, and thereby made them a members of a unified France.

Serious difficulties soon arose. France could extend decentralization to the colonies, but they in turn had only a handful of representatives in the Assembly which would keep legislative power, and would, doubtless, retain exclusive colonial rights. The universalist character of the Declaration of Rights indicated that men of colour—mulattoes and free Negroes—would lay claim to its benefits. And slavery? The 'Friend of the Negroes' did not ask for immediate emancipation, but they wanted to take steps in that direction, the first measure being suppression of the slave trade. In any case, it was unthinkable that this could be written into the constitution. The issue threw shipowners and traders from ports and large towns to the side of planters, whereas exclusive colonial rights divided them radically. On the other hand, racial prejudice was foreign to France, and its citizens were not disposed to deny equality of rights to people of colour. Amid these contradictions the Assembly hid behind inaction. No solution could have been worse, for the colonists took the initiative in an effort to force the issue and win autonomy.

At Paris the planters by-passed their powerless representatives and met as a club at the residence of the comte de Massiac, whose name the group adopted. On March 8, 1790, Barnave, reporter of the colonial committee and related to one of the most enterprising planters, was instrumental in obtaining passage of a decree authorizing colonial assemblies. Implemented by further instructions on March 23, the decree promised that the assemblies would be consulted on projected laws affecting their interests. They were to be elected by taxpaying 'personages'. The Assembly having declined to state whether men of colour were included among the personages, colonials and mulattoes cried victory. Overseas, however, the equivocal decree was already superseded.

In Saint-Domingue planters took advantage of France's lethargy by setting up an assembly at Saint-Marc. They named as president Bacon de La Chevalerie—Barnave's relative—and on March 28 produced a constitution which, ignoring the National Assembly, they submitted only for the king's approval. In Martinique a similar assembly took power into its hands and used military force to seize Saint-Pierre, where the traders were hostile. In Île-de-France the assembly passed laws with equal unconcern for the mother country. French unity was reduced to common loyalty towards the person of the king. Exclusive rights were to disappear at the expense of the bourgeoisie in France; the whites would rule alone, disqualifying men of colour and keeping their slaves.

They had gone too far or too fast. The royal governor of Saint-Domingue dispersed the Saint-Marc assembly with help from the military on August 8 and shipped some members back to France. On October 11 the Constituent declared the assembly dissolved; on November 29 it suspended that of Martinique, dispatching civil commissioners to the Windward Islands. On May 15, 1791, Barnave wrung a pledge from the Assembly not to pass legislation concerning individual civil status unless the colonists requested it. By that time the opposition had found its voice, and the Constituent conceded that men of colour born of free parents would enjoy civic rights. But an order of September 24 left determination of personal condition entirely to the colonial assemblies. On this point, at the very least, the Assembly had ended by capitulating.

Meanwhile anarchy raged. The 'red pompoms' of the Saint-Marc assembly clashed with the 'white pompoms', who refused to break with France. Mulattoes joined the battle: in October of 1790 Ogé returned from Paris after a sojourn in England and the United States and attempted a premature revolt. Defeated, he was broken on the wheel. In Guadeloupe and Martinique the governors Clugny and Behague joined counter-revolutionary forces and gained the upper hand through connivance with the planters. Agitation finally reached the slaves, who revolted in the area around Cap-Haïtien in Saint-Domingue at the end of August, 1791. Mulattoes often fought against them, but also turned upon the whites. The whole colony was gradually devastated, cutting off one of France's primary sources of wealth.

## FRANCE IN 1791

In the spring of 1791 Frenchmen realized that the structure raised by the Constituent Assembly was cracking before it was finished. Lafayette's policy was foundering upon resistance from the aristocrats, encouraged by religious division. Civil war was not severe enough to threaten the nation, but the ranks of the discontented were steadily growing. Disappearance of feudal rights and venality injured many bourgeois as well as nobles, and suppression of traditional institutions deprived even more of employment. They were not always able to find other means of earning a living. Abolition of the salt monopoly, for example, reduced smugglers to desperation: one of them was to lend his name to the *chouannerie*. More serious was the crumbling of the Third Estate, evident in the rising strength of the democrats.

Since 1789 the counter-revolutionaries had never failed to warn the bourgeoisie that arguments contesting advantages of birth, put forth in order to abolish noble privileges, would soon boomerang, for others would also argue that inheritance of wealth ensured a privilege in practice. In the early stages, however, it was not to censure the social order that the principle of equality proclaimed in the Declaration was invoked. That order was indirectly criticized, from the political angle, by attacks on an electoral system that was based on property qualifications. A very few deputies, among them Robespierre, defended universal suffrage, and some journalists raised the same cry, but the 'silver mark decree' that granted eligibility to merit only if it had financial backing was a greater issue with them. Clubs open to the people encouraged the development of a democratic party, and such clubs were the work of obscure leaders rather than of Assembly deputies or the Jacobin Club. The passage of time brought forth certain impatient or bold men who until then had not succeeded in gaining attention. Actors, writers, artists, or teachers, they were unable to find regular employment and often, being newcomers in a commune, were not held within the conformity that business, family, and local connections enforced. In Paris a poor schoolmaster named Dansard founded the first 'fraternal society of the two sexes' on January 2, 1790. In the next months similar groups appeared. The Cordeliers Club opened in April of 1790, the Indigents Club in March of the following year. They admitted 'passive' citizens and their entrance fees were minimal. When elections to the new Legislative Assembly were announced, agitation swelled. The popular societies set up a central committee in May, 1791. On June 15 they presented the Constituent with a petition objecting to property qualifications. A group called the Social Circle began holding public meetings at the Palais Royal, where abbé Fauchet lectured on the *Social Contract*. Bonneville defended democracy in the *Bouche de fer*. Marat gave support to the movement in the *Ami du peuple*. Some of the democrats—chiefly Robert, in the *Mercure national*—announced their support of republicanism in the autumn of 1790.

A few writers by implication touched upon the true social issue, that equality of rights was an illusion to those lacking the means to use it. In a way the aristocrats encouraged this conclusion by telling the people that without alms from the clergy or paternal protection from the lords they would regret the good old days. Soon came denunciation of the 'new feudalism' that economic freedom would bring, profiting rich employers and returning workers to servitude. The masses were not so far-sighted, but they applauded attacks on 'financial operators' and the 'hoarders', towards whom those bourgeois who had accumulated fortunes, as well as former officials and lawyers, showed as much hostility and were equally bitter as the democrats.

Yet, as usual, it was a confluence of circumstances that set the wage earners in motion. Food was not, for the time being, a source of wide concern, but economic activity, favoured by the early effects of inflation, persuaded the proletariat that the moment to improve earnings had come. The Paris printers organized to demand a minimum wage. When winter ended the building trade went on strike and the blacksmiths followed their lead. Journeymen's associations began to stir up the provinces. Fraternal societies and democratic broadsides lent their support, although no one defended the right to strike—wage earners were accustomed to having conflicts settled by the authorities and tended to request mediation. Another reason the democrats made themselves heard was that if the lower classes gained electoral equality, state power might pass into their service. This was exactly what frightened the bourgeoisie.

Mirabeau pressed his plans on the royal family with even greater energy. The court followed his advice only in using bribery: Talon enlisted agents and hired accomplices with funds from the king's civil list. Fortunately for his reputation with posterity, the 'tribune' died on April 2, 1791. This premature removal has saved his reputation as a statesman, for like Lafayette, he mistook the king's designs, and defeat lay in wait for him. Duport, Lameth, and Barnave immediately stepped into his place. Alarmed by democratic advances and labour agitation, the triumvirs in turn wanted to arrest the Revolution. They received money from the court to start a newspaper, the *Logographe*, and in May were on the verge of reconciliation with Lafayette. Under their direction the majority gave in to the right in passing the decree of May 7, which officially recognized services conducted by non-juring priests. At the same time passive citizens were barred from joining the National Guard in the future. Group petitions were forbidden. Bailly evicted the Cordeliers from their monastery. On June 14 the Le Chapelier law prohibited combinations and strikes. Constitutionalist newspapers now sided with counter-revolutionaries in denouncing the popular movement, which, they declared, foreshadowed 'agrarian law'—i.e., distribution of property by means of pillage. Frightened, the bourgeoisie wanted to quell the populace. Disintegration of the Third Estate was speeded. Lafayette and the triumvirate concluded that the work of the Constituent had to be revised, property qualifications made more stringent, clubs suppressed, the press bridled. But to check the

Revolution by smothering popular demands with help from the Blacks meant reversing its course: they planned to give the king larger powers and institute an upper house. Above all, they had to keep themselves in power—by authorizing re-election of Constituent members—and take over the ministry—by obtaining passage of the decree of November 7, which allowed deputies to become ministers. Robespierre, now the leader of the democratic party, succeeded in obtaining defeat of the motion for re-election and thereby defeated them. They pursued their plans. Like Mirabeau, they considered the principles of 1789 intangible, and their design, like Mirabeau's, presupposed that Louis would remain loyal to them. Suddenly the ground gave way beneath them. The king fled.

# Part III

The Revolution and Europe
up to the Formation of the
First Coalition

# 11

## THE CONSTITUENT ASSEMBLY AND EUROPE

Louis fled in hope of obtaining, at last, the support that he had been imploring from foreign rulers. There could be little doubt that sovereigns abroad opposed the Revolution: it announced and put into effect principles which redefined the law of nations as well as government and society. Yet the reigning heads of Europe were absorbed in their own rivalries until the king's escape abruptly focused attention on affairs in France. The flight to Varennes, which dealt a fatal blow to the French monarchy, proved no less decisive in the relations between Europe and the Revolution.

### REVOLUTIONARY PROPAGANDA

In the beginning it was the international influence of the Revolution that most disturbed foreign rulers. They lost no time in denouncing the 'clubists'' propaganda and blamed the French government for tolerating or even encouraging such publicity. Actually, revolutionary ferment spread spontaneously for months, much as the Enlightenment had moved across Europe earlier in the century. Events in France naturally excited great curiosity. The literary journals of Germany and Italy lost many of their readers, while French booksellers moved to cultivate the new public they could reach, with quick success: as early as August of 1789 Núñez, Spanish ambassador to Paris, mentioned that translations were being printed for the market in Catalonia. Distributors employed hundreds of ruses to elude the police, and not even the Spanish Inquisition could track down all smuggled literature. The Revolution found throngs of willing agents among French residents abroad. Perhaps it would find even more among the foreigners who were crowding into France.

No one could remember having seen so many newcomers. After July 14 arrived Campe, who had succeeded Basedow as canon of Dessau, with his student Wilhelm von Humboldt. Georg Forster, already famous for his travels with Captain Cook, came from Mainz to attend the Federation ceremony on July 14, 1790. Rhinelanders and Swabians were drawn to Strasbourg; there the Capuchin monk Eulogius Schneider, from the University of Bonn, took up residence in 1791. From England came Danton's friend Holcroft in 1789, and the next year Brissot's Quaker friend Pigott, along with Wordsworth and Miss Williams, who soon became an admirer of Madame Roland. From Russia came the writer Karamzin as well as Prince Stroganov's son, escorted by his tutor, Romme. Many of these visitors plunged into French quarrels, as was taken for granted in a cosmopolitan age, and the revolutionaries joyously welcomed all neophytes, believing that their own example was to regenerate the world. Of course there were foreigners who did not side with the Revolution. Baron Grimm never gave up his opposition towards it. The comte de La Marck bribed Mirabeau; the baronne de Korff and the Englishman Crawford applauded the king's flight; and Mallet du Pan, editor of the *Mercure*, ended by passing over to counter-revolution. Among the joiners were secret agents as well: Elliot and Miles from England, Ephraïm from Prussia, the baronne d'Aelders, spy for the Stadholder. But sincere enthusiasm moved many aliens to take up the cause of liberty. Wordsworth was an outstanding example. Some joined the '89 Club, others the Jacobin Club, the Social Circle, the Cordeliers Club. A few quickly earned personal reputations: we know of the role taken by Marat or by Baron Clootz, 'orator of mankind', who paraded a cosmopolitan group before the Assembly on June 19, 1790, and asked that it have the honour of representing the universe at the Federation ceremony. Through connections with their homeland or, if they returned, by taking active steps and telling of their experiences, these 'Patriots' assumed the role of publicists—without co-ordinating their activity and almost without reflecting on the part they played.

Conspicuous among them, however, were political refugees, and their purpose was more deliberate. After the uprisings of 1781 and 1782 some had come from Neuchâtel and Geneva; in 1787 others fled Holland, in 1790 more arrived from Savoy, Liége, and Brabant. Inflamed by persecution and embittered by exile, they took their revenge in revolutionary propaganda. Separation from their homeland induced errors of fact and judgment: they easily confused their desires with reality and passed their personal delusions on to French comrades. The Swiss formed a Helvetian Club at Paris in the first half of 1790, and the lawyer Castella stirred up the cantons. Bern and Freiburg entered formal protest against their activity during the summer.

Later in the fall, certain democrats evidently thought of imitating the Swiss example. Orators at the Social Circle and Bonneville's newspaper, the Bouche de fer, called upon all men to realize universal peace through freedom, and next Bancal des Issarts tried to set up a London branch of the Circle. The Social Circle had been founded by the Masonic lodge Friends of Truth, and Bonneville had considerable influence in the lodge St. John of Scotland, whose leaflets were distributed in Germany through the efforts of Dietrich, mayor of Strasbourg. In 1787 the Illuminati had attempted to proselytize among the French Masons, and Bonneville was in contact with them. Propaganda in Savoy seems also to have made use of the Scottish lodges, which after the fall of the Old Regime took their cue from Lyon, especially if they were among those affiliated with the French Grand-Orient. Since the revolutionary period polemicists have attributed enormous influence to secret societies but have not supplied us with any proof. Societies whose members were sufficiently united to play a political role were certainly few; they may have rendered some service to the Revolution, but even if so, their part should not be exaggerated. In any case, we can conclude that on the eve of Varennes propaganda was developing into an instrument of combat.

## SPREAD OF THE REVOLUTION

The strength of resistance to French propaganda was to be demonstrated by future events, and with the advantages of hindsight it has become a commonplace to accuse the revolutionaries of frivolity and blind fanaticism because they either overlooked or underestimated these barriers. But it is quite true that the storming of the Bastille had inspired enough foreign enthusiasm—in nobles as well as bourgeois—to mislead Frenchmen, and it was with good reason that the newly arrived 'pilgrims of freedom' assured France's revolutionaries that they had followers in every land.

Followers in Eastern Europe were obviously limited in number and had no influence. A handful of isolated Russians—Novikov, the poet Radishchev, Prince Gallitzin—showed liberal sympathies but looked only to the central government for reforms, expecting that action would perhaps come from Catherine's grandsons, whose education had been guided by Laharpe. The Czarina treated the Polish nobility, the *szlachta*, as Jacobin in character because they formed a club at Prince Radziwill's home and modelled the constitution of May 3, 1791, on Western lines. Yet, disregarding the timid requests made by towns and ignoring Kollontai's efforts, this nobility admitted to the Diet no more than a few bourgeois members who discussed only commercial and municipal affairs. The most it granted to the peasants was placing them under theoretical protection of the law.

There was still active ferment in Hungary during 1790. Hundreds of pamphlets demanded in the name of 'the people' that a representative system be reinstituted and Magyar be made the official language. Here again, 'the people' were the nobles. Perhaps a few lords admired Voltaire and Rousseau, as did Count Feketi of Galantha, one of the leaders of opposition to Joseph, but that did not prevent the magnates from demanding that peasant emancipation be revoked when they made peace with Leopold. Some of the writers, such as Batthiany and Hajnóczy, influenced by Joseph and certain Frenchmen, now raised their voices against the aristocracy; some even led open attacks—notably Laczkovicz, a former officer and son of a bureaucrat, and Martinovics, a scholar and teacher connected with the Illuminati, who had sided with Condorcet in Paris. But they had no effect on the masses.

Guarded by distance, these countries did not lend themselves to propaganda.

Actually, the response from Eastern Europe did not much concern the French revolutionaries. For the time being the essential thing was to win a public in the states bordering on France; hostility from them was to be feared, since foreign invasion would be impossible without their assistance. From this point of view it was especially important to win over Germany and England, and it was in these two countries that the Enlightenment's advance promised greatest success.

The Revolution undeniably awoke sympathetic curiosity in many prominent or illustrious Germans. Some were nobles or even princes, such as the duke and duchess of Gotha, but most were men of letters, journalists, and teachers. At Mainz, then the freest of intellectual centres, there was Johannes von Müller, Swiss historian and secretary to the archbishop Erthal, and Forster, university librarian. At Göttingen were Schlözer and the poet Stolberg; at Brunswick, Major Mauvillon, one of Mirabeau's agents; and at Hamburg, Klopstock. The Weimar group showed most reserve—Herder, vice-president of the Consistory, Wieland, editor of *Merkur*, and Johann Paul Richter all indicated their approval, but Goethe and Schiller hesitated, though they did not declare themselves opposed. East of the Elbe, Kiel University was also split: Niebuhr came out against the Revolution. Many Prussians took pleasure in flouting Wöllner by praising events in France. They were seconded by Archenholz, an editor of *Minerva*, by Nicolaï, editor of the *Deutsche Bibliothek*, and Reichardt, director of the Berlin Opera. The eminent philosophers Kant and Fichte supported the Revolution from its beginning. In Vienna the *Aufklärung* circles were deeply moved. Only Bavaria, dominated by the Jesuits, continued to resist the contagion.

Sympathy did not remain entirely intellectual in nature. The bourgeoisie of Hamburg celebrated July 14, 1790. Certain writers issued a call to action in terms of violence; without delay the Illuminati were accused of preparing insurrections. More serious, the masses of the Rhineland stirred. Famine moved town populations to rise up and challenge the authority of governing oligarchies. Peasants took their cue from Alsace and, in the Palatinate and along the Rhine, refused to pay fees. Active discontent spread to the depths of Germany. An outbreak resembling France's *jacqueries* erupted on the island of Rügen;

agrarian disturbances occurred around Meissen, in Electoral Saxony; strikes broke out in Hamburg during 1791.

The Revolution might have spread through Germany more easily if Belgium and Switzerland had aided propaganda by rebelling in turn. Paris at one time hopefully expected this to happen. At Liége the nobility was weak, and the bourgeoisie had acquired considerable power with industrial growth. There Lebrun, later to be a Girondin minister, published his *Journal général de l'Europe*. The bishopric had continued to be calm through 1787, but tension gradually mounted as news from France arrived. Then came accounts of the storming of the Bastille and of the night of August 4. Led by Bassange, Fabry, and Ransonnet, insurrection broke out on August 18. The bishop fled to Trèves, but disturbance soon followed him there. Peasants and workers rose to demand freedom from servitude. The principality was to all appearances about to adapt itself spontaneously to the French Revolution. It was the only one to do so; yet its example, following closely after revolution in France, in turn hardened Belgian resistance to the Holy Roman Emperor. The introduction of bureaucratic centralization in 1787 had already provoked a violent reaction which the clergy, hitherto obedient to 'Josephism', now used in order to rebel in its own interests. The provincial estates balked, and on July 18, 1789, Austria dissolved those of Brabant. A lawyer from the aristocracy named Van der Noot found asylum in Breda and launched an appeal on behalf of the estates to England and Prussia. Neither country discouraged him, as the occasion provided an opportunity to harass Austria. The estates in question consisted of three orders, dominated by the nobility. The Third did not truly represent the bourgeoisie—in Brabant its members were elected only by the trades corporations in the three chief cities of Brussels, Antwerp, and Louvain. But there did exist a Belgian reform party, which was supported by the wealthy burghers (French in culture even though this was a Flemish area), by part of the lower clergy, and by a few nobles. The party's leader was Vonck, another lawyer from Brussels. He had broken ground for the revolt by organizing troops in the Liége area. These forces were commanded by Vandermersch, a former officer who had done service for France and Austria. Van der Noot reluctantly agreed to accept their aid. In November the Vonckists took Ghent by surprise. Mons and Brussels rose up. In December the Austrians retreated from their Belgian provinces.

German Switzerland, like the Rhineland, caught the contagion from Alsace. In Basel, Ochs and Gobel, who was later to become bishop of the Paris department, stirred up enough agitation to alarm the bishop of Basel, who in 1790 called for Austria to occupy what territories remained under his authority. (The city of Basel had expelled its bishop and withdrawn from the bishopric during the Reformation.) In Zurich the Rolands' friend Lavater rallied round him supporters of the new France. The 'Negatives' in Geneva were forced to agree to constitutional changes first in February of 1789 and again during the following December. From St. Petersburg Laharpe exhorted citizens of the Vaud and Valais cantons. The leading cantons had a more immediate source of concern: famine threatened to ignite another revolutionary fire in the wake of disturbances in Savoy, where peasants refused to pay redemption fees when manorial rights were suppressed. Among many others, a doctor named Doppet fled Savoy to seek support at Paris.

England, on the other hand, witnessed neither disturbances nor popular agitation. The French Revolution could reach the masses only through the radical movement, and although events on the continent encouraged a revival of radicalism, more time was needed. The British ruling classes condescendingly approved early French efforts to transplant their constitutional system, while Fox and his friends—Sheridan, Stanhope, Lauderdale, Erskine—expressed sympathy with the Revolution. Bentham drew up a plan for judicial reform, which Mirabeau presented to the Constituent Assembly. The dissenters were the most excited: Price delivered a sermon on November 4, 1789, that persuaded the Society of the Revolution (of 1688) to address the French National Assembly. The Society celebrated July 14, 1790, and set up contact with clubs in France. Dissenters pressed more urgently than ever for promised reforms, but Tory opinion cooled as the Revolution advanced, and Pitt kept silent. The attitude of dissenters gradually hardened: in 1791 they revived the London Society for Promoting Constitutional Information, created earlier by partisans of electoral reform. There were in English cities during the late eighteenth century groups of cultivated men, usually nonconformists, who advocated varying degrees of political reform. In London, Horne Tooke, Godwin, Thomas

Paine, and Mary Wollstonecraft, the apostle of women's rights, sided with Price. In Birmingham, Priestley's liberal views were reaching a wider public, and a Constitutional Society was founded in Manchester during 1790. Interest in public life revived in Scotland, where it had formerly been curbed by the skilful and unscrupulous management of patronage and bribery by Dundas, a cabinet minister. But on the eve of Varennes, the masses in Britain gave no evidence of reaction to revolutionary propaganda. Not until the end of 1791 did they become concerned with affairs across the Channel.

Ireland offered more fertile ground. Agitation on the island had never subsided after 1782: its Catholics praised the French for having proclaimed religious tolerance and suppressed the tithe; meanwhile, national sovereignty gradually led the Catholic Fitzgerald and the Protestant Wolfe Tone to demand Irish independence. Beginning in 1789, Whig clubs sprang up in Dublin and Belfast. Grattan, Irish Parliamentary leader, had thus far succeeded in confining aspirations to legal means, but at the end of 1791 he began to lose complete control.

The countries of southern Europe were affected less than England. The Revolution awakened some sympathy among Italian literary circles; Ciaja and Count Gorani at Naples, and in the North, Parini, the two Pindemontes, and Alfieri all hailed it in its early stages. The resentment of papal authority demonstrated at the Council of Pistoia was still present. The bishop of Pistoia, Scipio Ricci, corresponded with Grégoire and with Clément, who became constitutional bishop of Versailles. Here and there a few, such as Buonarroti, were inclined to take active steps, but revolutionary infection long remained superficial. On the Iberian peninsula there was even less response. Of the followers of the Enlightenment—Jovellanos, Campomanes, the Voltairian Aranda—none dared come out for the Revolution.

The French revolutionaries knew that Italy was unarmed, and they scorned Spain. They had virtually nothing to fear from either country. But it was obvious that in Germany and England reaction was growing in direct proportion to their own increasing influence, and the revolution in the Netherlands bitterly disappointed them.

## REACTION AND PROPOSALS FOR A CRUSADE

The French had built their illusions on events of 1789, especially on popular insurrection. The people have risen, they said, and have overthrown tyrants. They forgot that the people were the last to rise, that the bourgeoisie itself had begun to act only because the Estates-General had met, and that the aristocracy had been responsible for convocation of the Estates. News of agrarian revolt and the night of August 4 disclosed the value of that 'philosophy' which Europe's eighteenth-century nobility had paraded to annoy absolutism. With few exceptions, the nobles swung to counter-revolution. The sale of Church lands soon terrified clerics throughout Europe. The leading personalities of almost every kingdom noted the errors committed by their French confrères, who, because they had paralysed the king, watched while the Old Regime collapsed about their heads. Muting their grievances against royal despotism, they threw support behind the throne to guard privileges and property. Their attitude discouraged any inclination of the bourgeoisie, still very weak, towards direct action. If the middle class did not entirely repudiate the new principles, it was frightened by popular disorder and thought first of its own business and welfare. Nineteen out of twenty Englishmen who had a roof over their heads and a whole shirt on their backs, said Macaulay, took a stand against the Revolution. Thenceforth, whenever the people happened to stir, their leaders throughout Europe agreed that they must be brought to their senses, as tradition dictated. The very success of the French Revolution provoked outside its borders a development exactly contrary to the series of events which had secured its victory in France.

French émigrés did their utmost to sound the alarm against revolution and found valuable assistance in the person of the comte d'Artois, at Turin, as well as cardinal de Bernis and the duc de La Vauguyon, ambassadors to Rome and Madrid, who promoted their cause in every way possible. In 1790 armed groups began to assemble on the domain of the elector of Trèves. But most of the émigrés, counting on a swift end to their exile, sought only to amuse themselves. Prodigal though soon without funds, they made life more expensive wherever they set up camp. Many were haughty and insolent, frivolous and irresponsible, and earned universal dislike. Yet they presented others of their class a living example of what had occurred, and the tales of horror which they fed to journals and broadsides eventually made an impression. Assuring others that their compatriots were resentfully enduring the tyranny of a handful of evildoers, they wagered that disciplined troops could reach Paris with no serious opposition. The role they played abroad bore close resemblance to that of political refugees in France.

Nothing should have been more instructive to the revolutionaries than the course of events in the Netherlands. When the Austrians had departed, Vonck submitted his programme to Van der Noot: equality of rights; reform of the provincial estates, including doubling of the Third and election of its representatives in local districts; the calling of a general assembly of the provinces. His plans contained no suggestion of following the French pattern as far as landed aristocracy or clergy were concerned. But, moderate as his reforms appeared to be, the Statists thought they boded no good, and when an independent United States of Belgium was proclaimed by them on January 12, 1790, they entrusted its government to a congress of delegates from the provincial estates, which were restored intact. The Statists refused to complete national unification by annexing Liége because its revolutionary citizens would have strengthened their opponents too decisively. Both parties sought foreign support, both in vain—Van der Noot from Prussia and England as before, Vonck from France. Vonck's efforts earned him nothing more than advice from emissaries sent by Lafayette plus an offer from Béthune-Charost to take the throne. The Vonckists were able to form committees in a few towns, but part of the bourgeoisie split: the trades corporations came out in favour of the Old Regime. Van der Noot played into the hands of Van Eupen, a canon, who with the Jesuit Feller led the clergy in a furious campaign against reform, which they said heralded the subversion of religion. They won over workers and peasants, who had found nothing to attract them in Vonck's programme nor in the man himself. Unlike his rival, Vonck had none of the attributes of a popular leader. The Statists distrusted the volunteers organized by Vandermersch and accused them of planning a conspiracy. Ultimately, on March 16–18, 1790, a few hundred rioters drove the Vonckists from Brussels. They emigrated to France. Power remained in the hands of the privileged, and they, powerless to organize defence against Austria, resigned themselves to the finishing stroke. In November and December of 1790 Austrian troops restored the prince-bishop's power at Liége and reoccupied Belgium.

In England, too, the Church apparently was the first to become frightened. The landed aristocracy quickly took up the alarm; elections in 1790 strengthened the Tory majority. New attempts to abolish the Test Act and to reform Parliament met worse defeat than before: Pitt denounced reforms as signals of weakness and declared that circumstances required their postponement—an adjournment that stretched on through another generation. Disagreement broke out among the Whigs. To Fox's great dismay, Windham terrified the Commons with a dramatic description of perils threatening the Church, and in April of 1791, as they were discussing a bill to organize constitutional government in Canada, Burke broke with Fox. The Whig schism had begun.

In the previous November, Burke had brought out his celebrated *Reflections on the Revolution in France*, which became and has remained the gospel of counter-revolution. Forcefully arguing that decrees do not suffice to give a sense of freedom and civic virtue, he introduced into history and politics the concept of evolution. His thought was profound. The book, however, found favour among contemporaries specifically because of the limits he assigned to society's evolution—class hierarchy to him seemed divinely ordained, and if he condemned the French Revolution as hellish and destructive of all social order, it was because the Revolution meant downfall of the aristocracy. Better than any of his contemporaries, he perceived the most essential and enduring aspect of the revolution in France. An unexpected counteraction followed his enormous success. Most of his numerous critics addressed themselves to the bourgeoisie, taking issue only with the narrow interpretation he gave to 1688 and to progressive evolution; this was the line that the Scotsman Mackintosh followed in his *Vindiciae Gallicae*. Another critic, however, was Thomas Paine, already famous for having sided with the American insurgents. His attacks on political and social injustice, on kings and lords, spoke directly to the people, and his *Rights of Man*, the first part of which appeared in 1791, distributed throughout Europe in cheap editions, showed the masses what they might learn from the French example.

In Germany, Schlözer, known as the 'Rhadamanthus of Göttingen', did not repudiate liberal principles, but in 1790 began to attack the 'ochlocracy', the democratic rabble running France. He encountered heavy criticism, yet more and more writers ranged themselves alongside him. Among them were Ottokar Reichard, Girthammer, Brandes, the privy councillor from Hanover, and notably Rehberg, Germany's Edmund Burke, who wrote for the Litteraturzeitung of Jena. At Vienna, Hoffmann had Leopold's protection in using the Wiener Zeitung to wage a virulent campaign against the liberals. Secret societies and universities became suspect; in 1791 an anonymous pamphlet entitled Letters of a Traveller blamed the societies for unleashing agitation in France. There was talk in Vienna of banning The Magic Flute, whose Masonic rites evidently tainted the libretto. Perhaps the most alarming symptom was that while liberals continued to praise the Constituent Assembly's reforms, they disclaimed any intention of wishing to introduce them forthwith in Germany and declared that progress lay solely in the cultural and moral advancement of men as individuals. The immediate, unmistakable objective of the Revolution, a change of institutions, they banished to a distant future, thereby testifying to their impotence.

The general trend of public opinion could not help but favour that reaction against the Aufklärung which had begun in Prussia before 1789. Frederick William II gave greater support to Wöllner's efforts to lead ministers and professors back into the path of religious conformity, over their protests. The king had his predecessor's code revised to purge it of clauses that might interfere with royal or Junker authority, and he made it clear that no changes would be introduced in the manorial system.

Within Habsburg territory the 1789 revolt in Belgium as well as a threatened rebellion in Hungary checked imperial reform policies. Before his death in February of 1790 Joseph revoked or suspended a number of changes. His brother and successor, Leopold II, came to Vienna from the duchy of Tuscany. There he had been regarded as one of the most enlightened of despots, but his primary obligation was to protect the dynastic heritage of his house. The only means he could conceive was to make peace with the aristocracy and satisfy particularism while salvaging as much as possible of Joseph's work. To soothe the clergy he suppressed the reformed liturgy, dissolved new seminaries, handed back to the monks management of their own cloisters, promised to abolish no more monasteries, left control over schools to the bishops, and re-established tithes. He did not, however, return what had already been secularized, or restrict religious tolerance, or modify the state's independent stand towards the papacy. Yet by restoring the *Landtags*, Hungary's constitution, the administrative districts called *comitats*, and even the traditional institutions of Belgium, he re-established chaotic diversity in his lands. At the same time he put an end to fiscal and agrarian reform. The manorial regime was secured, despite agrarian outbreaks in Bohemia and Hungary. Only abolition of personal serfdom remained.

Governments of other Catholic countries took up defensive stands. In December of 1790 Bavaria renewed its measures against the Illuminati and tightened censorship, even banning the Paris *Moniteur*. During the same year the king of Sardinia advised Masonic lodges to stop meeting, and Joseph de Maistre converted his friend Costa de Beauregard to the ranks of reaction. By ordering prayer and fasting for the welfare of the Church the pope indicated censure of all dissidents, which snuffed out what timid support had been given the Revolution in Italy. Journals and academies denounced without distinction all Freemasons, Jansenists, and liberals. Many Frenchmen were arrested or deported. Yet there were in Italy, as in Germany, rulers such as the duke of Tuscany who did not favour repression. In Spain, on the other hand, Florida Blanca and the Inquisition joined forces in 1789 to seize books and newspapers from France, open letters, and search imported goods. Jovellanos was exiled; Campomanes withdrew from the Council of Castile. All Frenchmen were kept under close watch; some, like Cabarrus, were imprisoned, more were expelled. A similar situation prevailed in Portugal. Officials tightened existing repressive laws when a French citizen whose motive has never been discovered wounded Florida Blanca on June 18, 1790. In March of 1791 the government stationed a cordon of troops along the Pyrenees to halt the 'French plague'.

Burke would have liked to see all the great powers take equally firm measures and wanted England to assume the lead in a peaceful blockade that would restrain propaganda. These steps he thought should be only a beginning. Against a nation returned to barbarism he preached a crusade. Soon Baron Grimm and Zimmermann, a Swiss doctor who had become a nobleman and a councillor in Hanover, repeated his call in Germany. Once Pius had formally condemned the Revolution's principles, in the spring of 1791, could kings fail to speak out and defend their own cause against new unbelievers? The question was well taken.

## LOUIS XVI AND THE ÉMIGRÉS: APPEAL TO FOREIGN POWERS

It was a question asked not only by polemicists and for reasons of state. The émigrés publicly, Louis XVI privately, implored rulers to proceed with active steps. At Turin, Artois had personally entreated the king of Sardinia and dispatched the comte de Vaudreuil first to Rome and then to Madrid. In May of 1791 he approached Leopold at Mantua. Appealing primarily for funds, he also demanded military intervention to support uprisings instigated in southern France. The next month he settled down with Madame de Polastron at the castle of Schönbornbust on the domain of his uncle, the elector of Trèves. While his extravagant and dissipated entourage enjoyed itself, émigrés who wanted to engage in military action were unable to obtain the bare necessities at Worms, where the prince de Condé assembled them. Calonne, who became minister to Condé at the end of 1790, did not neglect the emperor but counted more on Prussia, and offered England alliance with France as well as some French colony. With Condé's army to clear the way for foreign troops, invading forces would restore the Old Regime. The émigrés voiced horrible threats against their compatriots, using terms of scorn for a sovereign who docilely bore the Assembly's yoke.

Louis's obedience was in fact illusory. The fear of a new 'day' drove him to practise a duplicity that ultimately denied him respect from any quarter, but in a personal communication to his relation Charles of Spain, in November of 1789, he repudiated the concessions that had been imposed on him; and Marie Antoinette repeated endlessly to her friend, the Swedish count Axel de Fersen, and to the Austrian ambassador, the comte de Mercy-Argenteau, varying expressions of the hatred she bore Lafayette and the constitutionalists. The abbé de Fontbrune, who took the king's protestations to Madrid, was also charged to find out what aid Spain would promise and to ask for money. In 1790 Fontbrune again set out, this time for Vienna. Leopold succeeded

Joseph in February. Both were Marie Antoinette's brothers; a third ruled the archbishopric of Cologne; one of their sisters governed the Netherlands; another reigned at Naples. Nevertheless, Fontbrune received nothing more than pleasant words. This was at the end of June, too early for the Civil Constitution of the Clergy to bear responsibility for Louis's appeal to foreign powers. If we concede that religious scruples later reinforced his decision, other motives confirmed that choice of action: the administrative organization set up by the Constituent was beginning to function, and the ministers he appointed were departing one by one. He had to admit that the Revolution was not merely another Fronde. When in October the bishop of Pamiers, d'Agoult, having already emigrated, urged him to act, he had no difficulty in convincing Louis. The baron de Breteuil received full powers and assumed leadership of the secret project, with authority to accredit agents in foreign courts. Louis had resolved to flee. He ordered the marquis de Bouillé, conqueror of Nancy and commander at Metz, to make preparations for receiving him. In December Fersen began to arrange for the escape.

Louis and Marie Antoinette were proceeding at cross purposes with émigré diplomacy. A serious quarrel broke out between Artois and the marquis de Bombelles, ambassador to Venice, who was tending to the count's affairs at the expense of his ordinary ambassadorial duties but also obeyed the king's secret orders. Louis and his queen openly accused those who had fled France of having abandoned the royal family and compromised its safety by planning rash and premature enterprises; moreover, they were afraid of being thrown upon the mercy of a victorious aristocracy. To an invasion from Condé's troops they preferred a concert of the powers, which would order the Assembly to revise its decrees as Louis required and would back up threats with a demonstration of military force on the frontier. Louis, installed at Montmédy, would act as mediator and retain full control over events. Although he insisted that he did not want foreign forces to enter France, the queen, if not Louis, thought that monarchs who committed themselves to a concert would not hesitate to order invasion should the Assembly balk. France would, of course, bear the cost of foreign aid: reimbursement stood to reason. Louis did not wish to give up any of his provinces, but on the advice of Bouillé he ordered, in

May of 1791, that England be offered some colonial morsel in return for neutrality.

Rulers abroad were divided between Louis and the émigrés. Catherine welcomed the refugees warmly and enthusiastically supported a crusade without mercy—'To destroy French anarchy is to prepare one's immortal glory.' Gustavus of Sweden shared her views, and in the spring of 1791 settled as a sort of advance guard at Spa and at Aix-la-Chapelle. Victor Amadeus of Sardinia, like the pope, appeared to side with Artois. With a great show of chivalry Frederick William seemed burning to assist Louis, but he also listened to the émigrés, as did his helpmate Bischoffswerder and the Prussian court clique. In Spain, Florida Blanca held the émigrés aloof, judging them both costly and compromising. The emperor brushed aside any suggestions of co-operating with them. In January of 1791 he refused to see Calonne, then ordered him out of Vienna; in May he packed Artois off to Mantua. In England, king, ministers, and Parliament agreed that regardless of their own feelings they would not intervene unless national interest required it. When he spoke to his countrymen of a crusade Burke was preaching in the wilderness.

The friends of the émigrés were more spirited in opposing the Revolution, but, lacking the emperor's support, they were helpless. While Catherine urged others on, she was resolved not to follow. Frederick received the baron de Roll favourably in August of 1791 and in September made his first overtures to Vienna, but could make no definite commitment without Austria. Leopold seemed to be the natural leader of any coalition against France, considering the locality of his states and the relation he bore to Marie Antoinette, yet he was the least warlike of European sovereigns. After his own reforms in Tuscany, most of those passed by the Constituent inspired no horror in him; moreover, he considered restoration of the Old Regime in France neither possible nor practical. Of course he would under no circumstances vacate his own authority, but that the king of France was weakened did not discountenance him. And, finally, he had his hands full with settling the imperial estate left by his brother. Under these combined pressures he gave no encouragement to his brother-in-law, preferring that Louis come to terms with the constitutionalists, and he let matters drag out, offering as excuse the slowness of other powers, their disagreements, and the enigmatic attitude of England. The correspondence of Marie Antoinette and of Ambassador Núñez outlines the course of pitiful alternatives and fruitless efforts that the royal family, itself divided (Madame Elisabeth and the king's aunts favoured the émigrés), carried on month after month. The queen accused other monarchs and especially her brother of egoism and blindness. Since the Revolutionary period, many have tried to show that rulers outside France actually harboured no aggressive intentions—thus attributing full responsibility to the Revolution. In fact, Leopold was not unresponsive either to the danger that lay in propaganda or to the duties required by blood ties and monarchical solidarity. But like other sovereigns he thought— not without reason—that for the time being he had nothing to fear from the French Revolution. Forced to reconquer Belgium, to appease Hungary and end the Turkish war, he judged that before shouldering the burdens of Louis XVI he had the right and the duty to dispose of his own.

## THE FOREIGN POLICY OF THE CONSTITUENT ASSEMBLY

As it happened, conflicts of public law and territorial order rose between European monarchs and revolutionary France. The German princes who still held lands in Alsace found their interests endangered by abolition of manorial rights and appealed to the Imperial Diet under terms of the Westphalian treaties. The French bishops of Strasbourg and Verdun were not averse to following their example, but Avignon and its surrounding territory, the Comtat, took an opposite course. They renounced the Old Regime and ran headlong into conflict with the pope. On June 12, 1790, Avignon asked to be reunited with France; Carpentras, capital of the Comtat, was satisfied to adopt the French constitution but did not reckon on the pope's disapproval. When the Constituent failed to take a clear stand, war broke out between Avignon and Carpentras. Meanwhile, aristocrats and Patriots within Avignon came to blows.

These two struggles led the Revolution to draw from its principles a new international law, foreshadowed as early as 1789 when Corsica was admitted as a department of France. In November of 1790 the Constituent Assembly replied to the German princes, through the voice of Merlin de Douai, that Alsace was French not because the treaties of 1648 had ceded it to Louis XIV but because the Alsatians had certified, specifically by participating in the Federation, their desire to remain united with their compatriots. The Revolution thus liberated nations just as it liberated man and the citizen; it even called national entities into being. Hitherto only states had possessed legality; men followed the soil as it was conquered or ceded. On May 22, 1790, the Constituent Assembly formally renounced the right of conquest, declaring that man's will, freely expressed, was to determine the destiny of the soil. The territorial and dynastic state yielded to the nation. Following this principle, the left moved that Avignon be annexed, in view of the wishes expressed by its inhabitants. In May of 1791 a bare majority voted down the proposal. The Assembly decided to occupy Avignon and the Comtat to restore order and to consult the population. Union with France was finally voted in September. By then the pope had issued appeals to all Europe. Monarchs thought that this new international law was obviously calculated to benefit France by permitting it to annex, peacefully and at no cost, any territory whose inhabitants wished to start their own revolution, challenging their rulers. All treaties were torn up, all legal bonds between France and Europe broken. These possibilities naturally aroused indignation in diplomats and sovereigns.

Statesmen were not, however, contented with words. The issues concerning Alsace and Avignon would constitute an excuse to declare war should that course seem desirable, but they were not in themselves vital to the great powers. Only if French forces had remained intact would there have been any serious threat, and France had neither army, navy, money, nor virtually any alliance left. The claims of the revolutionaries were pathetic: they would be brought to their knees in one day.

The Constituent did seem to be afraid of war—on principle, no doubt, but also because open struggle would strengthen the king's position. The Assembly had turned away appeals from the Belgian Estates-General, and even though it denied passage to Austrian troops, it let them occupy the bishopric of Basel. After repudiating in principle the rights of the German princes it offered them an indemnity—Louis barely had time to send Augeard to keep the princes from accepting the offer—and postponed union with Avignon as long as possible. In May of 1790, to prevent the king from forcing its hand, the Assembly made his right to declare war subject to legislative approval; and although the constitution gave him control over foreign affairs, the Constituents formed a diplomatic committee on August 1. Finally, since alliances concluded under the Old Regime might involve the new France in disputes against its will, it preferred isolation instead. The Habsburg alliance died from natural causes, since the emperor no longer valued a powerless France, and also from a revival of the anti-Austrian tradition, which was fed by hatred towards the queen and which had been passed on to the revolutionaries in the works of Favier. That hatred made them turn towards Prussia, and Goltz, its ambassador, with Ephraïm, Frederick William's secret agent, stimulated French hopes for rapprochement. Even the émigrés followed this strong tradition by courting Prussia, as we have seen. The Spanish alliance had permitted France to defeat England during the recent American war and was not as objectionable as the Austrian one, but the Constituent let it lapse too. It is true that many revolutionaries regarded England sympathetically, and naturally financiers and merchants, Talleyrand among them, were Anglophiles. When in May of 1790 Spain, threatened by Pitt, invoked the family compact, as the Bourbon alliance was termed, the Assembly ended by voting on August 26 to arm forty-five ships. At the same time, however, it pronounced the dynastic agreement invalid: a new one would be negotiated to unite the two nations. The implications were not lost. Alliance between France and Spain was dead. Pitt's agents Miles and Elliot, who had rebuked and probably paid Mirabeau, congratulated themselves.

France's impotence seemed quite evident. Throughout history, it was remarked, this had always been the result of revolutions. Wisdom commanded rulers to leave the nation to its own devices while pursuing their plans as usual. There would always be time to restore the authority of a king who could, after all, thwart their designs.

## EUROPEAN POLITICS

In its early years the French Revolution did not monopolize European attention, because Europe seemed to be on the verge of a general war. Joseph, allied with Catherine since 1782, had ended by yielding to the temptation of the 'Greek project', a plan to restore the Byzantine Empire under Catherine's grandson and to create the Dacia that Potemkin had long anticipated. The project would grant Austria the Serbian provinces of the Ottoman Empire plus the territorial possessions of Venice. By uniting Austria with Lombardy, this would advance the Habsburg conquest of Italy, a goal that since 1715 had been a leading Austrian ambition.

Neither Vergennes nor Pitt approved the dismemberment of Turkey. France enjoyed a privileged position there; Pitt wanted to keep the Russians away from the Mediterranean Sea and routes to India. But the Stadholder, during his struggle with the burghers, had in 1787 appealed to England and Prussia for help. Prussia invaded the United Provinces and Pitt took this opportunity to restore the lustre of British diplomacy by alienating the Provinces from France, indicating that he would intervene if the French army challenged the Prussians. At that time Brienne was battling with the parlements, and Montmorin, who succeeded Vergennes when the minister died, gave in. Re-established, the Stadholder strengthened his authority and joined a Triple Alliance with Prussia and England. This disaster, which helped considerably to undermine the prestige of the monarchy in France, convinced Joseph that his ally claimed no role in Eastern affairs; in any case, he ruled out the possibility of an entente among Western powers.

Furthermore, if domestic affairs paralysed France, Pitt had his own share of troubles at home. In 1788 George III went insane and his son demanded the power to rule through a regency. The prince was a sorry figure, but it seemed difficult to refuse him. Pitt nevertheless maintained that the choice of regent belonged to Parliament and, without openly depriving the prince of power, had a bill passed to limit his authority. Pitt's reputation for having maintained the parliamentary system in spite of George III is in part due to this incident. In fact, he was skilled in responding to the king's wishes and was determined to obstruct both the prince, who certainly would have dismissed him, and Fox, his natural successor. These long disputes proved to be a waste of time: the king regained his sanity in February of 1789 and Pitt stayed in power. In the interval a European crisis had begun.

In August, 1788, the Turks, long irritated, moved forward, and the war turned in their favour. The Russians were unable to take the port of

Ochakov, which controlled access to the Dnieper and Bug Rivers; the Austrians fared worse, being defeated before Belgrade and forced to retreat, allowing the Turks to overrun the Banat. The Turkish forces ultimately weakened. Laudon took Belgrade, and Suvarov won Ochakov. But the Greek project nevertheless seemed a failure. Moreover, Joseph's resounding defeat had encouraged his subjects to revolt; the multi-national empire seemed already crumbling when the death of its ruler (February, 1790) introduced new possibilities of disruption.

Sweden and Prussia took advantage of these combined circumstances. Sweden attacked Russia and had advanced to the gates of St. Petersburg when its own nobility came to Catherine's rescue, utilizing the moment to snatch power from Gustavus, whereupon many Swedish officers refused to serve their king. In a subsequent coup d'état, however, Gustavus not only recovered but enhanced his position. The war was renewed, and the Swedes, defeated on land, were victorious at sea in 1790. Meanwhile Prussia seized the opportunity to prejudice Austria by backing the rebellion at Liége in 1789 and by fomenting intrigue in Belgium. It did not want Russia to dominate the Baltic— neither did Pitt, for that matter, considering that British and Dutch trade ruled unchallenged there. As a result the Danes found themselves forbidden to intervene against Sweden. However, Prussia decided that if Austria and Russia were expanding at Turkey's expense, it deserved to be compensated with Polish territory. Catherine, having occupied Poland since the partition, turned a deaf ear to any such proposal. The Prussians then encouraged the Polish aristocracy to revolt by promising an alliance. A party of Patriots was at that time growing in Poland. It improved the educational system, concentrated on stimulating an awakening national sentiment, and had just attempted to end anarchy by suppressing the liberum veto. Catherine's puppet king, Stanislas Poniatowski, did negotiate a treaty that would have sent as much as had been allowed to remain of the army of the 'republic' against Turkey. But when the Diet, which for this purpose had to be a full session, convened in September of 1788, the Patriots had listened to Frederick William's deceptive offers and were unwilling to assist Russia. In May of 1789 they demanded that the occupation troops leave. Everyone expected Prussia then to take matters in hand, thinking that its statesmen had not only a grand plan but the means to carry it out. The outcome, on the contrary, proved the mediocrity of Prussian leaders and composed a worthy prologue to the lamentable venture of 1792.

Prussia was in fact wavering between two policies. According to the 'Grand Design' that Herzberg presented to his king in May of 1789, Austria, being rewarded in Turkey, would restore Galicia to the Poles, who in turn would cede Danzig, Torun, and Posen to Frederick William. Herzberg thought a few military demonstrations sufficient to assure these exchanges. The king, either less credulous or more warlike, instead had visions of detaching the Netherlands from Austria and perhaps of taking Bohemia for himself. Inciting the Belgians and Hungarians and counting on England, he massed an army in Silesia in August, 1789; then, just when decision and boldness were needed, he postponed military action to the following spring. In the interim Joseph died and the alliance with England foundered.

Pitt valued the Prussian alliance because it curbed Russia and could aid him in the Netherlands. But he was not concerned with territorial aggrandizement, especially if it had to be won at the price of armed struggle. Holland was even more peaceably inclined, having lent huge sums to Catherine. Dissolution of the Austrian monarchy alarmed both countries because it would destroy the continental balance and direct a newly independent Belgium into the French orbit. They wanted to restore the status quo. Pitt, moreover, had his eyes on the sea and on colonial areas: administrator and financier above all, he did not want war. But he was capable of bold action when he sensed that an adversary was willing to yield, and the victors of the American wars were natural targets. In 1787 he had made France back down and had gained a stake in Holland. In 1790 Spain received similar treatment: the question of who controlled the bay of Nootka Sound, on the Pacific coast north of California, had long been contested, and when Spain seized several English ships there, Pitt demanded reparation. In May, 1790, he armed his forces. England then commanded ninety-three ships of the line; Spain had thirty-four. France being weakened, Madrid revoked the seizure and, under an ultimatum, surrendered the bay on October 24. Thus occupied, Pitt understandably informed the Prussians throughout that year that their plans did not fall under terms of the alliance.

Pitt would none the less have found it difficult to restrain Frederick William if the Prussian king had chosen to profit from Joseph's death.

Since Frederick William did nothing about it, the prime minister had time to reach an understanding with Leopold that allowed Pitt to act as mediator. The new emperor had fewer alarming ideas than his brother. In order to save Austria and still guard what he could of Turkish conquests, he first had to isolate Prussia. When in April the English offered their good offices on the basis of the status quo ante bellum, Leopold hastened to accept. In addition he distinguished between the simple status quo and an 'improved' status. For the latter he did not object to negotiations with Prussia. Kaunitz was against this, but Leopold had his own 'secret': the vice-chancellor, Philip Cobenzl, and the chief clerk, Spielmann, worked with him despite the 'old papa'. The conference opened at Reichenbach, in Silesia, where 170,000 Prussians faced 150,000 Austrians. Herzberg reworked his proposal to conciliate everyone: Austria would return no more than one-sixth of Galicia and would relinquish a proportionate part of its Turkish conquests; Prussia would be satisfied with Danzig and Torun. The English immediately disapproved; the Poles protested. Disturbed, Frederick William suddenly renounced any territorial gain, and Spielmann, greatly annoyed, had to accept the simple status quo on July 27.

Leopold in fact won everything he wanted by these arrangements. In June he made peace with the Magyar aristocracy. In November his army entered Belgium. At the beginning of December, Brussels and Liége fell to him. The Triple Alliance, meeting at The Hague on December 10, forced him to grant an amnesty and guarantee provincial privileges, but he did not ratify the convention. He carried on negotiations with the Turks at Sistova, but nothing was decided. The Austrian state was regaining its position. To Prussian eyes this spelled disaster.

Another setback was in preparation. Catherine, in turn called upon to accept mediation, had fully expected the request and, noting that Leopold was withdrawing from the game, made peace with Gustavus. Suvarov had been victorious at Focsani in 1789 and reached the Danube, then won Ismailia on December 22, where he ordered a horrible massacre of the garrison and of the town population. Catherine refused to compromise. When Prussia gave her to understand that it was ready to reach an agreement, this very nearly resulted in Polish dismemberment. On March 26, 1791, a dispatch was sent to Berlin proposing a second partition. All counter-revolutionary action would have taken another course had the offer been accepted, but the dispatch arrived too late.

Frederick William, chafing in uncertainty, grew more concerned. His court clique advised him to draw closer to Austria and thus isolate Catherine. He too now had his 'secret': Bischoffswerder, neglecting to inform Herzberg of his activity, made an initial offer to Leopold in September of 1790 and returned to Vienna the following February. Leopold did not want to quarrel with Russia, but thought it politic to handle Prussia carefully. He listened to the king's minion but promised nothing. This was, however, enough for the credulous and muddle-headed Bischoffswerder, who upon his return assured Frederick William that Austria would remain neutral if open conflict broke out. On March 11 the king summoned England to announce its stand on coercive action against Russia.

Pitt, having first humiliated France and Spain and then saved Austria, was reaching his zenith. The English fleet was still mobilized, and Whitworth, ambassador to St. Petersburg, assured him that Russia was exhausted. Pitt's previous bluffs having succeeded, he was evidently overconfident. Ewart, his ambassador to Berlin, pressed him to link Sweden, Poland, Turkey, and Prussia in a league that, under the aegis of England, would block Russian expansion permanently. Pitt let himself be persuaded. On March 21–22 the cabinet decided to send an ultimatum to Catherine. It was hastily seconded by Prussia. But Pitt had not taken the Whigs into account. With the complicity of Vorontzov, Russia's representative, they stirred up opposition to a war of this nature, arguing that England supplied three-quarters of Russia's imports and that it hardly seemed fitting to back the Turks, who were France's clients and were unbelievers besides, against Catherine. At that time Pitt was the only one to foresee danger concerning routes to India. His majority in the Commons crumbled; the cabinet split. By April 6, in the interests of his office, he was resigned to retracting the proposal and found a way to save face through the intervention of the Danish minister, Bernstorff, who offered assurance that Catherine would consent to remain behind the Dniester. Ewart returned to Potsdam on April 20 to notify Prussia that England was backing out. Catherine triumphantly announced that the barking dog did not always bite and agreed in the treaty of Jassy (January 9, 1792) to keep Ochakov and abide by the Dniester line.

This time Prussia was not the only wounded party: Poland felt that it had been handed over to Catherine's vengeance. Against this threat the king and Patriot leaders—Stanislas and John Potocki, Malachovski, Kollontai, and Czartoryski—buried their differences. On May 3, 1791, they passed through the Diet a new constitution abolishing the *liberum veto* and setting up a limited monarchy that granted royal succession to the elector of Saxony's daughter. It was obvious that Poland lacked time to prepare its defences and that Russia would again occupy the country. This prospect appeared catastrophic to Prussia and Austria, who drew together once more, this time decisively. Herzberg being in disgrace, Bischoffswerder gained consent on May 12 to treat with Leopold, and on June 11 met with the emperor at Milan. Leopold accepted alliance and promised to make peace with the Turks. It was agreed that the two rulers would meet at Pillnitz, in Saxony. In exchange Leopold asked Prussia to join him in recognizing the Polish constitution, including the proposed Saxon succession. The final treaty, which was supposed to be signed at Vienna, seemed to pit the two German powers against Russia. But their agreement rested on an equivocation: Leopold wanted to save Poland; Frederick William hoped to partition it. To Frederick the Polish alliance had lost all value when the Diet, on September 6, 1790, forbade cession of any part of national territory. The Polish constitution was to him even more worthless because it risked reviving the country. By separating Austria from Russia he planned to press Catherine towards a new partition—all things considered, events could follow the same course as in 1772: Austria would yield, and the restored Triple Alliance could throw its whole force against France. But already counter-revolutionary plans were entering into European politics: before settling the Polish question the two German courts incautiously committed themselves in the West—an act that benefited Catherine most and doomed their coalition to failure before it was formed.

On the morrow of its defeat at Reichenbach, Prussia drew up the first proposals for intervention in France. Frederick William posed two conditions—Austria's co-operation, and compensation for war expenses: Bavaria would cede him Jülich and Berg and would recoup its losses, as would Leopold, in Alsace and Lorraine. This idea led to the first overtures to Austria in September 1790. Undeniably, the personal feelings of the impulsive Prussian king towards Louis XVI and some of the émigrés contributed to this initiative, but his defeat at Reichenbach, by an odd twist, made counter-revolution seem revenge. It would procure for him both an ally to replace England and the territory necessary to his personal glory. New difficulties in the East later made these prospects seem all the more inviting. In February of 1791 Bischoffswerder again told the emperor that Prussia would follow him against France. He repeated this at Milan in June.

Leopold at first did not respond. On May 18, as we have seen, he sent the comte d'Artois off to Mantua. The fact that Catherine kept advising him to invade France was one more reason for postponement. Suddenly, at Milan, he welcomed Bischoffswerder's offers. The possibility of counter-revolutionary action formed one basis of their agreement. This was because he had just received a letter from Marie Antoinette telling him of her imminent flight from France. Leopold's indifference has been exaggerated. He would wisely have preferred to abstain and thus keep out of crossfire, but if the royal couple's position were threatened he had no doubt that his duty was to aid them. This attitude placed him at the mercy of Louis's discretion: by escaping, the French king forced Leopold's hand.

# 12

---

# FLIGHT OF THE KING AND DECLARATION OF WAR AGAINST AUSTRIA, JUNE, 1791–APRIL, 1792

The flight of Louis XVI was one of the most important events of the time—for Europe as well as for the Revolution. There was no doubt in France that Europe's kings opposed the Revolution, yet their involvement in other affairs would have permitted it to continue its work in peace for at least a while longer. The initiative of Louis XVI himself precipitated the conflict that brought his downfall.

## THE FLIGHT TO VARENNES AND ITS CONSEQUENCES IN FRANCE

During the several months that Fersen had been preparing for the royal family's escape, indiscretions could not be avoided. Marat among others kept predicting that the king would flee. On the evening of June 20 Bailly, somewhat worried, sent Lafayette to inspect the Tuileries. The general reported the palace well guarded, but at that very moment the fugitives were making good their escape. As a result of what negligence or what complicity? This point is the most important and, unfortunately, the most obscure of the whole affair.[1]

A massive, sumptuously furnished berlin coach carried Louis and his family along the road to Châlons, from which they were to go on to Montmédy, the final destination. Bouillé had set himself up at Stenay and from there had stationed detachments at intervals along the king's route to a point beyond Sainte-Menehould. But the berlin fell five hours behind schedule. The fears that had broken out repeatedly in eastern France since 1789 had made the populace nervous and defiant. Disconcerted, military commanders along the way abandoned their posts. Late that night the king reached the top of the hill outside Varennes and, failing to find the expected relay, halted. That was his downfall.

He had taken few pains to conceal his presence, but of those who recognized him no one dared act save Drouet, the posting master of Sainte-Menehould, whose quick initiative forced the hand of fate. Riding at top speed, he overtook the halted berlin, then went on into Varennes and ordered the bridge over the Aire, at the other side of the town, barricaded. When the king finally drew up he was stopped, and admitted his identity. Clanging bells called out the peasants. The hussars who rushed to the spot began to fraternize with the crowd. When day broke Lafayette's messengers appeared with orders from the Assembly. The party had to return to Paris. Their journey back was tragic: threatening crowds surrounded the coach and the comte de Dampierre, who came to greet the king, was murdered by a group of peasants. On June 25 the royal family re-entered the Tuileries under heavy guard.

The Assembly set an example of composure. After suspending the king and abolishing his veto, it gave orders to his ministers and to all purposes organized France as a republic, then returned to the business of the day. But a wave of feeling coursed through the nation, reaching far into the provinces. No one doubted that the king's flight heralded

[1] Historians who have treated the episode say nothing about this matter. In his *Mémoires* (2 vols., Paris, 1929), the comte de Saint-Priest explains that Lafayette had left one entrance to the Tuileries unguarded so that Fersen could have free access to the queen's rooms (Vol. II, pp. 91–93).

invasion. Garrisons along the frontier spontaneously prepared for siege, and as early as June 21 the Assembly ordered 169 infantry battalions drawn up from the National Guard. Again a 'great fear' and its attendant consequences swept France. The short-lived joy of the aristocrats provoked punitive reaction; nobles and refractory priests were often molested, chateaux went up in flames. But was not Louis himself now the worst enemy? With one outburst the people demanded that he be brought back—as hostage, not as king.

In Paris, news of the flight provoked a storm of invective, sometimes coarse, against the king and queen. Republicans exulted. 'At last we are free and kingless,' the Cordeliers announced in their proclamation. Hoping to sweep the democrats along with them, on June 21 they asked the Constituent to proclaim the republic or, failing that, to do nothing before consulting the primary assemblies. Brissot, Bonneville, and, on July 8, the marquis de Condorcet came out in favour of the republic. Among the provincial clubs, several expressed more or less similar feelings. But the king's return and the Assembly's attitude stemmed the tide, and, moreover, not all democrats agreed with the clubs: a republic without universal suffrage and with Lafayette as president was not what Robespierre wanted. Several men still looked to the duc d'Orléans; Marat, as usual, demanded a dictator. Robespierre insisted that action should stop with trial of the king and prompt elections to the Legislative Assembly to replace a Constituent that had become suspect.

The National Assembly, resolute, turned away all petitions. Proclamation of the republic meant certain war; it also meant opening the way to democracy, encouraging the mute peasant rebellion, and inciting strikes such as those which had frightened the bourgeoisie in the spring. The Constituent voluntarily took its stand at the beginning by denouncing the 'abduction of the king', thus inventing a piece of fiction that absolved him from blame. The triumvirs and Lafayette made peace, and on the evening of June 21 Barnave gave the watchword to the Jacobins: 'The constitution is our guide, the National Assembly our rallying point.' The Revolution is ended, he would soon tell the Assembly; beyond lies disruption of society. To prevent the electoral assemblies, which had already been arranged for, from passing resolutions in favour of the Republic, the Assembly postponed elections. When the king returned, Duport and Barnave prompted him in whispers, and Barnave started a secret correspondence with the queen; Louis recognized that he had misunderstood the attitude of Frenchmen and indicated that he would accept the constitution. Two decrees of July 15 and 16 arraigned the authors of the 'abduction' and exonerated the sovereigns.

But on the evening of July 15 the Jacobins, invaded by a crowd from the Social Circle headed by the Cordeliers, agreed to sign a new petition requesting the Assembly to replace Louis—'by all constitutional means', added Brissot, who drafted the text the next day. On the Champ-de-Mars, where they gathered to sign the request, the Cordeliers protested Brissot's amendment, which could benefit only the duc d'Orléans. The matter was referred to the Jacobins. Having just received the decree absolving the king, they repudiated the whole idea of a petition. Robespierre approved this decision, but the Cordeliers insisted and, on July 1, went ahead with their rally. A new text was drawn up on the Champ-de-Mars, upon the Altar of the Fatherland.

The crowd was unarmed, and in any case insurrection was doomed: the National Guard, composed only of the bourgeoisie, showed intense hostility towards 'the rabble'. But repeated petitions had provoked rowdy demonstrations that gradually mobilized workers from the recently disbanded labour centres. Threats and serious incidents were reported; that morning, when the new petition was signed, two men discovered under the Altar of the Fatherland were murdered. Bailly and Lafayette, encouraged by the Constituent, resolved to make an example. The red flag of martial law was hoisted. National Guardsmen invaded the Champ-de-Mars and opened fire. A number of petitioners were killed or wounded. In a fit of excess those who drew up the petition were accused of conspiracy, many new prisoners were taken, and several democratic newspapers were suppressed. The Cordeliers suspended their sessions briefly. Schism threatened to break up the Jacobins when most of the deputies left to start a new club, called the Feuillants. Robespierre was almost the only member who kept his head, and ended by preserving the society. The Patriot party was nevertheless cut into two parts: one the constitutionalists, those bourgeois who passed the electoral property qualifications and who, to maintain their compromise achievement, showed an inclination to reach some sort of agreement with the king and the Blacks; the other the democrats, among whom republicans were to assume more and more influence. Between them lay the blood spilled on the Champ-de-Mars and the 'tricoloured' terror.

Masters of the situation, Duport, Barnave, and the Lameths tried to rally the right to constitutional revision, proposing that royal power be increased, electoral qualifications raised, a second house created, the nobility re-established, and deputies permitted to be re-elected and accept ministerial portfolios. This effort achieved nothing substantial: the Blacks would not compromise at all, and some of the Patriots balked at so many concessions. Louis, however, resigned himself to accepting the constitution and was restored to his position. But there could no longer be any illusion as to his true feelings. Varennes had 'torn the veil aside'.

## THE DECLARATION OF PILLNITZ, AUGUST 27, 1791

Throughout Europe news of the king's arrest stirred passionate response, and, especially in England, shocked those loyal to the throne. Sovereigns paused to reflect on their own conduct. 'What a horrible example!' cried the king of Prussia. Spain intervened first with a threatening note dispatched by Florida Blanca on July 1. When Montmorin and Ambassador Núñez, equally concerned, softened its tone, Núñez was rebuked and called home. Charles did not insist, however: he turned upon the French residents in Spain, whom he summoned on July 20 to take an oath to him under penalty of expulsion.

All eyes turned to the emperor. Leopold was stunned by the king's capture but acted without hesitation. From Padua he issued a proposal on July 6 that the courts act in concert to save the royal family and the French monarchy, and on August 4 he signed a peace treaty with the Turks at Sistova. The Imperial Diet stirred once again and pronounced itself in favour of intervention on behalf of the German princes harmed by the Revolution. Bischoffswerder rejoiced to see Leopold now inclined to take the offensive and, without asking for authorization, signed, on July 25 at Vienna, the agreement arranged at Milan. Frederick William ratified it on August 12 over the protests of his ministers, then set out for Pillnitz with a staff of officers—and no diplomats.

Leopold, however, was already growing more moderate. The replies he received were not encouraging. From England, George responded that despite his concern for Louis XVI he would remain neutral. Charles of Spain and Victor Amadeus of Sardinia were waiting for Austria to start the war so they would avoid the initial fighting. Only Catherine of Russia and Gustavus of Sweden warmly agreed to concerted action. Leopold well knew that the Russian army, before fighting the French, would occupy Poland, and Prussia's designs on Poland disturbed him. In June, Frederick William had informed the Poles that their alliance of 1790 did not guarantee the constitution, which had been adopted before that date, and on August 9 he protested to the Austrians that he could not explain his views on the constitution so long as Russia remained silent.

Had the Constituent dethroned Louis, Leopold would have gone further, but the prudent moderation of the Assembly left him time to reflect on his own interests. On July 11 Barnave, Duport, Lameth, and Lafayette told Mercy, now the emperor's representative at Brussels, that a motion absolving Louis was about to be debated and warned him that if the European powers made matters worse they would expose their subjects to 'the contagious example of a dethroned king'. On July 30 they dictated to the queen a letter advising Leopold to keep peace. Then they sent the abbé Louis off to persuade Mercy to return to Paris.

The queen, it is true, privately repudiated her letter on the same day. 'By lulling them to sleep, by giving them confidence, we can better outsmart them later,' she wrote again on August 26. 'Now our only resources lie in the hands of foreign powers; they must at any cost come to our aid, but it rests with the emperor to take the lead.' Leopold found it wiser, for Louis and for himself, to accept the offers advanced by the Feuillants. On August 20 he made it known that the European powers would recognize the constitution accepted by Louis. At Pillnitz, Frederick William had to stop preaching armed intervention.

From that time on, wisdom commanded silence; a threat stipulating certain conditions could only bring the downfall of the Feuillants. That was just what the comte d'Artois wanted, and neither Leopold nor Kaunitz saw the trap. On the contrary, thinking that a manifesto would intimidate conspirators and enhance the authority of the constitutionalists, the two sovereigns decided to publish a declaration on

August 27. Re-establishment of order in France being a European concern, it stated, other monarchs were invited to join forces with them; 'then, and in that case', they would take action. Since England for one would still refuse to join the concert, Leopold kept his hands free. 'Then, and in that case,' he said, 'are for me the law and the prophets.' He was none the less satisfied when the Jacobins took fright, and he let the French princes interpret the declaration as an ultimatum.

On September 14 Louis accepted the constitution and by that act was restored to the throne. On September 30 the Constituent adjourned. Leopold was satisfied with the king's decision and dispelled any illusions that Marie Antoinette might still harbour. 'How terrible,' she wrote, 'that the emperor has betrayed us.' On December 3 Louis wrote the king of Prussia personally to ask help against his rebellious subjects. Frederick William declared himself incapable of taking action by himself. Leopold had not lost sight of the Prussian alliance: in November he reopened negotiations for a conclusive agreement. But he had to extract from Russia a guarantee of the new situation in Poland.

Meanwhile, convinced that he had saved Louis by intimidating the Constituent, the emperor continued the threats intended to restrain agitators. A circular of November 12 invited the ruling heads to reconsider forming a coalition. As the declaration of Pillnitz circulated across the continent it convinced most readers that the great powers would open war in the spring. It grew increasingly evident that Jacobin sentiment ran quite contrary to Leopold's design—instead of cringing before him they called his bluff, upsetting all his plans.

It has become a commonplace to damn the Jacobins for being either inept or foolish. Why didn't they rely on diplomats, who might have explained the rules of the game? Perhaps they should have. But they had good reason to believe the Revolution threatened. Especially by Prussia, it is true, and in this respect they were badly mistaken; still, once the Polish affair was settled, Leopold could turn upon them. Besides, the French knew nothing of court secrets and naturally interpreted the declaration as did the émigrés, an interpretation which the authors of the manifesto did not discourage. Lastly, it should not be forgotten that any threat of intervention, even if mild, was an offence. Caution perhaps advised that the declaration be ignored, but no nation would have pardoned it.

## THE LEGISLATIVE ASSEMBLY AND GIRONDIST POLICY, OCTOBER–DECEMBER, 1791

After the Champ-de-Mars incident the Feuillants appeared to be masters in France. No one any longer talked about a republic; Collot d'Herbois was free to publish his royalist *Almanach du père Gérard*. When the Legislative Assembly convened on October 1, 1791, the great majority of its members were sincere constitutionalists. Duport, Barnave, and Lameth thought they were guiding the king and queen and selected several ministers, notably de Lessart, who replaced Montmorin at the ministry of foreign affairs, and Narbonne, who succeeded Duportail at the war ministry. Actually, their influence was slight: Barnave condemned in vain the recruitment of counter-revolutionary elements for the king's Constitutional Guard and insisted, to no avail, that the civil household include a certain number of constitutionalists. The three men were not on good terms with Lafayette, who had not entirely agreed with them on constitutional revision; they let an avowed democrat, Pétion, win the election against him as mayor of Paris. Most important, they did not sit in the Assembly and did not have the majority in hand. Only 264 of the Assembly's members registered as Feuillants, while 136 signed as Jacobins and Cordeliers. An uncommitted 350 constitutionalists—half of the Assembly—remained, and they remembered Varennes and Pillnitz with deep-seated mistrust of the king.

Uneasiness still marked public opinion. Aristocrats and refractory priests were more active than ever: in August they had provoked disturbances in the Vendée; in February of 1792 they instigated uprisings in the Lozère. At Avignon on October 16, 1791, they killed the mayor, Lescuyer, and the Patriots avenged his death by a massacre at the Glacière. Since Varennes more and more citizens, especially from the military, were leaving France to take up residence abroad. The king's favourite, Bertrand de Moleville, remained in the cabinet as minister of the navy. New attacks on the 'Austrian Committee', in which popular suspicion confused royal agents with the triumvirs, disturbed even the moderates. The idea of foreign powers issuing peremptory demands offended Lafayette's sense of national dignity. The assignat fell. News from Saint-Domingue bewildered metropolitan France: now mulattoes too were fighting the whites; Port-au-Prince was laid waste in November. Uncertainty made the revolutionaries anxious, and when the left proposed 'strong measures' to restore security and confidence, the moderates easily consented.

New men rose to prominence within the left and until June of 1792 exercised decisive influence. First among them were Brissot, deputy from Paris, and Vergniaud, best known of the representatives from the Gironde. Brissot gave his name to the group; they were called Brissotins, and, especially after Alphonse de Lamartine's study, we name them the Girondins. They were a second generation of the Revolution, brought to power by the Constituents themselves when they ruled against re-election of deputies. Part of them came from the educated but poor lesser bourgeoisie of lawyers and writers. Something more than ambition and enthusiasm urged them to make public service their profession: more often than not they were receptive to the attractions of private salons, whose doors were opened to them by political life. They consorted with the business bourgeoisie—shipowners, wholesalers, bankers—who wanted to end counter-revolution and stabilize the assignat, and who did not regard with disfavour a war that would bring lucrative contracts to suppliers. This business group, however, approved of war on condition that hostilities be confined to the continent, leaving the ports free to carry on a prosperous trade. Marseille, Nantes, and especially Bordeaux were vital centres of capitalism in this period and played a large role in the history of the Girondin party.

While their origins and personal philosophy urged the Girondins to accept political democracy, their tastes and connections led them to demand that democracy respect wealth and talent. Certainly Brissot and Vergniaud possessed ability, but they lacked strength of character. After roaming about as a freelance journalist, Brissot became known through the 'Friends of the Negroes' and the *Patriote français*. Having no independent income, he had worked for the duc d'Orléans, for speculators such as Clavière, and even Lafayette. His moral principles have been questioned, but he died poor. Because he had travelled in England, Switzerland, and the United States, he thought himself familiar with various courts and peoples and styled himself the diplomat of the Gironde. He was the promoter of that region as well, owing to his wide connections, driving energy, and a certain lightheartedness and flexibility that lent him an engaging manner. He was also muddled, and the impression of flightiness, of irresponsibility, left by the conduct of the Girondins is largely his legacy, though their political romanticism agreed with the youth and the social origins of most of them.

Vergniaud's character was marked more by indolence and indecisiveness. The son of a merchant in Limoges, he had finally, after long trial and error, found his way into law practice at Bordeaux, where he became an intimate of Guadet, Gensonné, and Grangeneuve. The Revolution brought him together with merchants, Ducos and Boyer-Fonfrède. He was the party's best orator, and some of his speeches, with their passionate repetitions, are extremely moving. On many occasions he acted as the voice of the nation. He knew how to evoke the tragic decisions which his party's policy had to impose on the Revolution, and explained them with a relentless logic that seemed to make immediately necessary an action described. His elegant, restrained Epicureanism, however, tended to make him shun awesome measures. Through him the Girondins found a place to discuss their programme, at the table and in the luxurious salon of Madame Dodun, widow of a farmer-general, in the Place Vendôme. Caught in the spell of their own eloquence, they forgot to pass beyond words.

If they were to make the Assembly listen, the Girondins saw no means but to strike down the Revolution's enemies. Beginning on October 20, Brissot, Vergniaud, and Isnard attacked the comte d'Artois, the comte de Provence, who had fled when the king made his attempt, and the émigrés. Against this group they succeeded in passing two decrees, one on October 31, another on November 9. They turned upon the refractory clergy as well—not that they were strongly attached to the constitutional Church: most of them agreed with Voltaire and the Encyclopaedists rather than with Rousseau, and lacked a religious nature. Later, on March 26, 1792, Guadet severely reprimanded Robespierre for having declared, in a circular to the affiliated Jacobins, that Providence watched over the Revolution; at a later date Sonthonax exclaimed, 'No sermons!' In a report delivered to the Assembly on November 3, 1791, Gensonné indirectly criticized the Civil Constitution of the Clergy and recommended that a civil registry be established and that secular authority take over education and poor relief. He did not suggest that the government cease paying clerics, but several days earlier Ducos had asked that Church and state be separated. Because the Constituent Assembly had, in the course of revision, separated the Civil Constitution from the constitution itself, the Legislative could have annulled the former. But it did not intend to turn its back on priests who supported the Revolution, and besides, the oath prescribed on November 27, 1790, no longer applied to the Civil Constitution, which meant that protests of non-jurors lost some effect. None, however, would reconsider his refusal to take the oath: the conflict had obviously become political, and they were playing into the hands of the aristocrats. In defence the Assembly did not go so far as to order internment of the non-jurors, but on November 9 it abolished the *simultaneum* and authorized penal sanctions against them in the event of public disturbance.

The measures against the émigrés incurred the veto of the king and were in any case obviously illusory. A more effective course would be to summon the elector of Trèves to dissolve the armed companies of émigrés assembling on his territory. On November 29 the Assembly requested Louis to issue a summons to this effect. As the archbishop of Trèves was a prince of the Holy Roman Empire, he would certainly ask aid and advice of the Imperial Diet and the emperor. The end result of the Girondist offensive—an offensive that developed out of what Jaurès termed a form of 'shrewd daring'—was therefore to turn public opinion against Austria. What did they hope to gain from this tactic? Above all, popularity and a significant role, but they also hoped to drive the king into a corner and rid the Revolution of oppressive suspicion. If Louis agreed to summon the elector he would in effect retract his veto; with this accomplished they had only to force on him Patriot ministers pledged to a policy of war. Brissot thought a surprise attack against Austria would bring immediate uprisings by the empire's oppressed peoples and hand victory to the French. 'The time has come,' he said on December 31, 'for a new crusade, a crusade of universal freedom'. Political refugees responded with cheers and the banker Clavière from Geneva joined the Girondins; on December 18 an English deputation led by Watt's son met a hearty reception from the Jacobins. In the north, Belgians were organizing for combat and the inhabitants of Liége asked to form a legion. The first objective would be to liberate Belgium and the left bank of the Rhine. Nothing could have been better calculated to inflame idealists already confident of offering liberty to the world, or to win over realists lured by the advantages of French expansion.

Yet the Girondins might have failed to carry the government with them had they not worked with Lafayette's supporters and had the court not secretly made an about-face. Lafayette and his friends expected to take command of the armies: while the Gironde thought war would dethrone the king, they, on the contrary, thought it would enhance royal power—it would justify measures to bring agitators under control, and if necessary victorious troops could be used to stamp out radical factions. The salon of Madame de Staël was the focal point for their party, and on December 9 her lover, the comte de Narbonne, a court noble related to the Bourbons but pledged to the Revolution, was appointed minister of war. His basic sentiments put him in agreement with the Lafayettists. The marquis de Condorcet, Voltaire's publisher and a thinker in his own right who was to become the intellectual of the Gironde and the reformer of public education, served as liaison between the Staël group and the Brissotins. Before supporting the republic he belonged to the '89 Club, and as director of the government mint he had financial connections. It was he who led Brissot and Clavière to the Staël salon. The two parties pursued opposing aims but shared the same objective, war, and were capable of reconciling their differences long enough to provoke hostilities. In fact, it was a Lafayette partisan of Dutch Origin, Daverhoult, who on November 29 had proposed the summons to the elector of Trèves. Their compact threatened to dissolve, however, when Lafayette's friends, supported by the triumvirate, objected to the decree against refractory priests. Louis vetoed the decree on December 19 at the request of the department of Paris. The Gironde did not insist, and threw its whole support behind Narbonne.

Duport, Barnave, and Narbonne's colleagues disagreed with his policy but did not protest the summons, counting on Leopold. Duport and Barnave wrote the emperor a note recommending that he disperse the émigrés. This try marked the last of their collective efforts: Duport continued to oppose Narbonne and the Gironde, but Barnave retired to the Dauphiné and from there, reasoning as Lafayette had done, advised his friends to support the Patriot ministers.

On December 14 the king appeared before the Assembly to announce that he was sending the summons, and Narbonne promptly requested that three armies be called up, one under command of Lafayette. The Feuillants and Girondins would have been more than surprised if they had known that Louis had yielded with good grace. Despairing of a concert of powers, he resolved once more to force the hands of kings to whom he had addressed entreaties: if openly attacked they would be obliged to come to his aid. The revolutionaries were playing his game for him. On December 14 the queen wrote Fersen: 'The imbeciles! They don't even see that this serves our purpose'; and the same day Louis wrote Breteuil: 'Instead of civil, we will have political, war, and things will be much the better for it. France's physical and moral state renders it incapable of sustaining a semi-campaign.'

The war found its strongest opposition, and the only one to persist, within the left itself. Upon returning from Arras at the end of November, Robespierre did not at first oppose war, but the attitude taken by Lafayette, Narbonne, and the king soon showed him the reaction that armed struggle held in store. He delivered his first speech against war to the Jacobins on December 16. For a while Danton, Camille Desmoulins, and a few newspapers supported him, but their voices gradually faded. Robespierre remained unmoved to the end. With surprising foresight he outlined the potential dangers—popular resistance to 'armed missionaries', inevitable dictatorship, overwhelming burdens, weariness, and disgust. He exasperated the Gironde in particular by criticizing its ambivalent position: it offered itself as guarantor of Lafayette, the man of the Champ-de-Mars, and demanded that Narbonne, the king's minister, be trusted because war required unity of forces! Foreseeing the schemes of the Feuillants, Robespierre maintained that before opening hostilities the Assembly must gain mastery over the king and weed out counter-revolutionary officers.

He was none the less too harsh in disparaging the Girondins: they were not mistaken when they judged the Revolution menaced, while he insisted that foreign powers had peaceful intentions, and if propaganda had not produced the desired results, neither had it passed unnoticed. Although he did not actually say that Brissot was conspiring with the court, he aroused suspicions to that effect, and the Girondins retaliated in kind. In any case, his efforts did not prevent the majority of

Patriots from throwing their support behind war propaganda. The dangers he described, real but distant, did not alarm the French. The prospect of war failed to touch them directly—as long as volunteers were filling the armies they never thought that they might soon be called up. Robespierre still had backers among the Jacobins, but his popularity, which had been immense as the Constituent Assembly drew to a close, diminished noticeably until July.

The war of defence and of ideology preached by the Girondins undeniably worked its charms upon the revolutionary imagination, and its aura outshone any image of the disaster it would invoke. Those who promoted it are still admired because they seem to embody the young nation freshly delivered, proud to extend liberty to its 'sisters'. They failed not because their plans were rash but because they did not execute them properly. For in waging war they intended to unmask and strike down traitors: 'Let us designate the place for traitors beforehand, and let it be the scaffold,' cried Guadet on January 14, 1792; and Brissot had already announced, 'We need spectacular treason cases; the people are ready!' 'But you, representatives of the people,' countered Robespierre, 'aren't you ready too? And what are you doing in power, if you know nothing better than to deliver the people to the terrible law of insurrection?' At the crucial moment they were not to dare.

## THE AUSTRO-PRUSSIAN ALLIANCE, DECEMBER, 1791–APRIL, 1792

Louis XVI and those who backed war thought that the elector and the emperor would reject the summons. Instead, a horrible panic swept the Rhineland; aristocrats were sure that rebellion would break out at the first sight of French forces. When the elector turned to the emperor for help, Leopold, having neither respect nor sympathy for the émigrés, promised to protect him only on condition that he disperse them at the end of December. They accordingly disbanded, although they stayed close by, and only Louis's brothers were allowed to show themselves at Coblenz. The Legislative Assembly in return ordered the Brabant groups to dissolve.

Although he postponed intervention once more, Leopold persisted in his policy of intimidation. On December 10 he ratified the Diet's resolution granting imperial protection to princes who had rights in Alsace, and on the 21st he warned France that his troops in the Netherlands would defend Trèves. At the same time he stigmatized Jacobin behaviour, expressing hope that he would not be forced to humble them and renewing the threats made at Pillnitz. Kaunitz developed the same theme in stronger terms on February 17 and again on March 18.

On the other hand, Leopold followed up preliminary negotiations. On December 20 he urged Prussia to sign the treaty even though he had hitherto shown little concern for it. This time it was Frederick William who vacillated, indicating that Austria was mistaken as to the meaning of the agreement of July 25: it was not the free Polish constitution—that of May 3, 1791—which he had guaranteed, but a free constitution. Was Poland being abandoned? Leopold nevertheless made no objections and at that price won the treaty of February 7, which stipulated that 20,000 troops would be sent to aid either power if it were attacked. A defensive precaution, it was later said, and one which justified France's attitude but it should not be forgotten that this alliance was never brought into play, being no sooner concluded than superseded. On January 17 a ministers' conference at Vienna adopted plans for a European entente, submitted to Prussia on the 25th. That any such concert would be formed seemed more and more improbable: at the beginning of the year Russia, in agreement with Spain, announced that it would confine itself to giving the émigrés a free rein, promising them eventual support; and in any case the invitation was not sent out until April 12. Actually, Austria was proposing to Prussia a two-power offensive. Each power would furnish 50,000 men, 6,000 to be put into action immediately; France would be summoned to restore the rights of the German princes and of the pope in their respective territories, to send the royal family to a safe place, and to guarantee its monarchical form of government. Prussia immediately agreed and demanded in addition that Jacobin demonstrations be prohibited, a proviso that made war more certain. Even if we concede that Leopold still thought he would not have to fight—he probably considered the Jacobins 'too cowardly', as Marie Antoinette had been writing, to resist foreign armies—it is difficult to deny that the way was now paved for intervention. On February 16 Frederick William held council at Potsdam with the duke of Brunswick, whom he proposed as commanding general, and together they drew up a plan of campaign. Two days later he once more sent Bischoffswerder to encourage his ally in Vienna. Leopold died on March 1. The accession of Francis II could only hasten conflict, for he lacked any traces of the caution and liberalism of his father. To intervention in France he gave unqualified approval.

The Revolution surprised him by taking the initiative. On March 26 Marie Antoinette informed him that on the preceding day France's cabinet had decided to declare war and march into Belgium. Dismayed, the Aulic Council voted on April 13 to dispatch all available troops to Belgium and cut back the forces intended for the offence to 15,000 men.

The Prussians objected: invasion of France with 65,000 men was impossible; their troops would be fighting only to defend Austria. On April 18 Frederick William made it known that he would not mobilize until Austria announced precisely when its 50,000 men would be ready to invade France. Vienna promptly yielded, setting the offensive for the end of July. Prussia issued its order for mobilization during the night of May 4–5. France had three months' respite.

Now the die was cast. By rushing to affairs in the West, the Germans handed Poland over to Catherine. While warmly applauding their aggressive intentions towards France, on March 15 she received three Poles who, since the preceding summer, had been trying to gain her support against the new Polish constitution: Felix Potocki and Rzewuski, intent on preserving the aristocracy's power at any cost, and Branicki, whose avarice had accustomed him to practise treason. The 'Confederation' was drawn up at St. Petersburg on April 27, but to save face was dated from Targowice, May 17, the eve of the day set for invasion of Poland. As early as February 28 Catherine had spoken of Polish intervention in vague terms to the ambassadors Goltz and Louis Cobenzl, but as no one thought her capable of occupying all of Poland, the king of Prussia welcomed her action, thinking she would offer him an equitable share. On February 15 he learned from Goltz that she announced herself resolved upon a second partition, and the next day Frederick William made his fateful decision; without ceasing to speak of Jülich and Berg, of reimbursement in money and of territorial prizes from Louis in case the king lacked necessary resources, he decided to compensate himself in Poland for the expenses of a French campaign. On March 12 he notified Catherine of his intention.

Frederick William little suspected what reverses awaited him, and Austria was destined to experience a worse fortune, since it assumed all the territorial risks involved in war with France. Prussia's position left it free to abandon its ally at will, as it had recently demonstrated. Kaunitz, still faithful to Leopold's policy, did not want division of Poland and pressed for reimbursement in cash, which would rule out Prussian territorial gain. But in that case, if Catherine entered Poland— and how could she be stopped?—the Austro-Prussian alliance would not hold up. This was what Spielmann and Philip Cobenzl, Kaunitz's subordinates, clearly saw. Spielmann, accustomed under Leopold to negotiate on his own, notified Prussia on January 17 that Austria was willing to exchange Belgium for Bavaria; then, on March 28, made the first allusion to a partitioning of Poland by Russia and Prussia. But, thus divided, the Austrian chancellery did not specify its conditions and began the campaign against France before any formal treaty had settled the question of indemnities, an omission explained by the fact that until Valmy the allies did not believe France would resist or that the war would last long. The imprudence of the Girondins has been mercilessly criticized—but were their policies any worse than those of the Old Regime in Europe?[1]

[1] Heinrich von Sybel, in *Geschichte der Revolutionszeit* (5 vols., Düsseldorf, 1853–79), and Albert Sorel, in *L'Europe et la Révolution française* (8 vols., Paris, 1885–1904), agree that the Girondins alone were responsible for the war. Von Sybel was guided by his hostility towards France, Sorel by his antipathy towards the democratic party represented by the Gironde. To defend their viewpoint they argued that the declaration of Pillnitz had to remain a dead letter from the beginning; they attached no importance to the proclamation issued by the émigrés and to Leopold's subsequent steps to re-establish the concert, nor did they take any account of the conclusions which Frenchmen, whether for or against the Revolution, drew from these developments. Their thesis has been summarized without nuance by Adalbert Wahl in *Geschichte des europäischen Staatensystems im Zeitalter der französischen Revolution und der Freiheitskriege* (1789–1815) (Munich and Berlin, 1912), and has been repeated with no new arguments by H. A. Goetz-Bernstein in *La diplomatie de la Gironde, Jacques-Pierre Brissot* (Paris, 1912). The warlike views of the Gironde are incontestable, and Jaurès has laid them bare. But, on one hand, the importance of the declaration of Pillnitz and of the policy of intimidation pursued by Leopold and Kaunitz, in addition to, on the other hand, the aggressive frame of mind of Frederick William, who was looking for any opportunity to enhance his position, have been clearly outlined by Sir John Clapham in

## THE DUMOURIEZ CABINET AND THE
## DECLARATION OF WAR, APRIL 20, 1792

On January 6, 1792, when the Legislative Assembly learned that the émigrés were disbanding, de Lessart could confidently assert that France would obtain satisfaction. Since December 31, however, Paris had known of Leopold's dispatch containing new threats, which provided the Girondins with fresh ammunition against him. On January 13 Gensonné, speaking for the diplomatic committee, proposed that an ultimatum be issued requiring Austria to state by March 1 whether it intended to abide by the alliance of 1756 and renounce a European concert. Brissot and Vergniaud gave full support to the proposal. On January 25 the Assembly voted the necessary decree, then sequestered all émigré property on February 9. Narbonne declared that the army would be prepared, and he instructed the son of the comte de Custine to offer the duke of Brunswick command of the French forces. At the same time de Lessart agreed that Ségur should be dispatched to Berlin in order to win Frederick William's neutrality by bribing the king's favourites, and that Talleyrand should cross the channel to reassure the English and secure a loan. At London, Talleyrand negotiated a secret deal with financiers who were agents of British colonists at Tobago, arranging for France to return the island in exchange.

De Lessart still had trust in Leopold. On January 21 he cautiously protested the emperor's claim to intervene in domestic affairs of the French kingdom, assuring him that France wanted peace. Nothing was better suited to make Kaunitz more arrogant, and when on February 17 he 'publicly' denounced the 'sect' that refused to allow constitutional revision, he touched off an explosion. Protesting the humiliation dealt France, Lafayette and Narbonne broke with Duport and Bertrand de Moleville. In a cabinet meeting Narbonne read Louis a memorandum

The Causes of the War of 1792 (Cambridge, 1889), and especially by Hans Glagau in Die französische Legislative und der Ursprung der Revolutionskriege (Berlin, 1896), with letters of Mercy-Argenteau and of Pellenc, Mirabeau's former secretary, and also by Karl Heidrich, in Preussen in Kampfe gegen die französische Revolution bis zur zweiten Teilung Polens (Stuttgart and Berlin, 1908). It is strange that in discussing this point the authors attribute to the coalition powers only the traditional preoccupation with power, without ever introducing the motive of a passionate desire to crush the Revolution—a desire that the interests of their political and social dominance inspired in Europe's kings and aristocrats.

challenging the king to prove his loyalty to the constitution, specifically by purging his entourage and appointing Feuillants to the civil household. Instead of Bertrand, however, Narbonne himself was dismissed. Girondins and Lafayettists retaliated by starting impeachment proceedings against de Lessart on March 10. The other ministers, frightened, resigned. Duport advised Louis to try a coup d'état. But how? Frightened himself, the king retreated, but passed over Lafayette's candidates to present Dumouriez with carte blanche.

After serving brilliantly in the Seven Years War, Dumouriez had sought further fortune in secret diplomacy. He was afterwards appointed military commander of Cherbourg, where he was growing old, deprived of glory, when the revolution suddenly opened a new career to him. He rallied to it. While stationed in the Vendée he acted the part of a Jacobin and came into contact with Gensonné, who at the time was carrying out duties for the Constituent Assembly. Dumouriez, however, also offered his services to the king, through the agency of his friends Laporte, an intendant on Louis's civil list, and the banker Sainte-Foy, who put him in touch with de Lessart. Dumouriez's ultimate goal coincided with that of Lafayette and Narbonne: to conduct a brief war, then use his victorious army to restore royal power and govern in the king's name. The other two were distasteful to the court, whereas he, a fresh personality, pleased the king with his spirit and ready wit. To fortify himself with democratic support Dumouriez granted a few portfolios to the Gironde. There was even some talk of appointing Danton and Collot d'Herbois—Jacobins as ministers, said Sainte-Foy, will not be Jacobin ministers—but they were content to put Clavière in charge of the ministry of public contributions and Roland, former inspector of manufactures, in the interior ministry. The other ministers were king's men, but a few subordinate places were found for Jacobins: Bonnecarrère, Lebrun-Tondu, and Noël (Danton's friend), in the foreign office; Lanthenas and Pache in the interior.

Dumouriez had got his way. This time Robespierre had just grounds to decry the compromise between 'intriguers' and the court. The break became final: this was the germ of the mortal duel between Mountain and Gironde. The Brissotins mistakenly walked into a dangerous position, accepting the responsibility of power without the means to direct it. Misunderstanding concerning their role has persisted in the term

'Girondin cabinet', still used today. Madame Roland immediately grasped the situation and attempted to remedy it by having Servan appointed minister of war on May 9 while personally supervising the interior ministry through the agency of her husband. Even before, in the spring of 1791, at her salon on the Rue Guénégaud, she had been annoyed by the indolence her friends demonstrated. Now residing in the grand mansion that her husband occupied, formerly assigned to controllers-general of finance, she became the Egeria of the Gironde and urged it into action. She believed that her Cornelian will made her worthy of power, but active participation by a woman in politics was at that time ridiculed and her presence only weakened the party. Moreover, having no definite programme that we know of, she was more suited to reign than to govern. And although she preached unity her efforts only divided the democrats: judging men by their personal appearance and submission, she disliked Vergniaud, looked on Danton with horror, and imposed her own prejudices upon those beguiled by her charm.

But the heedless Gironde thought only of declaring war, which was now considered inevitable. Dumouriez opened with a rather moderate note on March 18, but it crossed the one from Kaunitz. One week later the cabinet decided to send Austria a final ultimatum. Vienna made no reply. On April 20, without serious opposition—such future Montagnards as Cambon and Carnot, Chabot, Basire, and Merlin de Thionville agreeing with the others—the Assembly voted war against the king of Bohemia and Hungary—i.e., against Austria, not the empire. A new period opened in the history of France and of Europe.

# 13

## THE SECOND FRENCH REVOLUTION, AUGUST–SEPTEMBER, 1792

War upset the plans of everyone who, for one reason or another, had brought it about. Except for a short interlude it lasted until 1815, and by then had convulsed all Europe. But its first effects were felt in France: there it brought the fall of the king and ushered in political democracy.

### FAILURE OF THE FRENCH OFFENSIVE, APRIL–JUNE, 1792

Dumouriez, who regarded himself as a diplomat first of all, was given charge of foreign affairs. He felt sure that he could isolate Austria and seize Belgium, where there were only 40,000 Habsburg troops, then make an early peace at the cost of little fighting. How he proposed to get Francis II in this position can be learned from the talks his agent Benoît held at Berlin concerning changes in the French constitution.

Prussia, Sardinia, and the Turks were the traditional and therefore seemed the most likely partners to an anti-Austrian coalition. Yet French envoys were rejected by all three, and England rebuffed Talleyrand, once more in London with the marquis de Chauvelin.

Although some encouragement could be drawn from the assassination of Gustavus III in Sweden by one of his nobles on March 16 and from the fall from favour of Florida Blanca, who was replaced by Aranda, Spain and Sweden could at best promise only neutrality. The diplomatic offensive had met defeat.

Dumouriez and Brissot expected great results from revolutionary propaganda, now conducted with official backing. Belgians, Liégois, Germans, Dutch, and Savoyards formed legions in France. Reaction against Austria, strong at Liége, had been less severe in Belgium, but the clergy still distrusted the Habsburg regime and discontent seethed. From Strasbourg, Mayor Dietrich, the Jacobin Laveaux, and the refugee Eulogius Schneider spread propaganda through Germany, and from Paris, Clavière and Doppet of the Helvetian Club—changed to the Allobrogian Club after August 10—concentrated on Switzerland and Savoy. Chantreau, a former professor at the Ávila military school, was charged with a secret mission to Catalonia and Miranda was welcomed when he proposed to inflame Spanish America with the French cause. Bribes were offered to encourage foreign deserters. The French confidently expected to be received as liberators beyond their borders—but first they had to cross the frontier.

Despite Narbonne's assurances to the contrary, the army was ill-prepared. Troops of the line were now below strength because most men preferred to enlist in volunteer battalions, which were better paid, elected their own officers, and could disband after the campaign. In spite of the attractions even these battalions were slow to form. The true volunteers who were fired with revolutionary enthusiasm filled only a part of the ranks: frequently National Guardsmen, not wishing to leave their firesides, offered bonuses to muster necessary quotas; and it took time for enough enlistments to come in. Equipment was furnished by local authorities and arrived slowly, nor were there enough arms. The new troops badly needed instruction. Their cadres were made up of the élite among the bourgeoisie and produced several generals for the Republic, but they had to learn everything concerning the waging of war.

Dumouriez recognized these shortcomings but thought that the army would get its training in combat; the most important thing to him was to act with boldness. Reasoning that the enemy had not more than 30,000 men to throw into a campaign and that foreign troops would be arranged in a cordon from the sea to Lorraine, he proposed to break through this barrier: one column each from Furnes, Lille, Valenciennes, and Givet, totalling more than 50,000 men, would set out on April 29 towards the enemy line. Unfortunately, the generals were trained for regular war and would hear nothing of this plan. Besides, the officers distrusted their undisciplined troops and the men suspected them in return: out of 9,000 officers at least half had already emigrated and a few deserted on the eve of the offensive. In May several others took three regiments into the enemy camp. On April 29, in sight of the first Austrian troops, Dillon and Biron ordered a retreat. Their men cried treason and disbanded; Dillon was murdered at Lille. Carle and Lafayette drew back without having caught a glimpse of the enemy. The Rhine army remained where it was in order to avoid provoking the Diet. Only Custine had any success: he took Porrentruy.

The generals laid entire responsibility on lack of discipline and a ministry that tolerated such conditions. In reply the Gironde ordered Dillon's murderers prosecuted, along with Marat, who had been exhorting the soldiers to get rid of their generals. A new decree tightened military justice and authorized the generals to issue regulations bearing penalties for infractions. The decree undeniably marked a surrender of legislative power—to no avail: on May 18 the heads of the armies, meeting at Valenciennes, disregarded repeated orders from the ministry and declared an offensive impossible, personally advising the king to make immediate peace. In June, Luckner ventured to take Courtrai, then promptly evacuated it. The military offensive, too, had failed. The generals' accusations cannot be denied; neither can their own incompetence. In any case they concealed their true reasons—Lafayette, for one, was executing a political about-face.

## ORIGINS OF THE SECOND REVOLUTION

Stirred by Girondist propaganda, unrest grew with each day. The Girondin appeal to 'sacred love for the fatherland' inflamed men's minds with an ardour that Rouget de Lisle captured in his *War Song for the Rhine Army*, written on April 26 at Strasbourg and destined to become, under the title the *Marseillaise*, the national anthem of the Republic. But the Patriots of 1792 were now the true champions of the Revolution. Aristocrats opposed king to fatherland and scoffed at the nation; they impatiently waited for the Germans to arrive in Paris, and some had already left to fight in Allied ranks. Rouget advised that magnanimity be shown the enemy—'Spare the sad victims who have regretfully taken up arms against you'—but he was obdurate toward traitors, 'parricides', 'the perfidious', accomplices of 'tyrants'. Nationalistic spirit and revolutionary fervour went hand in hand. The reverses of April were attributed to treason. A refractory priest was murdered at Lille, repeating Dillon's fate; on the same day the directory of the Nord department voted to imprison non-juring priests at Cambrai. The idea of an aristocratic conspiracy haunted the people more than ever as, exulting over defeat in their conversations and journals, aristocrats redoubled their activity. La Rouërie in the west, Monnier de La Quarrée in the south-east, the Charriers and others in the Vivarais, the Gevaudan, and the Velay, prepared to aid the invaders with insurrections. A revolt took place at Yssingeaux in May. The counter-revolutionaries of Arles, who had controlled the town since Varennes, now bolstered their forces.

Defensive and punitive reactions were renewed in strength. In February and March the Jacobins of Marseille voluntarily took matters in hand throughout Provence and, using armed force, quashed their opponents at Avignon and at Arles. From that time Marseille represented the highest hopes of the Patriots. The democratic movement gained ground. During the winter Girondins brought the red cap of liberty into fashion among sans-culottes and advised 'passive' citizens to arm themselves with pikes. The fraternal societies again swelled their membership. The Assembly pardoned the Swiss of Châteauvieux who had been incarcerated after the Nancy affair and who, despite André Chénier's invectives, were feted at Paris on April 15. The Constituent had granted amnesty for all acts connected with the Revolution: this was now extended to various murders committed in the Comtat so as to condone those who had perpetrated the massacre at the Glacière, in particular Jourdan the Headcutter, who returned to Avignon with the Marseille victors.

Within the popular classes revolutionary activity took on a social aspect that alarmed the bourgeoisie more than in 1789. Almost everywhere the wealthy were made to pay for reimbursing or equipping volunteers. Agrarian revolt continued to smoulder, and at winter's end broke out again in Quercy. When a ship used for transporting National Guards capsized in the Rhine on its way to aid the citizens of Marseille, the cry of treason rose afresh and a horrible *jacquerie* was unleashed in the regions of Gard, Ardèche, and Hérault. Couthon moved that landlords be constrained to produce the original title to their lands, which harked back to the proposal that all dues be abolished without indemnity. The Assembly did suppress redemption on June 18, but only for perquisites.

Of even greater consequence because it struck the towns, economic crisis again set the masses in motion. This time its cause was not scarcity but inflation, as currency had increased by 600 millions since October. Depreciation of the assignat continued and the exchange rate fell even more rapidly: in Paris, French money once worth 100 London pounds would buy only 70 on the eve of Varennes and only 50 by March; then its value rose a bit between April and August. The flood of paper notes, misused by speculators, aggravated unrest. In March the 'assistance house' at Paris defaulted; for one year afterwards the state had to provide for reimbursement. Fortunately, prices were not as inflated as gold—they rose 33–50 per cent, while gold rose 200 per cent—but in a period when workers had difficulty obtaining higher wages, this was enough to drive them to excess. Sugar grew scarce as disorder in the West Indies continued. On March 24 Brissot finally obtained equality of rights for men of colour, but it was too late. Shipments tapered off and hoarding kept colonial imports from the market. In January, Parisian mobs stormed the city's stores. In February a scarcity of soap provoked further riots. The lack of adequate grain supplies promised greater suffering. Large wheat-growers, paying neither dues nor taxes and meeting their rent payments with depreciated assignats, welcomed rising prices—the more so because they could sell their produce without leaving home territory, which meant that some areas received little or no grain. Grain shipments again were obstructed. In February a crowd gathered from ten leagues around the area of Noyon to stop wheat boats on the Oise; at Dunkirk a riot halted consignments destined for the west and south. Workers from Perche and Maine descended upon the rich wheat-growing area of Beauce and compelled the fixing of prices of foodstuffs. On March 3 Simoneau, mayor of Étampes, was murdered. War brought further difficulties—requisitioning of horses and vehicles slowed threshing and distribution; purchases for the army deprived public markets and drove up grain prices. New defenders arose to demand price controls and economic regulations, which were dear to the people. In May Jacques Roux, the vicar of Saint-Nicolas-des-Champs in Paris, demanded death penalties for hoarders. In June, Lange, a municipal official in Lyon, proposed that a national maximum price be established for grains. These attempts to rectify what were considered abuses on the part of proprietors led a few individuals to demand that ownership itself be restricted. Such was Pierre Dolivier, the parish priest of Mauchamp, who defended the rioters of Étampes and declared that landholders should be forced to split up their large farms.

With greater insistence Feuillant newspapers claimed that more than the Constitution was threatened and alarmed the bourgeoisie with the spectre of 'agrarian law'. The Girondins too were frightened: on June 3 they officially honoured the memory of Simoneau. They were responsible for the existing political order; their members held cabinet positions, were closely tied to the bourgeoisie, and expressed full devotion—Roland especially—to economic freedom. The appearance of sans-culottes scared them into taking a path that was to lead to conservatism. But for the moment danger of counter-revolution occupied their full attention.

## FALL OF THE DUMOURIEZ CABINET AND FAILURE OF THE GIRONDINS, JUNE–AUGUST, 1792

Lafayette could hardly endure a cabinet that he had no part in choosing and which included such petty personages as Roland. Military failure preyed on his mind. He began to share the feelings of Feuillants. At Givet he received Duport and agreed that the clubs should be closed and the constitution revised with the aid of a military coup d'état. To Mercy he sent an envoy to propose an armistice which would enable him to march on Paris. No response was made, in the knowledge that Louis had no desire to be saved by the general. Nothing, however, would prevent the king from taking advantage of Lafayette's breach with the Jacobins by dismissing the Girondin ministers. As soon as he realized that point, Dumouriez started to oppose his colleagues from the Gironde.

In the second half of May the Patriots feared that a show of force was imminent. The justice of the peace, Larivière, boldly ordered the arrest of the 'Cordeliers Trio', consisting of Basire, Chabot, and Merlin de Thionville, on May 18. The Girondins saw no choice but to fall back on the policy of intimidation which had brought them to power. On May 23 Vergniaud and Brissot denounced the Austrian Committee; on the 26th a decree ordered that any priest denounced by twenty citizens in a department be deported. Two days later the Assembly declared that it would sit in continuous session, and on the morrow it dissolved the king's Constitutional Guard. On the 30th Gensonné proposed to entrust the civil service with duties of political police, including the right to arrest suspects. Finally, on June 6, a measure initiated by Servan summoned 20,000 National Guards to attend the Federation ceremony and then set up camp outside Paris. This was done to protect the capital against enemy forces, but meanwhile it could aid the Patriots should an occasion arise. A petition called the Petition of Eight Thousand, started by the Parisian National Guard, insisted that they were capable of maintaining order. Louis refused either to sacrifice the non-jurors or to authorize the establishment of a military camp. On June 12 a letter from Roland urged him to yield on those two points, stating that his conduct would provoke the fall of the throne and a massacre of the aristocrats. The next day Roland was dismissed, Clavière and Servan along with him. On June 15 the reception of Dumouriez by the Assembly was hostile enough to convince him that he would be arraigned, and, since the king insisted on approving only the decree disbanding his guard, Dumouriez submitted his resignation and left to rejoin the army of the north. The Feuillants returned to power in a new ministry. Deciding that the moment had come, Lafayette summoned the Assembly on June 18 to break up the democratic movement.

Since the end of May the faubourgs had seemed on the verge of passing to direct action. While in power the Girondins restrained them through the agency of the mayor of Paris, Pétion; now they encouraged their part in the demonstration planned to celebrate the anniversary of the Tennis Court Oath on June 20. The directory of the Paris department prohibited the demonstration, but in vain. A mass of demonstrators marched before the Assembly, then invaded the Tuileries and sought out the king. With dignity Louis listened to curses and threats; with obstinacy he refused to withdraw his veto or recall the Girondins. The insults he suffered earned ardent declarations of loyalty from others; he proceeded to suspend Pétion and Manuel, *procureur* of the Commune.

On June 28 Lafayette, having left his army without authorization, appeared before the Assembly and tried to press it into taking strong measures. Repudiated by the court, he now failed to muster support from the National Guard of the wealthier, western areas of the city, and returned to the front severely disappointed. But he had not given up: at the end of July his troops and those of Luckner performed, in the face of the enemy, an incredible and useless manoeuvre that brought them near Compiègne. They entreated Louis to join them there, but he refused to change his mind. Nor would he listen to Feuillant proposals that he move to Rouen, where he would have access to the sea. Counting on the manifesto that he begged the Prussians to publish, on bribery, and on the forces still at his disposal, he believed that he could hold his position until the invaders arrived. He also relied on Girondin vacillation.

Briefly disconcerted over the failure of the demonstration on June 20, the Girondins resumed their assault on the ministry. A decree of July 2 authorized National Guards, many of whom were already on their way to Paris, to come to the Federation ceremony; another of July 5 declared that in the event of danger to the nation all able-bodied men could be called to service and necessary arms requisitioned. Six days later the Assembly declared 'the fatherland in danger'. Vergniaud on July 3 and Brissot on July 9 heatedly accused the king and his ministers of treason, asked that the ministers be declared collectively responsible for exercise of the veto, threatened to arraign them, and implied that there might be grounds for deposing the king. The immediate result was resignation of the ministry on July 10; all that remained was to get Louis to recall the Girondins. Then, like the triumvirate before them, Vergniaud, Guadet, and Gensonné entered into secret correspondence with the king. On July 20 they sent a letter through the painter Boze, who was in league with Thierry de Ville-d'Avray, royal valet. Vergniaud wrote a second on July 29, and according to some accounts Guadet met with the royal family at the Tuileries. Louis did not definitely promise them the ministry but gave enough encouragement to bind their hands. The Girondins were suddenly transformed; instead of attackers, they were defenders of the throne. But even if he called them back, who would prevent him from dismissing them again in the midst of an invasion? The Fédérés and sections, more clear-sighted, decided to put an end to the whole affair. A few Girondins tried to stop them: on July 26 Brissot threatened republicans with the full force of the law and declared himself against dethronement; on August 4 Vergniaud managed to annul a decree of the Mauconseil section which stated that it 'no longer recognized Louis XVI as king of the French'; Isnard spoke of an order for Robespierre's arrest and trial. The Gironde thus severed connections with the revolutionary people just when they were about to carry its own policy to a logical conclusion. Later, on January 3, 1793, Guadet explained his letter to the king on the grounds that, if insurrection failed, he feared its results would be far graver than those following the demonstration of June 20. There were, however, deeper reasons for the failure of the Gironde. At heart these 'statesmen' felt little more than distant sympathy for the sans-culottes, and the thought of insurrection terrified them because they foresaw that, unless they remained masters of the situation, private wealth would be endangered, just as the Feuillants had been predicting, and perhaps private property as well. But to reverse themselves at this crucial moment was to pronounce the death sentence on their party and on each man in it.

## THE REVOLUTION OF AUGUST 10, 1792

The provinces had offered republicans in Paris little aid after the flight to Varennes, but after June 20 the countryside was a main source of support. Although administrative personnel in departments and even in districts expressed indignation that the throne had been abused, many municipalities, especially in the south-east, came out against the king. When the sans-culottes felt their position threatened they appealed to the citizens of Marseille, famous for their victorious spring campaign, then to Montpellier and to Nîmes. From Paris, Barbaroux asked his fellow townsmen of Marseille for five hundred men who knew how to die well. The Jacobins of Montpellier sent Mireur, future general of the Republic, to cement relations with their brothers of Marseille. He taught them the *War Song*, which Rouget de Lisle had written and which they sang on the way to Paris. Scarcely had the future battalion of August 10 departed when its municipality—the first to do so—demanded establishment of the Republic. Well before this southern contingent arrived, other National Guards reached Paris, and on July 11 Robespierre published an address to the Fédérés. Fired with enthusiasm and organized as a military body, they formed an extremely valuable reserve. On July 17 and 23 they submitted petitions to the Assembly relating to deposition of the king. In this sense the revolution of August 10 was not Parisian, as that of July 14 had been, but national.

The Fédérés set up a central committee and a secret directory that included some of the Parisan leaders and thereby assured direct contact with the sections. Daily meetings were held by the individual sections, and on July 25 the assembly authorized continuous sessions for them. On the 27th Pétion permitted a 'correspondence office' to be set up in the Hôtel de Ville. Not all sections opposed the king, but passive citizens joined them, and on the 30th the section of the Théâtre Français gave all its members the right to vote. At the section meetings Jacobins and sans-culottes clashed with moderates and gradually gained the upper hand. On July 30 a decree admitted passive citizens to the National Guard.

One after another, forty-seven sections pronounced themselves for deposition of the king and appointment of an Executive Council. But Robespierre pointed out that to accomplish anything they first had to dispose of the Assembly: to replace it they must elect, by universal suffrage, a Convention—a term borrowed from America—meaning a Constituent Assembly. In the last days of July dramatic events aroused spirits to fever pitch. From the 22nd to the 24th it was announced in the streets that the fatherland was in danger. Military enlistment began. The Prussians were departing from Coblenz, and on August 1 came news of a manifesto signed by the duke of Brunswick threatening to deliver Paris 'to military execution and total destruction' if the 'slightest violence' were committed against the royal family. On July 25 the Fédérés from Brest arrived; on the 30th those of Marseille paraded through the 'faubourg of glory' singing the anthem which thenceforth bore their name and which they for ever linked to the fall of the monarchy and the advent of political democracy. Insurrection threatened to break out on the 26th, again on the 30th. It was postponed both times through the efforts of Pétion, who was to present the section petitions to the Assembly on August 3. The faubourg Saint-Antoine, section of the Fifteen Score, gave the Assembly until August 9 to prove itself. Gensonné later declared that he had come out in committee for dethronement, but he had no chance of convincing the Assembly to depose the king. On the 9th it refused even to indict Lafayette. That night the tocsin rang.

Sans-culottes leaders were far from convinced that victory would be easily won: on the contrary, up to the last moment they feared that the aristocratic conspiracy would provoke a fresh assault upon faubourgs and Assembly. This 'fear' was not without motive: a heavy concentration of Swiss guards had taken posts around the Tuileries, and they were joined by several hundred royalists, among them a number of future Vendéans. In addition, the court knew it could rely on Mandat, commander of the National Guard. This meant that anything short of a military offensive could be repulsed by the court, which could then disperse the Assembly, and with a firm and capable leader such as Barras or Bonaparte in command the 'day' would permit Louis to receive the Prussians as victor in his own right. In the sense that the revolutionaries saw a potential danger and resolved to meet it, the insurrection was another defensive reaction.

During the night of August 9–10 the faubourg Saint-Antoine invited other sections to send representatives to the Hôtel de Ville. They met in a room adjoining the official Commune and at daybreak took its place as the Paris Commune. Mandat was summoned, arrested, then murdered. The orders he had given were cancelled. At the Tuileries, National Guards either defected or left their posts. Roederer, *procureur-général-syndic* to the department of Paris, then stepped in, to the advantage of the Girondins: he persuaded the royal family to take refuge in the Assembly, hoping that this would head off armed conflict and leave the deputies power of decision.

Early that morning Chaumette and Gorsas led the Fédérés of Marseille to the palace. Few more than the Swiss Guards were left to meet them. The Fédérés were allowed to enter the courtyard and advance to the great staircase to fraternize. Suddenly the Swiss opened fire, repulsed the attackers, and cleared the court before the palace. Reinforcements finally arrived from the faubourgs; the Fédérés attacked again and drove the defenders back into the palace. As at the Bastille, a cry arose that conspirators had laid a trap. When around ten o'clock the king ordered the guards to cease fire and withdraw, they received no quarter from their opponents: many were massacred; fifty Swiss were taken to the Hôtel de Ville and there put to death. Part of the garrison, however, was spared and put into prison.

July 14 had saved the Constituent Assembly. August 10 passed sentence on the Legislative Assembly: the day's victors intended to dissolve the Assembly and keep power in their own hands. But because the new Commune, composed of unknowns, hesitated to alarm the provinces, where the Girondins still enjoyed popularity, the Brissotins were kept as security, and the Revolution was mired in compromise. The Assembly remained for the time being but recognized the Commune, increased through elections to 288 members, among them Robespierre. The king was suspended, not deposed. The Commune had him shut up in the Temple with his family, but final decision was deferred until a Convention could be elected by universal suffrage, following Robespierre's proposal. The Assembly appointed a provisional Executive Council and put Monge and Lebrun-Tondu on it, along with several former Girondin ministers. They were joined by Danton, who the Assembly thought would prove useful in dealing with the Commune.

The son of a *procureur* from Arcis, former advocate to the Council of State, a member of the departmental directory of Paris in 1791 and then assistant *procureur* to the Commune, Danton had been known as a democrat since 1789. But he had suddenly acquired a great deal of money—received, it was said, from the king. Mirabeau states in a private letter that he purchased Danton's services. Still, we have no knowledge of what the court may have obtained from him. In testifying before the revolutionary tribunal he boasted of having instigated the uprising of August 10, yet the witnesses to accredit his testimony are scarce and have been challenged. We do know, however, that for the Girondins to turn to him he must have had both popularity and commitments to the insurgents. Like Mirabeau, he was impetuous, inclined to indulge his taste for pleasure, and unencumbered by morality. In private company he seemed a hearty fellow. As he was not a writer, many of his political ideas and intentions are lost to us. He gives the impression of testing the political wind before taking sides, yet he undeniably possessed many of the qualities that mark a statesman: the ability to evaluate quickly, a talent for rapid and bold decision, a sense of realism unclouded by scruples, and an eloquence enriched with captivating phrases. He knew little of jealousy or bitterness and declared himself always willing to join with others for action. Known to enemies of the Revolution as the Mirabeau of the rabble, Danton has remained a popular figure for many average Frenchmen, who find in him their own patriotic sense and concern for concrete deeds to achieve progress at the cost of few sacrifices. He was in effect master of the Executive Council and there rendered service to the Revolution.[1]

---

[1] There are two opposing views on Danton's character. According to the first, Danton was an ardent democrat, an unswerving patriot, a great statesman. This opinion has been defended chiefly by J. F. E. Robinet (*Danton, Mémoires sur sa vie privée* [Paris, 1865, 3rd ed., 1884], *Procès des dantonistes* [Paris, 1879], *Danton émigré* [Paris, 1887], *Danton homme d'État* [Paris, 1889]), and by Alphonse Aulard (*Les orateurs de la Législative et de la Convention* [2 vols., Paris, 1885, 2nd ed., 1906], II, 165–225; *Études et leçons sur l'histoire de la Révolution française* [Paris: Series I, 1893, Series II, 1898, Series IV, 1904, Series V, 1907, Series IX, 1924). According to the second view, Danton was an unscrupulous politician, capable of betraying the Revolution and the fatherland as well, who at best sold himself to the court. This was maintained for more than twenty years by Albert Mathiez in a great many articles appearing in *Annales révolutionnaires* (15 vols., 1908–23), and in *Annales historiques de la Révolution française* (1924–), as well as in several books: *Études robespierristes*, I (Paris, 1917), 31–69, 70–97, 98–134, *Danton et la paix* (Paris, 1919), *Autour de Danton* (Paris, 1926). The reader will find a summary of Mathiez's conclusions in 'Danton, l'histoire et la légende', *Annales historiques de la Révolution française*, IV (1927), 417–61. He pointed out that Danton grew inexplicably wealthy, and he published the declaration that Talon, civil lieutenant of the Châtelet in 1789 and later distributor of the secret-service fund from the civil list, made to the police in the Year XII: 'I had contact with Danton and that contact was in fact to find out what might concern the king's personal security' (*Annales historiques de la Révolution française*, V [1928], 1–21: 'Talon et la police de Bonaparte'). Mirabeau's letter to the comte de La Marck, March 10, 1791 (*Correspondance entre le comte de Mirabeau et le comte de La Marck pendant les années 1789, 1790 et 1791*, ed. by A. F. Bacourt [Paris, 1851], III, 82), according to which Danton had just received 30,000 livres out of the bribery fund, is thus corroborated. It seems to be substantiated also by the fact that in purchasing Church land he paid in full on the spot, and by what we now know concerning his role in the king's trial (see Chapter 15). Louis Madelin (*Danton* [Paris, 1914]), and Georges Pariset (*La Révolution, 1792–1799* [2 vols., Paris, 1920]), admit that he was bribed but deny neither his revolutionary patriotism nor his political ability. This middle position has been taken by

The chief source of danger from the provinces was Lafayette, who had roused the Ardennes department and wanted to march on Paris, while his friend Dietrich tried to stir Strasbourg to revolt. Neither succeeded. Deserted by his troops, Lafayette went over to the Austrians on August 19 and was made their prisoner. Within France a few of the departmental directories balked; when suspended outright they caused no more trouble. A great many of the administrative bodies none the less remained in the hands of the constitutionalists and in conflict with the Jacobin clubs. As in Paris, the provinces often faced a confused situation of competing authorities: the Assembly sent them its 'representatives on mission', who were also attached to the army; the Executive Council sent commissioners chosen by Danton from the insurrectionaries; Roland had his agents; the Commune appointed its own. Some of the commissioners took revolutionary measures, arresting suspects, naming vigilance committees, purging local authorities, and—when officials resisted—on occasion ordering arrests.

A second revolution had, indeed, occurred, ushering in universal suffrage and, in effect, a republic. But it did not have the warm and virtually unanimous support that the nation had offered the first. Events since 1789 had brought difference and divisions: many had followed the refractory priests; of those who remained loyal to the Revolution some criticized August 10, while others stood by, fearing the day's aftermath. Those who had actually participated in the insurrection or who unhesitatingly approved it were few in number, a minority resolved to crush counter-revolution by any means. The Terror began. But it obviously lacked direction: the Committee of Public Safety had not yet formed.

Georges Lefebvre in his essay bringing the facts up to date—'Sur Danton', *Annales historiques de la Révolution française*, IX (1932), 385–424, 484–500.

In so far as August 10 is concerned, the same variety of opinion exists. Aulard thinks that Danton directed the insurrection, as Danton told the revolutionary tribunal (*Études et leçons*, Series IV, pp. 194–226: 'Danton et la Révolution du 10 août 1792'). Mathiez thinks that Danton played a minor role until the insurrection was successful. Danton was then assistant *procureur* to the Commune, but no one has detailed information on his activity. Nevertheless, if the Girondins thought it wise to bring him into the provisional Executive Council, they must have regarded him as one of the ringleaders.

## THE FIRST TERROR, SEPTEMBER, 1792

The victors of August 10 were concerned first with establishing their dictatorship. The Commune immediately silenced the opposition press, closed the tollgates, and by repeated house visits seized a number of refractory priests and aristocratic notables. On August 11 the Legislative Assembly gave municipalities the authority to arrest suspects. Application of the power depended on the local officials. In the Côte d'Or they ordered multiple arrests, but for the most part they seem to have exercised discretion and some ignored the decree altogether. The news of invasion plus concern for the approaching elections moved the Assembly to order all non-juring priests deported—or, more accurately, banished—on August 26. At Paris the priests were imprisoned; in the departments most but not all went into exile—some remained and in rare instances were hunted out: many of the arrests were subsequently overruled. Even the number of those imprisoned at Paris has been exaggerated: on September 2 the nine prisons visited by the bands intent on massacre held only about 2,600, and of that total fewer than a thousand had been committed after August 10. On the whole the first Terror, despite the fear it bred, would have been rather mild had it rested only with France's administrators, who with few exceptions had not been replaced by new elections and who as republican bourgeois were reluctant to suspend the rights of man and citizen.

Unfortunately the people were aroused and had to be considered. Before and after August 10 murderous riots had broken out in the provinces—when news of the capture of Longwy reached Cambrai on August 30 it provoked the near extermination of imprisoned priests. Volunteers often pressed for summary execution. In Paris a desire to avenge the victims 'ambushed' at the Tuileries on August 10 threatened more violence. From the first moment insurrectionists declared that they would eliminate the prisoners if they were not quickly tried before a popular tribunal. On August 17 the Assembly consented to set up a court with members to be elected by the sections, but its deliberation and clemency disappointed those who had asked for it. Announcement of the invasion spread the haunting idea of a massacre. Proposals involving violence were more and more frequently heard, even at the Assembly, where Merlin de Thionville demanded that wives and children of émigrés be seized as hostages, while Debry advocated a 'tyrannicide corps' to exterminate kings. Marat had many times insisted that the only way to save the Revolution was to slaughter the aristocrats en masse. The 'people's friend', embittered by failure and poverty, by judicial prosecution and illness, attracted an audience because his ominous predictions were being realized and because he demonstrated a keen sense of the sufferings and inarticulate desires harboured by the crowd. Responsibility for the September Days has been attributed to him, but the collective mentality that made them possible resulted from circumstances and not from the will of any particular individual.

Longwy had fallen to the enemy; on Sunday, September 2, news came that Verdun was about to surrender. Tocsin and cannon sounded the alarm. Volunteers massed to leave. Rumours circulated that their departure was to be the signal for prisoners to stage an uprising against Patriots. In reality the prisoners may have expected liberation at the hands of the Prussians, but did not consider insurrection. The state of prison management, however, entrusted to a small and inept staff, encouraged suspicion of revolt. Escapes and riots had repeatedly occurred, and authorities had already expressed fear that mobs of common criminals would roam the city. The populace detested such criminals as much as counter-revolutionaries because, access to prisons being relatively easy, they made a business of counterfeiting the assignats that circulated in the sections.

On the afternoon of September 2 a few prisoners in the mayor's residence were unwisely moved to the Abbaye prison. When they arrived a crowd attacked, murdering them all. At that moment section meetings were being held and the section of Poissonnière passed a motion demanding that the prisoners be immediately tried. In all likelihood other meetings ruled that they should hold trials on the spot. At the end of the afternoon groups went into action at the Carmelite monastery, then the Abbaye, the prison of La Force, the Châtelet, the Conciergerie, and others. They set up tribunals and carried out summary executions, which continued during the following days, spreading to the Salpêtrière and Bicêtre prisons, and ending on September 6.

The murderers, among whom were many Fédérés and petty bourgeois, seem to have been relatively few, yet no serious attempt was made to halt the movement. Danton let matters take their course; as for the Girondins, they were terrified, since suspicion spread to them. On September 2 Robespierre declared that Brissot and Carra were servants of the enemy—Carra because he had conceived the incredible idea of setting up Brunswick or the duke of York as king. A thorough search was made of Brissot's residence and there was evidently some question of making arrests, to which Danton objected.

The extant documents permit us only an approximate statement of the actual deaths: somewhere between 1,090 and 1,395, about half the total number of prisoners. There were 223 priests and other 'political' victims, accounting for no more than one-fourth of those killed; the rest were common criminals. On September 3 the vigilance committee of the Commune, on which Marat now served, published a circular that called on provincial Patriots to defend Paris and asked that, before leaving their homes, they eliminate counter-revolutionaries. The Girondins afterwards made much of this circular, but there is no evidence that it had any influence. As before, murders in the provinces continued: the blood-letting did not cease until the countryside was purged. The collective mentality is sufficient explanation for the killing.

The Terror accentuated the political, religious, and social consequences of August 10. No longer were there any who dared defend the monarchy. On September 4 the Legislative Assembly expressed hope that its successor would abolish the throne, and the new deputies from Paris were given a formal mandate to that effect. The latter were named by voice vote; in the departments a few electoral assemblies followed suit, and some began their meetings by purging certain members. The number of abstentions was enormous. Elections to the Convention signified less the institution of universal suffrage than the dictatorship of those who supported August 10.

On August 11 the Assembly closed the remaining monasteries; on the 15th it abolished teaching and charity orders and put into effect the decree against refractory priests, which had been refused by the king. Further arrests, massacres, and the August 26 decree on deportation eliminated the non-jurors. Priests who had not been required to take the oath of November 27, 1790, were obliged by a decree of August 14 to swear loyalty to liberty and equality. The decree originally applied to public officials but was broadened on September 3 to include all citizens. The pope did not issue official condemnation of this 'lesser oath', and one group of priests caused yet another split within the body of the clergy by swearing to it. Among them was Émery, director of Saint-Sulpice. After that, many refractory parishes accepted a constitutional priest rather than have none at all, but because there were not enough to fill all vacancies the Assembly, on September 20, ended its months of discussion on the subject and placed the register of births, marriages, and deaths in the hands of secular authorities. On the same day it authorized divorce. The Assembly's actions deprived the constitutional clergy of power at the very moment when it had seemed to emerge triumphant. State authority over it increased: clerics were denied perquisites, were not allowed to wear ecclesiastical dress unless conducting services, were forbidden to keep registers of Catholicism or to authorize marriage under any conditions except those provided by law, which meant they could not refuse to marry divorcés or their own priests. Bells and silver plate were taken from churches and ecclesiastical cloth was put up for sale. Rupture between republicans and constitutional clergy was now only a question of time.

The social order established by the Constituent Assembly also felt the after effect of popular victory. New measures advanced the peasants towards economic freedom. On August 25 manorial dues were suppressed without indemnity unless the landlord could produce original title to the land, and two days later a decree terminated the lords' rights to repossession of holdings in lower Brittany. Another of August 28 gave back to the communes any land which a seigneur had forced them to cede or had usurped. In addition, the rural proletariat was helped to acquire land: a decree of August 14 amended that of July 27 (which had put émigré property up for sale) by dividing such lands into small plots to be distributed in return for an annual rent, and authorized the division of commons. The Commune of Paris put the unemployed to work on fortifications around the city.

As the problem of finding sustenance was growing acute, on August 11 the Commune requested that trade in silver coin and the use of two prices be outlawed. A serious riot completely stopped traffic on the Midi Canal and other uprisings forced the introduction of fixed prices at Lyon and Tours. Through virtually all France the authorities reversed their policy and instituted economic controls. Finally, decrees of

September 9 and 16 authorized district directories to inventory grain supplies and order consignments to replenish markets. The only step that the Legislative Assembly dared refuse was price fixing. These measures seemed to foreshadow more drastic action to come, and some of the Jacobins made alarming comments to that effect. Commissioners Dufour and Momoro in the departments of Eure and Calvados stated that the nation guaranteed industrial and commercial property and for the time being respected landed property, but that it had the right to set up controls on produce. 'Beware the agrarian law,' wrote Bishop Lindet. In the department of Cher a parish priest named Petitjean urged his congregation to pool its possessions and pay no more rents.

The Montagnards elected at Paris found themselves unable to keep up with events. Even those who condoned the massacres did not favour anarchy in the streets, and certainly not one of them—Marat and Hébert included—ever considered suppression of private property. They were not wedded to economic controls, and particularly not to fixed prices. But to break with the people was to play into the hands of the moderates, much as the Feuillants had played into the hands of counter-revolution; moreover, they thought that in the interest of defending the Revolution some measures demanded by the people could be of use. For the enemy had accomplices of various kinds in France: on August 21 the first rightist insurrection in the Vendée gained control of Châtillon; Danton had learned of the conspiracy organized by La Rouërie in Brittany; and it was the royalists who had brought about the surrender of Verdun. Many people were encouraging resistance to enlistment and requisitions, were predicting an Allied victory and rejoicing at the prospect. The Terror must strike down all suspects and ensure total obedience. Requisitions and fixed prices would provision the armies, cut down expenses, and assure order. To achieve these purposes the regime of the Year II was sketched in outline in 1792.

In perfect agreement the Commune and the Assembly called up 30,000 men from the vicinity of Paris and moved their battalions nearer the border. In the north and east mass levies for the National Guard were ordered. The Commune went further, making an attempt at general mobilization, by requisitioning first arms and surplus horses, then bells, bronzes, and silver plate from the churches, and by setting up clothing centres. Finally, on September 4, the Executive Council ordered requisitions and price controls for grain and fodder to supply the army. It would take time for these efforts to produce full results, but at once they gave renewed energy to national defence. Twenty thousand men left for Champagne. The arrival of these reinforcements after the French victory at Valmy gave the Prussians pause to reconsider and greatly strengthened the Belgian front. The army felt that now the government was resolved to fight. Danton better than any other embodied the new will to win: until he intervened certain of his colleagues wavered and, on August 28, considered withdrawing to the Loire, a move that would have meant the moral dissolution of the nation. Less certain of victory than his words indicated, he rose to show the unfaltering character of a leader—and on that day merited well of the Revolution.

Whether it was an impulse from the people or a means of governing, the Terror, a temporary expedient adopted in the face of danger, was due to end when victory was won. Valmy sounded the signal for relaxation. The Girondins did not wait that long to take their revenge. Massacres and arbitrary arrests were provoking violent reactions while requisitioning and statements tinged with socialism frightened the bourgeoisie. Instinctively the latter rallied behind the Girondins, who, as the Feuillants had done before, raised the cry of social peril. Their party was largest in the Assembly, held a majority in the Council, and received fresh encouragement when most of those who were elected throughout the nation proved favourable to them. Revolutionaries in the departments did not follow every detail of their brothers' struggles in Paris; and now, when their numbers were less and the danger greater, unity took precedence over factional conflict. In their minds the Girondins were the men of August 10 because that day had put them back in the ministry.

On September 13 Roland denounced the Commune's commissioners and on the 17th Vergniaud attacked the vigilance committee. The Commune at once submitted, broke up its committee, and made due apology. But on September 20 it decided to elect a new committee. This skirmish was only the beginning. The Brissotins never forgave the sans-culottes of Paris for the worry the latter caused them, the political defeat the sans-culottes had dealt them, or the election of the Montagnards. Madame Roland developed a violent hatred of Robespierre and especially of Danton, who had left her husband no authority. It was she who started the idea of a departmental guard to protect the new assembly—and to facilitate indictment of the Montagnards. By the time it convened, the Convention was torn by irreparable party rifts.

# 14

## INVASION OF POLAND AND OF FRANCE. REVOLUTIONARY COUNTER-ATTACK: VALMY AND JEMAPPES, SEPTEMBER, 1792–JANUARY, 1793

French inaction let the Austrians and Prussians carry out their military preparations undisturbed. But the coalition members were not alert enough to profit fully from the respite: their delays gave the republicans time to dispose of the king, and their disputes soon permitted the revolutionary armies to seize the offensive again.

### INVASION OF POLAND AND THE QUESTION OF INDEMNITIES

The delays and conflicts that prevailed in Berlin were equalled only by affairs in Vienna. The emperor's successive coronation ceremonies at Buda, Frankfurt, and Prague took most of the summer. Francis did not care for council meetings with his ministers and was reluctant to make any firm decision. Spielmann had staked his fortune on the Prussian alliance, and Philip Cobenzl hesitantly agreed with him, while Kaunitz and his friends upheld the traditional policy and detested Spielmann as an upstart. The Prussian ministers were jealous of the king's favourites, especially of the incompetent Bischoffswerder, and bitterly criticized the alliance with Austria. Although they bowed before their king's desire to wage war in France, to them the whole enterprise seemed not only useless but dangerous now that the Polish question had been raised. And yet the boldness and unrestraint that Catherine displayed foiled all expectations.

The Czarina did not let events run ahead of her. While urging the Germans on against the Revolution, she prepared to enter Poland the moment they turned their backs, and on the day the Legislative Assembly declared war she sent a dispatch notifying the German powers that she was moving into Poland. During the night of May 18–19 approximately 100,000 Russians crossed the Lithuanian and Ukrainian borders. The Diet conferred dictatorial powers on Stanislas and then dissolved on May 29. The two Polish armies together numbered a little more than 30,000; Poniatowski, commander in the south, had neither experience nor decisiveness, although one of his lieutenants, Kosciusko, veteran of the American war, was adept at manoeuvring. Turned back again and again, the Poles warded off encirclement. For a time they held a line along the Bug River, but on July 18 it gave way and they had to fall back to Warsaw. Their cause was not altogether lost, since the Russians were far from their source of supplies and volunteers were rallying in great numbers: Poland began to stir. Its king unfortunately betrayed the nation. In the beginning he had decided that he would give up his country to protect his personal position. On June 19 he begged Catherine's clemency and on July 22 received the command to swear adherence immediately and irrevocably to the Confederation of Targowice. The next day he pressed an affirmative answer from his council. Russia occupied all Poland. The Confederates restored the old constitution, arrogated power to themselves, and dispersed the army through the country. Most of the Patriot leaders emigrated.

Prussians and Austrians alike were disconcerted. They had agreed not to defend the constitution of May 3 and had so informed Warsaw, but had hoped either that Catherine's success would be less swift and complete or that, at least, all three powers would decide the fate of Poland. They proposed that she join their February treaty and thus restore the Triple Alliance; she turned a deaf ear, offering only, on July 14, to renew her agreement with Austria, and then, on August 3, to join forces again with Prussia. In other words, she wanted to pursue negotiations with each separately. The two powers, neither trusting the other, now sought to deal tactfully with the all-powerful empress and find favour with her.

Catherine's entourage was not agreed on what fate should be dealt Poland, and she herself was probably undecided. It is commonly thought that she planned to preserve it intact as her protectorate, but the actual situation was more involved. She knew that Poland could at the first opportunity escape her with support from its neighbours, as it had in 1789. Annexation of the Ukraine would therefore prove more certain and would flatter her ego. Besides, she sincerely wanted the French to be brought to their senses and had no doubt that Prussia would abandon its plans against France if denied a portion of Poland. A second partition would, in all likelihood, have brought the three part-ners together and would have consolidated the coalition had not Spielmann, in a move to weaken Kaunitz, decided that instead of taking part of Poland, Austria should exchange the Netherlands for Bavaria, which the aged Kaunitz had long desired.

His idea had disastrous consequences. Seizing her opportunity, Catherine reasoned that a Polish state which was her protectorate deserved to be larger if the two other powers arranged an exchange. Thus, the Austrian move pushed her to reach a separate agreement with Prussia to obtain immediate possession of the territory involved, whereas the Bavaria–Netherlands exchange could not be concluded until peace was made with France, and even then there would be further complications: the duke of Zweibrücken, heir presumptive of Bavaria, in any case opposed the arrangement, and the maritime powers would object to a Belgian prince who could not defend his country. If the war dragged on, Austria would watch empty-handed while its allies took all they wanted. The alternative was to request that they wait until Austria could receive its due portion; either way the coalition would be weakened psychologically. At the time, however, they all thought that an expedition into France would be little more than a military exercise. Prussia readily agreed that Austria should receive an indemnity equal to Prussia's in value and at the same time, Spielmann was free to err at leisure. Error or not, he might have obtained a proper treaty from Prussia had he not been semi-disowned in Vienna.

After the Potsdam conferences of May 12–15 Schulenburg made official proposals, and Spielmann had to tell the emperor and Kaunitz of the arrangements he had been making. Stating that Austria would be playing the fool, Kaunitz opposed the agreement and refused to budge. In August, Francis accepted his resignation. This did not prevent the emperor from listening to the other ministers who indirectly attacked the exchange: because the income from Bavaria was less than from Belgium, Austria should demand a bonus—which was opportunely found in the margraviates of Ansbach and Bayreuth, which Frederick William had recently inherited. When it came time to leave for Frank-furt things were still unsettled and not until July 17 was a compromise adopted: Francis still demanded that England must first consent to the exchange. Schulenburg took offence at the request for a bonus but did not refuse to present the plan to his king, and the conference broke up. Nothing had been signed, and when Russia, at the beginning of August, inquired about the indemnities agreed upon at Frankfurt, Prus-sia replied that Austria's terms were not yet fixed but its own part was settled. This permitted negotiations to begin between Berlin and St. Petersburg. Then Schulenburg gave notice that the king would not give up the margraviates and that Austria had either to accept the original exchange or propose a substitute bonus. Intense discussions began again at Vienna. Finally, on September 9, the emperor made a firm pronouncement: without the margraviates there could be no question of an exchange or, consequently, of territorial indemnities; if Prussia did not give in, it would have to accept, like Austria, a financial indemnity. Spielmann departed on September 12 to present this fine programme to Frederick William. He travelled with Haugwitz, new Prussian ambassador to Vienna, who had hitherto seemed definitely to favour the alliance. They were not too discouraged: if necessary might the emperor not accept Alsace and Lorraine up to the Moselle? In fact, they were planning to rejoin the king of Prussia in Paris.

## THE COALITION ARMY

Europe offered no assistance whatever to the coalition powers. Counter-revolution had lost one of its main proponents when Gustavus of Sweden was assassinated on March 16; the duke of Sudermania, now regent, made overtures to France; and in Spain, Aranda tried to reach some sort of accommodation with the French government. Pitt was still unmoved. Sardinia and Russia were the only countries to respond favourably to the circular of April 12; even then, Victor Amadeus promised nothing more than to defend himself if France invaded his lands, and requested assistance in that event. Catherine offered 15,000 men, 3,000 more than stipulated in her alliance with Austria, but noted that they could not set out until Poland was pacified. When it was proposed that she instead give a subsidy, she generously offered 400,000 rubles.

To the Germans, and even more to the Italians, war against France had no national meaning. They viewed it as a war of classes or of ideologies; their rulers saw in it only a political struggle. Reaction had made some progress in Germany—its latest conquest was Friedrich von Gentz, who translated Burke's *Reflections* at the end of 1791—but the Revolution had numerous firm supporters, especially among the Rhinelanders, who denounced intervention and predicted a Jacobin victory. French setbacks in April severely disappointed them. Bürger expressed their bitterness in his *Song of Reproach*—'He who cannot die for liberty deserves nothing better than chains.' Counter-revolutionaries meanwhile attributed a new slogan to the sans-culottes: 'Conquer or run.' The German princes saw nothing to be gained from the affair and abstained. For similar reasons Victor Amadeus failed, in October of 1791, to unite the states of the Italian peninsula. The French still counted on co-operation from the Rhineland princes, who, so long as the Austro-Prussian forces were not prepared to protect them, negotiated with France to forestall invasion. Although they subsequently broke off talks, Hesse was the only state to place any regiments at the disposal of the coalition.

Neither Austria nor Prussia planned to throw its entire force, officially reckoned at 223,000 men for the former and 171,000 for the latter, into the campaign. Other than the Hessian troops and Netherlands garrisons, the duke of Brunswick had at his disposal only the

100,000 troops that had been promised him, and when he arrived at Coblenz in July he learned that he would actually have less. Prussia sent its contingent of 42,000 combat troops, excluding the munitions guards; Austria could not assemble its men because of opposition from the Hungarian diet and from the provincial estates of Belgium. The king of Prussia was not wealthy and had squandered part of Frederick the Great's treasury between 1789 and 1791, but he managed a loan from Holland. Austria, financially exhausted by the Turkish war, could not even meet current expenses and at the same time had to strengthen its position in the Netherlands. In addition, desertions lowered its troop strength. The most it could send Brunswick was 29,000 men, of whom 15,000 were under the command of Hohenlohe-Kirchberg and 11,000 were led from the Netherlands by Clerfayt. On Frederick William's insistence the duke accepted between four and five thousand émigrés, whose military value he considered negligible. There were 16,600 Austrians stationed on the Rhine and 25,000 more in the Netherlands, 13,000 of whom the governor, Duke Albert of Saxe-Teschen, used to attack Lille.

The quality of these forces compensated for quantity, in the minds of their commanders and even of the French. Prussian troops were thought the best in Europe because they performed with mechanical precision on the drill field and were regimented by a brutal but precise discipline that denied initiative to officers and men alike. Frederick the Great had perfected military training in the form of drillwork, admired and imitated by military leaders throughout Europe. Actually, his method was a product both of the men recruited to form his armies— uneducated peasants and volunteers inspiring distrust—and of the linear formations that were introduced to give the musket maximum effect, since linear orders permitted repeated salvos to be fired as fast as possible.

Yet Frederick William had waged no campaigns with his army, and when put to the test its lustre tarnished. Serious deficiencies became apparent—the artillery proved mediocre, its technicians inept, medical services non-existent; and general command was paralysed by official routine. The minister of war committed suicide in 1790 when mobilization exposed serious defects. The men did not live off the country, carried a nine-day supply of bread, and were expected to purchase the rest from their pay. At the end of nine days they either had to set up a new supply base and provide storehouses and ovens or food had to be brought by military transport. The huge baggage allowance granted to officers made any march a cumbersome affair.

Austria's army was considered inferior, being a mere copy of Frederick's machine. In 1753 Maria Theresa had imposed on her German provinces the system of recruiting by lots, an adaptation of the Prussian *Kantonisten* method, and had taken over the Prussian drill. Yet the Habsburg army had just returned from fighting the Turks and therefore possessed an undeniable advantage—the civil commissariat had been compelled to master the technique of feeding troops in territories that had few resources when transportation was not practicable. On the French frontier Austria acquitted itself better than Prussia.

The duke of Brunswick gave scarcely a thought to delays. In carrying out monarchical policy it was axiomatic that one did not gamble with an army that could be reformed only at the expense of much time and money. Besides, this army was intended less to destroy the enemy than to acquire securities for the forthcoming negotiations. Its training and infantry tactics did not encourage the leaders to seek a decisive battle: they had to have favourable terrain resembling a drill field. Linear formations were better suited to defence than to attack, since marching broke up the alignment and made it impossible to fire salvos; moreover, they lay at the mercy of a cavalry charge and could not easily pursue the enemy. These were old objections, and Frederick the Great himself had not surmounted the difficulties. A deep formation, the column, gave the infantry attacking power but interfered with firing, whereas a formation of skirmishers seemed risky: besides preventing formation of a square to resist cavalry attack, it made desertion an easy matter. It was used only to start an engagement or to begin entrenchment. In this respect, too, the Austrians held an advantage, for they had a light infantry composed of Tyroleans and Croats, although it was a small force. Under such circumstances military training advised that open battle be avoided, that manoeuvring be employed to threaten the enemy's communications, and that he be forced back, leaving behind fortified garrisons that could be besieged at leisure. Since the adversary would follow the same precepts, it was important to cover his flanks, and especially his supply stores, as well as the convoy routes. One's army, stretched out in a cordon, would lose all offensive power. In

France the comte de Guibert had earlier expressed hopes that an army transformed into a national organization composed of men burning with patriotism and confident of their mass strength would introduce new tactics and strategy. The Revolution alone could translate such hopes into reality. Even Frederick had left behind him no disciples in Prussia: his failures were remembered better than his successes, and many observers pointed out that he had become more and more cautious towards the end of his career. His victories went counter to principle and were attributed to the blunders of his enemies or to mere chance. The duke of Brunswick concurred in these opinions. As a general he was famous; he had courage and intelligence, but lacked the essential quality of a great man of war—he was afraid to gamble. Fearing that his personal glory might be compromised, he surrendered his authority in stipulating that Hohenlohe should act on his own responsibility to execute the plan they had agreed upon. Full of respect for the king, he dared neither disregard Frederick William's military judgment nor contradict him. The invading forces had not one but three leaders.

According to the plan outlined by the duke in February and defended by him again in May at Sans-Souci, the Prussians were to march by way of Longwy upon Verdun, separating the Metz army, which Hohenlohe would hold in check, from the Sedan army, which Clerfayt would guard. Upon reaching the Meuse they would lay siege to the forts abandoned by the enemy and would march upon Paris during the following spring. This plan conformed to precept. But general opinion considered the 'army of bunglers' incapable of effective resistance and expected France to suffer the fate that had struck Holland in 1787. Moreover, Bouillé offered assurance that he held the keys to the fortresses in his hands and that most Frenchmen were impatiently awaiting deliverance. A threatening manifesto would rally those who continued to hesitate. Frederick William therefore wanted to enter Paris at the end of the summer. Judging his effective force too small and the season too advanced, the duke said nothing but held to his original plan. His forces started off without a settled programme of action.

The final preparations were completed during the celebrations honouring the coronation of Francis—festivities that marked the last grand spectacle of the old Germany. During this final stage Mallet du Pan presented to the sovereigns the proposal for a manifesto which Louis XVI had received from the Feuillants. The marquis de Limon countered with one of his own, approved by Fersen. The diplomats looked absently at both and selected the second, for what reasons we scarcely know. On July 25 Brunswick took responsibility for its proclamation, an act he regretted the rest of his life.

## VALMY, SEPTEMBER 20, 1792

The army finally left Coblenz on July 30 but did not cross the border until August 19. They had no sooner entered France than rain began to fall, and an almost continuous downpour transformed the regions of Woëvre and the Argonne into a mud-hole, in which the advancing army gradually bogged down. Rain was one of the most precious allies the Revolution had. Brunswick attacked Longwy on August 22. Lacking proper equipment for a siege, he bombarded the town, which surrendered the next day. Verdun, besieged on the 29th, fell on September 2 after its commander, Beaurepaire, either committed suicide or was murdered.[1] Not that the Lorrainers hated the Revolution, as the invaders learned with chagrin, but Verdun's citizens weakened under bombardment and did not yet have a revolutionary government capable of pushing them to sacrifices and of humbling the royalists, who were able to cow the military command. If the 'virgins of Verdun', later guillotined, did not strew the road with roses for the king of Prussia, neither did they turn their backs upon him.

Brunswick had not yet given up his plan. Frederick William, however, was obstinate, and under the influence of Calonne and Breteuil the duke yielded, encouraged because the Sedan and Metz armies were

[1] Much ink has been spilled over the siege of Verdun and the death of Beaurepaire. Arthur Chuquet, in Les guerres de la Révolution (3 vols., Paris, 1886–87), declared himself convinced that Beaurepaire committed suicide, but the thesis of assassination has been strongly defended by Edmond Pionnier in Histoire de la Révolution à Verdun (Paris, 1906). His description was criticized by M. Sainctelette, La mort de Beaurepaire (Paris, 1908). The two theses are summarized by Xavier de Pétigny, Beaurepaire et le premier des bataillons des volontaires de Maine-et-Loire à Verdun, juin-septembre 1792 (Angers, 1912). Two facts are beyond dispute: the betrayal of the royalists, including some of the officers who had command of the defence, and the giving way of the population. If Beaurepaire was not assassinated, he was certainly driven to suicide by treason; but assassination is much more credible.

falling back and he no longer feared that he would be turned. He summoned Hohenlohe, who left a screen of troops before Thionville. On September 8 three sections of the coalition army entered the Argonne Forest: Hohenlohe at Les Islettes, on the road to Châlons; Brunswick near Grandpré, at the Aire pass; and Clerfayt to the north. All three ran into French forces commanded by Dumouriez.

Although forsaken by Louis and alienated from the Gironde, Dumouriez was not disturbed at finding his star eclipsed. In the camp at Maulde he worked wonders; by opposing Lafayette he regained the confidence of the Jacobins. The Sedan army needed a leader, so the Executive Council turned it over to him. He joined it on August 28. His designs were unchanged: convinced that Brunswick was rushing to aid the duke of Saxe-Teschen, he still wanted to march into Belgium. Servan, on the other hand, hoping to curry public favour, urged him to protect Paris. From a strategic point of view it was certainly doubtful that Brunswick would detour to defend the Netherlands, and if the Prussians reached Paris, what would become of Dumouriez in Belgium? Dumouriez changed his mind when he learned that the enemy had reached the Meuse. On September 1 he left Sedan, and by a flanking march that Clerfayt, with astonishing lethargy, did not even attempt to harass, reached the Argonne with his 23,000 men. Duval and Beurnonville joined him with 10,000 more from the north; Kellermann arrived from Metz with 18,000.

The French army had made progress since the previous spring. A war of position seasoned it, and although the Legislative Assembly obstinately refused to mix volunteers with troops of the line, amalgamation was beginning as generals grouped battalions of diverse origins in their formations. Panics continued to break out, and Dumouriez thought himself in no position to give battle in open country. He could, however, put up a defence, especially in country like the Argonne. The French artillery was on the whole superior to the enemy's, and Lafayette had provided it with horse-drawn batteries. French generals kept largely to traditional tactics: the regulations of August, 1791, based on Guibert's teachings, prescribed a shallow formation with the infantry drawn up in two lines of three ranks each, while permitting attack in deep order by battalion columns. But the pressure of events had already started to transform the mode of combat—defensive action, a stationary war, the need to employ volunteers who could not be drawn up in linear formation but were obviously filled with fervour and initiative, suggested that part of the forces be used as mobile riflemen who could be continually reinforced with effectives. The army had found a leader, and Dumouriez showed outstanding qualifications as a general: courageous, possessing great endurance, he knew how to speak the soldiers' language and win their affection. He was high-spirited and cheerful; he affected confidence at the most perilous moments and never lost his self-control. Unfortunately, in the army as in the cabinet, he retained a certain inconstancy and lack of foresight that all but undid him.

Relying on the commander who guarded the defile at Croix-aux-Bois, he let its garrison be withdrawn. Clerfayt seized it on September 12, and Dumouriez was turned. He escaped from Grandpré by a night march and camped outside Sainte-Menehould, backed by Dillon, who still held Les Islettes, and soon reinforced by Beurnonville and Kellermann. The Paris route lay open, but, since he could not leave his rearguard exposed to attack, Brunswick was unable to utilize the opportunity. He did nothing until September 17, then crossed the Argonne and surrounded the French positions, threatening the route to Vitry, their sole line of retreat, in an effort to force them back. Frederick William was in a hurry to finish off the campaign. Ignoring the rules of the game, on September 19 he ordered Brunswick to march straight upon the enemy. The next day the Prussians met Kellermann's troops, who had taken up battle positions on the heights of Valmy and Yvron. A furious cannon exchange started the action. After noon the infantry began to advance. French morale ran high; the defenders redoubled their fire and the attacking columns wavered. Thinking that his attempt had failed, Brunswick sounded retreat. It was not a great battle but the French had carried off a great victory, a moral victory for the Revolution even in the eyes of its enemies. Goethe, who witnessed the battle, at the time saw infinite repercussions. It was a military success as well and one much under-rated, for by gaining time for the French it worked to the disadvantage of their adversaries.

At first it was thought that matters were only postponed. Dumouriez, in no way reassured, wanted to temporize. With characteristic vanity he flattered himself that by urging the Prussians he could get them to retreat, enabling him to carry the war into Belgium and perhaps even conclude peace and form an alliance against Austria to boot. He sent out feelers for negotiations on September 22. The Prussians responded with alacrity, thinking that he, like Lafayette, wanted to march on Paris and restore the monarch. Let Louis be put back on the throne, they declared, and Prussia would be ready to talk of peace. But on the 23rd Dumouriez learned that the Republic had been proclaimed. He passed the news on to Frederick William, who on September 28 broke off preliminary talks with a strongly worded manifesto. Meanwhile Brunswick's troops, badly supplied from Verdun, exposed around the clock, in the barren region of Champagne, to drenching by autumn rains, and succumbing to dysentery, were diminishing with each day. He had 17,000 able-bodied men left. Retreat was decided upon for October 1. The situation appeared critical: as they crossed the Argonne, Dumouriez could swoop down on them. On the 29th the Prussians reopened discussions just as Dumouriez received instructions which the Executive Council, having learned of the talks, had issued on September 25 and 26.

Danton shared Dumouriez's misgivings; in the middle of the month Lebrun had tried to sound out the king of Prussia on an armistice; Servan still wanted to pull the army back behind the Marne or below Paris; the north of France was already invaded and Lille was under Austrian siege. The untoward effects of August 10 were now visible abroad: England, Russia, Spain, Holland, and Venice broke off all relations with France; the Swiss cantons armed themselves, and the Bernese took Geneva. An attack from Sardinia was expected momentarily. Montesquiou and Anselme received orders to advance on Savoy and towards Nice, and Custine was authorized to march on Speyer. But what purpose would such diversionary actions serve? Dumouriez's negotiations seemed an unexpected piece of good luck, and he was given full powers. The Council, however, thinking that the enemy would not willingly retreat, advised that guarantees must be obtained.

Guarantees were what Dumouriez and Westermann, Danton's envoy, did not secure. Their talks remain shrouded in mystery, but the facts speak for themselves: Prussia's army reached the Meuse without firing a shot. Custine meanwhile advanced beyond Speyer. The Austrians abandoned the Prussians; the Hessians rushed towards Coblenz. Brunswick, in a hurry to follow them, gave up Verdun on October 8 and Longwy on the 22nd, both to Kellermann. Negotiations proceeded along the way, but then, having brought a hornet's nest down about his ears, Frederick William refused to treat further. Had he been playing games with the French? No clear answer can be given. Certainly the fact that French territory had been evacuated, plus the opportunity to attack Belgium and the prospect of detaching Prussia from the coalition, persuaded Dumouriez and the Executive Council, which backed him, to spare the enemy. Some individuals suspected that this policy resulted from treachery and did not forget the pattern of events. But, rumours to the contrary, the Prussian retreat appeared to be a dazzling triumph for the young Republic. It must be acknowledged that it precipitated another.

## REPUBLICAN CONQUEST: JEMAPPES, NOVEMBER 6, 1792

Montesquiou seized Montmélian on September 22, entered Chambéry two days later, and was hailed throughout Savoy as its liberator. When ordered to drive the Bernese out of Geneva he chose to negotiate instead and succeeded in getting them to evacuate the city. Anselme arrived at Nice on September 29; Custine occupied Speyer the next day and, since the Austrians had recrossed the Rhine, continued on to Worms, then to Mainz on October 21, and finally to Frankfurt.

The duke of Saxe-Teschen had started to bombard Lille but could not shut off all access to the city. The electoral assembly of the Nord department, then in session at Quesnoy, voted to repair to Lille. Reduced to a handful of Jacobins under the leadership of Nolf, a curate, the assembly members headed off any signs of wavering. Representatives on mission mobilized one-quarter of the National Guards. On October 8 the Austrians withdrew to Mons. On November 6 Dumouriez led 40,000 troops in an attack on the enemy before Mons, near the hill town of Jemappes, which he took by assault. All Belgium fell to him. He occupied Aix-la-Chapelle and pushed on to the Roër.

In France and through Europe this continuation of French success had a profound effect. Jemappes, echoing Valmy, was a true revolutionary victory; it had been won in an open attack without astute manoeuvres and by the sans-culottes, who rushed the enemy to the martial strains of the *Marseillaise* and the *Carmagnole*, swamping the adversary with sheer force of numbers. Their achievement gave birth to the ideas of mass levy and a popular war which required neither military science nor formal organization.

The campaign nevertheless had been badly conducted. If Dumouriez had pursued the Prussians, if Custine had taken Coblenz, Brunswick would have been trapped and French troops could have marched up the Meuse and into Belgium to annihilate the Austrian army. Dumouriez had rolled back the coalition forces; he might have destroyed them. Unless peace were made, it was certain that spring would bring another attack upon France.

## THE SECOND POLISH PARTITION AND DISRUPTION OF THE COALITION

The entente was none the less weakened—another significant result of Valmy. When Haugwitz and Spielmann arrived at Verdun on October 8 they found the army in disorderly confusion, the king furious and stung with humiliation, Bischoffswerder disgraced and already supplanted by Lucchesini, who was Austria's enemy. Haugwitz immediately changed camp. It was no longer a question of Prussia invading France, but of defending the Netherlands and the Habsburg empire! From then on Austria was the 'principal party'; Prussia, now only an 'associate', could repudiate concomitant, if not equal, indemnities. It would have no qualms about looking after its own interests and disregarding those of its ally, and not until it had occupied its proper share of Poland would it be partner to a new campaign. Actually Frederick William, having more scruples than his ministers, declared that he would continue to combat the French. But he knew the Russians were impatient, and Goltz assured him that Catherine would deal separately with Prussia. On October 17 the king gave his ambassador full authority to negotiate, and on the 25th, at the Merl camp in Luxembourg, he made his intentions known to Austria: if rebuffed, he would furnish no more than the 20,000 men specified in the treaty of February 8, or a number equal to the empire's contingent if the Imperial Diet declared war on France.

The note from Merl reached Vienna on November 20 together with the news of Jemappes, which gave the note graver significance: Austria was faced with losing its ally or giving up all indemnity claims for the time being. Yet Spielmann and his colleagues did not despair of finding some way out of the gloomy dilemma. They banked on the king's inconstancy and, trying to gain time, did not reply until December 11, when they conceded that Prussia might occupy its share of Poland 'should an occasion arise'. Haugwitz expostulated and later maintained that he had received verbal consent to an 'immediate' occupation. Evidently he believed he had been given carte blanche. But Austria secretly asked England to oppose a Polish partition and requested Catherine both to postpone partition and to decrease Prussia's share, an action the more likely since it was known that she had described the losers at Valmy in terms of scorn. Austria, however, had waited too long. Upon reflection Catherine began to fear that Frederick William would make peace with France and that England would intervene. No later than December 13 she resolved to make an end to it. On December 16 Ostermann outlined to Goltz what sections she intended to take—the Ukraine and White Russia, an area four times larger than Prussia's part, with three million people compared to Prussia's one. Still, Frederick William's gain—Danzig, Torun, Posen, and Kalish—was hardly to be spurned. The treaty was drawn up in six days and signed on January 23, 1793. Prussia was committed to continue the war in the West; actually it sent part of its troops to Poland and thought only of refusing Austria any substantial aid or any indemnity. But the emperor was invited to add his signature, in consideration of which the famous Bavarian exchange would be facilitated, with such accompanying additions as were possible. When news of the treaty reached Vienna, consternation and indignation defied description.

# 15

## THE ORIGINS OF THE FIRST COALITION

If the revolution, victorious and possessing territorial securities, had chosen to temporize until Poland was partitioned a second time, in all probability it could have obtained peace from a quarrelling coalition by offering to hand back its spoils on condition that its own independence be respected. This prospect was no doubt what Danton anticipated early in October of 1792. To accomplish it, however, the French would meanwhile have to resist the intoxication of victory that urged them on to a war of propaganda, to further annexation, and hence to a breach with England. They would also have to spare Louis XVI. Any such policy required unity and concord among French republicans. Torn by factional conflicts, the Convention could not offer peace to Europe.

### THE BEGINNING OF THE CONVENTION: GIRONDINS AND MONTAGNARDS

The National Convention assembled for its first session on the afternoon of September 20, just as the battle of Valmy ended. The next day, having settled its rules of procedure, it replaced the Legislative

Assembly at the Manège. Towards the end of that day's session Collot d'Herbois, warmly seconded by Grégoire, rose to move that the monarchy be abolished. The motion was carried easily. The following day Billaud-Varenne had no difficulty in gaining consent to the proposal that decrees thenceforth be headed 'Year 1 of the Republic'. The first French republic was thus established by indirection, not out of judgment based on theory and formally stated, but because revolutionary France, which for its own safety had dethroned Louis XVI, now had to govern itself.

The Convention could not mirror the nation as a whole. The revolution of August 10 made it necessary to exclude royalist accomplices of foreign powers or suspects for treasonable activities. The masses, who had not voted, were vaguely troubled and mutely discontent: they would have preferred to enjoy the benefits of revolution and abjure the responsibilities it entailed. The new assembly emanated from a national minority resolved to spurn all compromise and to stand fast in the face of danger. It was a constituent assembly even in name—the embodiment of national sovereignty, according to Sieyes's theory, it enjoyed full and unqualified authority. By law and in fact it was invested with dictatorial powers.

But its composition failed to satisfy the Commune and the insurrectionary elements of August 10, partly because many of those elected called themselves republicans only in deference to events, and partly because the sans-culottes of the 'days', partisans of terror and of controls, did not have their own spokesmen: the Mountain represented them only to a limited degree, since it had no social and economic programme as yet, and the forlorn hope of agrarian law was denounced on all sides. Lacking representation in the Convention, extremists promptly took over the Cordeliers Club. In 1793 events were to permit them to sweep along with them both the Mountain and the sections in order to force the hand of the assembly.

Within the Convention two directing groups, the Girondins and the Montagnards, immediately came into conflict. They were not organized, disciplined parties; each had its dissidents and each lacked coordination. Nor did they defend clearly opposing doctrines; instead they revealed tendencies which their rivalry and the difficulties they faced made increasingly disparate.[1] Their antagonism dated back to reciprocal accusations of connivance with the court and to the conflict between Brissot and Robespierre over the advisability of war. August 10 and its aftermath then raised other issues. Madame Roland never forgave Danton for attaining his prominence and gathered round her an intransigent faction that included Barbaroux, Buzot, and Louvet. Pétion remained bitter towards the Parisians for not having elected him. And all still felt the fear of September.

The dispute soon grew venomous: to oppose a centralizing dictatorship the Girondins called on the support of local administrative bodies, controlled by the moderate bourgeoisie even after the Convention had decreed new elections, and they encouraged the passion for autonomy which had thrived since 1789. Although a few leaned towards federalism, the party never planned to introduce it in France, but its members relied on particularism for support, which was worse. The Gironde was bound to the business bourgeoisie, had little contact with the people, and had given up the Jacobin Club to meet at the homes of Madame Dodun, Madame Roland, or Valazé. Its members, Roland in particular, remained partisans of economic freedom, and they therefore parted with the people of small means who were wedded to economic controls. From then on, the conflict took on a social aspect. Virtually the entire bourgeoisie lined up behind the Girondins, whose name it used as a shield, in the Convention and even more in the provinces, for its royalist tendencies. The Montagnards were elected from Paris and naturally favoured the throng of sans-culottes *sectionnaires*. The Mountain controlled the Jacobin Club, where it carried on discussions with the sans-culottes, and it pleaded their cause. Threatened by the Gironde and deeming it incapable, if not of voting, certainly of applying with

---

[1] Between Girondins and Montagnards, Alphonse Aulard sees no difference beyond their idea of the role Paris should play in the political life of France (*Histoire politique de la Révolution française* [Paris, 1901, 5th ed., 1921], Part II, Chap. 7). Albert Mathiez sees in the Girondins representatives of the grand bourgeoisie and in the Montagnards representatives of the democracy of artisans, small rural landowners, and proletarians ('De la véritable nature de l'opposition entre les Girondins et les Montagnards', *Annales révolutionnaires*, XV [1923], 177–97). They should not be considered as organized, well-defined parties, and, most important, they should not have attributed to them ideas representing consistent doctrine or crystallized thought. Circumstances and personal rivalries exerted decisive influence upon them.

any conviction the measures that war required, the Montagnards ended by adopting—not without occasional regret—popular attitudes and by assuming leadership of the revolutionary extreme left which had no seats in the assembly. Their union was still not an intimate one, and as the group took on more provincial members it became even less homogeneous.

Between the two factions lay the centre. No majority could be formed without it, but it was an unstable group that never made a decision without later reversing itself. Resolved to defend the Revolution and the territorial integrity of the nation, its members were opportunists in selecting their means. Very bourgeois, they were at heart afraid of the people; arbitrary and bloody violence repulsed them; economic freedom they, too, considered dogma. But as long as the Republic was in danger they thought it unwise to break with the men of August 10, especially since those men demanded measures which could be of some use until victory was won. For these reasons a few—Barère, Carnot, Lindet, Cambon—rallied to the Mountain. More foresighted than the party leaders already enraged with hate, the largest block of deputies realized that the republicans were too few to escape perishing together if they tore one another to pieces. By changing sides at frequent intervals they forced the Convention to incredible reversals, but they were guided by a well-grounded sense of reality.

## THE STRUGGLE BETWEEN PARTIES AND THE DEATH OF THE KING, SEPTEMBER, 1792–JANUARY 21, 1793

For several weeks the Girondins preserved their popularity and appeared to be masters in the Convention. The jealousy that provincial deputies felt towards the Commune and sans-culottes of Paris, the fear that massacres had inspired, the anger that was provoked by remarks interpreted as threats against private property, the sense of security that was engendered by victory with its consequent reaction to terror—all aligned the majority behind the Gironde. When Danton withdrew from the Executive Council to take a seat in the assembly, Roland, 'the virtuous', judged himself leader in the Council. The Commune was not actually dissolved until the end of November, but it had lost its exceptional powers and had abolished its vigilance committee. The 'commissioners of executive power' were recalled to Paris. The high police force found that it was controlled by Roland and the assembly's Committee of General Security: prosecutions stopped, suspects were freed, many deported priests and émigrés were allowed to return. Next, the extraordinary tribunal of August 17 was suppressed, and as normal judicial processes were restored, special trials for counter-revolutionaries ended, for the High Court had already been abolished. Controls over the grain trade fell into disuse, and the September decrees had never been strictly applied. Roland continued to denounce grain controls, and when partisans of fixed prices resorted to violence between the Eure and the Loire he restored free trade on December 8.

Government controls relaxed in other areas as well. Private contractors had been enjoying immense profits from the war, especially when operations in Belgium provided lucrative opportunities for those employed by Dumouriez. The abbé d'Espagnac was the best known of the general's clients. When Pache, the new war minister, substituted a 'purchasing directory' for the contractors, Dumouriez protested unceasingly until the Convention granted him exclusive authority over expenditures allocated to supply his army. When it was decided not to fortify Paris, the labourers engaged for that purpose were dismissed. Roland restored piece-work wages in national manufactories and energetically denounced the prodigality of the Commune in keeping bread prices down to 3 sous a pound at the taxpayers' expense. The peasants, too, were affected by new measures: it was decided to postpone division of commons and sale of émigré lands. This general policy made the sans-culottes increasingly bitter towards the 'Rolandins', but within the Convention such measures did not encounter as much resistance as might have been expected. During the long debate on the grain trade, Saint-Just, orthodox economist, showed that the only way to check high prices was to curb inflation. Robespierre gave eloquent expression to the people's grievances and demanded that hoarding be stopped, but he proposed neither requisitions nor price controls.

The republicans seem to have agreed, with little dissent, as to their views on the clergy. They refused to abolish the budget of public worship, a course advocated by Cambon, but in December calmly discussed—without reaching any conclusion—the establishment of public, lay, free, and compulsory education, following the principles of the celebrated report delivered by Condorcet to the Legislative Assembly.

Danton did not share Robespierre's deep hatred of the Girondins; instead he offered them his support. At heart he belonged more to the centre, as Levasseur has noted. He only asked that extreme measures be avoided, and in October he promised Théodore de Lameth, who had returned from London to seek his assistance, that he would try to save the king. He well knew that this was a primary condition for peace, and to obtain a truce he might even have gone so far as to re-establish constitutional monarchy, perhaps with the duc de Chartres on the throne. As early as October 4 he proposed that the fatherland be declared out of danger. But, conversely, moderation and appeasement could not come before the end of hostilities. The dilemma could only be resolved by unity among the parties; in any case the Montagnards had to be silenced. On September 21 and 25 Danton criticized dictatorial powers and agrarian law as well as federalism. Wisdom advised the Girondins to come to terms with him.

Instead they wanted to crush their opponents. They forced Danton to move towards the left when they attacked him, demanding an account of his secret expenditures, which he could not provide, while Madame Roland charged that he had pilfered the royal storerooms, which had recently been broken into. On September 25 Marat and Robespierre heard themselves violently denounced as aspirant dictators. Attacks on the Commune increased. On October 29 Louvet launched a new campaign against Robespierre. It was obvious that the Girondins were seeking by every means to indict those among the 'instigators' of August 10 who had not rallied to them—as had Carra and Barbaroux—by attributing the September massacres and revolutionary dictatorship to them. The Girondins realized that by placing blame on the sans-culottes and driving them to a more desperate stand, they risked exposing themselves to a new 'day'. On this account Roland asked the Convention on September 23 to give him a private bodyguard, and Buzot, whose love for Madame Roland was turning him against his former comrades, proposed the formation of a 'departmental guard' to protect the national representatives.

Although the majority in the assembly shared the Girondin dislikes, it refused to hand over their opponents. A third party therefore emerged. Subsequently labelled the Plain, to contrast it with the Mountain, or else castigated as the Marsh, it implicitly agreed with the thesis brilliantly propounded by Robespierre on November 5: certain results of August 10 were regrettable, but there could be no question of outlawing the men who had overthrown the king and nipped treason in the bud; by prosecuting those leaders the Convention would tacitly denounce the insurrection and destroy the assembly's own basis of authority; furthermore, the deputies would place themselves at the mercy of the royalists if they employed force against the Parisian sans-culottes. The assembly, therefore, halted after expressing its contempt for Marat. Robespierre was not arraigned; having passed that test, he grew in stature and took over leadership of the Mountain. To avoid arousing the departments against the capital, the assembly cautiously limited itself to praise of departmental addresses favouring the Gironde and allowed the provinces to send a new throng of Fédérés to Paris.

Having failed to sway the Convention this time, the Girondins found their power on the wane: within the Council the ministers of war and navy, Pache and Monge, dissociated themselves from Roland. Since the Parisian bourgeoisie still refused to vote, the Jacobins gained control of the Paris departmental directory, and in the Commune a moderate mayor was flanked by Chaumette as *procureur* and Hébert as his assistant. Worse still, the embattled Montagnards answered their critics by accusing them of postponing the king's trial.

This was in fact what the Brissotins hoped to do, since the orientation of their domestic policy inclined them to spare Louis. But Danton had already said to Lameth: 'Can a king under indictment be saved? He's as good as dead when he appears before his judges.' And in reality the Convention had to declare him guilty if it wanted to avoid damning August 10, its own existence, and the proclamation of the Republic—as Robespierre reminded it, with irrefutable logic, in an address delivered on December 2: 'If the king is not guilty, then those who have dethroned him are ... The Constitution prohibited everything you have done ... Prostrate yourselves before Louis to invoke his clemency.' Once the Convention recognized Louis's guilt it could hardly refuse to pronounce the death penalty against a person who had summoned the aid of foreign powers and whom the sans-culottes considered responsible for the ambush at the Tuileries. To save the king they would have to avoid asking the question of his deserved punishment—in other words, he could not be put on trial. The Girondins wished to follow this course, but in trying to outlaw the Mountain they could not prevent the Montagnards from speaking. The king's head was at stake for each party.

Debate on Louis's trial did not begin until November, after undistinguished reports had been delivered by Valazé and Mailhe, and it was still dragging along when on November 20 an iron chest was discovered at the Tuileries. Roland committed the signal mistake of being the first to examine its compromising papers with no witnesses present. Trial was now inevitable. On December 11 Louis was brought before the Assembly. After either denying the charges or taking refuge behind the constitution, he was authorized to consult Tronchet and Malesherbes. On December 26 the lawyer Sèze gave the defence: he denied that treason had been committed, but devoted his argument to challenging the Convention's competence to try the king and invoking royal inviolability. As to the first point, the Convention was invested with full powers as a constituent assembly, and the majority had no doubts concerning its own legality. As to the second, after Varennes, Brissot and Robespierre agreed that the king's inviolability applied only to his constitutional acts countersigned by a minister. On July 3, 1792, Vergniaud had protested that the constitution's respectful silence on treason could be ridiculously interpreted as granting Louis immunity. But the Girondins resorted to obstruction. They asked that all Bourbons be banished, charging that those who wanted to do away with Louis intended to replace him with the duc d'Orléans, who was now a deputy from Paris and called Philippe Égalité—a change of position which forced the Mountain to defend him and in turn allowed it to be accused of royalism. Then the Girondins maintained that determination of the king's fate had to be ratified by the people. Barère rebutted that claim in the most distinguished of his speeches, that delivered on January 4, 1793. Surrendering hope of a legal case for acquittal, they ended by pointing out that regicide would rouse a general coalition against the Republic and would again endanger its life, This was a telling argument for avoiding the trial in the first place, but was no longer valid. Besides, it seemed to represent quibbling from the Girondins, who in November had demanded war to the finish.

Balloting on separate issues began on January 14, 1793. Each deputy explained his vote at the rostrum. The vote against the king was unanimous. There was to be no popular referendum. The fatal vote started on January 16, and continued until the next day. Of the 721 deputies present, 387 declared themselves for the death penalty, 334 were against. But 26 supporters of the penalty had proposed that an examination be opened to determine whether a case for granting reprieve existed. This skilful manoeuvre originated with Mailhe, the first to vote. If the 26 votes were taken to be contingent upon a new examination the margin was reduced to very little. The 26 had to be forced to take sides. It was then agreed to take a final vote on the sole question of reprieve: 380 votes were cast against; 310 for. Each time the Girondins had split.

Agitation by the sections had occurred during the trial, and charges have been made that the Convention was swayed by fear in its balloting. The only victim of violence, however, was a Montagnard, Lepeletier de Saint-Fargeau, assassinated by a royalist on January 20. On the other hand, bribery helped swell the minority in favour of reprieve: not content to use official channels, Ocariz, the Spanish chargé d'affaires, distributed two million livres advanced by the banker Le Couteulx. Until the last hour royalists had continued to hope. The final result took them by surprise.

On the morning of January 21 the Convention ordered the entire National Guard to line both sides of the route taken by the king to the scaffold. Louis was beheaded at the Place de la Révolution. With few exceptions the French people accepted the deed in silence, but it made a profound impression. Its effects will long be debated. Execution of the king aroused pity and exalted royalist convictions, yet it seems undeniable that monarchical sentiment was dealt a severe blow—a king had been put to death like any ordinary man; royalty lost, never to recover, the supernatural quality that even the Revolution had not yet eradicated. At the time, however, dismay seized many Frenchmen when they realized the implications of what had been done: within the nation, 'voters' and 'appellants' swore undying hatred of each other; abroad, the rest of Europe decreed a war of extermination against regicides. Fundamentally the king's trial opposed those who, in the interest of peace, were more or less consciously inclined to compromise with counter-revolution, against those who, remaining intransigent, gave the nation no hope of salvation save through total victory.

## ANNEXATIONS AND WAR OF PROPAGANDA

The Girondin policy of warding off dictatorship and sparing the king required peace. Yet theirs was, and remained, the war party, more so now than ever, because to win back the sans-culottes they rashly invoked the vision of France as liberator of the world. They were not inspired solely by party ambition, for the romantic dream of liberation dazzled them. Nevertheless, impulse served them well—a war of propaganda lay close to the hearts of the revolutionary populace, and indeed of many Montagnards; the people criticized the Gironde not for having launched the war but for having waged it poorly.

The Convention still held back, even though it was pressed from all sides to answer urgent problems with solutions binding on the future. Certainly the occupied countries aspired to be delivered from the Old Regime, but should they be left to accomplish this alone? Or should their desires be anticipated by 'municipalizing' them immediately? And should France liberate them at its own expense, exporting its currency to pay the costs? Or should it supply its troops by requisition-ing materials and demanding war contributions? The refugees in France were agitating, and Clavière, one of them who was now a minis-ter, had Montesquiou deprived of command when he treated the Genevese aristocracy too lightly. In November the inhabitants of Nice, Savoy, and the Rhineland raised a new issue by asking that their terri-tories be annexed to France. The generals had received no instructions and were proceeding to act on their own initiative. At Nice, Anselme replaced existing authorities, 'municipalizing' the town; on the other hand, Montesquiou, in Savoy, limited his activity to allowing the for-mation of new clubs and the convocation, on October 20, of a 'national assembly of Allobrogians'. In the Rhineland Custine organized clubs, best-known of which is that of Mainz, and wanted to abolish the feudal system. Later Dumouriez, who hoped to rule an independent Belgium, acted with the Vonckists in authorizing provincial assemblies to be elected in place of the Estates. This was enough to provoke a quarrel with the Statist party. Meanwhile he was unable to prevent anti-clerical democrats from triumphing at Liége and from starting troublesome clubs everywhere else, which immediately aroused strong opposition from the Church. Financial policies adopted by the military commanders were equally varied: Anselme, Montesquiou, and Dumouriez exacted as little as possible from the people—Dumouriez tried to obtain a loan from the clergy, and his contractors paid for their purchases in currency. But in the Rhineland Custine lived off the country by exacting money from privileged groups, usually members of the bourgeoisie, such as bankers in Frankfurt. Up to the middle of November the Convention had taken no definite stand.

Then came Jemappes, after which confidence and enthusiasm knew no bounds. The Montagnards exulted along with the rest and this time Robespierre did not try to resist the wave of popular opinion. No one took time to reflect. On November 19 Rühl informed the Convention that the Mainz club feared for its existence and wanted French protection; La Revellière-Lépeaux promptly proposed the famous decree offering 'fraternity and assistance' to all peoples who wished to regain their liberty. The decree was immediately voted, and the die was cast. Revolution in France donned warrior's garb to challenge the world. On November 27, while an English delegation was congratulating the young republic, Grégoire rose to salute another republic soon to emerge on the banks of the Thames. Brissot tried his utmost to force a complete break with Spain: 'Our liberty will never rest quietly as long as a Bourbon is enthroned. There can be no peace with Bourbons; with that understood, we must consider an expedition into Spain.' He demanded that Dumouriez send back his lieutenant, Miranda, to stir up Latin America. Nor were Germany and Italy ignored. 'We cannot be calm,' wrote Brissot on November 26, 'until Europe, all Europe, is in flames.' Ten days earlier Chaumette had prophesied that soon Europe would be municipalized as far as the borders of Russia. Refugees, first among them Clootz, pressed energetically for a crusade into Europe. Dutchmen asked that Dumouriez invade their country; at Bayonne Marcheña and Hévia arranged for propaganda to cover Spain.

The most practical course was first to decide the future of occupied lands, and as their boundaries reached the crest of the Alps and the banks of the Rhine, voices rose to demand that French expansion should be bounded by 'natural frontiers'. In the years to follow many historians were to defend this same doctrine, which would continue to attract partisans, on the grounds that France's natural borders constituted a monarchical legacy and a national tradition. There is in fact little evidence that the kings of France thought in terms of any such doctrine. Several of them pushed into the Low Countries, where until the sixteenth century the count of Flanders, as one of the French king's great vassals, ruled over a land whose border lay too close to Paris for safety. But in the eighteenth century Louis XV did not follow their example. It was chance that led Henry II into the three bishoprics of Metz, Toul, and Verdun, and Richelieu into Alsace. Farther north, French diplomacy sought only to secure dependent territories on the left bank of the Rhine.

Was it, then, the romantic excitement of Victory which led Frenchmen to maintain that nature had providentially framed the nation? The romantic element undeniably had influence, but it seems plausible to conclude that there had been ample preparation for the idea. The concept of natural limits dated back at least to certain writers who provided Richelieu with rationale for his policy; Mézeray, a historian whose works were honoured as classics in the eighteenth century, formulated it in clear terms. And there probably were other sources, such as the schoolbooks containing Caesar's *Commentaries*, which assigned to Gaul the same limits claimed by the revolutionaries. At any rate, Brissot wrote in November: 'The French Republic's only border should be the Rhine,' and on November 16 the Executive Council opened the Scheldt estuary to shipping in a gesture aimed to persuade the citizens of Antwerp that Belgium already belonged to France. The Council's act violated the treaties of Westphalia, which stipulated that the river should remain closed. Liberation therefore risked turning into conquest, and the pressures of setbacks to propaganda and military necessity hastened that development. Only a few more weeks were needed.

The Convention, like the Gironde, would have liked to see France surrounded by sister republics. But it soon became obvious that most of their neighbours were either opposed to the idea or kept silent out of caution. Occupation everywhere brought its own evils or else provoked a nuisance that they wished to avoid. Only Savoy stated its position clearly by abolishing the Old Regime and requesting annexation.

On the other hand, Belgium reacted by sending a delegation to ask the Convention, on December 4, to recognize its independence: the delegates themselves did not intend to adopt full revolutionary reforms, out of fear of the Church. A similar attitude prevailed in the Rhineland. In sum, the inhabitants were either incapable of freeing themselves or did not wish to be liberated. The republicans bridled. 'Just as it is our duty to give freedom to other peoples,' Danton had stated on September 28, 'I declare that we also have the right to tell them "you will have no more kings".' Foreigners friendly to the Revolution replied that independence as much as victory of the coalition would deliver them into the hands of their enemies. The citizens of Nice voiced this opinion on November 4. At Mainz the club found itself isolated and Forster finally proposed union.

On November 27 the Convention took the initiative and annexed Savoy. Grégoire justified the decree by invoking national sovereignty, the geographical reasons that made Savoy part of France, and the common interests they shared. If these were the conditions for annexation, then each occupied country would have to be considered individually; but the army's needs and those of the treasury made an immediate decision urgent.

At the height of a campaign led by Dumouriez and the contractors against the purchasing directory, which they accused of seriously cutting army supplies, the Convention had dispatched special commissioners to Belgium on November 30. Camus returned to report that the troops did lack the essentials, which was why Dumouriez was given a free hand despite Cambon's objections. But Camus also told the committee that there would not be enough creditors to cover Dumouriez's expenses, meaning that the Republic would have to bear the financial burden. Cambon replied that war could not continue under such conditions and that revolutionary steps had to be taken: property belonging to the Belgian clergy, the prince, and 'abettors and willing satellites' should be sequestered to guarantee assignats, which could be introduced into occupied countries to relieve France of the need to export its own currency. The tithe and manorial rights should be suppressed, and old duties replaced with taxes on the rich. New officials would carry out reforms: electors and candidates would be limited to those willing to swear an oath to liberty and to renounce all privileges.

Thus would popular masses realize the tangible benefits of revolution—'war for châteaux; peace for cottages'. This famous decree, voted with acclamation on December 15, instituted the dictatorship of revolutionary minorities under the protection of French bayonets, and undertook to secure the fortunes of other peoples without consulting them, at their expense. This time Dumouriez was the loser. Not content to make himself financially independent, he tried to treat the Belgians with care to pave the way for his candidacy should they obtain an independent government. Here the war was less than a year old, and already a Bonaparte was knocking at the door. With his plans endangered, Dumouriez hurried back to Paris on January 1; but he obtained nothing.

The result—already predicted by Robespierre—was calamitous. The Belgian populace itself rejected the gifts, which it considered quite worthless when priced in assignats. Thirty commissioners went to Belgium and forcibly applied the decree. Cambon congratulated himself on February 1 for having already obtained 64 million livres from the country, but by taking Church property the French had alienated the people much as Joseph had done. On the 17th the commissioners stated plainly that the populace would revolt at the first military setback the French received. The same was true elsewhere: disaffection spread even to Savoy. It seemed obvious that only annexation could stave off counter-revolution in the occupied countries. Nice was consequently annexed on January 31, and on the same day Danton requested a similar measure for Belgium. He also formulated, with expressive brevity, the doctrine subsequently followed by the Convention: the Republic was to expand within its limits 'as defined by nature'. On February 14 Carnot completed the declaration by an appeal to history, stating that within the natural domain 'the parts detached have been taken by usurpation'. The republicans did not dare summon a Belgian assembly: in elections supervised by French agents and those friendly to them, each province in turn voted on its own annexation. In the Rhineland a single assembly, similarly elected, consented on March 17 to union with France. The Convention approved annexation within the month. The bishopric of Basel, which had been made the Republic of Rauracia in November of 1792, became the department of Mont-Terrible on March 23, 1793.

The army of the Republic was the only instrument that could enforce this policy, but by now the coalition was ready to act and had already delivered its first blows against French forces. After six months of discussion the Convention chose its course just when military defeat began.

## THE BREAK WITH ENGLAND

Events took Pitt by surprise. While defending his budget on February 17, 1792, he confidently predicted that England could expect fifteen years of peace, and proceeded to reduce the country's armed forces by 2,000 sailors and more than 5,000 soldiers. When war broke out on the continent he maintained strict neutrality, probably thinking, along with everyone else, that the Revolution would quickly be crushed. And he was delighted at the prospect, for revolutionary defeat could be expected to stem agitation in the United Kingdom.

Democratic propaganda had been gaining ground. In April several Whig leaders formed a new Society of the Friends of the People. But radicals of this stripe found themselves outflanked: as in the case of their French brethren, English democrats were led by natural inclination to formulate a social programme. In February, Paine published the second part of his *Rights of Man*, which vigorously attacked the British aristocracy and proposed a severely graduated income tax that would take all income above 23,000 pounds. Godwin's *Human Justice*, bordering on utopian communism, appeared in 1793. At the end of 1791 a poor London cobbler named Thomas Hardy formed a labouring group, which held its meetings in a local tavern. On January 25, 1792, they founded the London Corresponding Society, consisting of eight members and requiring dues of one penny per week. At the same time five or six workers in Sheffield formed a similar group. This participation of the artisan class, if not of the proletariat, in public life was a development important because it revealed that the social question had become a political reality. 'By our labour are the monarchy, the aristocracy, and the clergy supported,' the Stockport club was soon to state; 'we are not the swinish multitude described by Mr. Burke.' The Scots poet Burns expressed popular sentiment more bluntly. Newcomers infused the democratic movement with fresh vitality. On

March 24 club delegates, in a meeting at Norwich, expressed hope that all friends of liberty would form a general union, an idea which suggested a popular convention and terrorized the aristocrats, who believed that the seventeenth-century Levellers had reappeared.

As in France, propaganda drew its effect from economic circumstances. The year 1791 brought heavier Corn Law duties and ended wheat exports from England. During the winter bread prices rose. The harvest of 1792 promised no relief. In May riots broke out and strikes spread. The soldiers, who had to live off their pay and were not quartered in barracks, suffered from rising prices. Clubs proselytized among them and gained their signatures on a number of petitions. Military discipline weakened. In Ireland the situation seemed no better: agrarian disturbances again shook the country, persuading the Catholic 'Defenders' and the Protestant 'Peep of Day Boys' to make common cause with political groups. Societies—the non-sectarian United Irishmen organized by Wolfe Tone at the end of 1791, and the Catholic Committee, which in February of 1792 called a meeting of all affiliated members—joined in demanding that Catholics be given the right to vote and that the Test Act be abolished. Grattan defended their programme before Parliament, although he also criticized agitation. The Catholics reached their goal shortly before war with France broke out, but the other demands failed.

Until May of 1792 Pitt evidently was not alarmed. In that month he allowed Fox's bill for jury trial of libel cases to pass, although he rejected a new motion from Grey favouring electoral reform, On May 21, however, a royal edict suddenly denounced inflammatory publications and ordered legal action against them. The government simultaneously began to subsidize conservative propaganda. In June, having got rid of his long-time opponent, Lord Chancellor Thurlow, Pitt opened discussions with the Whig right wing, led by Portland, in hopes of setting up a union cabinet. If the king had not objected, Pitt would have brought in Fox; without him the attempt fell through.

The triumph of French democrats made the situation worse. This time Pitt and Grenville made no secret of their personal opinions, which had always coincided with those of George III and the ruling groups. The ambassador to Paris, Lord Gower, was recalled and all official contact with Chauvelin was abruptly broken off. Pitt's icy reserve and Grenville's haughty arrogance made it difficult to carry on official conversations—especially since the French asked that their new government be recognized before talks proceeded. Besides, Chauvelin was accused of encouraging the Whig opposition and even of directing and financing democratic propaganda. The September massacres and the wave of émigrés—3,772, numbering among them 2,000 priests—inflamed public opinion. It was said that the Parisian Jacobins ate an hors d'œuvre ground from human flesh. Those well disposed towards the Revolution, Bishop Watson among others, grew alarmed; some began to recant. In the course of September, Noël, Danton's envoy, did not disguise the fact that the situation was becoming dangerous.

Yet democratic propaganda made rapid headway during the fall. The Revolution's military victories gave new heart to its supporters in England as well as in France, and they rejoiced publicly. Hardy's society sent a delegation to congratulate the Convention. Club representatives were summoned to a general assembly, scheduled for December 11. In Scotland, Thomas Muir set up a Society of the Constitution and of the People on October 3. Burns purchased cannons to send the French and on one occasion rose from a theatre seat to call for Ça ira. The manufacturing of arms drew denunciations; in December, Burke made accusations in the Commons, throwing a dagger to the floor as evidence. On November 24 Noël stated that a revolutionary movement was in the making.

These declarations were only flattery of the Convention's delusions. There is no proof that the English societies planned to revolt; furthermore, the strong reaction of aristocrats and bourgeois who believed the societies had such intent indicated that Pitt would retain control. The historian John Reeves founded an 'Anti-Leveller' society, and general panic even caused numerous loyalist and French-hating groups to spring up. As soon as war entered the realm of possibility it became popular among the ruling classes: not only would it serve their interests and promise revenge against France overseas (as well as new colonies), but also would provide an opportunity to suppress the democrats at home. Domestic considerations made a breach with France appear desirable to Pitt and Grenville: if they declared the French decree of November 19, offering fraternity and assistance to all peoples, a *casus belli*, English democrats virtually faced charges of high treason for their activities. Paine sat in the French Convention as a deputy from Pas-de-Calais, but was tried *in absentia*; in January of 1793 proceedings were started against Muir, recently departed for Paris. War would also reinforce the cabinet's position in Parliament by inducing a Whig faction to leave Fox and join the majority.

Yet, as it happened, Pitt decided to break with France only to safeguard Britain's particular interests. As late as November 6 Grenville told Auckland, ambassador to The Hague, that he could see no advantage in abandoning neutrality. Although Pitt had written on October 16 that if France kept Savoy the face of things might change, it can legitimately be asked if annexation of Alpine or even of Rhineland regions would have provoked him to take up arms. That Dumouriez and the Convention imagined Pitt would let them annex or control Belgium, however, was an extraordinary misjudgment. At most England might have permitted them to carry the war into Belgian territory under condition of a formal promise not to take any measures concerning its status without British consent. In vain did Lebrun send Maret to assure Pitt that the Republic would not keep Belgium: opening up the Scheldt flatly contradicted his reassurances and signified to Pitt what could be expected from France. The decree of December 15 confirmed his suspicions. In addition, England was allied with Holland, which had a direct interest in keeping the Scheldt closed. When a French squadron forced its way into the harbour channels and pushed out the Dutch, the Stadholder concluded that invasion threatened and called for English aid. Pitt promptly answered in the affirmative.

In December the Girondins wavered: they had counted on England and Prussia; the bourgeois of Bordeaux and other large ports, already weakened by anarchy in the colonies, did not relish war on the seas. But ever since Jemappes, Dumouriez had been pressing for entry into Holland, and as Amsterdam was Europe's largest banking centre some contended that carrying the war forward would make it 'pay its own way'. On December 5, none the less, the Council put off decision on invasion of Holland. After that the king's trial, as we have seen, led the Girondins to make much of the threat of danger from abroad, but on that issue, too, the party split. On January 1 Kersaint, a naval officer, listed the considerations that showed England vulnerable: a 'modern Carthage', whose power rested on credit, would collapse like a house of cards. The Montagnards raised no objection to any of the measures that would make extension of the war inevitable; several of them hailed the prospect. Robespierre kept silent. Disguising their own hesitation, the Girondins would quickly have risen to denounce any sign of resistance from their foes. Thus did antagonism between the two parties once more bear fruit. Dumouriez, back at Paris, obtained the Council's consent on January 10, although it did not give the official order until the 31st. The Gironde had lost two months—two months in which Holland could have been occupied with no difficulty.

Pitt and Grenville showed greater power of decision. On November 29 Grenville received Chauvelin to tell him that the edict of November 16 and the decree of the 19th must be revoked. On December 2 Pitt spoke to Maret in similar terms; the day before, he had called up the militia. On December 13 Parliament assembled. Almost to a man the Whigs voted to support the government. Fox, Lansdowne, and Sheridan criticized French moves but bravely spoke against war— qualifying their remarks, however, with the proviso that Holland be left untouched. Pitt easily carried the day. On December 20 he asked for 20,000 sailors; on the 31st he had the Alien Bill passed; in January he halted shipments of grain and raw materials to the Republic. The king's execution brought matters to a climax. On January 24 Chauvelin was given his passport; Lebrun, anticipating the next step, recalled him the following day. When he arrived, on February 1, the Convention voted for a declaration of war against England. It was Brissot who had defended the motion before the assembly!

## THE BREAK WITH THE STATES OF SOUTHERN EUROPE

To England, Louis's execution served as a pretext; to Spain it was the cause for war. After August 10 Aranda continued to deal with France on friendly terms and even took measures against refugee priests. Despite Brissot, Lebrun restrained the French ambassador, Bourgoing, and proposed that both nations agree to disarm, suggesting further that they sign a declaration of neutrality pending Spanish recognition of the Republic. But on November 15 a palace revolution replaced Aranda with Godoy, lover of Queen Maria Luisa. Soon Louis's trial provoked demonstrations against France, and Godoy made neutrality dependent upon the verdict. After January 21, he turned down the French proposals. Bourgoing left Madrid on February 22; on March 7 the Convention declared war against Spain. England now had access to the Mediterranean, and the princes of Italy thought themselves free to turn against the Republic.

Rupture with Rome was already assured. The pope imprisoned two students from the French Academy, whom he released shortly afterwards; in return Mackau, the French representative at Naples, sent a secretary, Hugou de Bassville, who conspicuously wore the cockade and claimed the right to fly the tricolour. He was murdered in a riot on January 13. Madame Roland drafted a message from the Council denouncing the 'insolent hypocrite of Rome'.

In December, Naples was threatened by a squadron led by Latouche-Tréville, and awaited the arrival of English ships. Ferdinand and his minister, Acton, joined the coalition. Tuscany and Venice had to break with France. Parma followed Spain; Modena, Austria. Choiseul-Gouffier, former French ambassador to the Ottoman Empire, had managed to make even the Grand Turk distrustful of the new envoy, Descorches. Except for Switzerland and the two Scandinavian countries, France found itself pitted against all Europe just when its army was dwindling with each day. Volunteers enlisted only for the length of the campaign; throughout the winter they returned to their homes, reassured that the fatherland no longer seemed in danger. The Gironde was no better prepared to fight than it had been the preceding spring.

The policy followed by the Gironde was a series of paradoxes. It tried to restore the liberal regime and spare the king, which presupposed peace, yet it provoked a general war. It could not spare Louis and conclude peace without the agreement of all republicans, yet by lashing out at the Montagnards and sans-culottes it killed any chance for unity. The coalition powers at first won a series of brilliant victories and thereby sealed the fate of this party which had failed to resolve any of its contradictions.

# BIBLIOGRAPHY

This is the bibliography prepared by Georges Lefebvre for the 1951 edition of *La Révolution française* and subsequently brought up to date by him for the 1957 reprinting of his work. The translator has added no new items, but publication facts have been brought up to date wherever possible.

See P. Sagnac, *La fin de l'Ancien Régime et la Révolution américaine* (Paris, 3d ed., 1952), Vol. XII of the series 'Peuples et Civilisations', and its bibliography. Pertinent sections may also be found in P. Muret and P. Sagnac, *La prépondérance anglaise* (Paris, 3d ed., 1949), Vol. XI of the same series; and G. Lefebvre, *Napoléon* (Paris, 4th ed., 1953), Vol. XIII of that series. The reader may also wish to consult general histories, such as the *Histoire générale*, published under the direction of E. Lavisse and A. Rambaud, Vol. VII (Paris, 1896); *The Cambridge Modern History*, Vol. VII (Cambridge, 1909); *Weltgeschichte in gemeineständlicher Darstellung*, published under the direction of L. M. Hartmann, Vol. VI, Part II (Stuttgart and Gotha, 1923); *Propyläen Weltgeschichte*, published under the direction of W. Goetz, Vol. VI: *Das Zeitalter des Absolutismus, 1600–1789* (Berlin, 1931); G. Barbagallo, *Storia universale*, Vol. V, Part I: *Riforme e Rivoluzione, 1699–1799* (Turin, 1940), with bibliography; R. R. Palmer, *A History of the Modern World* (New York, 1950; 2d ed., 1956), with an extensive bibliography, chiefly for works in English; A. J. Grant and H. Temperley, *Europe in the Nineteenth and Twentieth Century, 1787–1915* (London, 1939); R. Mousnier and E. Labrousse, *Le XVIIIe siècle, Révolution intellectuelle, technique, et politique (1715–1855)* (Paris, 1953), in the series 'Histoire générale des Civilisations'.

PART ONE. THE WORLD ON THE EVE OF THE FRENCH REVOLUTION

**Chapter I. European expansion**

*Knowledge of the globe*

General description in F. Marguet, *Histoire générale de la navigation du XVe au XXe siècle* (Paris, 1931). Technical advances and exploration are summarized in A. Wolf, *History of Science, Technology and Philosophy in the 18th Century* (New York, 1939).

For explorations, see Orjan-Olsen, *La conquête de la Terre*, 6 vols. (Paris, 1933–37), Vols. IV and V; J. N. Baker, *A History of Geographical Discovery and Exploration* (London, 1931); G. Roloff, *Geschichte der europäischen Kolonisation seit der Entdeckung Amerikas* (Heilbronn, 1913); A. Rein, *Die europäische Ausbreitung über die Erde* (Potsdam, 1931).

A bibliographic essay on discoveries appears in the *Bulletin of the International Committee of Historical Sciences*, Vol. VII (No. 27, 1935).

*The partition of overseas territories*

See above, and the general histories of particular states cited below. In addition, see A. Zimmermann, *Die europäischen Kolonien*, 5 vols. (Berlin, 1896–1903); Ch. de Lannoy and H. Van der Linden, *Histoire de l'expansion coloniale des peuples européens*, 3 vols. (Brussels, 1907–21); G. Roloff, *Geschichte der europäischen Kolonisation seit der Entdeckung Amerikas* (Heilbronn, 1913); W. C. Abbot, *The Expansion of Europe, A Social and Political History of the Modern World*, Vol. II (New York, 2d ed., rev., 1938).

For Latin America, bibliographies in P. Muret and P. Sagnac, *La prépondérance anglaise* (Paris, 3d ed., 1949), Book III, Chap. III; and P. Sagnac, *La fin de l'Ancien Régime* (Paris, 3d ed., 1952), Book I, Chap. V, Secs. 9 and 10, and Book II, Chap. II, Sec. 7; C. Pereyra, *Historia de la América española*, 7 vols. (Madrid, 1920–25), *Historia de América y de los pueblos americanos*, edited by A. Ballesteros y Beretta, 9 vols. (Barcelona, 1936–49); A. Ballesteros y Beretta, *Historia de España y su influencia en la historia universal*, 9 vols. (Barcelona, 1919–41); M. Ballesteros Gailbrois, *Historia de América* (Madrid, 1946); D. Ramos Pérez, *Historia de la colonización española en América* (Madrid, 1947); *Historia de América*, edited by R. Levene (Buenos Aires, 1940–), Vol. III: *Descubrimiento de América y América colonial hispanica*, by E. Gardia and R. Levene; S. de Madariaga, *Cuadro histórico de las Indias* (*Introducción a Bolivar*) (Buenos Aires, 1945); bibliography by P. Chaunu in *Revue historique*, CCIV (1950), 77–105.

For Holland, P. Blok, *Geschiedenis van het nederlandische Volk*, 8 vols. (Groninguen, 1892–1908; 3d ed., 4 vols., Leiden, 1923–26), Eng. tr., *History of the People of the Netherlands*, 5 vols. (New York, 1908–1912); H. T. Colen-brander, *Koloniale Geschiedenis*, 3 vols. (The Hague, 1925–26); F. W. Stapel, *Geschiedenis van Nederlandische India* (Amsterdam, 1930); E. S. de Klerck, *History of the Netherlands East Indies* (New York, 1938). On the decline of Holland and Portugal, see P. Muret and P. Sagnac, *La prépondérance anglaise* (Paris, 3d ed., 1949), Book III, Chap. II, Secs. 4 and 5.

For England, bibliography in P. Sagnac, *La prépondérance anglaise* (Paris, 3d ed., 1949), Book I, Chap. II, Sec. I and Chap. III; see also below, under The Colonial Empires; *The Cambridge History of the British Empire*, Vol. I: *The Old Empire from the Beginning to 1783* (Cambridge, 1929), Vol. II: *The Growth of the New Empire, 1783–1870* (1940), Vol. IV: *British India* (1928), Vol. VI: *Canada and Newfoundland* (1930), Vol. VII: *Australia and New Zealand* (1933); L. H. Gipson, *The British Empire before the American Revolution*, 7 vols. (New York, 1936–49), Vol. VII: *The Great War for the Empire: The Victorious Years, 1758–60*; for Anglo-Saxon North America, *The Cambridge Modern History*, Vol. VII (1903); D. Pasquet, *Histoire politique et sociale du peuple américain*, Vol. I (Paris, 1924); G. S. Graham, *Empire of the North Atlantic, The Maritime Struggle for North America* (Toronto and London, 1959); for India, *The Cambridge History of the British Empire*, Vol. IV (1928); W. Smith, *The Oxford History of India* (Oxford, 1919, 2d ed., 1923); for the wars, J. W. Fortescue, *History of the British Army*, 12 vols. (London, 1899–1938), Vol. III: *1763–1793* (1903).

For France, *Histoire des colonies françaises et de la France dans le monde*, published under the direction of G. Hanotaux and A. Martineau, 6 vols. (Paris, 1929–), Vol. I: *Amérique*, Vol. V: *Inde*; J. Trammond, *Manuel d'histoire maritime de la France des origines à 1815* (Paris, 1916, last ed., 1942); J. Sain-toyant, *La colonisation française sous l'Ancien Régime du XVe siècle à 1789*, 2 vols. (Paris, 1929), Vol. II: *De 1715 à 1789*; G. L. Jaray, *L'empire français d'Amérique, 1534–1803* (Paris, 1938); extensive critical bibliography by C.-A. Julien in *Bulletin de la Société des professeurs d'histoire et de géographie de l'Enseignement public*, XL (November, 1950), 67–79.

*The colonial empires*

See the section above, and, on the colonial system, P. Muret and P. Sagnac, *La prépondérance anglaise* (Paris, 3d ed., 1949), Book I, Chap. II, Sec. 5.

For Latin America, the publications of Alexander von Humboldt, *Voyage aux régions équinoxiales du Nouveau Continent,* [1799 to 1806], 4 vols. (Paris, 1814–17), and *Essai politique sur la Nouvelle Espagne,* 2 vols. (Paris, 1811) are invaluable. Vol. XIII of *Historia de América,* published under the direction of A. Ballesteros y Beretta, written by G. Alcázar Molino, is devoted to *Los Virreinatos en el siglo XVIII* (Madrid, 1945). Better is Vol. VI (*El imperio español*), Chap. VI, of *Historia de España,* 9 vols. (Barcelona, 1919–41), by A. Ballesteros, for institutions and economic and cultural life. See further: J. Sacre, *Le système colonial espagnol dans l'ancien Venezuela* (Paris, 1939); Astrogildo de Melo, *O trabalho de indigenas nas lavouras de Nova Hespanha* (Saõ Paulo, 1946); Caio Prado, *História econõmica do Brasil* (Saõ Paulo, 1945), and *Formaçao do Brasil contemporâneo* (Saõ Paulo, 2d ed., 1945); R. Levene, *Investigaciones acerca de la historia económica del Virreinato del Plata,* 2 vols. (La Plata, 1927–28); G. Espedes del Castillo, *Lima y Buenos Aires; recensiones politicas y economicas de la creacion del Virreinato del Plato* (Seville, 1947); R. Barón Castro, *La poblacion de El Salvador* (Madrid, 1942); W. Howe, *The Mining Guild of New Spain and Its Tribunal General, 1770–1821* (Cambridge, Mass., 1949). Historians of Mexico and the United States have written on Latin America—for example, see S. Zevala y Maria Castello, *Fuentes para la historia del trabajo en Nueva España,* Vol. VIII: *1650–1805* (Mexico, 1946); P. H. Ureña, *Historia de la cultura en la América hispánica* (Mexico, 1947); J. Whitefield Diffie, *Latin American Civilization: Colonial Period* (Harrisburg, 1945); A. Whitaker, *The Huancavelica Mercury Mine, A Contribution to the History of the Bourbon Renaissance in the Spanish Empire* (Cambridge, Mass., 1941). See also the fascicule in *Annales,* 111 (1948), 385–576, titled 'À travers les Amériques latines', which is also No. 4 of the 'Cahiers des Annales'.

For the West Indies, W. J. Gardner, *History of Jamaica* (London, 1873, 2d ed., 1909); H. G. Bell, 'British Commercial Policy in the West Indies, 1783–93', *English Historical Review,* XXXI (1916), 429–41; L. Vignols, 'Les Antilles françaises sous l'Ancien Régime', *Revue d'histoire économique et sociale,* XVI (1928), 720–95; P. de Vaissière, *Saint-Domingue* (Paris, 1909); M. Satineau, *Histoire économique et sociale de Guadeloupe sous l'Ancien Régime* (Paris, 1928); L.-P. May, *Histoire économique de la Martinique* (Paris, 1930); E. A. Banbuck, *Histoire économique et sociale de la Martinique sous l'Ancien Régime* (Paris, 1935).

For expansion in Asia and the East India companies, P. Muret and P. Sagnac, *La prépondérance anglaise* (Paris, 3d ed., 1949), Book III, Chap. V; H. Furber, *John Company at Work, A Study of European Expansion in India in the Late Eighteenth Century* (Cambridge, Mass., 1948).

For Holland, see above, and J. S. Furnival, *Netherlands India: A Study of*

*Plural Economy* (Cambridge, 1939); A. Hyma, *The Dutch in the Far East: A History of the Dutch Commercial and Colonial Empire* (Ann Arbor, 1942).

For the English and French Companies, C. H. Philips, *The East India, 1784–1834* (Manchester, 1940); C. Northcote Parkinson, *Trade in Eastern Seas, 1793–1813* (Cambridge, Mass., 1937); H. Weber, *La Compagnie des Indes* (Paris, 1904); J. Conan, *La dernière Compagnie des Indes* (Paris, 1942).

On slavery, A. von Humboldt, *Voyages aux régions équinoxiales du Nouveau Continent*, 4 vols. (Paris, 1814–17); G. Scelle, *Histoire politique de la traite négrière aux Indes de Castille*, 2 vols. (Paris, 1906); A. Tourmagne (pseudonym of A. Villard), *Histoire de l'esclavage ancien et moderne* (Paris, 1880); better is Gaston-Martin, *Histoire de l'esclavage dans les colonies françaises* (Paris, 1948), and *Nantes au XVIIIe siècle, L'ère des négriers* (Paris, 1931); P. D. Rinchon, *La traite et l'esclavage des Congolais par les Européens* (Wetteren, 1929), and especially *Le trafic négrier d'après les livres de commerce du Gantois Pierre-Ignace Liévin van Alstein*, Vol. I: *L'organisation commerciale de la traite* (Uccle and Paris, 1938). English authors refer to B. Edwards, *Civil and Commercial History of the British West-Indies*, 5 vols. (London, 1793, 5th ed., 1819). See also A. Alcalá y Henke, *La esclavitud de los negros en la América española* (Madrid, 1919).

For the missions, H. Lovett, *History of the London Missionary Society*, 2 vols. (London, 1899); E. Stock, *The History of the Church Missionary Society*, 3 vols. (London, 1899); J. Schmidlin, *Katholische Missionsgeschichte* (Steyl, 1924), with an appendix on Protestant missions; E. Descamps, *Histoire générale et comparée des missions* (Brussels and Paris, 1932).

## The empires in jeopardy and the American revolution

See appropriate sections above, and below, in Chapter Five, The American Revolution. Also, R. Couplard, *The American Revolution and the British Empire* (London, 1930); B. Moses, *Spain's Declining Power in South America, 1730–1806* (New York, 1919), and *South America on the Eve of Emancipation* (New York, 1908); M. Lina Pérez, *Las etapas ideológicas del siglo XVIII en México a través los papeles de la Inquisición* (Mexico City, 1945); P. Gonzales Casanova, *El misoneísmo y la modernidad cristiana en el siglo XVIII* (Mexico City, 1948).

## Foreign civilizations

For Islam, see *Encyclopédie de l'Islam*, published in French, English, and German by T. Houtsma, R. Basset, etc., 4 vols. and supplements (Leiden and Paris; 1908–38); M. Abd el-Jalil, *Brève histoire de la littérature arabe* (Paris, 1943); H. Massé, *L'Islam* (Paris, 1940). On the Ottoman empire, see P. Muret and P. Sagnac, *La prépondérance anglaise* (Paris, 3d ed., 1949), Book III, Chap. III; N. Jorga, *Geschichte des osmanischen Reiches*, 5 vols. (Gotha, 1908–13); H. Dehérain, *L'Egypte turque* (Paris, 1931), Vol. V of *Histoire de la nation égyptienne*, published under the direction of G. Hanotaux; H. A. R. Gibb and H. Bowen, *Islamic Society and the West* (Oxford, 1950).

For Asia, see P. Muret and P. Sagnac, *La prépondérance anglaise* (Paris, 3d ed., 1949), Book III, Chap. V; F. Grenard, *Grandeur et décadence de l'Asie* (Paris, 1939); K. S. Latourette, *A Short History of the Far East* (New York, 1946); P. E. Eckel, *Far East since 1500* (New York, 1947); H. Cordier, *Histoire générale de la Chine et de ses rapports avec l'étranger*, Vol. III (Paris, 1920); R. Grousset, *Histoire de la Chine* (Paris, 1942), and *Histoire de l'Extrême-Orient*, 2 vols. (Paris, 1929); H. Maspero, *Les institutions de la Chine* (Paris, 1950); C. Maybon, *Histoire moderne du pays d'Annam* (Paris, 1919); J. Murdoch and J. Yamagata, *History of Japan*, 3 vols. (Kobe and Yokohama, 1903–25), Vol. III: *The Tokugawa Epoch, 1656–1868* (London, 1925–28, in 2 vols.); Takai Tsuchiya, *An Economic History of Japan* (Tokyo, 1938); K. Asakawa, 'La place de la religion dans l'histoire économique et sociale du Japon', *Annales d'histoire économique et sociale*, V (1933), 125–40; N. Konrad, N. Staroselzef, F. Mesin, and G. Joukof, *Breve storia del Giappone politico-sociale* (Bari, 1936; abstract by M. Haguenauer, also in the *Annales*, X (1938), 234–48). There is a bulletin on historiography on the Far East from 1939 to 1948 by E. Gaspardone in *Revue historique*, CCII (1949), 238–68. H. Labouret, *Histoire des noirs d'Afrique* (Paris, 1946); H. Urvoy, *Histoire de l'Empire Bornou* (Dakar, 1949, 'Mémoires de l'Institut français d'Afrique noire', No.7).

### Chapter 2. European economy

See J. Kulischer, *Allgemeine Wirtschaftsgeschichte der Mittelalter- und Neuzeit*, 2 vols. (Munich and Berlin, 1928, in the series 'Handbuch der mittelalterlichen und neueren Geschichte', edited by G. von Below and F. Meinecke), Vol. II (bibliography); G. Luzzatto, *Storia economica dell'età moderna e contemporanea, Part I: L'età moderna* (Padua, 1932); H. Heaton, *Economic History of Europe* (New York, 1936); W. Bowden, M. Karpovitch, and A. Usher, *An Economic History of Europe since 1750* (New York, 1937); S. B. Clough and C. W. Cole, *Economic History of Europe* (New York, 1941, 2d ed., 1946); N. S. B. Gras, *History of Agriculture in Europe and America* (New

York, 1925); H. Sée, *Esquisse d'une histoire du régime agraire en Europe au XVIIIe et XIXe siècles* (Paris, 1921). For government economic policies, see general histories of particular states.

## The traditional economy and its development

On mercantilism, see E. F. Hecksher, *Merkantilismen*, 2 vols. (Stockholm, 1931), German tr. *Der Merkantilismus* (Jena, 1932), and English, *Mercantilism* (London, 1935); J. Morini-Comby, *Mercantilisme et protectionnisme* (Paris, 1938); J. Kulischer, 'Les traités de commerce et la clause de la nation la plus favorisée du XVIe au XVIIIe siècle', *Revue d'histoire moderne*, VI (1931), 1–29; and works concerning economists, cited below, in Chapter Four, Scientific Rationalism. A report on research appears in J. F. Rees, 'Mercantilism', *History*, XXIV (1939), 129–35.

On the origins of capitalism, see W. Sombart, *Der moderne Kapitalismus*, 3 vols. (Munich, 1902–8; 6th ed., 1924, 2 vols. in 4); a third book in 2 vols., on *Hochkapitalismus*, has been translated into French with a critical introduction by A. Sayous (Paris, 1932); H. Sée, *Les origines du capitalisme moderne* (Paris, 1926), with bibliography, and 'Le grand commerce maritime et le système colonial dans leurs relations avec l'évolution du capitalisme du XVIe au XIXe siècle', *Revue de Synthèse*, XXXIX (1925), 15–35; R. de Roover, 'La formation et l'expansion de la comptabilité à parties doubles', *Annales d'histoire économique et sociale*, IX (1937), 171–93, 270–304.

On the influx of precious metals, see A. Soetbeer, *Edelmetall Produktion und Werthverhältnis zwischen Gold und Silber seit der Entdeckung Amerika's bis zur Gegenwart* (Berlin, 1879).

On the change in prices in various countries, see—England: J. E. Thorold Rogers, *Six Centuries of Work and Wages; the History of English Labour*, 2 vols. (London, 1884, rev. ed., 1949); V. J. Silberling, 'British Prices and Business Cycles, 1779–1850', *Review of Economic Statistics*, V (1923), 223–61; W. Beveridge, *Prices and Wages in England from the 12th to 19th Century*, Vol. I: *Price Tables Mercantile Era* (London, 1939), 'The Trade Cycle in Britain before 1750', *Oxford Economic Papers*, No. 3 (1940), pp. 74–109, and No. 4 (1941), pp. 63–76, and *Full Employment in a Free Society*, Appendix A— Holland: N. W. Posthumus, *Inquiry into the History of Prices in Holland*, Vol. I: *Wholesale Prices of the Exchange of Amsterdam, 1585–1914; Rates of Exchange at Amsterdam, 1609–1914*, (Leiden, 1946)—France: C.-E. Labrousse, *Esquisse du mouvement des prix et des revenus en France au XVIIIe siècle*, 2 vols (Paris, 1932), and cf. G. Lefebvre, 'Le mouvement des prix et les origines de la Révolution française, 1782–1790', *Annales d'histoire économique et sociale,* IX (1937), 139–70, and also in *Études sur la Révolution française* (Paris, 1954); Labrousse, 'Le froment dans les régions françaises, 1782–1790', *Annales d'histoire sociale,* I (1939), 382–400; F. Simiand, *Recherches anciennes et nouvelles sur le mouvement général des prix du XVIe au XIXe siècle* (Paris, 1931); *Recherches et documents sur l'histoire des prix en France de 1500 à 1800,* under the direction of H. Hauser (Paris, 1936); *Assemblée générale de la Commission centrale et des Comités départementaux* [of the economic history of the Revolution], Vol. II, Sec. 4; 'Les mouvements des prix' (Paris, 1941), especially the study by W. E. Schaap on the price of grains in Champagne at the end of the Old Regime—Spain: E. J. Hamilton, *War and Prices in Spain, 1651–1800* (Cambridge, Mass., 1947); cf. P. Vilar, 'Histoire des prix, Histoire générale', *Annales,* IV (1949), 29–45— Belgium: H. van Houtte, *Documents pour servir à l'histoire des prix de 1331 à 1794* (Brussels, 1902)—Germany: J. Elsas, *Umriss Geschichte der Preise und Löhne in Deutschland vom ausgehenden Mittelalter bis zum Beginn des neunzehnten Jahrhunderts,* 2 vols. (Leiden, 1936–40); A. Pribram, *Materialen zur Geschichte der Preise und Löhne in Oesterreich* (Vienna, 1938), cf. M. Bloch, 'L'histoire des prix; quelques remarques critiques', *Annales d'histoire sociale,* I (1939), 141–51; E. Waschinski, *Währung, Preisentwickelung und Kaufkraft des Geldes in Schleswig-Holstein von 1226 bis 1864* (Neumünster, 1952); and P. Jeannin, 'Monnaies et prix en Slesvig-Holstein', *Annales, Économies, Sociétés, Civilisations* (1955), 99–102.

On banks, see H. Hauser, 'Réflexions sur l'histoire des banques à l'époque moderne', *Annales d'histoire économique et sociale,* I (1929), 335– 51; G. Van Dillen, *History of the Principal Public Banks* (The Hague, 1934), with bibliography, 'Amsterdam, marché mondial des métaux précieux au XVIIe et au XVIIIe siècle', *Revue historique,* CLII (1928), 194–201, 'La Banque d'Amsterdam', *Revue d'histoire moderne,* III (1928), 161–87, and 'Die Girobanken von Genua, Venetie aan Hamburg', *Tijdschrift voor Geschiedenis* (1927), pp. 32–58; J. Clapham, *The Bank of England,* 2 vols. (Cambridge, 1944), Vol. I: *1694–1797;* A. Sayous, 'La banque à Genève pendant le XVIIIe siècle', *Annales d'histoire sociale,* I (1939), 133–40; R. Bigo, *Les bases historiques de la finance moderne* (Paris, 1933); M. Vigne, *La banque à Lyon du XVe au XVIIIe siècle* (Lyon, 1903); J. Bouchary, *Le marché des changes à Paris à la fin du XVIIIe siècle, 1778–1800* (Paris, 1937); R. Filangieri, *I banchi di Napoli delle origini alla constituzione del Banco delle Due Sicilie, 1538–1806* (Naples, 1949). On the bank of San Carlo at Madrid, see G. Desdevises du Dézert, *L'Espagne d'Ancien Régime,* 3 vols. (Paris, 1899–1904), and the notices by J. Bouchary in *Les manieurs d'argent à la fin du XVIIIe siècle,* 3 vols. (Paris, 1939–43).

On the history of fiduciary notes, see M. Bloch, *Esquisse d'une histoire monétaire d'Europe* (Paris, 1954, 'Cahiers des Annales', No. 9).

On credit, see R. de Roover, *L'évolution de la lettre de change, XIVe–XVIIIe siècles* (Paris, 1953).

On science and technology, see A. P. Usher, *History of Mechanical Inventions* (New York, 1929); A. Wolf, *A History of Science, Technology, and Philosophy in the 18th Century* (New York, 1939); F. Russo, *Histoire des sciences et des techniques, Bibliographie* (Paris, 1954); P. Chaunu, 'Progrès technique et progrès scientifique en Europe de la fin du XVIe à la fin du XVIIIe siècle (bibliographie)', *Bulletin de la Société des professeurs d'histoire* (November, 1954); S. T. McCloy, *French Inventions of the Eighteenth Century* (University of Kentucky Press, 1952); F. Brunot, *Histoire de la langue française*, Vol. VI, Part I: *Le mouvement des idées et les vocabulaires techniques*, 2 vols. (Paris, 1930). For agriculture, see Chapter Three, The Peasantry; for England, the section below.

### The economic revolution in England

See P. Sagnac, *La fin de l'Ancien Régime* (Paris, 3d ed., 1952), Book I, Chap. II, Secs. 6–10, and the works cited above, especially those of Silberling, Beveridge, and Clapham. In addition: E. P. Lipson, *The Economic History of England*, 3 vols. (London, 1931–33), Vol.11: *The Age of Mercantilism*; N. S. B. Gras, *Industrial Revolution* (Cambridge, Mass., 1930); P. Mantoux, *La révolution industrielle en Angleterre* (Paris, 1905), Eng. tr. by Marjorie Vernon, brought up to date, *The Industrial Revolution in the Eighteenth Century* (London, 1928); T. S. Ashton, *The Industrial Revolution, 1760–1830* (Oxford, 1948), and *An Economic History of England, The 18th Century* (London, 1955); A. D. Gayer, W. W. Rostow, A. J. Schwartz, and I. Frank, *The Growth and Fluctuations of the British Economy, 1790–1850, An Historical, Statistical and Theoretical Study of Britain's Economic Development*, 2 vols. (Oxford, 1953); T. S. Ashton and J. Sykes, *The Coal Industry of the 18th Century* (Manchester, 1929); A. Wadsworth and J. de Lacy Mann, *The Cotton Trade and Industrial Lancashire, 1600–1780* (Manchester, 1931).

For the history of agriculture, see P. Sagnac, *La fin de l'Ancien Régime* (Paris, 3d ed., 1952), Book I, Chap. II, Secs. 4–5; W. Curtler, *The Enclosure and Redistribution of Land* (Oxford, 1929); E. Davies, 'The Small Landowner, 1750–1832', *Economic History Review*, I (1927), 87–113; J. Chambers, 'Enclosure and the Small Landowner', *ibid.*, X (1939), 118–27; E. Barger, 'The Present Position of Studies in English Fieldsystem', *English Historical Review*, LIII (1938), 385–411; W. Tate, 'Some Unexplored Records of the

Enclosure Movement', *ibid.*, LVII (1942), 250–63; G. Homans, 'Terrains ordonnés et champs orientés: une hypothèse sur le village anglais', *Annales d'histoire économique et sociale*, VIII (1936), 438–48; D. Grove Barnes, *A History of the English Corn-Laws, 1660–1846* (New York, 1930); R. E. Prothero and Lord Earle, *English Farming, Past and Present* (London, 1912; 9th ed. brought up to date by A. D. Hall, 1936); H. G. Hunt, 'La Révolution agraire en Angleterre au XVIIIe siècle', *Annales, Économies, Sociétés, Civilisatious* (1956), pp. 29–41.

For industry, see W. Hoffmann, *Wachstum und Wachstumformen der englischen Industriewirtschaft* (Jena, 1940).

For commerce, see W. Schlote, *Entwicklung und Strukturwandlungen des englischen Aussenhandels van 1700 bis zur Gegenwart* (Jena, 1938), Eng. tr. by W. O. Henderson and W. H. Chaloner, *British Overseas Trade from 1700 to the 1930s* (Oxford, 1952). Very important: A. H. Imlah, 'Real Values in British Foreign Trade', *The Journal of Economic History*, VIII (1948), 133–52. The value of British exports and imports has been left us from customs assessment, which was calculated according to a scale of prices set up at the end of the seventeenth century and the beginning of the eighteenth. These official values do not, consequently, correspond exactly to real values. Imlah has worked out a new method of calculating imports, exports, and re-exports according to real values, but he could do this only beginning with 1798. He concludes that, contrary to current belief, Britain's balance of trade was unfavourable, with rare exceptions. The thesis of F. Crouzet, *L'économie britannique et le blocus continental (1806–13)*, 2 vols. (Paris, 1958), gives a critical comparison of the studies of Schlote, Gayer, and Imlah.

For Ireland, see G. O'Brien, *The Economic History of Ireland in the Eighteenth Century* (Dublin, 1918).

### The backwardness of continental Europe

See J. Kulischer, 'La grande industrie aux XVIIe et XVIIIe siècles, France, Allemagne, Russie', *Annales d'histoire économique et sociale*, III (1931), 11–46.

For France, see P. Sagnac, *La fin de l'Ancien Régime* (Paris, 3d ed., 1952), Book III, Chap. III, Sec. 2; H. Sée, *Histoire économique de la France*, with extensive bibliographic contributions by R. Schnerb, 2 vols. (Paris, 1939–42), *La vie économique et les classes sociales en France au XVIIIe siècle* (Paris, 1924), *La France économique et sociale au XVIIIe siècle* (Paris, 1925), and *L'évolution industrielle et commerciale de la France sous l'Ancien Régime*

(Paris, 1925), *Esquisse d'une histoire économique et sociale de la France depuis les origines jusqu'à la première guerre mondiale* (Paris, 1929); H. Hauser, 'Les caractères généraux de l'histoire économique de la France du milieu du XVIe siècle à la fin du XVIIIe', *Revue historique*, CLXXIII (1934), 312–28; L. Cahen, 'Aspects économiques à la veille de la Révolution', *Annales d'histoire sociale*, I (1939), 238–50; J. Bouchary, *Les compagnies financières à Paris à la fin du XVIIIe siècle*, 3 vols. (Paris, 1940–42); H. Lévy-Bruhl, *Histoire de la lettre de change en France aux XVIIe et XVIIIe siècles* (Paris, 1933), and *Histoire juridique des sociétés de commerce en France aux XVIIe et XVIIIe siècles* (Paris, 1938); Ch. Ballot, *L'introduction du machinisme dans l'industrie française* (Paris, 1923); A. Rémond, *John Holker* (Paris, 1946); G. and H. Bourgin, *L'industrie sidérurgique en France au début de la Révolution* (Paris, 1920); A. Demangeon, 'La répartition de l'industrie du fer en France en 1789', *Annales de géographie*, XXX (1921), 401–15; B. Gille, *Les origines de la grande industrie métallurgique en France* (Paris, 1947); P. Léon, *La naissance de la grande industrie en Dauphiné (fin du XVIIIe siècle–1869)*, 2 vols. (Paris, 1954); F. Dornic, *L'industrie textile dans le Maine et ses débouchés internationaux, 1650–1815* (Paris, 1955); J. Vidalenc, *La petite métallurgie rurale en Haute-Normandie sous l'Ancien Régime* (Paris, 1946); M. Rouff, *Les mines de charbon en France au XVIIIe siècle, 1741–1791* (Paris, 1922); A. de Saint-Léger, *Les mines d'Anzin et d'Aniche pendant la Révolution*, 2 vols. in 4 (Paris, 1935–39); Yvonne Lefranc, *Essai sur l'industrie textile de la Ferté-Macé* (Alençon, 1934); J. Letaconnoux, 'Les transports en France au XVIIIe siècle', *Revue d'histoire moderne et contemporaine*, XI (1908–9), 97–114, 269–92; Gaston-Martin, *Capital et travail à Nantes au cours du XVIIIe siècle* (Paris, 1931), and *Nantes au XVIIe siècle* (Paris, 1931); Th. Malvezin, *Histoire du commerce de Bordeaux depuis les origines jusqu'à nos jours*, 4 vols. (Bordeaux, 1892); R. Boutruche, 'Bordeaux et le commerce des Antilles françaises', in *Trois siècles de vie française, Nos Antilles*, published under the direction of S. Denis (Orléans, 1935), pp. 83–124; H. Sée, 'Esquisse de l'histoire du commerce français à Cadix et dans l'Amérique espagnole au XVIIIe siècle', *Revue d'histoire moderne*, III (1928), 13–31; P. Masson, *Histoire du commerce français dans le Levant au XVIIIe siècle* (Paris, 1911); P. Roussier, 'Tableaux du commerce général de la France avec les colonies d'Amérique et d'Afrique, de 1716 jusqu'à 1788', *Revue de l'histoire des colonies françaises*, XV (1927), 440–43; P. Dardel, 'Le trafic maritime de Rouen aux XVIIe et XVIIIe siècles (1614–1771)', a statistical essay, in *Bulletin de la Société libre d'émulation du commerce et de l'industrie de la Seine-Inférieure* (Rouen, 1945), pp. 115–250.

For Paris, see L. Cahen, 'Ce qu'enseigne un péage du XVIIIe siècle: la

Seine entre Rouen et Paris et les caractères de l'économie parisienne', *Annales d'histoire économique et sociale*, III (1931), 487–518; L. Guéneau, 'Le rôle de Paris dans les industries et le commerce de la soie et des soieries à la fin de l'Ancien Régime', *Revue d'histoire moderne*, I (1926), 280–303, 424–43; D. Pinkney, 'Paris, capitale du coton sous le Premier Empire', *Annales*, V (1950), 56–60; L. Janrot, 'L'activite économique autour de Paris au XVIIIe siècle', *Bulletin du Comité de Seine-et-Oise pour l'histoire économique de la Révolution* (1938–39), pp. 89–117.

For Germany, see P. Sagnac, *La fin de l'Ancien Régime* (Paris, 3d ed., 1952), notes on p. 39; H. Brunschwig, *La crise de l'État prussien à la fin du XVIIIe siècle* (Paris, 1947) with bibliography.

For Belgium, see J. B. van Houtte, *Esquisse d'une histoire économique de la Belgique à la fin de l'Ancien Régime* (Louvain, 1943); L. Dechesne, *Histoire économique et sociale de la Belgique* (Paris and Liège, 1932); Z. W. Sneller, 'La naissance de l'industrie rurale dans les Pays-Bas aux XVIIe et XVIIIe siècles', *Annales d'histoire économique et sociale*, I (1929), 193–202; P. Lebrun, *L'industrie de la laine à Verviers pendant le XVIIIe siècle et le début du XIXe* (Liége, 1948), reviewed by G. Lefebvre in *Annales*, V (1950), 49–55.

For Denmark, A. Nielsen, *Dänische Wirtschaftsgeschichte* (Jena, 1933).

For Spain, P. Sagnac, *La fin de l'Ancien Régime* (Paris, 3d ed., 1952), Book I, Chap. V, Sec. 5; G. Desdevises du Dézert, *L'Espagne d'Ancien Régime*, 3 vols. (Paris, 1899–1904, 2d ed., 1928).

For Holland, E. Baasch, *Holländische Wirtschaftsgeschichte* (Jena, 1925).

For Italy, G. Prato, *La vita economica in Piemonte a mezzo il secolo XVIII* (Turin, 1908); G. Sonnino, *Saggia sulla industria, marina e commercio in Livorno sotto i primi due Lorenesi, 1737–1790* (Cortona, 1909).

For Poland, J. Rutkowski, *Histoire économique de la Pologne avant les partages* (French tr., Paris, 1927), and 'Les bases économiques des partages de l'ancienne Pologne', *Revue d'histoire moderne*, VII (1932), 362–89; G. Kurnatowski, *Les origines du capitalisme en Pologne, ibid.*, VIII (1933), 236–67.

For Russia, J. Kulischer, *Russische Wirtschaftsgeschichte* (Jena, 1925), R. Portal, 'Manufactures et classes sociales en Russie au XVIIIe siècle', *Revue historique*, CCI (1949), 161–85, and CCII (1949), 1–23, also *L'Oural an XVIIIe siècle, Étude d'histoire économique et sociale* (Paris, 1950).

For agriculture, see below, in Chapter Three, The Peasantry.

*The enrichment of Europe*

See M. Reinhard, *Histoire de la population mondiale de 1700 à 1948* (Paris, 1949). On urbanism, see P. Lavedan, *Histoire de l'urbanisme*, Vol. II: *Renais-*

*sance et temps modernes* (Paris, 1941); P. Lelièvre, *L'urbanisme et l'architecture à Nantes au XVIIIe siècle* (Nantes, 1942); and the local or regional
monographs in general history. On progress of well-being, see works relating to mores—usually anecdotes—and biographies; Dorothy George, *London Life in the Eighteenth Century* (London, 1925); A. S. Tuberville, *English
Men and Manners in the Eighteenth Century* (Oxford, 1926, 2d ed., 1943).

## Chapter 3. European society

See bibliography in P. Sagnac, *La fin de l'Ancien Regime* (Paris, 3d ed.,
1952), Book I, Chap. II, Sec. 2; Chap. V, Sec. I; Chap. VI, Sec. 3; Chap. VII,
Sec. 7; Chap. VIII, Sec. 2; Book III, Chap. III, Sec. 4; and, for France, the
bibliographies in H. Carrée, *Le règne de Louis XVI* (Paris, 1910, Vol. IX of
*Histoire de France*, published under the direction of E. Lavisse), Book III,
and Book IV, Sec. 7. Social history is the least advanced of any historical
field. For a long time descriptions of 'society' concerned mainly the upper
classes and portrayed only their customs and attitudes, based on memoirs
and letters (for example: L. Ducros, *La société française an XVIII siècle,
d'après les mémoires et correspondances du temps* [Paris, 1922]), without
trying to estimate their numbers or their income. Recent interest in economic history has thrown light on the general picture, but, as can be seen
in the bibliographies of Sagnac and Carré, authors usually lump economic
and social studies together (for example, H. Sée, in *Histoire économique de
la France*, R. Portal, in 'Manufactures et classes sociales en Russie au XVIIIe
siècle', *Revue historique*, CCI [1949], 161–85, and L. Dechesne, in *Histoire
économique et sociale de la Belgique*), or discuss moral and social life (for
example: Sagnac, *La fin de l'Ancien Régime*, Book III, Chap. III, Sec. 4) or
even discuss political, economic, and social developments concurrently, as
de Tocqueville, Taine, Sorel, and Jaurès have done, along with Sagnac in *La
formation de la société française moderne*, 2 vols. (Paris, 1945–46). From the
historian's point of view such syntheses stand to reason, but they indicate
the absence of any thorough studies of the different social classes or categories, which would require local or regional monographs using all statistics available from fiscal documents (a few attempts of this sort are cited
below, under The Bourgeoisie). General ideas concerning the condition of
people and property can be obtained from legal histories: P. Viollet, *Histoire de droit civil français* (Paris, 1885); E. Glasson, *Histoire du droit et des
institutions de la France*, 8 vols. (Paris, 1887–1903), Vol. VIII: *L'époque mon-
archique*; J. Declareuil, *Histoire générale du droit français des origines à 1789*
(Paris, 1925); M. Garaud, *Histoire générale du droit privé français*, Vol. I: *La*

*Révolution et l'égalité civile* (Paris, 1953); W. Holdworth, *A History of English Law*, 3 vols. (London, 1903–9; rev. ed., 12 vols., 1922–38).

Corporative organization has been the subject of general studies. See, for France, F. O. Martin, *L'organisation corporative de l'Ancien Régime* (Paris, 1938); H. Holland, *Essai sur l'organisation corporative et la vie économique à Blois au XVIIIe siècle* (Paris, 1938). And, for the comparative point of view, see the collective work *L'organisation corporative du Moyen Age à la fin de l'Ancien Régime*, published in 1937 by the 'Bibliothèque de l'Université de Louvain', Series II, fasc. 44; also, E. Lousse, *La société d'Ancien Régime*, Vol. I: *Organisation et réprésentations corporatives* (Louvain, 1943); in addition, the International Committee of Historical Sciences formed a committee at Bucharest in 1936 for the history of the assemblies of the Estates.

## The clergy

See above. For France: P. de Vaissière, *Curés de campagne de l'ancienne France* (Paris, 1933); and the works on religious history during the Revolution, below in Chapter Ten, Reform of the Clergy. On the tithe, see H. Marion, *La dîme ecclésiastique en France au XVIIIe siècle et sa suppression* (Paris, 1912); P. Gagnol, *La dîme ecclésiastique en France au XVIIIe siècle* (Paris, 1911). See bibliography by R. Schnerb in H. Sée, *Histoire économique de la France*, 2 vols. (Paris, 1939–42).

## The nobility

For orientation of research, see M. Bloch, 'Sur le passé de la noblesse française; quelques jalons de recherche', *Annales d'histoire économique et sociale*, XIII (1936), 366–78; K. Jelusec, 'La noblesse autrichienne: avant et après la guerre', *ibid.*, 355–65; T. H. Marshall, 'L'aristocratie britannique de nos jours', *ibid.*, IX (1937), 236–56; K. Denholm-Young, 'L'aristocratie anglaise: le Moyen Age', *ibid.*, pp. 257–69; Neufbourg, 'Les noblesses', *ibid.*, X (1938), 238–55.

For France: H. Carr, *La noblesse de France et l'opinion publique au XVIIIe siècle* (Paris, 1920); P. de Vaissière, *Gentilshommes campagnards de l'ancienne France* (Paris, 1903); L. Tuetey, *Les officiers sous l'Ancien Régime, Nobles et roturiers* (Paris, 1908); E. G. Léonard, 'La question sociale dans l'armée française au XVIIIe siècle', *Annales*, 111 (1948), 135–49; H. Lévy-Bruhl, 'La noblesse de France et le commerce à la fin de l'Ancien Régime', *Revue d'histoire modern*, VIII (1933) 209–35; P. Ardascheff, *Les intendants de province sous Louis XVI* (Paris, 1909); A. Colombet, *Les parlementaires bourguignons à la fin du XVIIIe siècle* (Dijon, 1937). On venality of office, general observations in the conclusion of R. Mousnier, *La vénalité des offices sous Henri IV et Louis XIII* (Rouen, 1945).

On manorial rights, see P. Sagnac, *La législation civile de la Révolution* (Paris, 1898); J. de La Monneraye, *Le régime féodal et les classes rurales dans le Maine au XVIIIe siècle* (Paris, 1922); J. Millot, *Le régime féodal en Franche-Comté* (Besançon, 1937). See bibliography by R. Schnerb in H. Sée, *Histoire économique de la France*, 2 vols. (Paris, 1939–42), and works on France cited in Chapter Five.

*The bourgeoisie*

Several studies have been devoted to the bourgeoisie: W. Sombart, *Der Bourgeois* (Leipzig, 1913); J. Aynard, *La bourgeoisie française* (Paris, 1934); B. Groethuysen, *Origines de l'esprit bourgeois en France*, Vol. I: *L'Église et la bourgeoisie* (Paris, 1927). Groethuysen concentrates on showing the development of religious concepts in terms of the moral ideal inspired in the bourgeoisie by its professional activity. Much broader is the study by F. Borkenau, *Die Übergang vom feudalen zum bürgerlichen Weltbild; Studien zur Geschichte der Philosophie der Manufacturperiode* (Paris, 1934). Among works based on documentary research in France are the studies of F. Mireur, *Le Tiers État à Draguignan* (Draguignan, 1911); C. Pouthas, *Une famille de bourgeoisie française de Louis XIV à Napoléon* (Paris, 1931), on the Guizots; L. Cahen, 'La population française au milieu du XVIIIe siècle', *Revue de Paris*, V (1919), 146–70. For publications on financiers, see P. Sagnac, *La fin de l'Ancien Régime* (Paris, 3d ed., 1952), Book III, Chap. III, Sec. 6; J. Bouchary, *Les manieurs d'argent à la fin du XVIIIe siècle*, 3 vols. (Paris, 1939–43); on businessmen, F. Vermale, *Le père de Casimir Périer, 1734–1801* (Grenoble, 1935); on liberal categories, F. Delbeke, *L'action politique et sociale des avocats au XVIIIe siècle* (Louvain and Paris, 1927); J. Pellisson, *Les hommes de lettres au XVIIIe siècle* (Paris, 1911). In addition, L. Abensour, *La femme et le féminisme avant la Révolution* (Paris, 1923). The *Souvenirs* of Cournot (Paris, 1913) contain valuable material.

Special studies based on documents, as mentioned above at the beginning of this chapter, include H. Sée, 'La population et la vie économique à Rennes vers le milieu du XVIIIe siècle d'après les rôles de la capitation', *Mémoires de la Société d'histoire de Bretagne*, IV (1923), 89–135; R. Gauthet, 'Château-Gontier à la veille de la Révolution', *Bulletin de la Commission historique de la Mayenne*, XLI (1925), 257–77, XLII (1926), 62–102;

L. Fournier, *Histoire politique de la municipalité de Guingamp de la révolte parlementaire de 1788 à l'organisation révolutionnaire de 1790–1791* (Saint-Brieuc, 1934); six studies concerning the French bourgeoisie in *Assemblée générale de la Commission centrale et des Comités départementaux* [d'histoire économique de la Revolution], *1939*, Vol. I (Besançon, 1942); F. Popelka, *Die Bürgerschaft der Stadt Graz von 1720 bis 1819* (Baden bei Wien, 1941).

For orientation of research, see A. Chatelain, 'Les fondements d'une géographie sociale de la bourgeoisie française', *Annales*, 11 (1947), 455–62.

### The peasantry

See N. S. B. Gras, *History of Agriculture in Europe and America* (New York, 1925); H. Sée, *Esquisse d'une histoire du régime agraire en Europe au XVIIIe et XIXe siècles* (Paris, 1921).

For France: M. Bloch, *Les caractères originaux de l'histoire rurale française* (Oslo and Paris, 1931; new ed., Paris, 1952); G. Lizerand, *Le régime rural de l'ancienne France* (Paris, 1942); J. Loutchisky, *La propriété paysanne en France à la veille de la Révolution* (Paris, 1912); G. Lefebvre, 'Les recherches relatives à la répartition de la propriété et de l'exploitation foncières à la fin de l'Ancien Régime', *Revue d'histoire moderne*, III (1928), 103–25 (and in *Études sur la Revolution française* [Paris, 1954], pp. 201–22); E. Patoz, 'La propriété paysanne dans les bailliages de Semur, Saulieu et Arnay-le-Duc', *Bulletin de la Société des sciences de Semur*, 1908–9; G. Lefebvre, *Les paysans du Nord pendant la Révolution française*, 2 vols. (Lille, 1924), which describes conditions at the close of the Old Regime; J. Loutchisky, 'Régime agraire et populations agricoles dans les environs de Paris à la veille de la Révolution', *Revue d'histoire modern*, VIII (1933), 97–142; R. H. Andrews, *Les paysans des Mauges au XVIIIe siècle* (Tours, 1925); G. Sangnier, *L'évolution de la propriété rurale dane le district de Saint-Pol [Pas-de-Calais] pendant la Révolution* (Blangermont, Pas-de-Calais, 1951), which describes conditions at the close of the Old Regime; see bibliography by R. Schnerb in H. Sée, *Histoire économique de la France*, Vol. I (Paris, 1939); G. Afanassiev, *Le commerce des céréales en France au XVIIIe siècle* (Paris, 1894); J. Letaconnoux, *Les subsistances et le commerce des grains en Bretagne au XVIIIe siècle* (Rennes, 1909); G. Debien, *En Haut-Poitou, Défricheurs au travail, XVe–XVIIIe siècles* (Paris, 1952, 'Cahiers des Annales', No. 7); M. Faucheux, *Un ancien droit ecclésiastique perçu en Bas-Poitou: le boisselage* (La Roche-sur-Yon, 1953); M. Chamboux, *Répartition de la propriété foncière et de l'exploitation dans la Creuse, Les paysans dans la Creuse à la fin de l'Ancien Régime* (Paris, 1955); G. Lefebvre, *Questions agraires au temps de la Terreur*

(Strasbourg, 1932, 2d ed., La Roche-sur-Yon, 1954). For landholding, sharecropping, and farming controls: M. Lacoste, *La crise économique dans le département de la Meurthe à la fin de l'Ancien Régime et au début de la Révolution* (typewritten thesis, Paris, 1951). For the tithe, see above, The Clergy; for manorial rights, see The Nobility; and for duties, the bibliography by R. Schnerb, mentioned above. See also below, in Chapter Ten, Agrarian Reform.

For Germany: G. Knapp, *Die Bauernbefreiung und der Ursprung der Landarbeiter in den älteren Teilen Preussens*, 2 vols. (Leipzig, 1887).

For Belgium: P. Recht, 'Quelques aperçus sur les classes rurales du Namurois à la fin du XVIIIe siècle', *Annales de la Société archéologique de Namur*, XLII (1937), 199–286; and *Les biens communaux du Namurois et leur partage à la fin du XVIIIe siècle* (Brussels, 1950); J. Ruwet, *L'agriculture et les classes rurales au Pays du Herve sous l'Ancien Régime* (Liége, 1943); J. Delatte, *Les classes rurales dans la principauté de Liége au XVIIIe siècle* (Paris, 1945).

For Spain: G. Desdevises du Dézert, *L'Espagne d'Ancien Régime*, 3 vols. (Paris, 1899–1904, 2d ed., 1928); J. Klein, *The Mesta, 1273–1856* (Cambridge, Mass., 1920).

For Italy: G. Prato, *La vita economica in Piemonte a mezzo il secolo XVIII* (Turin, 1908).

For Norway: H. Koht, *Les luttes des paysans en Norvège du XVIIe au XIXe siècle* (French tr., Paris, 1929).

For Poland: J. Rutkowski, 'Le régime agraire en Pologne au XVIIIe siécle', *Revue d'histoire économique et sociale*, XIV (1926), 473–505, and XV (1927), 66–113, and published together (Paris, 1928).

For Russia: A. von Tobien, *Die Livländische Ritterschaft* (Berlin, 1930), Chap. I; A. Schwabe, *Grundriss der Agrargeschichte Lettlands* (Riga, 1928), Fr. tr., abr., *Histoire agraire de la Lettonie* (Riga, 1929). See also below, The Proletariat.

*British society*

See P. Muret and P. Sagnac, *La prépondérance anglaise* (Paris, 3d ed., 1949), Book I, Chap. II, Sees. 3 and 4; P. Sagnac, *La fin de l'Ancien Régime* (Paris, 3d ed., 1952), Book I, Chap. II, Sec. 2; W. Holdsworth, *History of English Law*. Some material may be found in H. D. Trail, *Social England*, Vol. V: *From the Accession of George I to the Battle of Waterloo* (London, 1896, 2d ed., 1898); G. M. Trevelyan, *Social History from Chaucer to Queen Victoria* (London, 1942, 3d ed., 1945); E. Halévy, *Histoire du peuple anglais au XIXe siècle*, Vol. I (Paris, 1913), Eng. tr. by E. I. Watkin and D. A. Barker, *A History of the English People in the Nineteenth Century*, Vol. I (New York, 1949); B. and S. Webb, *English Local Government*, 3 Vols. (London, 1903–8); C. R. Fay, *The Corn Laws and Social England* (Cambridge, 1922), and *Great Britain from Adam Smith to the Present Day* (London, 1928); L. B. Namier, *The Structure of Politics at the Accession of George III*, 2 vols., (London, 1919), and *England and the Age of the American Revolution*, 2 vols. (London, 1930); A. S. Tuberville, 'Aristocracy and Revolution, The British Peerage, 1789–1832', *History*, XXV (1942), 240–53.

### The proletariat

The many works cited above in Chapter Two, on industry and agriculture, contain material on proletarians. On England, see for example T. S. Ashton, *The Industrial Revolution, 1760–1830* (Oxford, 1948); E. W. Gilboy, *Wages in 18th Century England* (Cambridge, Mass., 1934); D. Marshall, *The English Poor in the 18th Century* (London, 1926).

For Prussia: H. Brunschwig, *La crise de l'État prussien à la fin du XVIIIe siècle* (Paris, 1948).

For France: L. Guéneau, *L'organisation du travail à Nevers aux XVIIe et XVIIIe siècles, 1660–1790* (Paris, 1919), and *Les conditions de vie à Nevers à la fin de l'Ancien Régime* (Paris, 1919); J. Godart, *L'ouvrier en soie à Lyon* (Lyon, 1901); Germain-Martin, *Les associations ouvrières au XVIIIe siècle* (Paris, 1900); Martin-Saint-Léon, *Les compagnonnages* (Paris, 1901); C. Bloch, *L'État et l'assistance a la fin de l'Ancien Régime* (Paris, 1908); H. Sée, 'Les classes ouvrières et la question sociale à la veille de la Révolution', *Annales révolutionnaires*, XIV (1922), 373–86. Statistics may be found in H. Sée, 'Statistique des pauvres de Rennes vers la fin de l'Ancien Régime', *Annales de Bretagne*, XLI (1934), 474–77; F. Braesch, 'Essai de statistique de la population ouvrière de Paris en 1791', *La Révolution française*, LXIII (1912), 289–321; A. Mathiez, 'Notes sur l'importance du prolétariat en France à la veille de la Révolution', *Annales historiques de la Révolution française*, VII (1930), 497–524. On the proletariat, begging, and migration from the countryside, G. Lefebvre, *Les paysans du Nord, pendant la Révolution française*, 2 vols. (Lille, 1924), and *La Grande Peur de 1789* (Paris, 1932).

### Chapter 4. European thought

See P. Muret and P. Sagnac, *La prépondérance anglaise* (Paris, 3d ed., 1949), Book II, Chap. IV, and Book IV, Chap. VII; P. Sagnac, *La fin de l'Ancien Régime* (Paris, 3d ed., 1952), Book I, Chap. I, Sec. 4; Preserved Smith, *A History of Modern Culture: The Enlightenment, 1687–1776*, 2 vols. (New York, 1924–30, rev. ed., 1934); E. Cassirer, *Die Philosophie der Aufklärung* (Tübingen, 1933); P. Hazard, *La pensée européenne au XVIIIe siècle, de Montesquieu à Lessing, 3 vols. (Paris, 1946); C. Becker, The Heavenly City of the Eighteenth Century Philosophers* (New Haven, Conn., 1932); H. Laski, *Faith, Reason and Science, An Essay in Historical Analysis* (London, 1944); É. Bréhier, *Histoire de la philosophie*, Vol. II: *Le XVIIIe siècle* (Paris, 1930); K. Fischer, *Geschichte der neueren Philosophie*, 6 vols. (Heidelberg, 5th ed., 1909–10); W. Windelband, *Die Geschichte der neueren Philosophie in ihrem Zusammenhang mit der allgemeine Kultur* (Leipzig, 1878–80, rev. ed., 1922); J. Delvaille, *Essai sur l'histoire de l'idée de progrès jusqu' à la fin du XVIIIe siècle* (Paris, 1910); F. Meinecke, *Geschichte des Historismus in XVIII. und XIX. Jahrhundert* (Berlin, 1927), and *Die Entstehung des Historismus* (Berlin, 1936).

## The mind of the past and the awakening of the modern mind

On Freemasonry, see bibliography in B. Fay, *La franc-maçonnerie et la révolution intellectuelle du XVIIIe siècle* (Paris, 1935).

For England, see 'Freemasonry' in the *Encyclopædia Britannica*, Vol. IX (14th ed., 1929).

For France, see Gaston-Martin, *Manuel d'histoire de la franc-maçonnerie française* (Paris, 1932); A. Lantoine, *Histoire de la franc-maçonnerie française* (Paris, 1925), primarily from the point of view of Scottish Rite Masonry; R. Priouret, *La Franc-maçonnerie sous les lys* (Paris, 1951); A. Mornet, *Les origines intellectuelles de la Révolution française* (Paris, 1933), Part III, Chap. VII.

For Germany, see P. Sagnac, *La fin de l'Ancien Régime* (Paris, 3d ed., 1952), Book III, Chap. IV, Sec. 7; F. J. Schneider, *Die Freimaurerei und ihr Einfluss auf die geistige Koltur in Deutschland am Ende des XVIII. Jahrhunderts* (Prague, 1909); R. Le Forestier, *Les illuminés de Bavière et la francmaçonnerie allemande* (Dijon, 1914).

For Italy, see P. Sagnac, *La fin de l'Ancien Régime* (Paris, 3d ed., 1952), Book I, Chap. III, Sec. 2.

On religious history, see P. Sagnac, *La fin de l'Ancien Régime* (Paris, 3d ed., 1952), Book I, Chap. VI, Sec. 2 (the papacy and Italy), Chap. II, Sec. II (England), Chap. IV, Sec. 3 (France), Chap. V, Sec. 4 (Spain), Chap. VII, Sec. II (Germany and Austria); L. Pastor, *Geschichte der Päpste seit dem Ausgang des Mittelaltern*, Vol. XVI, in three parts, the third on the pontificate of Pius VI (Freiburg im Breisgau, 1931–33); F. Mourret, *Histoire générale de l'Église,*

Vol. VI (Paris, 1911); A. Gazier, *Histoire générale du mouvement janséniste depuis ses origines jusqu' à nos jours* (Paris, 1922); E. Préclin, *Les jansénistes du XVIIIe siècle et la constitution civile du clergé* (Paris, 1928), and 'L'influence du jansénisme français à l'étranger', *Revue historique*, CLXXXII (1938), 25–71; B. Matteucci, *Scipione de Ricci* (Rome, 1941); A. C. Jemolo, *Il giansenismo nel Italia prima della Rivoluzione* (Bari, 1928); A. Cordignole, *Illuministi, giansenisti e giacobini nell'Italia del' Settecento* (Firenze, 1947).

On Protestantism in general, see É.-G. Léonard, bibliographic review in *Revue historique*, CCXII (1954), 279–326, and 'Le protestantisme français de la Révocation à la Révolution, Position de problèmes et bibliographie', *L'Information historique* (1950), pp. 134–40, and *Le Protestant français* (Paris, 1953).

For England and Germany, see appropriate sections below.

On unorthodox mysticism and occultism, see M. Lamm, *Swedenborg* (Leipzig, 1922); G. van Rijnberg, *Un thaumaturge au XVIIIe siècle, Martines de Pasqually: Sa vie, son oeuvre, son ordre*, 2 vols. (Paris and Lyon, 1935–38); J. Blum, *La vie et l'œuvre de J.-G. Hamann, le mage du Nord, 1730–1788* (Paris, 1912); R. Le Forestier, *La franc-maçonnerie occultiste au XVIIIe siècle et l'Ordre des Élus Cohens* (Paris, 1928); J. Buche, *L'école mystique de Lyon* (Paris, 1935); A. Joly, *Un mystique lyonnais et les secrets de la franc-maçonnerie: Willermoz* (Mâcon, 1938); A. Viatte, *Les sources occultes du romantisme: Illuminisme, Théosophie, 1770–1820* (Paris, 1928).

*Scientific rationalism*

See P. Sagnac, *La fin de l'Ancien Régime* (Paris, 3d ed., 1952), Book I, Chap. I, Sec. 4, Book III, Chap. III, Sec. 3; A. Wolf, *A History of Science, Technology, and Philosophy in the 18th Century* (New York, 1939); Vols. XIV and XV of *Histoire de la nation française*, published under the direction of G. Hanotaux (Paris, 1924); M. Caullery, *La science française depuis le XVIIIe siècle* (Paris, 1933); Hélène Metzger, *Les doctrines chimiques en France, du XVIIe siècle à la fin du XVIIIe* (Paris, 1923); A. Meldrum, *The Eighteenth Century Revolution in Science* (New York, 1929); N. Nielsen, *Les géomètres français du XVIIIe siècle* (Copenhagen, 1935); M. Berthelot, *La révolution chimique: Lavoisier* (Paris, 1890); E. Grimaux, *Lavoisier* (Paris, 1888); S. J. French, *Torch and Crucible, The Life and Death of Antoine Lavoisier* (Princeton, 1941), which also describes the work of English chemists; M. Daumas, *Lavoisier* (Paris, 1941), and *Lavoisier théoricien et expérimentateur* (Paris, 1953); D. Mackie, *Antoine Lavoisier* (London, 1952); R. Guyenot, *L'évolution de la pensée scientifique: Les sciences de la vie* (Paris, 1941), which describes

advances in classification and the birth of the concept of evolution;
D. Mornet, *Les sciences de la nature en France au XVIIIe siècle* (Paris, 1911);
H. Daudin, *Études d'histoire des sciences naturelles*, Vol. I: *De Linné à Jussieu,
1740–1790*; Vol. II: *Cuvier et Lamarck, 1790–1830*, 3 books (Paris, 1926);
M. Daumas, *Les instruments scientifiques aux XVIIe et XVIIIe siècles* (Paris,
1953); and bibliographies in F. Russo, *Histoire des sciences* (Paris, 1954), and
in P. Chaunu, 'Progrès technique et progrès scientifique en Europe', in
*Bulletin de la société des professeurs d'histoire* (November, 1954).

For scientific rationalism, see above, at the beginning of this chapter.

For the economists, see G. Weulersse, *Le mouvement physiocratique en
France de 1756 à 1770* (Paris, 1910), and *La physiocratie sous les ministères de
Turgot et de Necker, 1774–1781* (Paris, 1950); C. Gide and C. Rist, *Histoire des
doctrines économiques depuis les physiocrates* (Paris, 1909); G. Gonnard,
*Histoire des doctrines monétaires du XVIIe siècle à 1914*, 2 vols. (Paris, 1936);
P. Harsin, *Les doctrines monétaires et financières en France du XIVe au XVIIIe
siècle* (Paris, 1928); E. Cannan, *A History of the Theories of Production and
Distribution in English Political Economy from 1776 to 1848* (London, 1893);
C. R. Fay, *Great Britain from Adam Smith to the Present Day* (London, 1928);
R. M. Manfra, *Pietro Verri e i problemi economici del tempo suo* (Milan, 1932).

## Deism and natural law

On natural law, see the extensive bibliography in R. Derathé *Jean-Jacques
Rousseau et la science politique de son temps* (Paris, 1950). General surveys
may be found in P. Janet, *Histoire de la science politique dans ses rapports
avec la morale*, 2 vols. (Paris, 1872, 4th ed., 1913); G. Sabine, *A History of
Political Theory* (New York, 1937, rev. ed., 1955); R. Stintzing and E. Lands-
berg, *Geschichte der deutschen Rechtswissenschaft*, 6 vols. (Munich, Leipzig,
and Berlin, 1880–1910).

On the origins of natural law, see E. Troeltsch, 'Das stoisch-christliche
Naturrecht und das moderne profane Naturrecht', *Historische Zeitschrift*,
CVI (1911), 237–67. On the medieval concept of natural rights, see O. von
Gierke, *Rechtsgeschichte der deutschen Genossenschaft*, 3 vols. (Berlin, 1868–
81); one section of Vol. III has been translated in English by M. Maitland as
*Political Theories of the Middle Ages* (Cambridge, 1900), with introduction.
The concept of natural law was developed in the seventeenth century by
Protestant writers, mainly lawyers—Grotius, Althusius, Hobbes,
Puffendorf—and some of their works were later translated and com-
mented on by Barbeyrac and Barlamaqui. See O. von Gierke, *Johannes
Althusius und die Entwicklung der naturrechtlichen Staatstheorien* (Breslau,

1880); E. Barker, *Natural Law and the Theory of Society, 1500–1800* (Cambridge, 1934); B. Freyd, *The Development of Political Theory* (London, 1939); J. W. Gough, *The Social Contract, A Critical Study of Its Development* (Oxford, 1936).

Authors of the seventeenth century were criticized by Rousseau, who drew logical conclusions from natural right by formulating the idea of inalienable and indivisible sovereignty of the people and, consequently, the idea of the democratic republic. Concerning his debt to them and his originality, see R. Derathé, cited above.


*England and Germany*

For England, see P. Muret and P. Sagnac, *La prépondérance anglaise* (Paris, 3d ed., 1949), Book I, Chap. I; P. Sagnac, *La fin de l'Ancien Régime* (Paris, 3d ed., 1952), Book I, Chap. II, Sec. II; and Book III, Chap. II, Sec. 3; L. Stephen, *History of English Thought in the Eighteenth Century*, 2 vols. (London, 1876–80, 3d ed., 1902); H. J. Laski, *Political Thought in England from Locke to Bentham* (London, 1919); A. Cobban, *Edmund Burke and the Revolt against the Eighteenth Century* (London, 1929); P. Magnus, *Edmund Burke* (London, 1939); É. Halévy, *La formation du radicalisme philosophique en Angleterre*, 3 vols. (Paris, 1901–4), Eng. tr., *The Growth of Philosophical Radicalism* (London, 1928); P. Larkin, *Property in the Eighteenth Century, with Special Reference to England and Locke* (Cork, 1930); J. Overton, *The English Church from the Accession of George I to the End of the Eighteenth Century* (London, 1906); N. Sykes, *Church and State in England in the Eighteenth Century* (Cambridge, 1935).

For Germany, see P. Sagnac, *La fin de l'Ancien Régime* (Paris, 3d ed., 1952), Book I, Chap. VII, Sec. I; L. Lévy-Bruhl, *L'Allemagne depuis Leibnitz* (Paris, 1890); J.-E. Spenlé, *La pensée allemande* (Paris, 1934); E. Ermatinger, *Deutsche Kultur im Zeitalter der Aufklärung*, Vol. I (Potsdam, 1934); A. Ritschl, *Geschichte des Pietismus in der lutheranischen Kirche des XVI. und XVII. Jahrhunderts*, 3 vols. (Berlin, 1880–86), especially Vol. III, on Zinzendorf and the Moravian brothers; F. Lichtenberger, *Histoire des idées religieuses en Allemagne depuis le milieu du XVIIIe siècle*, 3 vols. (Paris, 1873); J. Küntziger, *Febronius et le fébronianisme* (Brussels, 1889); P. Klassen, *Justus Möser* (Frankfurt, 1936); G. Goyau, *L'Allemagne religieuse, Le catholicisme*, 4 vols. (Paris, 1905–9), Vol. I, Chaps. I and II. In addition, see K. Bidermann, *Deutschland in XVIII. Jahrhundert* (Leipzig, 1854–80, 2d ed., 1881); J. Hansen, *Quellen zur Geschichte des Rheinlandes im Zeitalter der französischen Revolution, 1780–1801*, 4 vols. (Bonn, 1931–38), Vol. I;

H. Brunschwig, *La crise de l'État prussien* (Paris, 1947); W. H. Bradford, *Germany in the Eighteenth Century, The Social Background of the Literary Revival* (New York, 1935).

*France*

See P. Sagnac, *La fin de l'Ancien Régime* (Paris, 3d ed., 1952), Book I, Chap. I, Sec. 4, and Chap. IV, Sec. 3; Book III, Chap. III, Secs. 3 and 4; and *La formation de la societé française moderne*, 2 vols. (Paris, 1945–46); H. Carré, *Le règne de Louis XVI* (Paris, 1910), Books III and IV; Bibliography by L. Gottschalk, 'Studies since 1920 of French Thought in the Period of Enlightenment', *The Journal of Modern History*, IV (1932), 242–60; D. Mornet, *La pensée française au XVIIIe siècle* (Paris, 1926), and *Les origines intellectuelles de la Révolution française, 1755–1787* (Paris, 1932); H. Sée, *Les idées politiques en France au XVIIIe siècle* (Paris, 1920), and *L'évolution de la pensée politique en France au XVIIIe siècle* (Paris, 1925); É. Carcassonne, *Montesquieu et le problème de la constitution au XVIIIe siècle* (Paris, 1927); A. Schinz, *La pensée de J.-J. Rousseau; essai d'interprétation nouvelle* (Paris, 1929), and *État présent des travaux sur J.-J. Rousseau* (Paris, 1941); R. Derathé, *Le rationalisme de J.-J. Rousseau* (Paris, 1948), and *Rousseau et la science politique de son temps* (Paris, 1950); B. Fay, *L'esprit révolutionnaire en France et aux États-Unis à la fin du XVIIIe siècle* (Paris, 1925), Eng. tr. by Ramon Guthrie, *The Revolutionary Spirit in France and America* (New York, 1927); G. Bonno, *La constitution britannique devant l'opinion française, de Montesquieu à Bonaparte* (Paris, 1932); É. Ruff, *Jean-Louis de Lolme und sein Werk über die Verfassung Englands* (Berlin, 1934); F. Acomb, *Anglophobia in France, An Essay in the History of Constitutionalism and Nationalism* (Durham, N.C., 1950); A. Lichtenberger, *Le sociolisme au XVIIIe siècle* (Paris, 1899); A. Espinas, *La philosophie du XVIIIe siècle et la Révolution française* (Paris, 1898); Eva Hoffmann-Linke, *Zwischen Nationalism und Demokratie, Gestalten der französischen Revolution* (Munich, 1927); K. Martin, *French Liberal Thought in the Eighteenth Century: A Study of Political Ideas from Bayle to Condorcet* (London, 1929); R. R. Palmer, *Catholics and Unbelievers in the Eighteenth Century in France* (Princeton, 1939).

On the spread of new ideas, see D. Mornet, cited above; F. Brunot, *Histoire de la langue française*, Vol. VII: *La propagation du français en France jusqu'à la fin de l'Ancien Régime* (Paris, 1926); J.-P. Belin, *Le mouvement philosophique de 1748 à 1789*, and *Le commerce des livres prohibés à Paris de 1750 à 1789* (Paris, 1913); H. Sée, 'La diffusion des idées philosophiques à la fin de l'Ancien Régime', *Annales révolutionnaires*, XV (1923), 482–502;

M. Bouchard, *De l'humanisme à l'Encyclopédie, Essai sur l'évolution des esprits dans la bourgeoisie bourguignonne sous les règnes de Louis XIV et de Louis XV* (Paris, 1929); P. Grosclaude, *La vie intellectuelle à Lyon dans la seconde moitié du XVIIIe siècle* (Paris, 1933); R. Tisserand, *L'Académie de Dijon* (Vesoul, 1936).

On religion, see P. Sagnac, *La fin de l'Ancien Régime* (Paris, 3d ed., 1952), Book I, Chap. IV, Sec. 3; *Histoire de la nation française*, published under the direction of G. Hanotaux, Vol. VI: *Histoire religieuse*, by G. Goyau (Vesoul, 1922); G. Le Bras, 'Les transformations religieuses des campagnes françaises depuis la fin du XVIIe siècle', *Annales sociologiques*, Series E, Fasc. 2 (1937), pp. 15–70.

*Arts and letters*

See P. Van Tieghem, *Histoire littéraire de l'Europe et de l'Amérique de la Renaissance jusqu'à nos jours* (Paris, 1941), and *Le préromantisme, Études d'histoire littéraire européenne*, 3 vols. (Paris, 1924–27); Vol. VI of *Histoire de la langue et de la littérature française*, published under the direction of Petit de Julleville (Paris, 1909); G. Lanson, *Histoire de la littérature française* (Paris, 1895); J. Bédier and P. Hazard, *Histoire de la littérature française illustrée* (Paris, 1923–24, rev. ed. published under the direction of P. Martino, Paris, 1950), Vol. II; F. Brunot, *Histoire de la langue française*, Vol. VI: *Le XVIIIe siècle*, 4 vols. (Paris, 1930, 1932–33); D. Mornet, *Le sentiment de la nature de J.-J. Rousseau à Bernardin de Saint-Pierre* (Paris, 1907); L. Bertrand, *La fin du classicisme et le retour à l'antique dans la seconde moitié du XVIIIe siècle* (Paris, 1898); F. Badolle, *L'abbé Jean-Jacques Barthélemy (1716–1793) et l'hellénisme en France dans la seconde moitié du XVIIIe siècle* (Paris, 1927); H. T. Parker, *The Cult of Antiquity and the French Revolutionaries* (Chicago, 1937); A. Monglond, *Histoire intérieure du préromantisme français de l'abbé Prévot à Joubert*, 2 vols. (Grenoble, 1929); *The Cambridge History of English Literature* (Cambridge, 1907–18), Vols. IX–XI; E. Legouis and L. Cazamian, *Histoire de la littérature anglaise* (Paris, 1924); W. Scherer, *Geschichte der deutschen Literatur* (Berlin, 1883, 15th ed., 1922); J. Schmidt, *Geschichte der deutschen Literatur von Leibnitz bis auf unsere Zeit*, Vol. III (Berlin, 1886); A. Köster, *Die deutsche Literatur der Aufklärungszeit* (Heidelberg, 1925); O. Walzel, *Deutsche Dichtung von Gottsched bis zur Gegenwart* (Berlin, 1926); G. Natali, *Il Settecento*, 2 vols. (Milan, 1929); F. De Sanctis, *A History of Italian Literature*, 2 vols. (New York, 1931); P. Hazard, *La Révolution française et les lettres italiennes* (Paris, 1910).

On plastic arts: P. Lavedan, *Histoire de l'Art* (Paris, 1944), with bibliography and notes, Vol. II, *Moyen Age et temps modernes; Histoire générale de l'art*, published under the direction of A. Michel, Vol. VII: *L'art en Europe an XVIIIe siècle*, 2 vols., (Paris, 1924); L. Réau, *Histoire générale des arts* (Paris, 1935), Vol. III, and *L'ère romantique, Les arts plastiques* (Paris, 1949), Introduction and Book I; L. Hautecœur, *Rome et la renaissance de l'antiquité à la fin du XVIIIe siècle* (Paris, 1912); P. Sagnac, *La fin de l'Ancien Régime* (Paris, 3d ed., 1952), Book I, Chap. I, Sec. 7; L. Hautecœur, *Histoire de l'architecture classique en France*, 3 vols. (Paris, 1950–54), Parts III and IV, and *Louis David* (Paris, 1954); P. Verlet, *Les meubles français du XVIIIe siècle*, 2 vols. (Paris, 1956).

On music: J. Combarieu, *Histoire de la musique*, Vol. II (Paris, 1913, 2d ed., 1919); H. Prunières, *Nouvelle histoire de la musique*, Vol. II: *La musique des XVIIe et XVIIIe siècles* (Paris, 1936).

*Cosmopolitanism and nationalities*

See P. Muret and P. Sagnac, *La prépondérance anglaise* (Paris, 3d ed., 1949), Book III, Chap. IV, and Book IV, Chap. VII, Sec. I; P. Sagnac, *La fin de l'Ancien Régime* (Paris, 3d ed., 1952), Book I, Chap. I, Secs. 5 and 6; F. Brunot, *Histoire de la langue française*, Vol. VIII: *Le français hors de France au XVIIIe siècle*, 2 vols. (Paris, 1934–35); L. Réau, *L'Europe française au siècle des lumières* (Paris, 1938); L. Reynaud, *Histoire générale de l'influence française en Allemagne* (Paris, 1914); F. Meinecke, *Weltbürgertum und National-staat* (Berlin, 1908), and *Geschichte des Historismus*, 2 vols. (Berlin, 1927); O. Vossler, *Der Nationalgedanke von Rousseau bis Ranke* (Munich and Berlin, 1937); R. Reinhold Ergang, *Herder and the Foundation of German Nationalism* (New York, 1913); G. Maugain, *L'évolution intellectuelle en Italie de 1657 à 1750 environ* (Paris, 1909); H. Bédarida and P. Hazard, *L'influence française en Italie au XVIIIe siècle* (Paris, 1936). The origins of the Risorgimento in Italy have been the subject of many works in Italy: general treatment in C. Barbagallo, *Storia universale*, Vol. V, Part I: *Riforme e Rivoluzione, 1699–1799* (Turin, 1946), Book IV, Chap. II, with bibliography, and in conjunction, G. Lesage, 'La production historique en Italie de 1940 à 1945', *Revue historique*, CXCVII (1947), 79–117; I. Kont, *Étude sur l'influence de la littérature française en Hongrie, 1770–1896* (Paris, 1902); A. Eckhardt, 'Le Contrat social en Hongrie', *Revue des études hongroises* (1924), pp. 117–37; H. Tronchon, *Un voltairien d'Hongrie, le comte Jean Fekete de Galántha* (Paris, 1924); H. Cidade, *Ensaio sôbre a crise mental do seculo XVIII* (Coimbra, 1929); L. Pingaud, *Les Français en Russie et les Russes en France* (Paris, 1885); E. Haumant, *La culture française en Russie* (Paris, 1910);

K. Waliszewski, *Autour d'un trône* (Paris, 1913), Part II. Further bibliographic information may be found in J. Mathorez, *Les étrangers en France sous l'Ancien Régime*, especially Vol. II (Paris, 1921); in A. Mathiez, *La Révolution et les étrangers* (Paris, 1918); and the general histories cited at the beginning of this bibliography.

### Chapter 5. The states and social conflicts

On the concept of the dynastic and absolutistic state, see F. Meinecke, *Die Idee der Staatsräson* (Berlin, 1924); P. Janet, *Histoire de la philosophie morale et politique*, 2 vols. (Paris, 1858); A. Sorel, *L'Europe et la Révolution française*, Vol. I (Paris, 1885, 12th ed., 1908); J. Jaurès, *Histoire socialiste de la Révolution française*, 4 vols. (Paris, 1901–4), Vol. III (Vol. V of the new ed., prepared by Mathiez); the Introduction to H. Michel, *L'idée de l'Etat* (Paris, 1895), discusses the eighteenth century and the Revolution.

*Enlightened despotism*

Enlightened despotism was part of the programme of the International History Congress held in Warsaw in 1933. Reports were presented for most of the continental countries; these, along with the general report by M. Lhéritier, were published in the *Bulletin of the International Committee of Historical Sciences*, Vol. V., No. 20 (1933), and Vol. IX, Nos. 34 and 35 (1937). The best general work is L. Gershoy, *From Despotism to Revolution, 1763–1789* (New York, 1944, in the series 'The Rise of Modern Europe', edited by W. Langer). See also the works cited below, under State Rivalry; C. Morazé, 'Finance et despotisme, Essai sur les despotes éclairés', *Annales*, III (1948), 279–96; G. Lefebvre, 'Le despotisme éclairé', *Annales historiques de la Révolution française*, XXI (1949), 97–115.

For the condition of the peasants, see Chapter Three above, The Peasantry.

For Germany, see P. Muret and P. Sagnac, *La Prépondérance anglaise* (Paris, 3d ed., 1949), Book III, Chap. III, Sec. 2; P. Sagnac, *La fin de l'Ancien Régime* (Paris, 3d ed., 1952), Chap. VII, Secs. 1, 4–8; Book III, Chap. IV, Sec. 6. The basic work on Frederick the Great is R. Koser, *Geschichte Friedrichs des Grossen*, 4 vols. (Stuttgart and Berlin, 1921–25). See also K. Bidermann, *Deutschland im XVIII. Jahrhundert* (Leipzig, 1854–80, 2d ed., 1881); C. Perthes, *Politische Zustände und Personen in Deutschland zur Zeit der französischen Revolution*, 2 vols. (Gotha, 1862–69); W. Wenck, *Deutschland vor hundert Jahren*, 2 vols. (Leipzig, 1887–90); K. Deutschmann, *Die Rhein-*

*lande vor der französischen Revolution* (Berlin, 1902); M. Doeberl, *Entwick-elungsgeschichte Bayerns*, 2 vols. (Munich, 1912, 3d ed., rev., 1928), Vol. II; F. Schnabel, *Deutsche Geschichte im neunzehnten Jahrhundert*, Vol. I (Freiburg-im-Breisgau, 1929).

For the Rhineland countries, see J. Hansen, *Quellen zur Geschichte des Rheinlandes im Zeitalter der französischen Revolution, 1780–1801*, 4 vols. (Bonn, 1931–38), Vol. I.

For Austria, see P. Muret and P. Sagnac, *La prépondérance anglaise* (Paris, 3d ed., 1949), Book III, Chap. III, and P. Sagnac, *La fin de l'Ancien Régime* (Paris, 3d ed., 1952), Book I, Chap. VII, Secs. 9 and 11, Book III, Chap. IV, Sec. 1, and Chap. V, Sec. 7; I. Beidtel, *Geschichte der oester-reichischen Staatsverwaltung*, Vol. I: *1740–1848*, 2 vols. (Innsbrück, 1896–98); L. Sommer, *Die oesterreichischen Kameralisten in Dogmen geschichtli-cher Darstellung*, 2 vols. (Vienna, 1921–25); A. W. Small, *The Cameralists* (Chicago, 1909). On Joseph II, in addition to P. von Mitrofanov, *Joseph II, Seine politische und kulturelle Tätigkeit*, translated from the Russian by V. von Demelič, 2 vols. (Vienna and Leipzig, 1910), and E. Benedickt, *Kaiser Joseph II* (Vienna, 1936), see S. K. Padover, *The Revolutionary Emperor, Joseph the Second* (New York, 1934), and E. Winter, *Der Josephismus und seine Geschichte, Beiträgen zur Geistesgeschichte Œsterreichs, 1740–1848* (Vienna, 1943). Winter relates Josephism to an ecclesiastical reform movement originating in Italy and the Low Countries and comparable to the Erasmian movement of the sixteenth century; yet it seems unlikely that among Joseph's achievements one can attribute to that movement either his attitude towards the papacy, in which he demonstrated the tradition of absolutist Caesaro-papism, or the emancipation of the Protestants, which corresponded to the philosophical current of the eighteenth century. See also E. Denis, *La Bohême depuis la Montagne Blanche*, 2 vols. (Paris, 1903, 2d ed., 1930); R. J. Kerner, *Bohemia in the 18th Century* (New York, 1932); H. Marczali, *Magyarorszag II. Joseph koraban*, 3 vols. (Budapest, 1888–89), Vol. I translated into English with introduction by H. Temperley, *Hungary in the 18th Century* (Cambridge, 1910); F. Valsecchi, *L'assolutismo illuminato in Austria e in Lombardia*, 2 vols. (Bologna, 1931–34); C. Vianello, *La riforma finanziaria nella Lombardia austriana del XVIII secolo* (Milan, 1940); H. Pirenne, *Histoire de Belgique*, Vol. V (Brussels, 1921); Mme Tassier-Charlier, 'L'esprit public en Belgique de 1725 à 1789', *Revue de l'Université de Bruxelles*, IV (1934–35), 391–413.

For Italy, there is an extensive bibliography in P. Sagnac, *La fin de l'Ancien Régime* (Paris, 3d ed., 1952), Book I, Chap. VI; N. Bianchi, *Storià della monarchia piemontese dal 1773 al 1861*, 4 vols. (Rome, 1877), Vol. I;

M. Bruchet, *L'abolition du régime seigneurial en Savoie* (Paris, 1908); C. Tivaroni, *L'Italia prima della Rivoluzione francese, 1735–89* (Turin, 1888); S. Ortolani, *L'Italie au XVIIIe siècle* (Paris, 1929); P. Orsi, *L'Italia moderna* (Milan, 1901, 3d ed., 1910); E. Rota, *Le origini del Risorgimento* (Milan, 1950); A. Pingaud, *Bonaparte, président de la République italienne* (Paris, 1914), Vol. I, pp. 1–131, with bibliography; R. Mori, *Le riforme leopoldine nel pensiero degli economisti toscani* (Florence, 1951); H. Holdack, 'Die Reformpolitik Leopolds von Toskana', *Historische Zeitschrift*, CXLV (1941), 23-46; B. Croce, *Storia del regno di Napoli* (Bari, 1925); M. Scipa, *Il regno di Napoli al tempo di Carlo III di Borbone*, 2 vols. (Rome, 1923); E. Pontieri, *Il riformismo borbonico nella Sicilia del Settecento e dell' Ottocento* (Rome, 1945), and *Il tramonto del baronaggio siciliano* (Florence, 1943).

For Spain: P. Muret and P. Sagnac, *La prépondérance anglaise* (Paris, 3d ed., 1949), Book I, Chap. V and Book II, Chap. II, Sec. 7; G. Desdevises du Dézert, *L'Espagne d'Ancien régime*, 3 vols. (Paris, 1899–1904, 2d ed., 1928); A. Ballesteros y Beretta, *Historia de España*, 9 vols. (Barcelona, 1936–49); R. Altamira, *Historia de la nación y de la civilisación española*, 4 vols. (Barcelona 1906–11, 5th ed., 1935), Vol. IV; L. Sánchez Agesta, *El pensamiento politico del despotismo ilustrado* (Madrid, 1951); J. Sarrailh, *L'Espagne éclairée de la seconde moitié du XVIIIe siècle* (Paris, 1954); R. Leonard, *Agrarpolitik und Agrarreform in Spanien unter Carlos III* (Munich, 1909); D. Villar Grangel, *Jovellanos y la reforma agraria* (Madrid, 1925); M. C. Alcazar, *El conde de Florida Blanca* (Madrid, 1929); A. Fugier, *Napoléon et l'Espagne*, 2 vols. (Paris, 1930), Vol. I, Introduction.

For Portugal: P. Sagnac, *La fin de l'Ancien Régime* (Paris, 3d ed., 1952), Book I, Chap. V, Sec. 10; F. de Almeida, *Historia de Portugal*, 4 vols. (Coïmbra, 1922–26).

For Russia: P. Sagnac, *La fin de l'Ancien Régime* (Paris, 3d ed., 1952), Book I, Chap. VIII, and Book III, Chap. V; P. Miliukov, C. Seignobos. and L. Eisenmann, *Histoire de Russie*, 3 vols. (Paris, 1932); M. N. Pokrovsi, *Russkaya Istoria*, 4 vols. (Moscow, 1924), and *Brief History of Russia*, 2 vols. (New York, 1931–33); A. Brükner, *Katharina II* (Berlin, 1883); J. Kulischer, *Russische Wirtschaftsgeschichte* (Jena, 1925); R. Portal, *L'Oural au XVIIIe siècle* (Paris 1950); and, on serfdom, H. Sée, *Esquisse d'une histoire du régime agraire* (Paris, 1921).

For Poland: P. Sagnac, La fin de l'Ancien Régime (Paris, 3d ed., 1952), Book I, Chap. IX, Secs. 1 and 2, Book III, Chap. V, Sec. 6; *The Cambridge History of Poland*, Vol. II: *From Augustus II to Pilsudski, 1687–1935* (Cambridge, 1941); D. C. Niewenglowski, *Les idées politiques et l'esprit public en Pologne à la fin du XVIIIe siècle* (Paris, 1901); L. Knopczinsnki, *Le 'Liberum*

veto', *Étude sur le développement du principe majoritaire* (Paris, 1930);
J. Fabre, *Stanislas-Auguste Poniatowski et l'Europe des lumières* (Paris, 1952).

For Denmark: P. Sagnac, *La fin de l'Ancien Régime* (Paris, 3d ed., 1952),
Chap. IX, Sec. I; E. Holm, *Danmark-Norges Historie*, Vol. V: *1720–1814*
(Copenhagen, 1902); L. Krabbe, *Histoire du Danemark* (Paris, 1950).

For Sweden. P. Sagnac, *La fin de l'Ancien Régime* (Paris, 3d ed., 1952),
Book I, Chap. IX, Sec. I; R. Swanshöm and C. F. Palmierstierna, *Histoire de
Suède*, French tr. by L. Maury (Paris, 1942).

On reaction in Germany, see M. Philippson, *Geschichte des preussischen
Staatswesens vom Tode Friedrichs des Grossen bis zu den Freiheitskriegen*, 2
vols. (Leipzig, 1880–82), an unfinished work, which stops at the death of
Frederick William II; P. Schwartz, *Die erste Kulturkampf in Preussen in Kirche
und Schule, 1788–1798* (Berlin, 1925); R. Le Forestier, *La franc-maçonnerie
occultiste* (Paris, 1928).

*Great Britain*

See P. Sagnac, *La fin de l'Ancien Régime* (Paris, 3d ed., 1952), Book I,
Chap. II, Secs. 1–3 and 11; Book II, Secs, 4–7; L. Cahen, 'L'évolution de la
Grande-Bretagne dans la seconde moitié du XVIIIe siècle', *Revue d'histoire
moderne*, XI (1936), 60–77; *Cambridge Modern History*, Vol. VI; W. H. Lecky,
*History of England from the Peace of Utrecht to the Peace of Versailles*, 7 vols.
(London, 1878–90, rev. ed., 1918–25); W. Hunt, *Political History of England
from the Accession of George III to the Close of Pitt's First Administration*
(London, 1905); C. Grant Robertson, *A History of England under the Hano-
verians* (London, 1911, 14th ed., 1944); G. M. Trevelyan, *British History in the
19th Century and after, 1782–1919* (London, 1922, rev. ed., 1937); M. A.
Thompson, *A Constitutional History of England, 1642–1801* (London, 1938),
Vol. IV of *Constitutional History*, published under the direction of R. Tre-
harne; L. B. Namier, *Structure of Politics at the Accession of George III*, 2 vols.,
(London, 1919); J. H. Rose, *Pitt and the National Revival* (London, 1911);
D. G. Barnes, *George III and William Pitt, 1783–1806* (Stanford, Cal., 1939);
K. Feiling, *The Second Tory Party, 1714–1832* (London, 1938); A. Hope-Jones,
*Income-tax in the Napoleonic Wars* (Cambridge, 1939); F. Halévy, *Histoire du
peuple anglais au XIXe siècle*, Vol. I (Paris, 1913), Eng. tr., *A History of the
English People in the Nineteenth Century*, Vol. I (New York, 1949).

For Ireland: P. Sagnac, *La fin de l'Ancien Régime* (Paris, 3d ed., 1952),
Book I, Chap. III, Sec. 6; H. McAnally, *The Irish Militia* (Dublin and London,
1949).

*The united provinces and continental patriciates*

For Holland: P. Sagnac, *La fin de l'Ancien Régime* (Paris, 3d ed., 1952), Book II, Chap. I, Sec. 9; P. Blok, *Geschiedenis van het nederlandische volk*, Vol. IV (Leiden, 1926); A.-E. Sayous, 'Le patriciat d'Amsterdam', *Annales d'histoire sociale*, II (1940), 177–98, with bibliography; H. de Peyster, *Les troubles de la Hollande à la veille de la Révolution française* (Paris, 1905).

For Switzerland: P. Sagnac, *La fin de l'Ancien Régime* (Paris, 3d ed., 1952), Book II, Chap. III, Sec. 6; J. Dirauer, *Geschichte der schweizerischen Eidgenossenschaft*, 6 vols. (Gotha, 1887–1922), Vols. III and IV; E. Gagliardi, *Geschichte der Schweiz von den Anfängen bis auf die Gegenwart*, 3 vols. (Zurich, 1920–27, 2d ed., 1937), Vol II: *1519–1798;* J. C. Mörikofer, *Die schweizerische Literatur des XVIII. Jahrhunderts* (Leipzig, 1861); V. Rossel, *Histoire littéraire de la Suisse romande*, Vol. II (Geneva, 1891).

For Genoa: F. Donaver, *La storia della repubblica di Genova*, 3 vols. (Genoa, 1913–14); P. Nurra, *Genova nel Risorgimento* (Milan, 1948), Chap. II.

For Venice: H. Kretschmayer, *Geschichte von Venedig*, 3 vols. (Stuttgart, 1934), Vol. III: *Der Niedergang;* K. Schillmann, *Venedig, Geschichte und Kultur Venetiens* (Leipzig and Vienna, 1933); P. Molmenti, *Venezia nella vita privata* (Turin, 1905); C. Diehl, *Une république patricienne: Venise* (Paris, 1918); G. MacClellan, *Venice and Bonaparte* (Princeton, 1931).

*The American revolution*

For bibliography, see S. Morison and H. S. Commager, *The Rise of the American Republic* (New York, 1942), and R. R. Palmer, *A History of the Modern World* (New York, 1950). In addition to Vol. I of Morison and Commager, see H. Adams, *History of the United States*, 9 vols. (New York, 1890–1917), Vol. I; E. Channing, *History of the United States*, 5 vols. (New York, 1905–25), Vol. III; S. M. Bemis, *A Diplomatic History of the United States* (New York, 1936, rev. ed., 1950); *The Cambridge Modern History*, Vol. VII (1903); *The Cambridge History of the British Empire*, Vol. I (1929); *A History of American Life*, published under the direction of A. Schlesinger, D. R. Fox, and C. Becker, Vol. IV: *The Revolutionary Generation, 1763–90*, by E. B. Greene (New York, 1945); D. Pasquet, *Histoire du peuple américain* (Paris, 1924); F. J. Turner, *The Frontier in American History* (New York, 1920); C. W. Wright, *Economic History of the United States* (New York, 1941); H. V. Faulkner, *American Economic History* (New York, 7th ed., 1954); H. Bell, 'The West India Trade Before the American Revolution', *The American His-*

*torical Review*, XXII (1917), 272–87; K. W. Porter, *John Jacob Astor, Businessman*, 2 vols. (Cambridge, Mass., 1931); J. B. MacMaster, *The Life and Times of Stephen Girard, Mariner and Merchant*, 2 vols. (Philadelphia, 1918); *The Cambridge History of American Literature*, 3 vols. (1933), Vol. I; C. Becker, *The Declaration of Independence: A Study in the History of Political Ideas* (New York, 1922, rev. ed., 1941); A. C. MacLaughlin, *Confederation and Constitution* (New York, 1905), and *Foundations of the American Constitution* (New York, 1932), and *Constitutional History of the United States* (New York, 1935); C. A. Beard, *Economic Interpretation of the Constitution* (New York, 1923), which is very important; F. Jameson, *The American Revolution Considered as a Social Movement* (Princeton, 1926, rev. ed., 1940); B. Fay, *George Washington, gentilhomme américain* (Paris, 1931), and *Franklin*, 3 vols. (Paris, 1930–31); O. Vossler, *Die amerikanischen Revolutionsideale in ihrem Verhältnis zu den europaischen Untersucht an Th. Jefferson* (Munich and Berlin, 1929).

On the influence of the American Revolution, see L. Gottschalk, *Lafayette Comes to America* (Chicago, 1935), *Lafayette Joins the American Army* (Chicago, 1937), *Lafayette and the Close of the American Revolution* (Chicago, 1942), *Lafayette between the American and the French Revolution* (Chicago, 1950), and *The Place of the American Revolution in the Causal Pattern of the French Revolution* (Easton, Pa., 1948); R. de Crévecoeur, *Saint-John de Crévecoeur, Sa vie et ses ouvrages* (Paris, 1883); L. M. Gidney, *L'influence des États-Unis d'Amérique sur Brissot, Condorcet et Madame Roland* (Paris, 1930).

### France

See P. Sagnac, *La fin de l'Ancien Régime* (Paris, 3d ed., 1952), Book I, Chap. IV, Book II, Chap. II, Secs. 1–6, Book III, Chap. III; general bibliography in E. Préclin and V. Tapié, *Le XVIIe siècle* (Paris, 1943); in addition, D. Dakin, *Turgot and the Ancien Régime in France* (London, 1939); J. Égret, *Le Parlement du Dauphiné et les affaires publiques dans la seconde moitié du XVIIIe siècle* (Grenoble, 1942). For French institutions on the eve of the Revolution, see P. Viollet, *Histoire des institutions politiques et administratives de l'ancienne France*, 2 vols. (Paris, 1889–98), Vol. II; M. Garaud, *Histoire du droit privé français*, Vol. I (Paris, 1953).

### Rivalry of states

See P. Sagnac, *La fin de l'Ancien Régime* (Paris, 3d ed., 1952), Book I,

Chap. IX, Book II, Chap. III, Secs. 5, 6, 9; Book III, Chap. III, Secs. 3–5, and Chap. IV, Sec. 7; H. Carré, *Le règne de Louis XVI* (Paris, 1910), Book II; A. Sorel, *L'Europe et la Révolution française*, Vol. I (Paris, 1885); É. Bourgeois, *Manuel de politique étrangère*, 3 vols. (Paris, 1892–1905, 6th ed., 1910), Vol. I: *Jusqu'en 1789;* Vol. II: *1789–1830;* C. Dupuis, *Le principe d'équilibre européen de la paix de Westphalie à l'acte d'Algésiras* (Paris, 1909); M. Immich, *Geschichte des europäischen Staatensystems von 1660 bis 1789* (Munich and Berlin, 1905); Häusser, *Deutsche Geschichte vom Tode Friedrichs des Grossen bis zur Gründung des Bundes, 1786–1815,* 4 vols. (Berlin, 1854–57, 4th ed., 1869), Vol. I; K. von Heigel, *Deutsche Geschichte vom Tode Friedrichs des Grossen bis zur Auflösung des alten Reiches,* 2 vols. (Stuttgart, 1899–1911), Vol. I.

For Prussia and Austria, see above, under Enlightened Despotism. For Austria, see also F. Krones, *Handbuch der Geschichte Œsterreichs,* 5 vols. (Berlin, 1876–79), Vol. IV; shorter, but with a bibliography, is K. and M. Uhlirz, *Handbuch der Geschichte Œsterreichs und seiner Nachbarländer Böhmen und Ungarn,* 3 vols. (Graz and Vienna, 1929), Vol. I; A. Beer, *Joseph II, Leopold II und Kannitz* (Vienna, 1873).

For Belgium, see H. Pirenne, *Histoire de Belgique,* Vol. V (Brussels, 1921). For Denmark, Spain, and Holland, see above, under Enlightened Despotism; in addition, for Holland, see H. De Peyster, *Les troubles de Hollande à la veille de la Révolution française* (Paris, 1905); H. T. Colenbrander, *De Patriottentijd,* 3 vols. (The Hague, 1897–99).

For Italy, see above.

For Poland, see above and O. Halecki, *La Pologne de 963 à 1914* (Paris, 1933); W. Sobieski, *Histoire de la Pologne des origines à nos jours* (Paris, 1934); E. Krakovsky, *Histoire de la Pologne* (Paris, 1935); A. Beer, *Die erste Theilung Polens* (Vienna, 1873); R. H. Lord, *The Second Partition of Poland* (Cambridge, Mass., 1915).

For Russia, see above.

For Sweden, see above, and A. Geffroy, *Gnstave III et la Cour de France,* 2 vols. (Paris, 1867).

For the Eastern question, see A. Beer, *Die orientalische Politik Œsterreichs seit 1774* (Prague, 1883); A. Sorel, *La question d'Orient au XVIIIe siècle* (Paris, 1878); N. Jorga, *Geschichte des osmanischen Reiches,* Vol. V (Gotha, 1913).

For the blockade, see G. Lefebvre, *Napoléon* (Paris, 4th ed., 1953), Book I, Chap. II, Sec. 4.

PART TWO. THE ADVENT OF THE BOURGEOISIE IN FRANCE

The general histories cited at the beginning of this bibliography devote one volume or several chapters to the revolutionary period. The works of Sybel and Sorel cited below, at the beginning of Chapter Eleven, also cover the whole period, but focus on European politics.

Among the histories of the French Revolution should be cited those of F. Mignet, 2 vols. (Paris, 1824); A. Thiers, 10 vols. (Paris, 1823–27); J. Michelet, 7 vols. (Paris, 1847–53); Louis Blanc, 12 vols. (Paris, 1847–62). Neither Thomas Carlyle, *The French Revolution*, 3 vols. (London, 1837), E. Quinet, *La Révolution*, 2 vols. (Paris, 1865), nor H. Taine, *Les origines de la France contemporaine*, 6 vols. (Paris, 1876–93), presents a continuous narrative: the first is a series of tableaux, the other two are more doctrinal than historical. For more recent bibliography see P. Caron, *Manuel pratique pour l'étude de la Révolution française* (Paris, 1912, rev. ed., 1947). The reader may also consult L. Villat, *La Révolution et l'Empire, 1789–1815*, Vol. I: *Les assemblées révolutionnaires, 1789–1799* (Paris, 1936); A. Monglond, *La France révolutionnaire et impériale; annales de bibliographie méthodique et descriptions des livres illustrés*, 4 vols. (Grenoble, 1930–35); A. Martin and G. Walter, *Bibliothèque nationale, Département des imprimés, Catalogue de l'histoire de la Révolution française*, 4 vols. (Paris, 1936–43); cf. Anne Terroine, 'L'œuvre bibliographique de M. G. Walter', *Annales historiques de la Révolution française*, XX (1948), 1–26. The reader should note the following works: A. Aulard, *Histoire politique de la Révolution* (Paris, 1901, 5th ed., 1921); J. Jaurès, *Histoire socialiste de la Révolution française*, Vols. I–IV (Paris, 1901–4, new ed. by A. Mathiez, 8 vols., 1922–24, reprinted in 1939), which stops at 9 thermidor, but is continued by Vol. V of the *Histoire socialiste*, written by G. Deville (1905); P. Sagnac, *La Révolution, 1789–1792*, and G. Pariset, *La Révolution, 1792–1799* (both: Paris, 1920), forming Vols. I and II of *Histoire de France contemporaine*, published under the direction of E. Lavisse; A. Mathiez, *La Révolution française*, 3 vols. (Paris, 1922–27), which the author's death in 1932 regrettably did not permit him to continue beyond 9 thermidor, completed by G. Lefebvre, up to 18 brumaire, in *Les Thermidoriens* (Paris, 1937, 2d ed., 1947), and *Le Directoire* (Paris, 1946, 2d ed., 1950); G. Salvemini, *La Rivoluzione francese* (Milan, 1905, new ed., Bari, 1954); Crane Brinton, *A Decade of Revolution, 1789–1799* (New York, 1934, in the series 'The Rise of Modern Europe', edited by W. Langer); L. Gershoy, *The French Revolution and Napoleon* (New York, 1933); J. Thompson, *The French Revolution* (Oxford, 1944); M. Goehring, *Geschichte der grossen Revolution*, Vol. I: *Vom Ancien Régime zum Sieg der Revolution* (Tübingen, 1950), Vol. II: *Vom Liberalismus zur Dictatur* (Tübingen, 1951). The publication of

P. Sagnac and J. Robiquet, *La Révolution de 1789*, 2 vols. (Paris, 1934), contains rich illustrations, some not published before.

Between regions and even among neighbouring communes there was great variety of public opinion and of events. The reader should therefore consult local histories and the histories of clubs, which are for the most part imperfect; there is no profound synthesis of this diversity in France. Note, for example, R. Doucet, *L'esprit public dans le département de la Vienne pendant la Révolution* (Paris, 1910); abbé H. Pommeret, *L'esprit public dans le département des Côtes-du-Nord pendant la Révolution* (Saint-Brieuc and Paris, 1921).

For institutions, we now have the work of J. Godechot, *Les institutions de la France sous la Révolution et l'Empire* (Paris, 1951, in the series 'Histoire des institution', directed by L. Halphen), with bibliography.

## Chapter 6. The aristocratic revolution, 1787–1788

H. Carré *Le règne de Louis XVI* (Paris, 1910); P. Sagnac, *La fin de l'Ancien Régime* (Paris, 3d ed., 1952), Book III, Chap. III; F. Droz, *Histoire du règne de Louis XVI;* 3 vols. (Paris, 1839); A. Chérest, *La chute de l'Ancien Régime*, 3 vols. (Paris, 1884); A. Wahl, *Vorgeschichte der französischen Revolution*, 2 vols. (Tübingen, 1905–7); H. Glagau, *Reformversuche und Sturz des Absolutismus in Frankreich, 1774–1788* (Munich, 1908); A. Mathiez, *La Révolution française*, Vol. I: *La chute de la royauté* (Paris, 1927), Chaps. I and II; G. Lefebvre, *Quatre-vingt-neuf* (Paris, 1939), Eng. tr. by R. R. Palmer, *The Coming of the French Revolution* (Princeton, 1947); J. Égret, *Le Parlement du Dauphiné et les affaires publiques dans la seconde moitié du XVIIIe siècle*, 2 vols. (Grenoble, 1942), 'L'aristocratie parlementaire à la fin de l'Ancien Régime', *Revue historique* CCVII (1952) 1–14, and 'La prérévolution en Provence', Annales historiques de la Révolution française, 1954, pp. 97–126, and 'La seconde Assemblée des notables', *ibid.*, 1949.

On the financial situation, see R. Stourm, *Les finances de l'Ancien Régime et la Révolution*, 2 vols. (Paris, 1885); C. Gomel, *Les causes financières de la Révolution*, 2 vols. (Paris, 1892–93); M. Marion, *Histoire financière de la France depuis 1715*, Vol. I: *1715–1789* (Paris, 1913); R. Bigo, *Les bases historiques de la finance moderne* (Paris, 1933); J. Bouchary, *Les manieurs d'argent à la fin du XVIIIe siècle*, 3 vols. (Paris, 1939–43). Of capital importance: F. Braesch, *Finances et monnaie révolutionnaires*, Vol. II: *Les recettes et les dépenses du Trésor pendant l'année 1789; le compte rendu au roi de mars 1788; le dernier budget de l'Ancien Régime* (Paris, 1936).

*Calonne and the notables*

See above, and the accounts by H. Carré, *Le règne de Louis XVI* (Paris, 1910), Book V, Chap. I, and by P. Sagnac, *La fin de l'Ancien Régime* (Paris, 3d ed., 1952), Book III, Chap. III, Secs. 5–8; G. Suzane, *La tactique financière de Calonne* (Paris, 1901); Assemblée générale de la Commission centrale et des Comités départementaux, 1939, Vol. II (Paris, 1945); F. Nussbaum and W. Pugh, *Finance et politique dans les dernières années de l'Ancien Régime en France*, pp. 485–98; W. Pugh, 'Calonne's New Deal', *Journal of Modern History* (1939), pp. 289–312; statement of the problem and bibliography in A. Goodwin, 'Calonne, the Assembly of French Notables of 1787 and the Origins of the *révolte nobilaire'*, *English Historical Review* (1946), pp. 329–77.


*Brienne and the parlements*

See the works cited above, and H. Carré, *Le règne de Louis XVI* (Paris, 1910), Book V, Chap. II; P. Sagnac, *La fin de l'Ancien Régime* (Paris, 3d ed., 1952), Book III, Chap. III, Sec. 9; M. Marion, *Le garde des sceaux Lamoignon et la réforme judiciaire de 1788* (Paris, 1905); P. Renouvin, *Les assemblées provinciales de 1787* (Paris, 1921), and *L'assemblée des notables de 1787, La conférence du 8 mars* (Paris, 1921); J. Égret, *Les derniers État du Dauphiné, Romans, septembre 1788–janvier 1789* (Grenoble, 1942). On propaganda methods used by the nobles in their revolution, see A. Cochin, *Les sociétés de pensée et la Révolution en Bretagne, 1788–1789* (Paris, 1925).

**Chapter 7. The bourgeois revolution**

*Formation of the patriot party*

See the accounts by H. Carré, *Le règne de Louis XVI* (Paris, 1910), Book V, Chap. III, Sec. 3, and P. Sagnac, *La fin de l'Ancien Régime* (Paris, 3d ed., 1952), Book III, Chap. III, Secs. 11 and 12. Consult J. Égret, *La révolution des notables, Mounier et les monarchiens* (Paris, 1950); P. Filleul, *Le duc de Montmorency-Luxembourg* (Paris, 1939). On associations at the end of the Old Regime, see D. Mornet, *Les origines intellectuelles de la Révolution* (Paris, 1932), Part III, Chaps. III, IV, and VII, as well as the work of Cochin, cited above. For propaganda of the Patriot party, see, for example, A. Cochin and C. Charpentier, *La campagne électorale de 1789 en Bourgogne* (Paris, 1904).

### Necker and the doubling of the third estate

J. Flammermont, 'Le second ministère Necker', *Revue historique*, XCVI (1891), 1–67; O. Becker, *Die Verfassungspolitik der französischen Regierung der grossen Revolution* (Berlin, 1910), covers September, 1788, to June 27, 1789; J. Égret, 'La seconde Assemblée des notables', *Annales historiques de la Révolution française* XXI (1949), 193–228.

### The elections and the cahiers

See P. Sagnac, *La Révolution, 1789–1792* (Paris, 1920), Book V, Chap. IV, Secs. 2–5, and *La fin de l'Ancien Régime* (Paris, 3d ed., 1952), Book III, Chap. III, Secs. 14–15. See also B. Hyslop, *French Nationalism in 1789 according to the General Cahiers* (New York, 1934), and 'French gild opinion in 1789', *American Historical Review*, XLIV (1939), 252–71.

The 'Commission d'histoire économique de la Révolution' has published a good number of collections of *cahiers*; some of the more recent are those of the bailiwick of Pont-à-Mousson, by Z.-E. Harsany (Paris, 1946), and those of the bailiwick of Romorantin, by B. Edeine (Blois, 1949). B. Hyslop has published for the Commission a *Répertoire critique des cahiers de doléances pour les États généraux de 1789* (Paris, 1933), with a supplement (Paris, 1952); this work was annotated and completed by her in *Annales historiques de la Révolution française*, 1955, pp. 115–23. She has also prepared a *Guide to the General Cahiers of 1789 with the Texts of Unedited Cahiers* (New York, 1936), and has published the *cahiers* of the gilds of Montargis, 'Les élections et les cahiers inédits de la ville de Montargis en 1789', *Annales historiques de la Révolution française*, IX (1946), 115–48.

### The victory of the bourgeoisie

For the history of the Estates General and the National Assembly, add G. Lefebvre, *Quatre-vingt-neuf* (Paris, 1939), Eng. tr., *The Coming of the French Revolution* (Princeton, 1947); F. Braesch, *1789, L'année cruciale* (Paris, 1941); article by J. Flammermont, *Le second ministère Necker*, cited above, which stops on the eve of the June 23 session; A. Aulard, 'Le serment du Jeu de Paume', *Études et leçons sur la Révolution française*, Series I (Paris, 1893); A. Brette, *Le serment du Jeu de Paume, Fac-similés du texte et des signataires* (Paris, 1893). Volume I of the *Recueil de documents relatifs aux séances des États généraux (mai–juin 1789)*, prepared by the Institut d'histoire de la Révolution française, in the Faculté des lettres of Paris, under the directon of G. Lefebvre and Anne Terroine, appeared in 1953 (Paris, 'Publication du Centre national de la recherche scientifique'); it covers the preliminaries and the royal session of May 5.

For the deputies, see A. Brette, *Les constituants, Liste des députés et des suppléants élus à l'Assemblée nationale de 1789* (Paris, 1897); A. Aulard, *Les orateurs de la Constituante* (Paris, 1882, 2d ed., 1906); J. Égret, *Mounier et les monarchiens* (Paris, 1950); É. Dumont, *Souvenirs sur Mirabeau et sur les deux premières assemblées législatives*, prepared by J. Bénétruy (Paris, 1951). Among the many biographies, see especially E. D. Bradby, *The Life of Barnave*, 2 vols. (Oxford, 1915); G. Michon, *Adrien Duport* (Paris, 1924); L. and C. de Loménie, *Les Mirabeau*, 5 vols. (Paris, 1878–90); A. Stern, *Das Leben Mirabeaus*, 2 vols. (Berlin, 1889); L. Barthou, *Mirabeau*, (Paris, 1913); O. G. Welch, *Mirabeau, A Study of a Democratic Monarchist* (London, 1951); E. Hamel, *Histoire de Robespierre*, 3 vols. (Paris, 1865); J. M. Thompson, *Robespierre*, 2 vols. (Oxford, 1935); G. Walter, *Robespierre*, 2 vols. (Paris, 1936–39, rev. ed., in one volume, 1946); P. Bastid, *Sieyes et sa pensée* (Paris, 1939); E. Lebègue, *Thouret* (Paris, 1910); A. Brucker, *Bailly, Revolutionary Mayor of Paris* (Urbana, Ill., 1950). Vols. I, II, and III (up to September 20, 1792) of the publication of *Discours de Robespierre*, prepared by G. Lefebvre, M. Bouloiseau, A. Soboul (Paris, 1951–54), are also Vols. VI, VII, and VIII of *Œuvres de Robespierre*, published by the 'Société des études robespierristes'.

*Appeal to armed force*

To the works cited above, add P. Caron, 'La tentative de contrerévolution, juin–juillet 1789', *Revue d'histoire moderne*, VIII (1906), 5–34, 649–78.

**Chapter 8. The popular revolution**

*The economic crisis*

See the works of C.-E. Labrousse and of F. Simiand, and the article by Lefebvre, cited in Chapter Two, under The Traditional Economy; C.-E. Labrousse, *La crise de l'économie française à la fin de l'Ancien Régime et au début de la Révolution*, Vol. I: *La crise viticole* (Paris, 1943), and 'Le froment, 1782–1790', *Annales d'histoire sociale*, I (1939), 382–400; L. Cahen, 'Une nouvelle interprétation da traité franco-anglais de 1786–1787', *Revue historique*, CLXXXV (1939), 257–85; P. Dardel, 'Crises et faillites à Rouen et dans la Haute-Normandie de 1740 à l'an V', *Revue d'histoire économique et* sociale, 1948, pp. 53–71; M. Lacoste, *La crise économique dans la Meurthe* (typewritten, Paris, 1951).

### The 'good news' and the great hope

See J. Belin, *La logique d'une idée-force, L'idée d'utilité sociale pendant la Révolution française, 1789–1792* (Paris, 1939), and *Les démarches de la pensée sociale d'après les textes inédits de la période révolutionnaire 1789–1792* (Paris, 1939); F. Brunot, 'Le mysticisme dans le langage de la Révolution', in *Cahiers rationalistes*, No. 38 (Paris, 1935).

### The aristocratic conspiracy and the revolutionary mentality

See G. Lefebvre, *La Grande Peur de 1789* (Paris, 1932) and 'Foules révolutionnaires', in *La foule*, published by the Centre international de synthèse (Paris, 1934), and in *Annales historiques de la Révolution française*, XI (1934), 1–26, and *Études sur la Révolution française* (Paris, 1954), pp. 271–87.

### The Parisian revolution

On July 14, the best work still is J. Flammermont, *La journée du 14 juillet 1789* (Paris, 1892). See also E. Funck-Brentano, *Légendes et archives de la Bastille* (Paris, 1898); P. Chauvet, *L'insurrection parisienne et la prise de la Bastille* (Paris, 1946); J. Durieux, *Les vainqueurs de la Bastille* (Paris, 1911); A. Chuquet, *Historiens et marchands d'histoire* (Paris, 1914); R. Farge, 'Camille Desmoulins au jardin du Palais-Royal', *Annales révolutionnaires*, VII (1914), 646–74, published separately in 1916.

### The municipal revolution

We do not yet have any general study of municipal development. See histories of provinces and towns, especially: F. Mourlot, *La fin de l'Ancien Régime dans la généralité de Caen* (Paris, 1913); L. Dubreuil, 'Le Comité permanent d'Évreux', *Annales révolutionnaires*, XII (1920), 372–99; H. Millot, *Le Comité permanent de Dijon* (Dijon, 1925).

### The peasant revolution and the great fear

General study by G. Lefebvre, *La Grande Peur de 1789* (Paris, 1932), with bibliographic notes. For the agrarian disturbances, add F. Mourlot, *La fin de l'Ancien Régime dans la généralité de Caen* (Paris, 1913); P. de Vaissières, *Lettres d'aristocrates* (Paris, 1907); G. Lefebvre, *Les paysans du Nord*, 2 vols. (Lille, 1924); the collection on manorial rights, published by P. Sagnac and P. Caron, cited below, Chapter Ten, under Economic Work of the Constituent; F. Évrard has reviewed the disturbances in the Mâconnais in 'Les paysans du Mâconnais et les brigandages de juillet 1789', *Annales de Bourgogne*, XIX (1947), 7–39, 97–121; H. Diné, *La Grande peur dans la généralité de Poitiers* (Paris, 1951); J. Palou, 'La Grande peur dans les Hautes-Alpes', *Annales historiques de la Révolution française*, 1952, pp. 502–5; and 'La Grande peur dan l'Oisans', *ibid.*, 1955, pp. 50–54.

### The night of August 4 and the declaration of the rights of man and the citizen

See works cited above, at the beginning of Part Two. For the Declaration see below, at the beginning of Chapter Ten.

### The October days

The best contribution is that of A. Mathiez, 'Étude critique sur les journées des 5 et 6 octobre', *Revue historique*, LXVII (1898), 241–81, but he does not survey the whole subject. The reader should also consult the work of baron de Villiers, *Les 5 et 6 octobre; Reine Audu* (Paris, 1917); that by dom H. Leclerq, *Les journées d'octobre* (Paris, 1925), covers more than those events. W. Güthling, *La Fayette und die Ueberführung Ludwigs XVI von Versailles nach Paris* (Halle, 1931), is devoted solely to denouncing Lafayette as the instigator of the movement.

## Chapter 9. Lafayette's year

### Lafayette and the patriots

See É. Charavay, *Le général La Fayette* (Paris, 1898); the biographies of Lafayette by L. Gottschalk (4 vols., Chicago, 1935–50), go only up to July 14; G. Michon, *Adrien Duport, Essai sur l'histoire du parti feuillant* (Paris, 1924); G. Ramon, *Frédéric de Dietrich, premier maire de Strasbourg sous la Révolution française* (Nancy, 1919). For the municipal history of Paris, see G. Garrigues, *Les districts parisiens pendant la Révolution* (Paris, 1931).

*Progress of the revolution*

On the Jacobin Club, see the collection of documents put out by A. Aulard, *La société des Jacobins*, 6 vols. (Paris, 1889–97). An important and original general study is that by Crane Brinton, *The Jacobins* (New York, 1930). On the origins of the club of the Rue Saint Honoré: H. Lemoine, 'L'origine du club des Jacobins d'après un document nouveau', *La Révolution française*, LXXXVII (1934), 17–28; Gaston-Martin, *Les Jacobins* (Paris, 1940, No. 140 in the series 'Que sais-je?').

There are many publications concerning provincial societies. See, for example, P. Leuilliot, *Les Jacobins de Colmar, Procès-verbaux de la Société populaire* (Strasbourg, 1923); M. Henriot, *Le club des Jacobins de Semur* (Dijon, 1933); G. Lefebvre, 'La société populaire de Bourbourg', *Revue du Nord*, 1913, pp.181–235, 273–323; G. Aubert, 'La Société populaire de Douai', *Annales historiques de la Révolution française*, Vols. XII–XV (1935–38). Attempt at synthesis by L. de Cardenal, *La province pendant la Révolution, Histoire des clubs jacobins, 1789–95* (Paris, 1929). On the fraternal societies in Paris, Isabelle Bourdin, *Les Sociétés populaires de Paris pendant la Révolution jusqu'a la chute de la royauté* (Paris, 1937).

On the federations, there are only particular studies, such as M. Lambert, *Les fédérations en Franche-Comté et la fête de la Fédération du 14 juillet 1790* (Paris, 1890); J. Trévédy, 'Les deux fédérations de Pontivy', *Revue morbihannaise*, Vol. IV (1894) and Vol. V (1895), published separately at Rennes, 1895; P.-H. Thore, 'Fédérations et projets de fédérations dans la région toulousaine', *Annales historiques de la Révolution française*, XXI (1949), 346–68. See also A. Mathiez, *Les origines des cultes révolutionnaires* (Paris, 1904).

On workers' agitation, see G. Jaffé, *Le mouvement ouvrier à Paris pendant la Révolution française, 1789–1791* (Paris, 1924).

*The aristocratic conspiracy*

See H. Carré, *La fin des Parlements, 1788–1790* (Paris, 1912); S. Ratenic, *Thomas de Mahy, marquis de Favras und seine Gemahlin* (Vienna, 1881); G. Cléray, *L'affaire Favras* (Paris, 1932); A. Challamel, *Les clubs contre-révolutionnaires* (Paris, 1895); E. Daudet, *Histoire des conspirations royalistes dans le Midi* (Paris, 1881); J. Barruol, *La contre-révolution en Provence et dans le Comtat* (Cavaillon, 1928); and especially E. Vingtrinier, *Histoire de la contre-révolution*, 2 vols. (Paris, 1924–25), which goes up to the eve of Varennes. Add P. de Vaissières, *Lettres d'aristocrates* (Paris, 1907); D. Walther, *Gouverneur Morris, témoin de deux Révolutions* (Lausanne,

1932). On emigration: H. Forneron, *Histoire générale des émigrés* (Paris, 1884), hasty and unreliable; E. Daudet, *Histoire de l'émigration*, 3 vols. (Paris, 1904–5), of which Vol. I goes to 18 fructidor.

## Disintegration of the army

See L. Hartmann, *Les officiers de l'armée royale et la Révolution* (Paris, 1903); L. de Chilly, *Le premier ministre constitutionnel de la Guerre, La Tour du Pin* (Paris, 1909); H. Chopin, *Les insurrections militaires en 1790* (Paris, 1903); O. Havard, *La Révolution dans les ports de guerre*, 2 vols. (Paris, 1911–13); G. Bourdeau, 'L'affaire de Nancy', *Annales de l'Est*, XII (1898), 280–92.

## Chapter 10. The work of the constituent assembly, 1789–1791

For general works, see those cited at the beginning of Part Two, especially J. Godechot, *Les institutions de la France* (Paris, 1951); and, for political institutions, A. Aulard, *Histoire politique de la Révolution* (Paris, 1901, 5th ed., 1921).

## The principles of 1789

See P. Sagnac, *La législation civile de la Révolution* (Paris, 1898); R. Redslob, *Die Staatstheorien der französischen Nationalversammlung von 1789* (Leipzig, 1912); Egon Zweig, *Die Lehre vom Pouvoir Constituant* (Tübingen, 1909), examines all the revolutionary constitutions from that aspect; K. Löwenstein, *Volk und Parlament nach der Staatstheorie der französischen Nationalversammlung von 1789* (Munich, 1922); E. Thompson, *Popular Sovereignty and the French Constituent Assembly* (Manchester, 1952).

On the Declaration, see in particular the works of Aulard and Godechot, above; L. Walch, *La Déclaration des droits de l'homme et du citoyen et l'Assemblée constituante; travaux préparatoires* (Paris, 1903); G. Jellinek, *Die Erklärung der Menschen- und Bürger-rechte* (Leipzig, 1890, French tr., Paris, 1902); V. Marcaggi, *Les origines de la Déclaration des droits de l'homme de 1789* (Paris, 1904); F. Klövekorn, *Zur Entstehung der Erklärung der Menschen- und Bürger-rechte* (Berlin, 1911).

The members of the Constituent Assembly were familiar with Anglo-Saxon precedents and especially the Declaration adopted in 1776 by the Virginia representatives. Jellinek concludes from this that the Declaration of 1789 offers nothing original, simply reflecting Christian thought as interpreted by German Protestantism. A lively controversy ensued at the beginning of the twentieth century. É. Boutmy rejoined in 'La Déclaration des droits de l'homme et du citoyen et M. Jellinek', *Annales des sciences politiques*, XVII (1902), 415–43; Jellinek replied in *Revue du droit public*, XVIII (1902), 385–400. Gilbert Chinard pointed out that their discussion was not conclusive and that the texts should be compared: the Constituents, and Boutmy later, had before them only the Virginia plan, dated June 5, 1776, and including 16 articles, whereas Jellinek referred to the text adopted on June 12, including 18 articles (*Year Book of the American Philosophical Society*, 1943, pp. 88–106, printed separately; reviewed in *Annales historiques de la Révolution française*, XXII [1950], 288–90). Whatever interest a literal comparison may offer, it is not sufficient to resolve the issue of origins. First of all, the affiliation would be Calvinist rather than Lutheran; second, the 'philosophic' current had become international and had, in France, taken on its own traits; and, most important, Jellinek's thesis bears a non-temporal characteristic which is only too usual in historians of ideas: the philosophic value of the declarations aside, it is still true that the mentality and particular interests of the bourgeoisie entered into their formulation of principles, and one therefore cannot maintain that the French bourgeoisie, even without the Anglo-Saxon example, would have been unable to draw up its own declaration.

On the relativity of rights, see G. Lefebvre, *Quatre-vingt-neuf*, pp. 241–42 (Paris, 1939), Eng. tr., *The Coming of the French Revolution* (Princeton, 1947); A. Mathiez, 'La Révolution française et la théorie de la dictature', *Revue historique*, CLXI (1929), 304–15. On application of the rights: P. Sagnac, *La législation civile de la Révolution* (Paris, 1898); J. Godechot, *Les institutions de la France* (Paris, 1951); M. Garaud, *La Révolution et l'égalité civile* (Paris, 1953); P. Duclos, *La notion de constitution dans l'histoire de l'Assemblée constituante de 1789* (Paris, 1932); A. Aulard, *Histoire politique* (Paris, 1901, 5th ed., 1921), Chap. III; A. Tecklenburg, *Die Entwickelung des Wahlrechts in Frankreich seit 1789* (Tübingen, 1911); E. Seligman, *La justice en France pendant la Révolution*, Vol. I (Paris, 1910); C. Durand, *Histoire du protestantisme français pendant la Révolution et l'Empire* (Paris, 1902); H. Lucien-Brun, *La condition des juifs en France depuis 1789* (Paris, 1900, 2d ed., 1901); Alma Söderhjelm, *Le régime de la presse pendant la Révolution française*, 2 vols. (Paris, 1900–1901); G. Le Poitevin, *La liberté de presse depuis la Révolution* (Paris, 1901); J. Letaconnoux, 'Le Comité des députés extraordinaires des manufactures et du commerce et l'oeuvre de la Constituante', *Annales révolutionnaires*, VI (1913), 149–208; L. Deschamps, *L'Assemblée constituante et les colonies* (Paris, 1898).

*Organization of the government*

Besides the works of Aulard, Godechot, Duclos, Mathiez, and Tecklen-burg, cited above, see M. Deslandres, *Histoire constitutionnelle de la France de 1789 à 1870*, Vol I: *De la fin de l'Ancien Régime à la chute de l'Empire, 1789–1815* (Paris, 1932).

*Organization of the administration*

On the new administrative districts, see E. Lebègue, *Thouret* (Paris, 1910). There are a good many departmental monographs, such as: C. Porée, *Formation du département de l'Yonne* (Paris, 1905), with a map of bailiwicks and *élections*; D. Jouany, *La formation du département du Morbi-han* (Vannes, 1920); J.-E. Gerock, 'La formation des départements du Rhin en 1789', in *Revue d'Alsace*, LXXII (1925), 193–212; M. Peyre, 'Le départe-ment de l'Aube, Son origine et ses transformations jusqu'en l'an VIII', in the *Mémoires de la Société de l'Aube*, XCI (1928), 119–82, printed separately (Troyes, 1928); L. Merle, *La formation territoriale du département des Deux-Sèvres* (Niort, 1938); E. Desgranges, *La formation territoriale du département de la Haute-Vienne, 1789–an X* (Paris, 1942).

On the operation of administrative bodies, see local histories, which unfortunately do not usually contain much information on anything but political life; see, for example, A. Claude, *L'administration du district de Neufchâteau-Monzon-Meuse* (Clamecy, 1943).

On the reorganization of the judiciary, E. Seligman, *La justice en France pendant la Révolution*, Vol. I (Paris, 1910); J. Lucas de Peslouan, *Histoire de la juridiction administrative sous la Révolution et l'Empire* (Dijon, 1907); bib-liographic information on tribunals and private law may be found in A. Mater, 'L'histoire juridique de la Révolution', *Annales révolutionnaires*, XI (1919), 429–58. There are a few studies relating to composition and activity of the tribunals: P. Viard, 'Les tribunaux de famille dans le district de Dijon', *Nouvelle revue historique de droit français*, XLV (1921), 242–77; M. Ferret, *Les tribunaux de famille dans le district de Montpellier, 1790–an IV* (Montpellier, 1926); A. Grivel, *La justice civile dans le district de Montpellier en 1790–1791* (Montpellier, 1928); J. Forcioli, *Le tribunal de famille d'après les archives du district de Caen* (Caen, 1932); H. Thomas, *Le tribunal criminel de la Meurthe sous la Révolution* (Nancy, 1937).

*Finances*

The standard works are still useful: R. Stourm, *Les finances de l'Ancien Régime*, 2 vols. (Paris, 1885); C. Gomel, *Histoire financière de l'Assemblée constituante*, 2 vols. (Paris, 1896–97); M. Marion, *Histoire financière de la France depuis 1715* (Paris, 1919), Vol. II. But financial history has been partly revised by: F. Braesch, *Finances et monnaie révolutionnaires*, Vol. I: *Les exercices budgétaires de 1790 et 1791 d'après les comptes du Trésor* (Nancy, 1934); R. Schnerb, *La péréquation fiscale de l'Assemblée constituante* (Clermont-Ferrand, 1936), and *Les contributions directes à l'époque de la Révolution dans le département du Puy-de-Dôme* (Paris, 1933), and *Recueil de textes et de tableaux relatifs à la patente à l'époque de la Révolution dans le département du Puy-de-Dôme* (Paris, 1933); S. E. Harris, *The Assignats* (Cambridge, Mass., 1930); J. Morini-Comby, *Les assignats* (Paris, 1925); G. Hubrecht, *Les assignats dans le Haut-Rhin* (Strasbourg, 1932). In addition, see M. Minoret, *La contribution personnelle et mobilière* (Paris, 1900); and, on the patriotic levy, R. Brouillard, *Les impositions extraordinaires sur le revenu pendant la Révolution* (Bordeaux, 1910); A. Boidin, *La contribution patriotique en Lorraine* (Nancy, 1910); P. Hugues, *Histoire de la contribution patriotique dans le Bas-Languedoc* (Paris, 1919). We still do not have a technical study on the movement of public funds and the dealings of the treasury.

*Economic work of the Constituent Assembly: agrarian reform*

The reader should consult collections of legislative and administrative texts and of documents published by the 'Commission pour la recherche et la publication des documents relatifs à l'histoire économique de la Révolution', founded in 1904 on the proposal of Jean Jaurès. A representative sampling includes: F. Gerbaux and C. Schmidt, *Procès-verbaux des Comités d'agriculture et de commerce de la Constituante, de la Législative et de la Convention*, 4 vols. (Paris, 1906–10); P. Sagnac and P. Caron, *Les Comités des droits féodaux et de législation et l'abolition du régime seigneurial, 1789–1793* (Paris, 1907); G. Bourgin, *Le partage des biens communaux* (Paris, 1908); C. Bloch and A. Tuetey, *Procès-verbaux du Comité de mendicité de la Constituante* (Paris, 1911).

General survey in H. Sée, *Histoire économique de la France*, Vol. II (Paris, 1942). On the abolition of manorial rights, besides the collection of Sagnac and Caron, see P. Sagnac, *La législation civile de la Révolution* (Paris, 1898); A. Aulard, *La Révolution et la féodalité* (Paris, 1914); A. Ferradou, *Le rachat des droits féodaux dans la Gironde, 1790–93* (Paris, 1928); J. Millot, *L'abolition des droits seigneuriaux dans le département du Doubs et la région comtoise*

(Besançon, 1941). On the division of land, see bibliography and statement of progress achieved in the two articles of G. Lefebvre, 'Les recherches relatives à la répartition de la propriété et de l'exploitation foncières à la fin de l'Ancien Régime', and 'Les études relatives à la vente des biens nationaux', in *Revue d'histoire moderne* (1928), pp. 103–30 and 188–219; and in *Études sur la Révolution française* (Paris, 1954), where there is a résumé of later publications. See also abbé C. Girault, *Les biens d'église dans le départ- nent de la Sarthe à la fin du XVIIIe siècle* (Laval, 1953); M. Gallix, *La vente des biens nationaux dans les districts de Montpellier et de Lodève* (Montpellier, 1951); P. Cambon, *La vente des biens nationaux dans les districts de Béziers et de Saint-Pons* (Montpellier, 1951); G. Sangnier, *Révolution de la propriété rurale* (Blangermont, 1951). By Lefebvre also: 'La place de la Révolution dans l'histoire agraire de la France', in *Annales d'histoire économique et sociale*, I (1929), 506–23, as well as 'La Révolution française et les paysans', in *Annales historiques de la Révolution française*, X (1933), 97–128, and in *Cahiers de la Révolution française*, 1934, pp. 7–49. G. Lefebvre has reviewed the question of church property and the agreement on sharecropping and tenant farming in *Questions agraires au temps de la Terreur* (Strasbourg, 1932). For all that concerns agriculture and the peasants, see also G. Le- febvre, *Les paysans du Nord pendant la Révolution française*, 2 vols. (Lille, 1924); O. Festy, *L'agriculture pendant la Révolution française, Les conditions de production et de récolte des céréales, 1789–1795* (Paris, 1947), and *L'agri- culture pendant la Révolution française, L'utilisation des jachères, 1789–1795* (Paris, 1950), and *L'agriculture pendant la Révolution française, Les journaux d'agriculture et le progrès agricole, 1789–an VIII* (Paris, 1950). On collective rights, see M. Bloch, 'La lutte pour l'individualisme agraire dans la France du XVIIIe siècle', *Annales d'histoire économique et sociale*, II (1930), 329–83, 511–56.

On food supplies, see C. Porée, *Les subsistances dans l'Yonne et par- ticulièrement dans le district d'Auxerre pendant la Révolution* (Auxerre, 1903); G. Lefebvre, introduction to Vol. I of *Documents relatifs à l'histoire des subsistances dans le district de Bergues, 1789–an V*, published by the 'Com- mission d'histoire économique', 2 vols. (Lille, 1913, 1921); Gaston-Martin, *La politique nantaise des subsistances sous la Constituante et la Législative* (Paris, 1924); O. Karmin, *La question du sel pendant la Révolution* (Paris, 1912); R. Werner, *L'approvisionnement en pain de la population et l'armée du Rhin pendant la Révolution* (Strasbourg, 1951). A large part of Vol. II of the publication titled *Assemblée générale de la Commission centrale et des Comités départementaux, 1939*, of the 'Commission d'histoire économique' (Paris, 1945), is devoted to the question of food (grain and bread) and its prices.

On industry and commerce, see E. Levasseur, *Histoire des classes ouvr-ières et de l'industrie de 1789 à nos jours*, 2 vols. (Paris, 1859, 1867, rev. ed., Paris, 1903–4), and *Histoire du commerce en France* (Paris, 1912); J. Bou-chary, *Le marché des changes à Paris* (Paris, 1937); G. and H. Bourgin, *L'industrie sidérurgique en France* (Paris, 1928); C. Ballot, *L'introduction du machinisme* (Paris, 1923); P. Reynoard, *Les ouvriers des manufactures nationales pendant la Révolution* (Paris, 1917); Letaconnoux, 'Le comité des députés extraordinaires', *Annales révolutionnaires* VI (1913), 149–208; M. Treille, *Le commerce de Nantes et la Révolution* (Nantes, 1908); L. Nuss-baum, *Commercial Policy in the French Revolution; a Study of the Career of G. J. A. Ducher* (Philadelphia, 1924); J.-B. Manger, *Recherches sur les rela-tions économiques de la France et de la Hollande pendant la Révolution française* (Paris, 1923); P. Masson, 'Marseille depuis 1789', *Annales de la Faculté d'Aix*, X (1916), 1–211.

On poor relief, C. Bloch, *L'État et l'assistance* (Paris, 1908); A. Tuetey, *L'assistance publique à Paris pendant la Révolution*, 4 vols. (Paris, 1895–97); L. Lallemand, *La Révolution et les pauvres* (Paris, 1898); E. Chaudron, *L'as-sistance publique à Troyes à la fin de l'Ancien Régime et pendant la Révolution* (Paris, 1923).

*Reform of the clergy*

Religious history of the revolutionary era has been and remains the subject of numerous publications. There are even many general histories, almost all written from the point of view of Roman Catholicism: L. Sciout, *L'Église et la constitution civile du clergé*, 4 vols. (Paris, 1873–81); abbé A. Sicard, *L'ancien clergé de France*, Vol. I: *Les évêques avant la Révolution* (Paris, 1893, 5th ed., rev. 1912); Vol. II: *Les évêques pendant la Révolution* (Paris, 1894); Vol. III: *De l'éxil au Concordat* (Paris, 1903); also by the same author, *Le clergé de France pendant la Révolution*, Vol. I: *L'effondrement* (Paris, 1912) and Vol. II: *La lutte religieuse* (Paris, 1927); P. de La Gorce, *Histoire religieuse de la Révolution*, 5 vols. (Paris, 1909–23); abbé F. Mourret, *Histoire générale de l'Église*, Vol. VII (Paris, 1913); dom H. Leclercq, *L'Église constitutionnelle* (Paris, 1934); A. Latreille, *L'Église catholique et la Révolution française*, Vol. I: *Le pontificat de Pie VI et la crise française, 1775–1799* (Paris, 1946), and bibliography in Vol. II (Paris, 1950); K. D. Erdmann, *Volks-souveränität und Kirche* (Cologne, 1949); chanoine J. Leflon, *La crise révolu-tionnaire, 1789–1846* (Paris, 1949), Vol. XX of *Histoire de l'Église*, published under the direction of A. Fliche and V. Martin; chanoine J. Gendry, *Pie VI, sa vie, son pontificat*, 2 vols. (Paris, 1906). From a different point of view:

A. Debidour, *Histoire des rapports de l'Église et de l'État de 1789 à 1870* (Paris, 1898); A. Gazier, *Études sur l'histoire religieuse de la Révolution* (Paris, 1887); A. Mathiez, *Rome et la Constituante* (Paris, 1910), *Contributions à l'histoire religieuse de la Révolution* (Paris, 1906), and *La Révolution et l'Église* (Paris, 1910); A. Aulard, *Le christianisme et la Révolution* (Paris, 1924); E. Préclin, *Les Jansénistes du XVIIIe siècle et la Constitution civile du clergé; Le développement du richérisme, sa propagation dans le bas-clergé (1713–1791)* (Paris, 1929); G. Le Bras, 'Les transformations religieuses', *Annales sociologiques*, Series E, Fasc. 2 (1937), pp. 15–70; A. Lajusan, 'La carte des opinions françaises', *Annales*, IV (1949), 406–14, with observations by L. Febvre.

Among the biographies and local monographs, beside the invaluable collection of chanoine P. Pisani, *Répertoire biographique de l'épiscopat constitutionnel* (Paris, 1907), we will cite only J. Robinet, *Le mouvement religieux à Paris pendant la Révolution*, 2 vols. (Paris, 1896–98); abbé O. Delarc, *L'Église de Paris pendant la Révolution française, 1789–1801*, 3 vols. (Paris, Lille, 1895–97); chanoine P. Pisani, *L'Église de Paris pendant la Révolution*, 2 vols. (Paris, 1908–9); abbé M. Giraud, *Essai sur l'histoire religieuse de la Sarthe de 1789 à l'an IV* (La Flèche, 1920); abbé E. Sevestre, *L'acceptation de la Constitution civile du clergé en Normandie* (Laval, 1922), and *Liste critique des ecclésiastiques fonctionnaires publics insermentés et assermentés en Normandie* (Laval, 1922); R. Reuss, *La constitution civile et la crise religieuse en Alsace*, 2 vols. (Strasbourg, 1923); abbé E. Sol, *Le clergé du Lot et le serment exigé des fonctionnaires publics ecclésiastiques* (Paris, 1926); abbé G. Charrier, *Histoire religieuse du département de la Nièvre pendant la Révolution*, 2 vols. (Paris, 1926); abbé J. Peter and dom C. Poulet, *Histoire religieuse du département du Nord pendant la Révolution*, 2 vols. (Lille, 1930–33); chanoine P. Lesprand, *Le clergé de la Moselle pendant la Révolution*, 3 vols. (Montigny-les-Metz, 1933–35); C. Constantin, *L'évêché du département de la Meurthe de 1791 à 1802*, Vol I: *La fin de l'Église d'Ancien Régime et l'établissement de l'Église constitutionelle* (Nancy, 1935); C. Aimond, *Histoire religieuse de la Révolution dans le département de la Meuse et le diocèse de Verdun, 1789–1802* (Paris and Bar-le-Duc, 1949); C. Ledré, *Une controverse sur la Constitution civile du clergé, Charrier de la Roche, métropolitain des Côtes de la Manche et le chanoine Baston* (Paris, Lyon, 1943); H. Lacape, *Pierre Pontard, évêque constitutionnel de la Dordogne* (Bordeaux and Paris, 1952); abbé E. Lavaquery, *Le cardinal de Boisgelin*, 2 vols. (Paris, 1920); J. Leflon, *Monsieur Émery*, Vol. I: *L'Église d'Ancien Régime et la Révolution* (Paris, 1944); marquis de Roux, *Histoire religieuse de la Révolution à Poitiers et dans la Vienne* (Lyon, 1952); G. Pioro, 'Institution canonique et consécration des premiers évêques constitutionnels', *Annales historiques de la Révolution française*, 1956.

*The colonies*

General survey in J. Saintoyant, *La colonisation française pendant la Révolution*, 2 vols. (Paris, 1930). In addition: L. Deschamps, *L'Assemblée constituante et les colonies* (Paris, 1898); Gaston-Martin and P. Roussier, *La doctrine coloniale de la France en 1789, Les colonies pendant la Révolution, Notes bibliographiques*, No. 3 of 'Cahiers de la Révolution française' (Paris, 1935); C. L. Lokke, *France and the Colonial Question, A Study of Contemporary French Opinion, 1763–1801* (New York, 1932); various articles by L. Leclerc ('La politique et l'influence du club de l'Hôtel Massiac', *Annales historiques de la Révolution française*, XIV [1937], 342–63; 'Les Lameth et le club Massiac', *ibid.*, X [1933], 461–63; 'La "trahison" des colons aristocrates de Saint-Domingue en 1793–1794', *ibid.*, XI [1934], 348–60); and G. Debien, *Les colons de Saint-Domingue et la Révolution, Essai sur le club Massiac* (Paris, 1953).

*France in 1791*

On the history of the party of constitutionalists, see G. Michon, *Adrien Duport* (Paris, 1924). On the democratic and republican movement, A. Aulard, *Histoire politique de la Révolution* (Paris, 1901, 5th ed., 1921), Chap. IV; A. Mathiez, *Le club des Cordeliers pendant la crise de Varennes* (Paris, 1910), with a supplement (1913); I. Bourdin, *Les Sociétés populaires de Paris* (Paris, 1937); A. Espinas, *La Philosophie sociale du XVIIIe siècle et la Révolution française* (Paris, 1898); A. Lichtenberger, *Le socialisme et la Révolution française* (Paris, 1899).

On workers' agitation, see G. Jaffé, *Le mouvement ouvrier* (Paris, 1924); C.-H. Pouthas, 'La Constituante et la classe ouvrière', *Annales révolutionnaires*, IV (1911), 153–82.

On agrarian disturbances, see H. Sée, 'Les troubles agraires en Bretagne, 1790 et 1791', *Bulletin d'histoire économique de la Révolution*, 1920–21 (fascicule published 1925), pp. 231–370; E. Sol, *La Révolution en Quercy*, Vol. I (Paris, [1929]), Book I, Chap. VI. On the popular mentality, see R. Baehrel, 'Epidémie et terreur: histoire et sociologie', *Annales historiques de la Révolution française* (1951), pp. 113–46.

PART THREE. THE REVOLUTION AND EUROPE UP TO THE
FORMATION OF THE FIRST COALITION

See works cited at beginning of Part Two. In addition, see A. Sorel,
*L'Europe et la Révolution française*, 8 vols. (Paris, 1885–1904); H. von Sybel,
*Geschichte der Revolutionszeit*, 5 vols. (Düsseldorf, 1853–79), Eng. tr. by
W. C. Perry, *History of the French Revolution*, 4 vols. (Leipzig, 1867–69); brief
survey in A. Wahl, *Geschichte des europäischen Staatensystem im Zeitalter der
französischen Revolution und der Freiheitskriege* (Munich and Berlin, 1912);
A. Fugier, *La Révolution française et l'Europe* (Paris, 1954), Vol. IV of 'His-
toire des relations internationales', published under the direction of
P. Renouvin.

### Chapter 11. The Constituent Assembly and Europe

For Germany, works by Bidermann, Perthes, and Wenck, cited in Chapter
Five, under Enlightened Despotism, and by Häusser and Heigel in Chapter
Five, under Rivalry of States.

For Austria, A. Beer, *Leopold II, Franz II und Katharina* (Leipzig, 1874); A.
von Vivenot, *Quellen zur Geschichte der deutschen Kaiserpolitik Œsterreichs
während der französischen Revolution (1790–1801)*, incomplete, 5 vols.
(Vienna, 1873–90), Vol. I.

For England, besides the appropriate section in Chapter Five, see J.
Holland Rose, *Pitt and the Great War* (London, 1911); A. W. Ward and G. P.
Gooch, *The Cambridge History of British Foreign Policy*, Vol. I (Cambridge,
1912); R. W. Seton-Watson, *Britain in Europe, 1789–1914* (Cambridge, 1937).

For Denmark, see appropriate section in Chapter Five.

For Spain, besides the appropriate section in Chapter Five, see
A. Muriel, *Historia de Carlos IV*, 6 vols. (Madrid, 1893–95); H. Baumgarten,
*Geschichte Spaniens zur Zeit der französischen Revolution* (Berlin, 1861);
A. Tratchevsky, 'L'Espagne pendant la Révolution française', *Revue
historique*, XXI (1886), 1–55.

For Holland, see appropriate sections in Chapters One and Five, and
L. Legrand, *La Révolution française en Hollande* (Paris, 1894).

For Italy, see appropriate section in Chapter Five, and F. Lemmi, *Le
origini del Risorgimento italiano, 1789–1815* (Milan, 1906, 2d ed., 1924);
E. Rota, *Le origini del Risorgimento* (Milan, 1938, 2d ed., 1950).

For Portugal, see appropriate section in Chapter Five.

For Russia, besides the appropriate section in Chapter Five, see C. de la
Rivière, *Catherine II et la Révolution française* (Paris, 1895).

For Sweden, see appropriate section in Chapter Five.

For Switzerland, see appropriate section in Chapter Five, and W. Œschli, *Geschichte der Schweiz im XIX. Jahrhundert*, Vol. I (Leipzig, 1903); H. Büchi, *Vorgeschichte der helvetischen Republik mit besonderer Berücksichtigung des Kantons Soleures* (Soleure, 1925), Vol. I; G. Steiner, introduction to *Korrespondenz des Peter Ochs* (Basel, 1927–38), Vol.1.

For the United States, see appropriate section in Chapter Five.

### Revolutionary propaganda

A. Mathiez, *La Révolution et les étrangers* (Paris, 1918), which lists many special works; F. Vermale, 'La franc-maçonnerie savoisienne à l'époque révolutionnaire', *Annales révolutionnaires*, III (1910), 375–94, and 'Joseph de Maistre franc-maçon', *ibid.*, II (1909), 356–76; J. Venedey, *Die deutschen Republikaner unter der französischen Republik* (Leipzig, 1870), Chap. II (on the influence of Strasbourg).

### Spread of the revolution

See the sketch by Jaurès, in *Histoire socialiste de la Révolution française*, Vol. III (Paris, 1903), and the last chapter, written by G. P. Gooch, of Vol. VIII (1904) of the *Cambridge Modern History*, devoted to revolutionary expansion; also A. Mathiez, *La Révolution et les étrangers* (Paris, 1918); J. Godechot, *La Grande Nation, L'expansion révolutionnaire de la France dans le monde (1789–1799)*, 2 vols. (Paris, 1956); and works cited at the beginning of this chapter.

For Germany: J. Schmidt, *Geschichte der deutschen Literatur*, Vol. III (Berlin, 1886), Chap. VIII; G. P. Gooch, *Germany and the French Revolution* (London, 1920); A. Stern, *Der Einfluss der französischen Revolution auf das deutsche Geistesleben* (Berlin, 1927) with an important bibliography; R. Aris, *History of Political Thought in Germany from 1789 to 1815* (London, 1936); J. Droz, *L'Allemagne et la Révolution française* (Paris, 1949); A. Chuquet, *Études d'histoire*, Series I: *G. Forster* (Paris, 1903), Series II: *Adam Lux, Klopstock* (Paris, 1903), Series VI: *Les écrivains allemands et la Révolution* (Paris, 1913), Series VII: *Stolberg* (Paris, 1914); Robinet de Cléry, *Frédéric de Gentz* (Paris, 1917); P. Sweet, *Friedrich von Gentz* (Madison, Wis., 1941), which is much more important; X. Léon, *Fichte et son temps* (Paris, 1922), Vol. I, Chap. V. On demonstrations and disturbances: F. Remmling, *Die Rheinpfalz in der Revolutionszeit* (Speyer, 1865), Vol. I; J. Venedey, *Die deutschen Republikaner* (Leipzig, 1870); A. Wohlwill, *Neuere Geschichte der Freien- und Hansestadt Hamburg, insbesondere von 1789 bis 1815* (Gotha,

1914); H. Schmidt, *Die sächsischen Bauernunruhen des Jahres 1790* (Meissen, 1907).

For England: J. Deschamps, *Les Iles britanniques et la Révolution française* (Paris, 1949); *The Debate on the French Revolution*, edited by A. Cobban (London, 1950); *The Cambridge History of Literature*, Vol. XI (Cambridge, 1914); C. Cestre, *La Révolution et les poètes anglais* (Paris, 1906); E. Legouis, *La jeunesse de Wordsworth* (Paris, 1896); A. Angellier, *R. Burns*, 2 vols. (Paris, 1893); L. D. Woodward, *Hélène Maria Williams et ses amis* (Paris, 1929); R. J. White, *The Political Thought of S. T. Coleridge* (London, 1938); W. P. Hall, *British Radicalism, 1791–97* (New York, 1912); P. A. Brown, *The French Revolution in English History* (London, 1918); H. W. Meikle, *Scotland and the French Revolution* (Glasgow, 1912); É. Halévy, *La formation du radicalisme philosophique*, Vol. II: *Evolution de la doctrine utilitaire de 1789 à 1815* (Paris, 1901), Eng. tr., London, 1928; M. C. Conway, *The Life of Thomas Paine*, 2 vols. (New York, 1932); Thomas Paine, *The Complete Writings*, edited with introduction by P. Foner, 2 vols. (New York, 1945); W. E. Woodward, *Tom Paine, America's Godfather* (New York, 1945); H. Roussin, *W. Godwin* (Paris, 1913); J. Russell, *The Life and Times of Fox*, 3 Vols. (London, 1867); A. Chardon, *Fox et la Révolution française* (Paris, 1918); Ghita Stanhope and G. P. Gooch, *The Life of Charles, Earl of Stanhope* (London, 1914); G. Pariset, 'La Société de la Révolution de Londres dans ses rapports avec Burke et l'Assemblée constituante', *La Révolution française*, XXIX (1895), 297–325.

For Spain: O. Miguel de los Santos, *Los Españoles en la Revolucion francesa* (Madrid, 1914); L. Sánchez Agesta, *El pensamiento politico* (Madrid, 1951); M. Menendez Pelayo, *Historia de los heterodoxos españoles*, Vols. VI and VII (Madrid, 1948).

For Portugal: O. Karmin, 'La Révolution française vue de l'intendance de Lisbonne', *Revue historique de la Révolution française* (1922), pp. 81–107.

For Hungary: works of I. Kont and H. Tronchon, cited in Chapter Five, Cosmopolitanism and Nationalities; E. Bencze, 'Un poète hongrois de la Révolution française: Bacsanyi', *Annales historiques de la Révolution française*, XVI (1939), 529–35.

For Italy, besides the works cited in Chapter Five, see A. Franchetti, *Storia d'Italia dal 1789 al 1799* (Milan, 1907); M. Monnier, 'Le comte Gorani d'après ses Mémoires', *Revue des Deux Mondes*, 1874, pp. 854–80; M. Vaussard, 'Les jansénistes italiens et la Constitution civile du clergé', *Revue historique*, CCV (1951), 243–59; E. Codignola, *Illuministi, giansenisti e giacobini* (Florence, 1947).

For Switzerland: H. Büchi, *Vorgeschichte der helvetischen Republik*, Vol. I

(Soleure, 1925); E. Chapuisat, *Genève et la Révolution française* (Geneva, 1912); M. Peter, *Genève et la Révolution* (Geneva, 1921); A. Boethlingk, *Der Waadtländer F. C. Laharpe*, 2 vols. (Bern, 1925); C. Finnsler, *Lavaters Beziehungen zu Paris in den Revolutionsjahren* (Zurich, 1898); G. Steiner, *Korrespondenz des Peter Ochs*, Vol. I (Basel, 1927); G. Gautherot, *La Révolution dans l'ancien évêché de Bâle*, Vol. I: *La République rauracienne* (Paris, 1908); J. Moriköfer, *Die schweizerische Literatur* (Leipzig, 1861); V. Rossel, *Histoire littéraire de la Suisse romande*, Vol. II (Geneva, 1891).

On the revolutions in Brabant and Liége, see H. Pirenne, *Histoire de Belgique*, Vol. V (Brussels, 1921); S. Tassier, *Les démocrates belges* (Brussels, 1930), 'Le prince de Béthune-Charost, candidat au trône de Belgique', *Revue d'histoire moderne*, XI (1936), 31–43, and 'Édouard de Walckiers, promoteur de l'union des Belges et des Liégeois', *Revue de l'Université de Bruxelles*, XLIV (1938–39), 139–65; P. Recht, *1789 en Wallonie* (Liége, 1933); D. Brouwers, 'La Révolution dans les campagnes wallonnes de la principauté de Liége, 1789–90', *Annales de la Société archéologique de Namur*, Vol. XXXVII (1926); P. Harsin, *La révolution liégeoise* (Brussels, 1954).

For the United States: C. D. Hazen, *Contemporary Opinion of the French Revolution* (Baltimore, 1897).

For Latin America: L. de Herrera, *La Revolucion francesa y Sud América* (Paris, 1910); R. Caillet-Bois, *Ensayo sobre el Rio de la Plata y la Revolución francesa* (Buenos Aires, 1930); H. Barbagelata, *La Révolution française et l'Amérique latine*, No. 5 of 'Cahiers de la Révolution française', (Paris, 1936).

### Reaction and proposals for a crusade

See works cited at beginning of Part Two and of Part Three; also F. Braune, *Edmund Burke in Deutschland* (Heidelberg, 1917).

For Belgium, add F. van Kalken, 'Origines du sentiment anti-révolutionnaire en 1789 dans les Pays-Bas autrichiens et ses effets sur la révolution brabançonne', *Revue d'histoire moderne*, II (1927), 161–76.

For the other Austrian territories: I. Beidtel, *Über die Veränderungen in den Feudalverhältnissen in den österreichischen Staaten unter der Regierung Leopolds II, 1790–92* (Vienna, 1853); R. Kerner, *Bohemia in the 18th Century* (New York, 1932); R. Mori, 'Il movimento reazionario in Toscana alle riforme economiche leopoldine nel 1790', *Archivio storico italiano*, 1942.

*Louis XVI and the émigrés: appeal to foreign powers*

See general works cited at the beginning of Part Two and of Part Three. See also A. Mousset, *Le comte de Fernan Nuñez, ambassadeur d'Espagne à Paris, 1787–1791* (Paris, 1923); Mme Arnaud-Boutteloup, *Le rôle politique de Marie-Antoinette* (Paris, 1924); A. Geffroy, *Gustave III et la Cour de France*, 2 vols. (Paris, 1867); B. Mallet, *Mallet du Pan and the French Revolution* (London, 1902). On emigration, see E. Daudet, *Histoire de l'émigration, Coblentz (1789–1793)* (Paris, 1890); L. Pingaud, *Le comte d'Antraigues* (Paris, 1893); P. de Vaissière, *À Coblence* (Paris, 1894); D. Greer, *The Incidence of the Emigration during the French Revolution* (Cambridge, Mass., 1951).

*The foreign policy of the Constituent Assembly*

See general works, particularly those of A. Sorel, H. von Sybel, É. Bourgeois, A. Ward and G. Gooch, R. Seton-Watson, cited at the end of Part One and the beginning of Part Three. See also F. Masson, *Le Département des Affaires étrangères pendant la Révolution, 1789–1804* (Paris, 1877); M. Dufraisse, *Histoire du droit de guerre et de paix de 1789 à 1815* (Paris, 1867); G. de Grandmaison, *L'ambassade de France en Espagne pendant la Révolution, 1789–1804* (Paris, 1892); J. Basdevant, *La Révolution française et le droit de la guerre continentale* (Paris, 1901); A. Aulard, J. Basdevant, and B. Mirkine-Guetzévitch, *La Révolution française et l'Europe* (Paris, 1930).

On foreign agents at Paris, see A. Mathiez, *La Révolution et les étrangers* (Paris, 1918). On the affairs of the German princes, see T. Ludwig, *Die deutschen Reichstände im Elsass und der Ausbruch der Revolutionskriege* (Strasbourg, 1898); P. Muret, 'L'affaire des princes possessionnés d'Alsace et les origines du conflit entre la Révolution et l'Europe', *Revue d'histoire moderne*, I (1899–1900), 433–56, 566–92.

On the events in Avignon, see P. Charpenne, *Les grands épisodes de la Révolution dans Avignon et le Comtat*, 4 vols. (Avignon, 1902); J. Viguier, 'La réunion d'Avignon et du Comtat-Venaissin à la France', *La Révolution française*, XXI (1891), 424–49, XXIII (1892), 149–60, and XXVI (1894), 150–68; P. Vaillandet, *Correspondance des députés d'Avignon près l'Assemblée Nationale*, 3 vols. (Avignon, 1933–37); A. Mathiez, *Rome et la Constituante* (Paris, 1910).

*European politics*

See the beginning of Part Three, and particularly R. H. Lord, *The Second Partition of Poland* (Cambridge, Mass., 1915), with important bibliography.

On Austrian and Prussian policies and on their relations with Russia after 1790, see K. Heidrich, *Preussen im Kampfe gegen die französische Revolution bis zur zweiten Teilung Polens* (Stuttgart and Berlin, 1908).

On internal affairs in Poland, see J. Klotz, *L'œuvre législative de la Diète de Quatre ans* (Paris, 1913); A. Jobert, *La commission d'éducation nationale en Pologne, 1773–1794* (Paris, 1941).

For Belgium, see H. Pirenne, *Histoire de la Belgique*, Vol.V (Brussels, 1921).

## Chapter 12. Flight of the king and declaration of war against Austria, June, 1791–April, 1792

*The flight to Varennes and its consequences in France*

On the flight, the chief work is that by Mgr. C. Aimond, *L'énigme de Varennes* (Paris, 1936). On events before that: V. Fournel, *L'événement de Varennes* (Paris, 1890), which G. Lenotre (*Varennes*, 1905) failed to make less important; and cf. G. Bord, *La fin de deux légendes, L'affaire Léonard* (Paris, 1909).

On the attitude of the parties and the Champ-de-Mars affair, A. Aulard, *Histoire politique* (Paris, 1901, 5th ed., 1921), Chaps. V and VI; A. Mathiez, *Le club des Cordeliers pendant la crise de Varennes* (Paris, 1910); G. Michon, *Adrien Duport* (Paris, 1924); F. Braesch, 'Les pétitions du Champ-de-Mars', *Revue historique*, CXLII (1923), 192–209, CXLIII (1923), 1–31, 181–97; cf. Mathiez, *ibid.*, CXLIV (1923), 87–91; H. Chobaut, 'La pétition du club de Montpellier en faveur de la République', *Annales historiques de la Révolution française*, IV (1927), 547–60.

Concerning relations of the constitutionalists, and especially of Barnave, with the queen, the publication of O. de Heidenstam, *Marie-Antoinette, Fersen, et Barnave* (Paris, 1913), based on documents taken from Fersen's papers, has given rise to lengthy discussion because the authenticity of the texts is generally doubted. The debate has been settled by Alma Söderhjelm, *Marie-Antoinette et Barnave, Correspondance secrète (juillet 1791–janvier 1792) Première édition complète établie d'après les originaux* (Paris, 1934), whose introduction sums up this argument.

G. Lefebvre, 'Le meurtre du comte de Dampierre (22 juin 1791)', *Revue historique*, CXCII (1941), 241–52.

*The declaration of Pillnitz*

See works cited in Chapter Eleven, under European Politics.


*The Legislative Assembly and Girondist policy*

For the history of the Legislative Assembly, see general works cited at the beginning of this chapter. A list of the deputies appears in A. Kuscinski, *Les députés à l'Assemblée législative* (Paris, 1924). The policy of the Feuillants is studied by G. Michon, *Adrien Duport* (Paris, 1924); on Narbonne's ministry, see E. Dard, *Le comte de Narbonne* (Paris, 1943); J. Poperen and G. Lefebvre, 'Études sur le ministère de Narbonne', *Annales historiques de la Révolution française*, XIX (1947), 1–36, 193–217, 292–321. See also works concerning Madame de Staël, especially Lady Blennerhassett, *Frau von Staël, ihre Freunde und ihre Bedeutung in Politik and Literatur*, 2 vols. (Berlin, 1887–89), Vol. II, Book II, Chap. II; D. G. Larg, *Madame de Staël, la vie dans l'œuvre* (Paris, 1924).

On the king's negotiations with foreign powers, see J. Flammermont, *Négociations secrètes de Lovis XVI et du baron de Breteuil, décembre 1791–juillet 1792* (Paris, 1885).

On the Girondins, general works are outdated or polemical: J. Gaudet, *Les Girondins*, 2 vols. (Paris, 1861); E. Biré, *La légende des Girondins* (Paris, 1881). See works by A. Aulard, *Histoire politique* (Paris, 1901, 5th ed., 1921), Part II, Chap. VII, and *Les orateurs de la Législative et de la Convention*, 2 vols. (Paris, 1885, 2d ed., 1906), Vol. I, Books III–V, Vol. II, Books VI–VII. In addition, see various biographies, among which are E. Ellery, *Brissot* (Cambridge, Mass., 1915); E. Lintilhac, *Vergniaud* (Paris, 1920); E. Chapuisat, *Figures et choses d'autrefois* (Geneva, 1925), which offers a study of Clavière, pp. 9–170; Clavière often appears, in connection with his financial dealings, in the 3 vols. of J. Bouchary, *Les manieurs d'argent*, 3 vols. (Paris, 1939–43), and occupies a prominent part of Vol. I. On the Egira of the Gironde, we have no general study that is entirely satisfactory; see instead the publications of C. Perroud, *Mémoires de Madame Roland*, 2 vols. (Paris, 1905); *Lettres de Madame Roland, 1780–1793*, 2 vols. (Paris, 1900–1903); *Roland et Marie Phlipon, lettres d'amour, 1777–1780* (Paris, 1909); 'Une amie de Madame Roland; souvenirs de Sophie Grandchamp', *La Révolution française*, XXXVII (1899), 65–89, 153–70. In addition, see Edith Bernardin, *Les idées religieuses de Madame Roland* (Paris, 1933).

On Dumouriez, see A. Chuquet, *Dumouriez* (Paris, 1914).

On Robespierre's opposition to the war, see biographies cited in Chapter Seven; G. Michon, 'Robespierre et la guerre', *Annales révolutionnaires*,

XII (1920), 265–311, and *Robespierre et la guerre révolutionnaire* (Paris, 1937); M. Eude, 'La politique de Robespierre en 1792, d'après "Le Défenseur de la Constitution"', *Annales historiques de la Révolution française*, 1956.

On the refugees: A. Mathiez, *La Révolution et les étrangers* (Paris, 1918), O. Lee, *Les comités et les clubs des patriotes belges et liégeois, 1791–an III* (Paris, 1931).

### The Austro-Prussian alliance

See works cited in Chapter Eleven, under European Politics, especially those by R. H. Lord and K. Heidrich.

### The Dumouriez cabinet and the declaration of war

In addition to works cited, see F. L. Nussbaum, 'L'arrière-plan de la mission de Talleyrand à Londres en 1792', in *Assemblée générale* (Paris, 1945), Vol. II, pp. 445–84.

## Chapter 13. The second French revolution, August–September, 1792

### Failure of the French offensive

The foreign policy of Dumouriez is discussed by A. Sorel in *L'Europe et la Révolution*, 8 vols. (Paris, 1885–1904), Vol. II, Book IV, Chap. I. The condition of the French army in 1792 is described by A. Chuquet, in Vol. I of *Guerres de la Révolution: La première invasion prussienne* (Paris, 1886), Chap. II. The reader may also consult Capt. J. Colin, *La tactique et la discipline dans les armées de la Révolution, Correspondance du général Schauenbourg du 4 avril au 2 août 1793* (Paris, 1902), Introduction; and, by the same author, *L'infanterie française an XVIIIe siècle* (Paris, 1907); Commandant E. Picard and Lt. Jouan, *L'artillerie française au XVIIIe siècle* (Paris, 1906). On strategy in the eighteenth century, see J. Colin, *L'éducation militaire de Napoléon* (Paris, 1900), and *Les transformations de la guerre* (Paris, 1911); M. Reinhard, *Le grand Carnot*, Vol. I: *De l'ingénieur au conventionnel, 1753–92* (Paris, 1950), and Vol. II: *L'organisateur de la victoire, 1793–1823* (Paris, 1952).

There are many monographs on the volunteers. For example, for Paris, C.-L. Chassin and L. Hennet, *Les volontaires nationaux pendant la Révolution*, 3 vols. (Paris, 1899–1901); Lt. Col. R. Tournès, *La garde nationale dans le département de la Meurthe pendant la Révolution* (Angers, 1921). General description appears in É. Déprez, *Les volontaires nationaux* (Paris, 1908), which is extensively criticized by A. Chuquet in *Historiens et marchands d'histoire* (Paris, 1914), pp. 42–109, and in the *Revue critique* (November 12, 1908). Many recollections and letters of soldiers during the Revolution have also been published, for example *Journal de marche du sergent Fricasse, 1792–1802*, ed. by Lorédan Larchey (Paris, 1882); *Journal du cannonier Bricard, 1792–1802*, ed. by his grandsons A. and J. Bricard (Paris, 1891); Lt. Col. Picard, *Au service de la nation, 1792–1798* (Paris, 1914).

On the high command, see G. Six, *Dictionnaire biographique des généraux et amiraux de la Révolution et de l'Empire* (Paris, 1948).

On military operations: *Victoires, conquêtes, désastres, revers et guerres civiles des Français, de 1792 à 1815, par une société de militaires et de gens de lettres*, 27 vols. (Paris, 1817–21), Vols. I–IV; H. Jomini, *Histoire critique et militaire des guerres de la Révolution*, 15 vols. (Paris, 1820–24), Vols. I–VI; H. Dumoulin, *Précis d'histoire militaire*, Vol. I: *Révolution* (Paris, 1901); Gen. Descoins, *Étude synthétique des principales campagnes modernes* (Paris, 1901), and the 7th ed., rev., Vol. I: *1674–1807* (Paris, 1928).

On operations along the northern frontier in 1792: P. Foucart and J. Finot, *La défense nationale dans le Nord de 1792 à 1802*, 2 vols. (Lille, 1890); *Krieg gegen die französische Revolution*, Vol. II (Vienna, 1905), published by the Austrian general staff. For the eastern frontier, A. Chuquet, cited at the beginning of this chapter.

## Origins of the second revolution

See works cited at the beginning of this chapter. For economic and social history see A. Mathiez, *La vie chère et le mouvement social sous la Terreur* (Paris, 1927), Chaps. I and II, as well as works concerning the food supply cited in Chapter Ten, especially the introduction by G. Lefebvre to *Documents relatifs à l'histoire des subsistances dans le district de Bergues*, Vol. I (Lille, 1913).

## Fall of the Dumouriez cabinet and failure of the Girondins

See works cited at the beginning of this chapter. On June 20 and its immediate consequences: Mortimer-Ternaux, *Histoire de la Terreur*, Vol. I (Paris, 1862); and F. Braesch, *La Commune du 10 août; étude sur l'histoire de Paris du 20 juin au 2 décembre 1792* (Paris, 1911). There is no monograph on June 20 besides that by L. B. Pfeiffer, *The Uprising of June 20, 1792* (Lincoln, Neb., 1913). See also 'Mémoires de Ch. Alexandre sur les journées révolutionnaires de 1791 et 1792', ed. by J. Godechot, in *Annales historiques de la Révolution française*, 1952, pp. 123–251.

On the events of June 20 and August 10, J. Chaumié has published the letters of Domingo de Yriarte, Spanish chargé d'affaires in France, to his prime minister, Aranda (June–August, 1792), in *Annuaire-bulletin de la Société de l'histoire de France*, 1944, pp. 129–258.

On the relations of the Girondins with the court on the eve of August 10, the reader should examine the Convention's session of January 3, 1793 (*Moniteur*, XV, 41), and the trial of the Girondins (Buchez and Roux, *Histoire parlementaire de la Révolution française*, 40 vols. [Paris, 1834–38], Vols. XXIX–XXX). Thiers published, at the end of his *Histoire de la Révolution*, the letter of the Girondins to Louis XVI.

### The revolution of August 10, 1792

Besides the general works cited at the beginning of this chapter, see Mortimer-Ternaux, *Histoire de la Terreur*, Vol. II (Paris, 1863); J. Pollio and A. Marcel, *La bataillon du 10 août* (Paris, 1881); A. Tuetey, *Répertoire général des sources manuscrites de l'histoire de Paris pendant la Révolution française*, Vol. IV, Introduction (Paris, 1889); P. Sagnac, *La chute de la royauté* (Paris, 1909); F. Braesch, *La Commune du 10 août* (Paris, 1911); A. Mathiez, *Le Dix août* (Paris, 1931).

On events leading up to that day, we now have the memoirs of Étienne-Louis-Hector Dejoly, last keeper of the seals under Louis XVI, edited by J. Godechot, in *Annales historiques de la Révolution française*, XVIII (1946), 289–382. In addition, see the publication of J. Chaumié, cited above.

On the day's immediate political consequences, see A. Aulard, *Histoire politique de la Révolution* (Paris, 1901, 5th ed., 1921), Part II, Chap. I; P. Mautouchet, *Le gouvernement révolutionnaire* (Paris, 1912), containing documents, with an introduction.

### The first Terror

There is no general study on the first Terror. For Paris, see Mortimer-Ternaux, *Histoire de la Terreur*, Vols. III (Paris, 1868), and IV (Paris, 1870), and F. Braesch, *La Commune du 10 août* (Paris, 1911). For the provinces, see A. Mathiez, 'L'arrestation des suspects en Côte d'Or pendant la crise de la première invasion', *Annales historiques de la Révolution française*, II (1925), 113–30, and various local histories.

The activity of the commissioners sent by the Executive Council, by the

Commune, and by Roland is studied by P. Caron, *La première Terreur*, Vol. I: *Les missions du Conseil exécutif provisoire et de la Commune de Paris*, 2 vols. (Paris, 1950–53). Carnot's mission to Alsace is discussed by M. Reinhard in *Le grand Carnot*, Vol. I.

The September massacres have been studied in many works, for example, J. Grente, *Les martyrs de septembre à Paris*, (Paris, 1919), and J. Hérissay, *Les journées de septembre 1792* (Paris, 1945). We now have a solid critical study by P. Caron, *Les massacres de septembre* (Paris, 1935), which lists most of the popular executions preceding or succeeding those in Paris.

On Marat, to whom full responsibility is usually attributed, see F. Chévremont, *Jean-Paul Marat*, 2 vols. (Paris, 1880); A. Cabanès, *Marat inconnu, L'homme privé, le médecin, le savant* (Paris, 1891, 2d ed., 1911); L. R. Gottschalk, *Jean-Paul Marat, A Study in Radicalism* (New York, 1927), and 'Quelques études récentes sur Marat', *Annales historiques de la Révolution française*, XIII (1936), 97–122.

On the role played by Danton: A. Aulard, *Études et leçons* (Paris, 1893), Series II, pp. 39–106; and the opposite view in A. Mathiez, *Autour de Danton* (Paris, 1926), Chaps. VI–VII; see also G. Pioro, 'Sur la fortune de Danton', *Annales historiques de la Révolution française* (1955), pp. 324–43.

On the political movement from August 10 to September 20: A. Aulard, *Histoire politique* (Paris, 1901, 5th ed., 1921), Part II, Chap. II; A. Mathiez, *La Révolution française*, 3 vols. (Paris, 1922–27), Vol. II.

On religious measures: A. Mathiez, *Les conséquences religieuses de la journée du 10 août* (Paris, 1911); L. Misermont, *Le serment de liberté-égalité* (Paris, 1914), and *Le serment à la Constitution civile du clergé; le serment civique [de 1792]* (Paris, 1917).

On reforms favouring the peasants, see above, Chapter Ten, under Agrarian Reform.

The economic and social movement has been studied by A. Mathiez, *La vie chère* (Paris, 1927), Chap. III; E. Campagnac, 'Un prêtre communiste; le curé Petitjean', *La Révolution française*, XLV (1903), 425–46.

## Chapter 14. Invasion of Poland and of France. Revolutionary counterattack: Valmy and Jemappes, September, 1792–January, 1793

See works cited at the beginning of Part III (Vol. III of Sorel's work begins with the Prussian invasion), and particularly those of R. Lord and K. Heidrich. Vol. II of the collection of documents published by A. Von Vivenot, cited at the beginning of Part III, is titled *Von der französischen*

*Kriegserklärung und dem Rücktritt des Fürsten Kaunitz-Rietberg bis zur zweiten Theilung Polens (April 1792–März 1793);* its supplement is *Zur Genesis der zweiten Theilungs Polens.*

*Invasion of Poland and the question of indemnities*

See works cited at the beginning of this chapter.

*The coalition army*

A good study of the Austrian army can be found in *Geschichte der Kämpfe Oesterreichs, Krieg gegen die französischen Revolution,* Vol. I: *Einleitung* (Vienna, 1905); a briefer description appears in M. E. von Angeli, *Die Heere des Kaisers und der französischen Revolution im Beginne des Jahres 1792,* new series, Vol. IV of the *Mittheilungen des kais. und kön. Kriegsarchives* (1889). The Prussian army is described by A. Chuquet, *Les guerres de la Révolution,* Vol. I (Paris, 1886), Chap. III. In addition: C. Jany 'Die Gefechtsausbildung der preussischen Infanterie vor 1806', in *Urkundliche Beiträge und Forschungen zur Geschichte des preussischen Heeres,* published by the German general staff, Vol. I (1903), Fasc. 5; and 'Der preussische Kavalleriedienst vor 1806', in the same series, Vol. III (1904), Fasc. 6.

*Valmy*

There is no individual study of the condition of the French army on the eve of Valmy. For military operations, besides the general works cited at the beginning of Chapter Thirteen, see A. Chuquet, *Les guerres de la Révolution,* Vol. I: *La première invasion prussienne* (Paris, 1886), Vol. II: *Valmy* (1887), Vol. III: *La retraite de Brunswick* (1887); and, by the same author, *Dumouriez* (Paris, 1914); *Krieg gegen die französische Revolution, cit.,* Vol. II (Vienna, 1905); Goethe, *Campagne in Frankreich* (1882), edited with introduction by A. Doves in *Goethes sämtliche Werke, Jubiläums Ausgabe,* Vol. XXVIII (Stuttgart, 1903); see also the edition by A. Chuquet (Paris, 1884).

*Republican conquest: Jemappes*

See A. Chuquet, *Les guerres de la Révolution,* Vol. IV: *Jemappes et la conquête de la Belgique* (Paris, 1890), Vol VI: *L'expédition de Custine* (1891); *Krieg gegen die französische Revolution,* Vol. II (Vienna, 1905). The reader will find nothing new in H. Libermann, *La défense nationale à la fin de 1792* (Paris, 1927).

*The second Polish partition and disruption of the coalition*

See works cited at the beginning of this chapter.

## Chapter 15. The origins of the first coalition

See general works cited in Chapter Eleven. Especially important are J. Holland Rose, *Pitt and the Great War* (London, 1911), and J. Déchamps, *Les Iles britanniques et la Révolution française* (Paris, 1949).

*The beginning of the Convention: Girondins and Montagnards*

For the history of the Convention, see general works on the Revolution, especially G. Pariset and A. Mathiez (Vols. II and III). See also: Mortimer-Ternaux, *Histoire de la Terreur*, Vols. IV–VIII (Paris, 1866–81); C.-A. Dauban, *La démagogie à Paris en 1793* (Paris, 1868); A. Kuscinski, *Dictionnaire des conventionnels* (Paris, 1919); A. Aulard, *Les orateurs de la Législative et de la Convention*, 2 vols. (Paris, 1885, 2d ed., 1906).

In addition to the biographies already cited in sections above, see E. N. Curtis, *Saint-Just, Colleague of Robespierre* (New York, 1935); G. Lefebvre, *Études sur la Révolution française* (Paris, 1954); L. Cahen, *Condorcet et la Révolution française* (Paris, 1904); G. Bouchard, *Un organisateur de la victoire, Prieur de la Côte-d'Or, membre du Comité de salut public* (Paris, 1946); L. Lévy-Schneider, *Jean Bon Saint-André*, 2 vols. (Paris, 1901); Stéfane-Pol, *Autour de Robespierre, Le conventionnel Lebas* (Paris, 1901); A. Montier, *Robert Lindet* (Paris, 1899); A. Tournier, *Vadier* (Paris, 1896); L. Madelin, *Fouché*, Vol. I (Paris, 1900), and the *Mémoires* of Fouché, ed. by L. Madelin (Paris, 1945); G. Avenel, *Anacharsis Cloots*, 2 vols. (Paris, 1865); S. Stern, *Cloots* (Stuttgart, 1914). On Carnot, M. Reinhard, *Le grand Carnot*, Vol. II (Paris, 1952); on Saint-Just, A. Soboul, 'Les Institutions républicaines de Saint-Just d'après les manuscrits de la Bibliothèque Nationale', *Annales historiques de la Révolution française*, 1948, pp. 193–262, 'Un manuscrit oublié de Saint-Just', *ibid.*, 1951, pp. 323–59, 'Sur la mission de Saint-Just à l'armée du Rhin', *ibid.*, 1954, pp. 193–231, 298–337; on David, D. L. Dowd, *Pageant-Master of the Republic: Jacques-Louis David and the French Revolution* (Lincoln, Neb., 1948), which treats David as an artist. See also Mme S. Tassier, 'Aux origines de la première coalition, Le ministre Lebrun-Tondu', *Revue du Nord*, 1954.

The diversity mentioned at the beginning of Part Two reached its height at the time of the Convention; consequently, local histories, histories of clubs and of the representatives on mission and the commissioners are more essential than before. See A. Troux, *La vie politique dans le départe-ment de la Meurthe d'août 1792 à octobre 1795*, 2 vols. (Paris, 1936); more will be cited below.

On the first sessions of the Convention and on the parties, see A. Aulard, *Histoire politique* (Paris, 1901, 5th ed., 1921), Part II, Chaps. II, VI–VIII; A. Mathiez, *Girondins et Montagnards* (Paris, 1930); on conflicts with the Commune, see F. Braesch, *La Commune du 10 août* (Paris, 1911).

On Girondins and Montagnards, see A. Aulard, *Histoire politique* (Paris, 1901, 5th ed., 1921), Part II, Chap. VII, and A. Mathiez, 'De la véritable nature de l'opposition entre les Girondins et les Montagnards', *Annales révolutionnaires*, XV (1923), 177–97.

### The struggle between parties and the death of the king

See Mortimer-Ternaux, Histoire de la Terreur, Vol. V (Paris, 1874); E. Seligman, *La justice en France pendant la Révolution*, Vol. II (Paris, 1913); P. de Vaissière, *La mort du roi* (Paris, 1910); A. Sevin, *Le défenseur du roi: Raymond De Sèze, 1748–1828* (Paris, 1936), and *La défense de Louis XVI* (Paris, 1936).

On Danton's role and the attempts at bribery during the trial, see A. Mathiez, in *Études robespierristes*, Vol. II (Paris, 1918), Chap. IV; Théodore de Lameth, *Mémoires* (Paris, 1913), and *Notes et Souvenirs* (Paris, 1914), both edited by E. Welvert; the letter of M. le Couteux de Canteleu, pub-lished in *La Croix* (December 9, 1926), and reprinted in *Annales historiques de la Révolution française*, III (1926), 179–83, and in *La Révolution française*, LXXX (1927), 146–49; the letters of Ocariz, published as an appendix by A. Chabaud, in his edition of *Mémoires de Barbaroux* (Paris, 1936), pp. 291–94. On the assassination of Lepelletier de Saint-Fargeau, see A. de Lestapis, *Revue des Deux Mondes*, February, 1953.

### Annexations and war of propaganda

See general works cited at the beginning of this chapter and those con-cerning the Gironde cited in Chapter Twelve, especially those of E. Ellery, É. Lintilhac, and H. Goetz-Bernstein. On the policy of Dumouriez and on supplying the armies, see A. Chuquet, *Dumouriez* (Paris, 1914), and *Les guerres de la Révolution*, Vols. IV and VI (Paris, 1890, 1891); C. Poisson, *Les fournisseurs aux armées sous la Révolution, Le directoire des achats, 1792–93* (Paris, 1932); J. Stern, *Le mari de Mademoiselle Lange: Michel-Jean Simons* (Paris, 1933).

On the question of natural frontiers: G. Zeller, 'La monarchie d'Ancien Régime et les frontières naturelles', *Revue d'histoire moderne*, VIII (1933), 305–33.

For Belgium: S. Tassier, *Histoire de la Belgique sous l'occupation française en 1792 et 1793* (Brussels, 1934), and 'La Société des Amis de la Liberté et de l'Égalité en Belgique en 1792–93', *Annales historiques de la Révolution française*, X (1933), 307–16, and 'La technique des révolutions nationales et le duel Cornet de Grez-Verlooy, Une cause inconnue de la première coalition', in *Miscellanea L. Van der Essen* (Brussels, 1947), pp. 901–13.

For the Rhineland, see the collection of documents by Hansen, cited in Chapter Four, in the section on Germany; and works by J. Venedey and F. X. Remmling, cited in Chapter Eleven, under Spread of the Revolution. See also J. Hashagen, *Das Rheinland und die französische Herrschaft* (Bonn, 1908); M. Springer, *Die Franzosenherrschaft in der Pfalz, 1782–1814* (Stuttgart, 1926); K. Bockenheimer, *Die Mainzer Klubisten der Jahren 1792 und 1793* (Mainz, 1896); P. Sagnac, *Le Rhin français pendant la Révolution et l'Empire* (Paris, 1917), with bibliography.

For Switzerland: G. Gautherot, *La Révolution dans l'ancien évêché de Bâle*, Vol. I (Paris, 1908).

For Spain: A. Morel-Fatio, 'José Marcheña et la propagande révolutionnaire en Espagne', *Revue historique*, XLIV (1890), 72–87; A. Richard, 'Marcheña et les Girondins', *Annales révolutionnaires*, XV (1923), 126–45.

Books on Miranda are numerous but often vindicatory. See J. Mancini, *Bolivar et l'émancipation des colonies espagnoles des origines à 1815* (Paris, 1912), Book II, Chap. II; W. S. Robertson, *The Life of Miranda*, 2 vols. (Chapel Hill, N.C., 1929); C. Parra Perez, *Miranda et Madame de Custine* (Paris, 1950). Miranda's papers are in the archives at Caracas; some have been published as *Archivio Miranda* (15 vols., 1929–38).

A study of plebiscites organized by the revolutionaries can be found in Sarah Wambaugh, *A Monograph on Plebiscites* (New York, 1920).

On the coalition powers, see above, at the beginning and end of Chapter Eleven. In addition: A. Bryant, *The Years of Endurance, 1793–1802* (London, 1942); H. McAnally, *The Irish Militia, 1793–1816* (Dublin, 1949); A. von Vivenot, *Quellen zur Geschichte der Kaiserpolitik*, 5 vols. (Vienna, 1873–90), Vol. II, Vol. III (May–December, 1793), and *Vertrauliche Briefe des Freiherrn von Thugut*, 2 vols. (Vienna, 1872); R. Petiet, *Gustave IV Adolphe et la Révolution française, Relations diplomatiques de la France et de la Suède de 1792 à 1800 d'après des documents inédits* (Paris, 1914).

*The break with England*

See works pertaining to England cited at the beginning of Chapter Eleven, especially those by J. H. Rose and J. Déchamps. In addition, see J. H. Rose, 'Documents Relating to the Rupture with France', *English Historical Review*, XXVII (1912), 117–23 and 324–30; E. D. Adams, *The Influence of Grenville on Pitt's Foreign Policy, 1787–1798* (Washington, 1904).

On the last attempts at negotiation, see Baron Ernouf, *Maret, duc de Bassano* (Paris, 1878).


*The break with the states of southern Europe*

See works cited at the beginning of this chapter. In addition, see A. Sorel, 'La diplomatie française et l'Espagne, 1792–1797', *Revue historique*, XI (1879), 208–330, XII (1880), 279–313, XIII (1880), 41–80, 241–78; G. Grosjean, 'Les relations de la France avec les Deux-Siciles de 1788 à 1793', *La Revolution française*, XV (1888), 9–45; F. Masson, *Les diplomates de la Révolution: Hugou de Bassville à Rome; Bernadotte à Vienne* (Paris, 1882); R. Trinquet, 'L'assassinat de Hugou de Bassville', *Annales révolutionnaires*, VII (1914), 338–68; F. Bornarel, 'Les relations de la France et de la Toscane de 1792 à 1795', *La Révolution française*, XIV (1888), 673–706; G. Grosjean, 'La mission de Sémonville à Constantinople, 1792–93', *ibid.*, XII (1887), 888–921; A. Rufer, *Novate* (Zurich, 1941)—Novate is the village where the Austrians arrested Maret and Sémonville, violating the Swiss frontier, with the complicity of aristocrats from the canton of Grisens—; L. Pingaud, *Choiseul-Gouffier* (Paris; 1887), Chap. VI.

# INDEX

# Routledge Classics
## Get inside a great mind

### The Great War
**1914–1918**
Mark Ferro

'A work of genius ... Succeeds supremely well in reflecting a new understanding of the nature of war.'
*Arthur Marwick, author of* The Nature of History

This overview of the apocalyptic conflict in which millions died is unrivalled in vision and scope. Mapping the realities faced by these men and their families at home, and charting the social changes arising from the war, Ferro travels well beyond the remit of most historians. This is one of the most significant reappraisals of the Great War ever to be written and one that rightfully takes its place as a Routledge Classic.

Hb: 0–415–26734–X    Pb: 0–415–26735–8

### Madness and Civilization
**A History of Insanity in the Age of Reason**
Michel Foucault

'Michel Foucault's *Madness and Civilization* has been, without a shadow of a doubt, the most original, influential, and controversial text in this field during the last forty years. It remains as challenging now as on first publication. Its insights have still not been fully appreciated and absorbed.'
*Roy Porter*

*Madness and Civilization* was Foucault's first book and his finest accomplishment. The themes of power and imprisonment, explored in his later work are established here. *Madness and Civilization* will change the way in which you think about society.

Hb: 0–415–25539–2    Pb: 0–415–25385–3

For these and other classic titles from Routledge, visit
**www.routledgeclassics.com**